Dartmouth Veterans

DARTMOUTH VETERANS

Vietnam Perspectives

Edited by Phillip C. Schaefer
with David S. deCalesta, Frederick C. Gray,
James P. Stewart, Robert J. Woodruff

Dartmouth College Press | Hanover, New Hampshire

Dartmouth College Press
An imprint of University Press of New England
www.upne.com
© 2014 Trustees of Dartmouth College

Manufactured in the United States of America
Designed by April Leidig
Typeset in Aldus by Copperline Book Services, Inc.

For permission to reproduce any of the material in this book,
contact Permissions, University Press of New England,
One Court Street, Suite 250, Lebanon NH 03766;
or visit www.upne.com

Library of Congress Cataloging-in-Publication Data
Dartmouth veterans: Vietnam perspectives / edited by
Phillip C. Schaefer with David S. deCalesta, Frederick C.
Gray, James P. Stewart, Robert J. Woodruff.
    pages cm
Includes index.
ISBN 978-1-61168-549-7 (pbk.: alk. paper)
ISBN 978-1-61168-550-3 (ebook)
1. Dartmouth College. Class of 1964. 2. Vietnam War,
1961–1975 — Veterans — United States — Biography.
3. Vietnam War, 1961–1975 — Personal narratives,
American. I. Schaefer, Phillip C.
DS559.5.D37 2014
959.704'30922—dc23
[B]   2013036505

5 4 3 2 1

In dedication to the men of the Class of 1964
who died because of the Vietnam War

William Brewster (Bruce) Nickerson
 March 17, 1942–April 22, 1966
 U.S. Navy Pilot/Navigator
 Downed over South China Sea

Peter Whitcomb Morrison
 December 29, 1942–June 9, 1967
 U.S. Air Force Pilot/Navigator
 Downed over South Vietnam

John Wheeler Griffin III
 January 14, 1943–November 15, 2011
 U.S. Army Infantry, Vietnam
 Felled by cancer attributed to
 Agent Orange exposure

Contents

1965

Foreword

"Where have all the young men gone?"

The Class of 1964 arrived at Dartmouth in September 1960. It was, culturally, still the 1950s, and would remain so for the next few years. This class was rooted in the Eisenhower era but would graduate in the age of the Beatles and of Bob Dylan.

September 26, 1960, at convocation, 806 matriculants heard President John Dickey affirm his confidence in their generation of undergraduates. He stressed the need for leadership—and for responsibility. Always interested in reminding students of the relevance of international affairs and the importance of international obligation, Mr. Dickey on this occasion had little comment on the world's problems. He did assure the class that he had no complaint over the conduct of the Cold War. And he acknowledged that he shared "with most of our countrymen the enormously important confidence that, in the main, America has both the right friends and the right enemies."

Surely few members of the Class of 1964 thought of war in September 1960. Few Americans did. It was a time of insecurity, but not of immediate danger. Those who did think of imminent war focused on Europe and the Soviet threat. Just as their freshman year was beginning, Nikita Khrushchev was disrupting a session of the United Nations by banging his shoe on the table. Gary Powers and his U-2 had recently been shot down while flying surveillance over the Soviet Union.

In the presidential election campaign of 1960 there was little real foreign policy difference between the candidates, Vice President Richard Nixon and Senator John Kennedy. Kennedy accused the Eisenhower administration of allowing a "missile gap" to develop. Nixon disputed this. In the presidential debates that fall, Nixon and Kennedy asserted their commitment to the islands of Quemoy and Matsu off the coast of

Formosa (Taiwan). There was little strategic difference here: the shared assumption was that the United States would protect Quemoy and Matsu. The debate was over who would be the stronger leader in doing this.

In his inaugural address in January 1961, President John Kennedy focused almost exclusively on the responsibility of the United States in the world. And he committed his generation and his country: "Let every nation know, whether it wishes us well or ill, that we shall pay any price, bear any burden, meet any hardship, support any friend, oppose any foe, to assure the survival and the success of liberty."

At the time this seemed a statement of principle, of values, not an expanded assumption of military obligation. And certainly not a commitment of military obligation in Vietnam. In 1960 there were nine hundred American advisers in Vietnam. Four servicemen had died that year. President Kennedy sometimes reminded Americans of threats in Thailand and in the old French Indochina empire, including Vietnam. But the Cuban Missile Crisis in 1962 served as reminder that America's primary threats were to the east—and then, briefly, south.

The undergraduate years of the '64s were a time of change—and, although only clear in retrospect, profound change. The year 1963 was marked by events that would resonate for a lifetime. In February 1963 Betty Friedan published *The Feminine Mystique*. As the Class of 1964 prepared for their senior year, Martin Luther King Jr. stood on the steps of the Lincoln Memorial and proclaimed to a quarter of a million on the Mall, and to the nation, "I have a dream"—and it was one that could no longer be denied. Before Dartmouth's Thanksgiving holiday, President Kennedy was assassinated in Dallas. That season the Beatles were planning their first American tour.

As 1963 ended there were 16,300 American military personnel in Vietnam. That year 118 had died. The level of commitment and the pace of death were quickening. Quietly. Seventy-one additional Americans died between January 1 and graduation day, 1964. Nonetheless, the country was not focused closely on these engagements involving American military "advisers."

At graduation in June 1964 neither President Dickey nor class valedictorian Michael Landay sounded any alarms. Dickey told the 615 graduates that he had confidence even in the "long shots" among the class. He assured that "the world will find you out as a man." Michael Landay spoke of values and assured the audience that he and his classmates "face the future with courage and with hope." Before this class's tenth—indeed, fifth—reunion, courage and hope would be tested.

On Saturday, June 13, 1964, the day preceding commencement, members of the class and their families gathered for the armed forces commissioning ceremony. Ninety-two received commissions that day, with another eleven scheduled to receive commission upon completion of "additional requirements."

It is impossible to speculate what those 103 men and their families were thinking on this occasion. Some share their memories in the essays that follow. On that graduation weekend few were planning to go to war. James Laughlin remembered, "Little did I know that the Vietnam War would explode during that time span. In 1964, I don't think anyone knew much about the place or the armed conflict that was beginning to boil up there." Michael Parker, on the other hand, recalled, "The prospect of serving in the war was a looming shadow almost from the time of my commissioning." Each would serve in Vietnam.

I had joined the Marines in June 1957, just two weeks after my high school graduation. Four classmates joined me, and three of us were still seventeen years old. I hadn't thought of going to war necessarily but was prepared to do it, in an innocent, even naïve, kind of way. My unit of the First Marine Brigade was deployed to Atsugi, Japan, from Kaneohe Bay, Territory of Hawaii, late in 1958 when American units were sent down to Formosa (Taiwan). We were positioned as backup for those units. In Atsugi we watched U-2 planes take off on "weather reconnaissance" missions. And my unit specifically replaced the one in which Lee Harvey Oswald served, moving into his barracks.

Military service was part of the life plan for my generation in my culture. We faced the imminence of the draft and elected to serve in the branch of our choice and at the timing that worked best for us. Members of the Class of 1964 considered the same choices. Electing the service branch and serving as an officer was a preferred option for many. In addition, at Dartmouth the scholarships provided by the military officer training corps were attractive at a time when financial aid was less widely available than it would be later.

Less than two months following graduation, in August 1964, Lyndon Johnson responded to North Vietnamese torpedo boat attacks on the U.S. naval destroyer *Maddox* and two days later alleged attacks on the *Maddox* and the *Turner Joy*. We now know that it is highly unlikely that the second attack ever happened, but nonetheless Congress reacted with an open authorization, the Gulf of Tonkin Resolution, to use military force not only to repel any attack on American forces, but to "take all necessary steps" to assist Southeast Asia Treaty Organization allies who requested "assistance in defense of its freedom."

In February 1965 the Viet Cong attacked the American Camp Holloway at Pleiku Air Base. This was the home of U.S. support troops. The assault killed 9 Americans and wounded 128. This would prove to be a pivotal moment: following this, President Johnson ordered conventional ground troops to Vietnam to protect our bases. Thirty-five hundred Marines began to come ashore at Da Nang on March 8.

Over the next nine years, 8.7 million Americans served in the armed forces, 2.6 million in Vietnam. More than 58,000 died in Vietnam or as a result of injuries suffered in Vietnam. Over 300,000 Americans were wounded in action. Neither the death nor the "wounded in action" statistics include the Agent Orange casualties, such as John Griffin of the Class of 1964, or the PTSD casualties. Each would prove substantial. Some estimates place the casualties (killed and wounded) at 1.4 million military, both sides, and the civilian casualties at 4 million.

According to Phil Schaefer's research, 157 members of the Class of 1964 served in the armed forces. Fifty-five of them have contributed accounts for this publication. Robert Hager ('60), who was in Vietnam as a reporter, and current Dartmouth undergraduate and veteran William Peters ('15) also wrote essays for this book.

Thirty-five of the classmates who wrote for this book served in Vietnam. (Phil Schaefer determined that at least nineteen more members of the class served there.) Two members of the class died in Vietnam, and their names are recorded on the Vietnam Veterans Memorial in Washington. Sage Dunlap Chase wrote an essay for this book about one of them, her friend Bruce Nickerson.

The other classmate lost in Vietnam, Peter Whitcomb Morrison, needs to be remembered as well. He was a Keene, New Hampshire, native who struggled at Dartmouth. One of my history students, Matthew Robinson

('13), did a paper on Morrison. Pete Morrison was an economics major and a member of Bones Gate. He joined the Air Force upon graduation and completed Officer Candidate School and training as a navigator. Morrison wanted to go to law school after his discharge, but that was not to be. His B-57 crashed in the Hao Chu mountains after taking hostile fire. He had been in Vietnam for only two days. At Dartmouth he had come to be close to Dean Thaddeus Seymour, who wrote to his parents following Pete's death to say how much he "deeply valued" Morrison.

The recollections and reflections gathered here are a testament to the work of Phil Schaefer. It is a thankless job to gather personal essays from a group of busy people who have mixed feelings about how much they will share about an often still-emotional experience. Phil's commitment and patience paid off, and not only his classmates but all who seek to know better the Vietnam generation will be grateful for that. This book provides an important source for those who seek to understand a generation caught in a world of change—and in a war that was sometimes hard to understand. When I wrote my book a few years ago I learned that the years that had passed had not really made understanding Vietnam much easier. In these essays we can sample some of the conflicting tensions that members of the Class of 1964 experienced.

In the years since I stepped down from the Dartmouth presidency, I have focused my energies, as a historian and a veteran, on reminding Americans of the human face of war. Complicated wars in unfamiliar places fought by unknown men—and women—are too easy for the rest of us to ignore. Vietnam, of course, was hard to ignore. In fact it was impossible to ignore. But aggressive visibility does not always result in understanding. Nor does time always soften the memory.

For many who served overseas, homecomings were anything but welcomes. Some veterans learned not to wear their uniforms, or talk about their service and experiences, and to avoid political discussions. The questions of why were not always easily answered. Karl Winkler remembers the experience in his essay. When asked by a wounded veteran who had apparently lost an eye, an arm, and possibly a leg and was on his way home, whether they had done the right thing, Winkler recalled, "I didn't want this conversation. . . . They've given so much of themselves when so few have. They were the boys without college or graduate school or political pull or a huge metropolitan draft pool. This war never made sense to me or my fellow trainees from officer's basic course. We proudly served. We didn't have to believe. But what to say? 'You were right, soldier,' I said as I shuffled forward to the passenger section, thinking of the price each of them had paid."

In 2009 I was invited to speak on Veterans Day at the Vietnam Veterans Memorial in Washington. I spoke there about our obligation not to allow war memorials to become silent tabulations of the forgotten dreams of anonymous lives.

That day I remembered two names on the Wall, one a young man from my hometown of Galena, Illinois. I had worked for his father when I was in the mines and knew the son as a high school student. This soldier, Michael Lyden, died on Hamburger Hill in May of 1969.

I also described Billy Smoyer, Dartmouth '67. I did not know Smoyer personally, but I came to know well his mother and father, brother and sister. Billy came from a comfortable New Jersey family and was a true student leader at Dartmouth. He was captain of both the soccer and the hockey teams, played rugby, and was in Theta Delta Chi and Casque and Gauntlet. Billy Smoyer joined the Marines because he didn't think that the war should be fought only by the sons of factory workers, miners, and farmers. Lieutenant Smoyer was killed when his platoon was ambushed while crossing a rice paddy in Quang Nam in July 1968, two weeks after he had arrived in Vietnam. Eighteen other Marines died with him in that fight.

In preparing for that Vietnam Memorial presentation, I looked into all of the Dartmouth names on the Wall. There are fifteen of them. Each shared in the experiences of life at Dartmouth and of death far from home. I wondered about the full lifetime of dreams that they brought to Vietnam—and left there. At the time, I read all that I could about these men. This past winter, I assigned one of these names to each of the students in my history seminar on America's wars. Their assignment was to describe the Dartmouth life of this Vietnam casualty. The description of Peter Morrison above was the result of this assignment.

John Ceremsak ('13) wrote about William Bruce Nickerson. He described Nickerson speaking at Dartmouth Night in October 1963. Bruce's classmates will recall that this was the Dartmouth Night without a bonfire because the Hanover Fire Department had refused to issue a permit owing to dry conditions that fall. Nickerson said this was OK, because the spirit of Dartmouth would bind for their lifetimes all who were there. Lifetimes are hard to project.

Less than two years after graduation, from his carrier, the USS *Kitty Hawk*, off the coast of Vietnam, Bruce Nickerson wrote to his friend Sage Dunlap. She would receive the letter following his death, and she quotes from it in her remembrance in this book. It captures as well as anything ever could the cruel cost of war: "I now look at life much more positively than I did in June of '64, and I picture myself as standing in the small end of a cornucopia with all of life opening up before me, to be lived, loved and learned about. I may have just turned 24, but I feel younger and more excited about life and all that it has to offer than ever before."

Just a few days after he wrote this optimistic embrace of life, his A-6 Intruder went down in the Gulf of Tonkin as a presumed result of hostile fire. His body was not recovered.

I conclude my observations by quoting from the closing of my remarks at the Vietnam Veterans Memorial on Veterans Day 2009.

Late this past summer my wife, Susan, and I visited Normandy, where we spent a lot of time walking through the American cemetery at Colleville. The white marble crosses and Stars of David filled the hillside with a sense of order and tranquility—and whispered of lives lost. We walked among the graves for some time, reading the names, observing where they were from and how old they were. We thought of lives cut short and of dreams unrealized and wanted to know more about them.

Casualties of war cry out to be known—as persons, not as abstractions called casualties or as numbers entered into the books, and not only as names chiseled into marble or granite. We have carried in our memories the stories of those recorded here. But memories fade—as do those who remember. We are graying. After all of us who knew them are gone, the names on this Wall will endure.

It is essential that the Education Center planned for this site sparkle with the human records of those whose sacrifice was forever. We need to ensure that here, in this place of memory, lives as well as names are recorded. Lives with smiling human faces, remarkable accomplishments, engaging personalities, and with dreams to pursue.

We do this for them, for history, and for those in the future who will send the young to war.

Thanks to Phil Schaefer and to all of the contributors to this volume, to this human record that is history. And thanks to all who served.

James Wright '64a
President Emeritus and
Eleazar Wheelock Professor of History
U.S. Marine Corps, 1957–60

Preface

Ten years ago I took an oral history project about World War II to the local elementary school. A fifth-grade teacher, an enthusiastic history buff, integrated the project into the curriculum and worked very diligently with me to guide that project to fruition. That exercise involved fourth and fifth graders interviewing local World War II veterans, printing a book (*Local American Heroes of World War II*, Borderlands Press, 2004), and celebrating their accomplishments together on Veterans Day 2004. The veterans were invigorated by their weekly interactions with the youngsters and grateful because, as they said, "We thought we'd been forgotten." The students learned about the war and developed an appreciation for their seniors, most older than their own grandparents. One even said, "I didn't know old people could be so interesting." Those children are now in college, and they have not forgotten. Only half of the veterans remain. The impact of this project on the student-writers and the veterans persists.

As secretary for the Dartmouth Class of 1964 it is my privilege to submit a column about classmates to the *Dartmouth Alumni Magazine* every two months. Three years ago, while searching for a topic for a few columns, it occurred to me that the veterans in our class would be a good focus. The vets cooperated and filled a database of information, which became the basis for writing six columns, a whole year's worth. However, only a few of our vets could be featured in the brief columns.

One way to include all our veterans was to publish a book of their essays. Ours is not a class that shrinks from the challenge of writing. We have already published two volumes, edited by current class president Ron Schram: *Sports: A Generation's Common Bond* (AuthorHouse, 2007) and *Generational Bridges to the World's Troubles* (AuthorHouse, 2012). As we approach our fiftieth class reunion in June 2014, what better way to reflect on our experiences than by sharing the one experience that shaped not just our class, but our generation?

Thus began a rather short eight months of collecting and editing veteran classmates' essays. It could not have been done so quickly without the concerted efforts of my classmate coeditors: Jim Stewart, Dave deCalesta, Bob Woodruff, and Fred Gray. They never complained when I reminded them, sometimes with less grace than I should have, that work was backing up. They made serious suggestions to raise the level of their classmates' work, and their recommendations were almost always accepted with appreciation. The writers were very cooperative and generally timely with their submissions. As a group, the editors selected the title and decided to arrange the book chronologically, approximately by the service years of the writer. We also thank classmate Bob Bartles for suggesting that we publish with the University Press of New England, who have raised the level of this book well beyond what we could have done on our own.

Firsthand recollections are a valuable resource for historians. Writing about one's involvement with or during a war can be cathartic for the author. Sharing the writer's sentiments can be thought provoking and inspirational to the readers. Acknowledging the angst and tragedy of this war, the Vietnam War, the one our country would like to forget, is a necessary step on the road to breaking the narcotic sensation that war is always the correct answer. This collection of essays, written by my classmates from the Dartmouth Class of 1964, is an attempt to address all these goals.

There are fifty-five essays by classmates and three extras: one by Sage Dunlap Chase, friend and correspondent of classmate Bruce Nickerson, who died in Vietnam; another by Robert Hager, '60, an "on the ground" news correspondent, who reported from Vietnam for NBC News; and finally an essay by William Peters, '15, who served in Iraq, which may become his generation's Vietnam. Each of them adds a special perspective and context.

As a studious, focused student, I graduated Dartmouth with fewer friendships than I should have. After working with these fifty-eight authors, I feel that I have more good friends than at any time in my life. There might have been more essays, which would have gladly been accepted, but some classmates could not, even now, write about their experiences of almost fifty years ago. Similarly, I value my connection with these men.

I would not want to hurt the feelings of even one of these writers. However, and I hope all will understand and agree, some of these essays are extraordinary, in the feelings they share, the experiences endured and related, and the life-changing transformations that occurred as a result of the Vietnam War. To give yourself a broad view, read all the essays about the numerous responsibilities required to "execute a war" and the many places that American men were engaged during that war. Then, return and reread the especially telling essays of Lee Chilcote, Willard Cook, Glen Kendall, Neal Stanley, Charles Williams, and Karl Winkler. I think you will be affected by them as I am still.

I thank Leo Caproni, '42, and his wife, Joanna, who offered very helpful advice based on their experience as editors of *Dartmouth at War* (2011), the collected essays from the Dartmouth Class of 1942 about their engagement in World War II. Finally, I would like to acknowledge my personal guiding light and sometimes coeditor, my wife, Mary Lou, and two adopted classmates, President Emeritus James Wright, '64a, and Professor Edward Miller, '64a. These two scholars are fully engaged with issues related to this book. President Wright, who wrote an invited essay, is an author (*Those Who Have Borne the Battle*, PublicAffairs, 2012) and has championed veterans' issues, including opening Dartmouth's doors to recent veterans like William Peters, '15. Professor Miller, who wrote the introduction, is also an author (*Misalliance: Ngo Dinh Diem, the United States, and the Fate of South Vietnam*, Harvard University Press, 2013) and carries a full teaching load, including his "sold-out" history class, The Vietnam War. The Dartmouth Class of 1964 thanks them for their contributions to this book.

Phillip C. Schaefer

Introduction

When the members of Dartmouth College's senior class assembled for commencement exercises on the morning of June 14, 1964, the Vietnam War seemed very far away. For the newly minted graduates, as for many Americans, there appeared to be good reason to believe that the United States stood on the threshold not of war, but of a new era of peace and prosperity. The country was enjoying a long economic boom that would last for the rest of the decade. The African American freedom struggle neared a historic breakthrough, as Congress inched closer to passing a landmark Civil Rights Act. Americans were also encouraged by recent developments in international affairs. Although the Cold War was far from over, tensions between the United States and the Soviet Union appeared to be subsiding after a period of heightened confrontation earlier in the decade. To the men of the Dartmouth Class of 1964, their departure from Hanover seemed to be taking place at a particularly auspicious moment. War was not very much on their minds.

With hindsight, of course, it is obvious that the Vietnam War was not nearly as distant as it appeared on that June morning. Although Vietnam did not yet occupy a central place in Americans' thinking about the world, it had already gained a reputation as a place of Cold War crisis and danger. By 1964, the United States had been allied with the anticommunist state of South Vietnam for a decade, and had furnished its government with billions in military and economic aid. But that aid had so far failed to transform South Vietnam into the stable, secure, and prosperous ally that Washington envisioned. As a result, U.S. leaders were already planning more direct and massive forms of military intervention in Southeast Asia.

The signs of trouble in South Vietnam had been evident as early as the fall of 1960, around the time the Dartmouth '64s arrived on campus to begin their studies. Newspaper accounts then had indicated that the Saigon regime of Ngo Dinh Diem was losing ground to the Communist-led

Viet Cong insurgency in the countryside. In 1961, President John Kennedy approved large increases in aid and sharply expanded the number of U.S. military advisers in South Vietnam. At first, these measures seemed to tip the military balance in Diem's favor; however, in 1963, South Vietnam was plunged into a new crisis by emergence of an anti-Diem protest movement led by Buddhist monks. After months of demonstrations— including the shocking self-immolation of the monk Thich Quang Duc, captured in a famous photograph by the American journalist Malcolm Browne—Diem decided to suppress the protesters by force. His crackdown on the Buddhists convinced Kennedy and other U.S. officials that the war against the Viet Cong could not be won under Diem's leadership. In early November 1963, Diem was ousted and killed in a military coup that had been green-lighted by Washington. But the South Vietnamese generals who succeeded Diem proved even less effective than he had been. In May 1964, the Central Intelligence Agency warned senior American officials that new Viet Cong gains and the "tide of deterioration" in South Vietnam could lead to the collapse of the Saigon government before the end of the year.

Lyndon Johnson, who had succeeded Kennedy after the latter's assassination in late 1963, was determined not to lose South Vietnam to communism. During his first months in office, the new president quietly took the first steps to turn the Vietnam War into an American war. In addition to further increases in aid and advisers, Johnson approved a covert campaign of sabotage against Communist North Vietnam, the main sponsor of the insurgency. To collect intelligence for these sabotage operations in the north, U.S. warships began patrols in the Gulf of Tonkin, sailing within a few miles of the North Vietnamese coast. On August 2, 1964, an American destroyer, the USS *Maddox*, repelled a brief assault by North Vietnamese torpedo boats. Two nights later, the *Maddox* reported that it was under attack again. Although we now know that the second attack never took place—the captain of the *Maddox* informed his superiors a few hours later that the initial report was the result a false sonar reading— administration officials seized on the incident to press for retaliation. Within days, they had persuaded Congress to authorize the use of force against North Vietnam to block its "deliberate and systematic campaign of aggression." In February 1965, Johnson used this authority to launch Operation Rolling Thunder, a massive strategic bombing offensive against

North Vietnam. A few weeks later, he sent the first U.S. ground combat units to South Vietnam. By the end of 1965, there were 184,000 American troops in Vietnam, with hundreds of thousands more on the way.

This book documents the far-reaching consequences that Johnson's decisions would have for the Dartmouth Class of 1964. More than 150 members of the class served in the U.S. armed forces during the Vietnam War era. Although not all of them fought in Vietnam, they were all profoundly affected by the war, in diverse and complicated ways. Not surprisingly, these veterans grappled with the same physical and emotional demands that war has always imposed on human beings, no matter where or when the fighting takes place. But for the Dartmouth men who served, the burdens of wartime military service were compounded by their status as members of the emerging "Vietnam generation." Along with others in their generational cohort, they fought the war while also struggling over its moral meaning.

As the essays in this volume demonstrate, the Dartmouth '64s who went to Vietnam were involved in all aspects of the U.S. war effort. They encountered famous commanders such as General William Westmoreland and Admiral Elmo Zumwalt; they also participated in "search and destroy" operations, commanded swift boats on South Vietnamese rivers, set up ambushes along the Ho Chi Minh Trail, walked point on jungle patrols, rode helicopters into "hot" landing zones, flew bombing missions over North Vietnam, and fought in the Tet offensive of 1968. Other Dartmouth men studied Vietnamese, built bridges and roads, conducted civic action missions to provide aid to refugees, and worked as broadcasters on Armed Forces Radio Saigon. Most of the '64s who went to Vietnam did so as officers. By their own testimony and that of their peers and commanders, they served with competence, leadership, courage, and distinction.

Yet the essays in this volume also speak to the war's more controversial and morally problematic aspects. Some authors raise troubling questions about the U.S. military's reliance on "body counts," free-fire zones, Agent Orange, napalm, and the forced relocation of Vietnamese civilians. Many contributors have retrospective doubts about the wisdom and the moral defensibility of the entire U.S. intervention in Vietnam. Of course, to express such doubts is not to disparage one's own service, nor that of one's comrades-in-arms. Hugh Savage, who served in the Army Corps of Engineers, was skeptical even from the outset that "the cause we fought for in Vietnam was glorious and honorable." Nevertheless, he remembers his six months in command of a platoon of combat engineers as "one of the most satisfying periods of my life."

The diversity of views and memories in these pages reflects the fact that the Vietnam War remains a deeply contested and controversial topic in the United States today. In many ways, the Vietnam War stands in the same relationship to twentieth-century U.S. history as the Civil War did to nineteenth-century America. Like the Civil War, the war in Vietnam opened deep political and cultural divisions in U.S. society; in both cases, moreover, those political and cultural divisions endured long after the guns had fallen silent. In this respect, these individual recollections of the members of the Class of 1964 provide an illuminating glimpse into the broader currents of American collective memories about Vietnam.

As much as these essays reveal about America, they may reveal even more about Dartmouth—not only about the institution that the college was in 1964, but also about the ways that the Vietnam War shaped its subsequent history. As several of the contributors point out, military service is no longer integrated into the fabric of Dartmouth life to the extent that it was during the early 1960s. The seemingly casual way in which some '64s decided to join one or the other of the college's Reserve Officer Training Corps programs stands in marked contrast to the post-Vietnam history of ROTC at Dartmouth. In the early 1970s, as a result mainly of the war's unpopularity, the faculty voted to end all on-campus ROTC programs. While the Army ROTC program was permitted to return to campus in 1981, its presence remained controversial—especially during the 1990s, when U.S. military leaders refused to end the Pentagon's long-standing ban against gay and lesbian service members. In recent years, the number of Dartmouth students participating in ROTC and other officer commissioning programs has remained relatively small. However, sympathy for these programs among the student body has grown considerably, as demonstrated by the rising attendance at the commissioning ceremonies each year on graduation weekend. In addition, these programs have benefited immensely from the steadfast support of Dartmouth president Jim Wright, who in 2006 successfully lobbied the Army to provide full tuition scholarships to all Dartmouth ROTC cadets.

Although the controversies of the Vietnam era no longer define student life at Dartmouth, the legacies of the Vietnam War are still present on campus today. Dartmouth students remain strongly and even intensely interested in the history of the war, as reflected in the continued large enrollments in the Vietnam War course I have taught since 2004. In part, this enduring interest reflects the questions that students have about America's recent wars in Afghanistan and Iraq, and about the validity of drawing historical analogies to Vietnam. But it also reflects Dartmouth students' recognition that the Vietnam War remains a central event in the modern history of the United States and in the living memory of Americans. In this respect, the essays that appear in the pages that follow are much more than a collection of reminiscences. They are a window onto the connections between Dartmouth's past and present. They also invite us to revisit questions of war and peace that remain as immediate and as critical today as they were in 1964.

As a historian and a member of the Dartmouth faculty, I am deeply grateful to all those who contributed to this volume, both for their military service and sacrifice and for their willingness to share their personal experiences. Thanks also to Phil Schaefer, '64, for his leadership of this worthy project, and to all the members of the Class of 1964 who have supported it.

Edward Miller
Department of History, Dartmouth College

Abbreviations and Glossary

AFB	Air Force base
Airborne	paratroopers
ARVN	Army, Republic of Vietnam
AWOL	absent without leave
BOQ	bachelor officers' quarters
chopper	helicopter
choy oy	multi-meaning exclamation, such as "good grief"
CICV	Combined Intelligence Command, Vietnam
click	kilometer
CO	commanding officer
deuce and a half	2½ ton U.S. Army truck
DIA	Defense Intelligence Agency
DOD	Department of Defense
Huey	Bell UH-1 Iroquois helicopter
IED	improvised explosive device
IG	inspector general
I Corps	("eye-core") northernmost region of South Vietnam, II–IV Corps being progressively farther south
JAG or JAGC	Judge Advocate General's Corps, the legal branch or specialty of the U.S. Air Force, Army, Coast Guard, and Navy
JG	lieutenant junior grade
Jolly Green Giant	Sikorsky HH-3E (and variant models) helicopter
KIA	killed in action

LCDR	lieutenant commander
LZ	landing zone
MACV	Military Assistance Command, Vietnam
MAF	Marine Amphibious Force
MI	Military Intelligence
MIA	missing in action
MOS	military occupation specialty
MP	military police
MRE	meal, ready-to-eat (field ration)
MSTS	Military Sea Transportation Service
NCO	noncommissioned officer
NSA	National Security Agency
NVA	North Vietnamese Army
OCS	Officer Candidate School, institution that trains civilians and enlisted personnel in order for them to gain a commission as officers
PFC	private first class
POW	prisoner of war
Puff the Magic Dragon	Douglas AC-47 gunship aircraft
PX	post exchange (military base store)
R&R	rest and relaxation/recuperation
ROTC	Reserve Officer Training Corps
RPG	rocket-propelled grenade
SDS	Students for a Democratic Society
SJA	Staff Judge Advocate
USAA	United Services Automobile Association
USAID	United States Agency for International Development
VC	Viet Cong (guerrilla forces)
XO	executive officer

1961–1963

"Ask what you can do for your country."
--John Fitzgerald Kennedy

Cuban Missile Crisis

U.S. military employs Agent Orange.

Buddhist monk Thich Quang Duc sets himself on fire
in Saigon protesting the Diem government.

Military Service

TOM SEYMOUR : U.S. MARINE CORPS

t was December 22, 1962, about one o'clock in the morning, when I alighted from the train that had taken me from Hartford, Connecticut, to Beaufort, South Carolina, to begin my Marine Corps basic training at Parris Island. Strangely, I had been given a private room for the long train ride, which took me through Washington, D.C., in the middle of a huge snowstorm, the cause of my late arrival at Beaufort. It was the last sense of luxury I was to feel for a long time.

At the little receiving station for recruits there was no one to be seen inside. Calling out to indicate my presence, I had the first encounter with my new life when a very large Marine came bounding into the anteroom, screaming his displeasure at seeing me—probably because I'd interrupted what he thought was going to be the rest of an uneventful evening just before Christmas, a time when virtually no new recruits had the poor sense to darken his doorstep. In fact, I was the only one who spent the night there before being taken by bus to Parris Island early the next morning, and I was the only one who got off that bus to be warmly welcomed by three drill instructors who must have enjoyed themselves immensely as they circled around me screaming like hyenas that I was just about the worst, lowliest, foulest, ugliest, and most disgusting piece of shit they had ever laid eyes on.

Thus began a three-year experience that was to change my life forever, in ways that I never could have imagined.

Boot camp training itself, once it began three weeks later, well after the holidays, consisted of ten grueling weeks of marching, hard exercise, learning how to fire a rifle, sliding down cables over muddy water to see if we would fall in (few of us did), learning the history of the Corps, and endless verbal and physical abuse by our drill instructors. The tone changed

Tom Seymour

over time, though, and most of us became more confident that we could survive the ordeal and even, maybe, become real Marines. In retrospect, of course, the purpose of the training was clear—to break us all down to the same level and then to build us back up in the mold of what the Marine Corps wanted us to become. On graduation day, when my family came down to see me, I was already a much different person—both physically and mentally. I experienced an enormous satisfaction in having made it through Parris Island—even winning my PFC stripes before leaving.

I had dropped out of Dartmouth after my sophomore year, demonstrating the only iota of good sense I still possessed—a realization that I was wasting a wonderful opportunity at college and needed a good kick in the ass. My upbringing had been WASP middle class, private day school—and then on to Dartmouth without any thought as to what a huge gift a liberal arts college education was. I decided that the Marine Corps was probably the best instrument to administer the boot to my posterior.

Boot camp was followed by infantry training in North Carolina, which, in turn, was followed by a special communications school for six months in Florida. It was secretive work that we were being readied for, and, apparently deemed not to be a security risk, I was sent home for a month's leave and then on to Japan, arriving at a small inland Naval Security Group base near Yokohama on January 9, 1964. During the next two years, the Marine Corps sent me to various places around the world and in various modes of transport for the purpose of doing what we had been trained to do. While never in ground combat, we were told our work was important, and it was often dangerous when on deployment. We were on the very front lines of the Cold War.

The Japan experience was for me divided into two distinct parts. The first was the purely military one of doing my job as a Marine and being one of a group of people who became—and remain—some of my very closest and dearest friends. The other was my exposure to Japan as the first foreign country I had ever been in. These two parts were nonexclusive, because much of what I learned about Japan was done while in the company of my Marine Corps buddies. When growing up in Connecticut—and also at Dartmouth—I had been exposed almost exclusively to people who were very much like me, never having to worry about whether there'd be enough food on the table or what we'd do if Dad lost his job. It was, of course, not "wrong" that my friends and I were so fortunate, but in my case, anyway, it had walled me off from most of the rest of the world where other young people's experiences were very different. Being in the military ended forever that isolation, and it was for me one of the greatest gifts I ever received. It opened my eyes to so many things that I certainly would never have seen or understood otherwise.

Japan took me to itself slowly and with some resistance. When I first started to venture off base, it was for only brief periods—a couple of hours or so—until I could return to a little America of Coke machines, cheap cigarettes, a small club for enlisted men, and our barracks close by. Gradually, I branched out for walks into parts of Yokohama where the Japanese themselves lived, and I started to eat their food. Some guys on our base had rented a small cottage down on the coast—in a place called Hayama—and we would go there when on liberty for parties on the beach with newfound Japanese friends—of both genders. It was great. In addition, we would go off for whole days to visit temples and shrines in and around nearby Tokyo, frequently ending up at a jazz or folk-song coffee shop where we could talk, smoke, listen to the music—and luxuriate in the joy of being away from the military and experiencing something new and really exciting.

During the spring of my second year in Japan, a Marine friend and I decided to take leave for a couple of weeks and tour around western and southern Japan. Part of this adventure took us to the city of Matsuyama on Shikoku, Japan's fourth-largest island, where we went to stay for a couple of nights. It was there that I met my wife-to-be, but of course I didn't have any inkling of that then. It happened when the manager at a hotel we wanted to stay at, but couldn't afford, asked if we were students.

We sensed that something good might happen, so we lied and said yes. Well, in that case, he said, he'd call a couple of ESS (English Speaking Society) students from the local university who could show us around town and practice their English at the same time. We naturally expected a couple of guys to appear and were quite pleasantly surprised when it turned out to be two girls—one of whom is now my wife of forty-five years. She became a high school English teacher in Japan, and we married three years later, long after the Marine Corps was history for me. I recall that my friend then returned to our base while I went on alone to the next port of call. There I was able to find an affordable inn and was ushered into the huge public hot-springs bath after depositing my bag in the room. All by myself, I thought this was what heaven would be in the unlikely case I was ever invited in. But, just then, the door opened and in came a Japanese couple, both completely as they had been born, only bigger and better developed. Well, so embarrassed was I to climb out of the water in their presence, I waited until they left—at which point I had turned as red as a lobster—my first encounter, though happily not the last, with mixed bathing in Japan.

Into the midst of this idyll intruded a war—the Vietnam War. There had been rumblings of trouble for some time—an increase in the military advisers sent by President Kennedy, the coup that toppled the South Vietnamese government, a growing bellicosity from the North. And then there were the Gulf of Tonkin incidents. The first involved the USS *Maddox*, attacked by PT boats from North Vietnam. This caught our attention in Japan because of the similarity between our work and the mission of the *Maddox*. Then, in 1965, the United States began bombing the North, followed by the Marine landing at Da Nang. By August there were 125,000 U.S. troops in country, and the buildup was just beginning. In the following year, the total had reached over 400,000.

We suddenly realized that we were serving our country in the *military*. I personally had not seriously contemplated that my joining the Marines might actually involve being in a war. Neither I nor my Marine buddies were afraid, but we were concerned. We knew that this situation could put all of our personal plans on hold, and, sure enough, an order very shortly came down informing all Marines that their enlistments were to be extended "for the duration." This was especially upsetting to me because I had applied for, and been granted, what was called an "early out," designed for soldiers who had been accepted into or, in my case, back into an accredited college or university. So, instead of ending my Marine Corps career in December 1965, I had been scheduled to leave in September, in time for Dartmouth's fall term.

As Marines, our first instinct was to accept what our government decided it needed to do, ours not to reason why. Despite this, the drumbeat of war news from Southeast Asia did not always seem to be in accord with facts we were hearing from other quarters or, in some cases, not even to make sense. Nevertheless, we were not overburdened by doubts, and many career Marines were happy that they might soon be asked to use their military training in a real war.

Then, something that "never" happens in the military happened to me—a lone exception to the "extended for the duration" requirement came down from above in late August 1965. Those who had previously been approved for an "early out" to go to university were told they could go. Given the war situation, it was with very mixed feelings that I alone walked off the base in Japan, leaving behind all my friends who faced a very uncertain future. A couple of weeks later I was back in Hanover, housed in a small, college-owned house on lower Main Street with a number of other military veterans. The contrast with my life in the Corps could not have been greater.

The New England autumn of 1965 was an especially beautiful one and helped ease the transition back to Dartmouth. To me, though, the students appeared very young and immature and fraternities a kind of joke. I found the budding campus antiwar activists totally out of touch with the "real world," looking upon their demonstrations as some big party. It was all kind of fun for them, or so it seemed to me, and I can recall one professor who brought his son on his shoulders to an antiwar event that I had come to observe. He told someone standing next to him that his greatest fear was that his son would become a "hawk," the world to him at that time being divided into hawks and doves. Ha, ha, I thought, really funny—especially, had they been there, to see my friends and all the others fighting in Asia. I was sure they would have gotten a big laugh. I was, in short, quite turned off.

Then one evening, I went to see a film on the war being shown on campus by a professor of mine who himself had only recently returned from a stint as an officer in the Navy. The film showed South Vietnamese troops moving and engaging the enemy in battle. One scene was of several soldiers raking their still living North Vietnamese prisoners at point-blank range with their weapons on automatic. The bodies of the victims as they died bounced several inches off the ground because of the force of the bullets, a scene I will never forget. I thought, this *couldn't* be what our troops would do. It was a turning point for me, as it brought into question all the government justifications for the war and how it was being executed. Gradually, as I studied and talked more about the war, I came to believe it was probably the biggest foreign policy and military blunder ever committed by my country. Especially I recall General Lewis B. Hershey, then head of the Selective Service Administration, visiting Hanover to give a speech telling Dartmouth students why it was in the national interest that they be given deferments to continue their education. In truth I had been a beneficiary of this philosophy without knowing it because that policy must have been behind my "early out" from the Marine Corps. While most students, naturally, were strongly in favor of this government policy, it didn't require a Dartmouth education to realize that those fighting and dying for their deferred peers would be the younger, less affluent, and disproportionately minority males—which, of course, is exactly what happened.

That was how I came to oppose the war—though quietly to myself, mostly. I didn't go to demonstrations. I didn't write letters to editors. I just couldn't. And I never once felt anything but respect for those Marines I had known and not known—and all the others in the military—who were serving their country during this difficult time. I remember when, two years later as a grad student at the University of Michigan, I saw a Marine Corps officer friend off to Vietnam and, about ten months later, welcomed back a person so changed by his experience that he was completely unable to talk about it or to be a part of the world around him. That virtually no one in the United States wanted to acknowledge his—and others'—service, because opposition to the war had grown so strong, is one of the blackest marks against us as a people in the last century. The wounds of the Vietnam conflict have not yet healed, and they likely never will.

So, after all this, what did serving in the Marine Corps mean to me? Without question it was the great turning point of my life. First, my Japan years gave me my wife (and two children) and, eventually, after much study and some experience, provided the basis for a business career that kept me in that country for almost all my adult life. Nearly as important, the comradeship with those I knew and who survived the conflict in Southeast Asia is one of the most precious gifts I have received. So strong is this feeling that it makes completely clear the theory of why soldiers and Marines fight and die in combat. They don't fight primarily for the lofty principles of their mission or even to protect their country—though these are important to them. No, they fight to save their friends, their buddies, their comrades. Even for those of us, like myself, who never saw real ground combat, the strength of those bonds of friendship is so great that it absolutely never wavers, never weakens, never breaks. It is not encumbered by doubts or by concern with one's social standing, education, income, career success (or its lack), color of skin, religion, marital status, political differences. It just is.

Equally, the timing of my service and its intersection with the Vietnam War—a war that I came to strongly oppose—caused me in time to become much more skeptical of what my government was telling me. To many in my generation, the election of President Kennedy and his appointment of such apparently intelligent and qualified people reassured us that our national leaders were rational, fair, and unambiguously dedicated to doing what was right for the United States and for the world. This idealism and naïveté were so greatly diminished by the loss of fifty-eight thousand young men and women who were killed in Vietnam—some of whom were my good friends—for reasons that did not make sense. None of this changes the feelings of gratitude I have at being able to serve in the Marine Corps for three years, but my time in service also led me never again to accept without a great deal of doubt and skepticism my government's call for measures that put the lives of our military young people at risk.

Tom Seymour ended active duty in September 1965 to return to Dartmouth. He graduated in 1967, having majored in government. In July 1968 he married Reiko Shiraishi in Japan at the start of a year of language study, part of a master's program in Japanese Studies at the University of

Michigan. The couple had two children, both raised in Japan: Lisa, born 1969, since married, with one son, living in Malaysia; and Daniel, born in 1973, married with one daughter, living in Honolulu.

In the summer of 1966, under the aegis of the Ledyard Canoe Club, Tom participated with five other Dartmouth students and four students from Cambridge University in England in a fifteen-hundred-mile kayak adventure up Japan's Inland Sea and on to Tokyo, chronicled in the September 1967 issue of *National Geographic*.

Having spent nearly thirty-five years of his adult life living in Tokyo as a businessman in subsidiaries of U.S. corporations, Tom is now semi-retired, residing in Amherst, Massachusetts, with his wife Reiko.

Tom was president of the Dartmouth Club of Japan from 1988 to 1997 and is a hospice volunteer and a board member of the Veterans Education Project.

An Undergrad in Vietnam

ANTHONY B. THOMPSON : U.S. ARMY

n 1963, with a firm push from Thad Seymour, dean of the college, I found myself suspended from the Hanover Plain. The plan was to "grow up" during two years, preferably in the U.S. Army, and return to Dartmouth ready to absorb something more valuable than Tanzi's best. So, in the spring of 1963 I volunteered for the draft. However, because my basic training was in Fort Dix, New Jersey, and many of my friends were working in New York City, the first six months of those twenty-four contributed little to growing up. For the most part I had a pretty good time, almost a continuation of the good times at the Big Green. But the Army was not all fun and games. They tried hard to make us soldiers, physically and mentally, and gave us batteries of tests to determine where we would best serve our country with our innate abilities. At one point I was asked to extend my two-year enlistment and go to Fort Benning, Georgia, for OCS. No way. I did score high as a medic, and soon was enrolled, yes, in radio training school, learning to be a radio telephone operator (RTO), a fateful MOS (Military Occupational Specialty).

After basic training I received my orders: I was going to be on the ski patrol in Garmisch, Germany, at an Army R&R facility. Life is good. That fantasy came to an end when those orders were revised; I was to report to Military Assistance Advisory Group, Vietnam—MAAG Vietnam—later to become MAC-V. I would be paid by the Navy and attached to the Army of the Republic of Vietnam, stationed in I Corps, near the DMZ and headquartered in Hue. What happened is that the powers that be did not want skilled American Army officers to be alone in the field—or to double up, so they attached to each adviser a lowly grunt, frequently an RTO, like me.

During my first six months in country, I rotated in and out of two outposts, Aloui and Tabat, on the Ho Chi Minh Trail in the A Shau Valley

Tabat from the air; airstrip is at upper right

on the Laotian border. These outposts were essentially accessible only by air, either by helicopter or by de Havilland Otter or Beaver, the workhorse aircraft in Vietnam. They landed in a hewn-out dirt strip covered with perforated steel planking. I was the radioman for the other American assigned as an adviser to that ARVN unit, typically a career officer with Ranger/Airborne training. At that time in 1964, typically the officer was in need of combat experience to further his checkered career.

MAAG's mission was to make the ARVN a complete army, capable of protecting the South, as well as protect U.S. interests in Southeast Asia. To the South Vietnamese the NVA were invaders from a despotic, socialist country focused on throwing out the Americans and making the South Vietnamese bend to their way of life. For us to do our job, we had to earn the respect of the ARVN soldiers, done mainly by fighting alongside them. Only then could we, maybe, advise them how to maintain their vehicles, set up effective chains of command, create a sound administration, etc. The mission of I Corps was to satisfy Saigon's and Washington's intent to keep North Vietnam's (Chinese and Russian) war matériel out of South Vietnam and to pacify I Corps. Finally, our mission in the A Shau Valley was simply to avoid inadvertently giving the VC a reason

Trunk made by Private Bua

to annihilate our small force. We had about one hundred soldiers in our command, and at any one time about forty-five of them were manning the three listening posts, up to a mile away, ringing our outpost. The balance of the unit was left to conduct patrols and defend. Many times, because we didn't have the manpower to relieve them first, we had to bring the men in from those posts, and only then send the relief force to retake our own posts.

It was, however, a rewarding time, an opportunity to learn the language, to meet true South Vietnamese people, to eat only their food, and to live the daily life that the ARVN soldier lived. To this day I have—rather, my son has—a trunk made for me by Private Bua, an ARVN soldier, out of wood from 105 mm howitzer boxes, made entirely without tools. That was also a time when, sleeping in my Army-issue, mosquito-netted hammock in our semi-underground bunker, we were mortared. In my haste to pop out of the hammock, I literally spun myself into a cocoon. That same bunker was visited by a colorful but small snake, which, when I went to pick it off the center post, was preemptively cut in two by a soldier who knew it was a (very dangerous!) coral snake. The next day, someone threw a four-foot worm the size of your arm into our bunker

Lieutenant Mowrey and Private Bua;
our bunker at Tabat

for laughs. It also was a time when, offered the opportunity to carry a Thompson submachine gun, I found out—when I released the bolt but a fraction of an inch from the chamber—that a Thompson has a fixed firing pin. It blew a six-inch hole in the dirt floor of the bunker right next to my foot. It was in Aloui, one of the two compounds in the valley, where I first heard bullets fly by my head as I was taking a leak out on the perimeter (protected by a six-foot-wide trench filled with punji sticks). On another occasion an ARVN soldier, squatting next to me on a resupply Huey, had his entire back barely creased by a bullet fired by a VC on the ground. It was also where Raymond Burr, aka Perry Mason, choppered in, just to say hello to two lone American soldiers and take well wishes home to our families. During that duty I saw no combat per se, but we lived each day expecting the worst. I was in the valley when the United States bombed Haiphong harbor, and we went on red alert, fearing being overrun.

In 1964–65, a typical tour in Vietnam consisted of six months "out" (field operations) and six months "in" (some administrative duty). At the start of my six months "in" I volunteered to replace an Aussie sergeant major adviser who feared going on a particular ARVN chopper mission into the boonies. That led me to a reassignment with that ARVN unit for the rest of my tour. It was the only ARVN unit to my knowledge to receive a U.S. Presidential Distinguished Unit Citation, for "extraordinary heroism in action defending their homeland against an opposing force in Quang Tri province from Aug. 1964 to Oct. 1965." This was a unit with superior leadership. It was a motivated, aggressive, disciplined regiment (First Regiment, I Corps), and a unit with many successful operations against the NVA and the VC. In the Cua Valley, shortly after a battle that resulted in many enemy KIA and a large haul of weapons, we were

APC that carried First Regiment's command element,
destroyed by RPGs

notified that Saigon was on its way to review the results, a wartime photo
op for the big boys. Along with Vietnam's biggest boy, General Nguyen
Khanh, came Ambassador Henry Cabot Lodge's personal secretary, Tony
Lake, whom I recognized as an old boyfriend of my sister. Tony went on
to become a strong voice in our State Department, at one time earning
a cover on the Sunday *New York Times Magazine*. We had a revealing
discussion about this battle. It appeared that, as the KIA count proceeded
up the chain, the numbers increased dramatically. This was back when
kill count determined Congress's willingness to spend dollars in and on
Vietnam, and those in charge had no shame in doctoring statistics. This
was to me an early hint of a looming problem.

The First Regiment was rightfully feared from the DMZ in the north,
down to Phu Bai in the south, to the A Shau Valley in the west, and it
owned the coast. However, one night in March 1965, an NVA unit mortared our command post. With armored personnel carriers serving more
as tanks than as personnel carriers, we went after them. Using the mortar
fire as bait, the NVA had set up an ambush predicated on the First's un-
failing aggressiveness, and we drove right into it. As a result, our entire
command element was either killed by RPGs or captured. I was neither.
That day the First Regiment was effectively wiped out. With reinforcements and the remnants of the regiment, we pursued the NVA, hoping
to avenge the loss and free those captured, but we were not successful. A

side note—my family in Vermont found out about the loss of the First Regiment via my maternal grandfather, who lived in Budapest and read the news of this NVA victory in the Communist press in Hungary.

Shortly after, and without a functioning ARVN unit, I went to Hong Kong for a five-day R&R and DEROS'd (Date Eligible for Return from Overseas) as scheduled, back to California and the United States. Certainly two years older and pretty certainly somewhat wiser.

My return to the Dartmouth campus, a few short weeks later, had many disappointments. My readmission meeting was a mess; the main discussion was about what I had been doing over the past two years to maintain my academic major. Ironically, it was Thad who convinced me to rejoin Dartmouth. Once again a student, I had to contend with the SDS, including, at my own fraternity, being called a moral coward for going to Vietnam as a soldier. The static I saw and felt on campus drove me to take an apartment in White River Junction, Vermont, where I resided until my graduation.

On graduating, Anthony Thompson was an election aide to Vermont governor Richard Snelling, worked in New York City, went to Australia for six years, then returned to Stowe with his wife and daughter to run the family heating oil business and to have their second child, a son. Active in town affairs, he was a Stowe Area trustee, chaired the Stowe Grand Prix tennis tournament (won twice by Jimmy Connors), served on the board of a local bank, chaired the District Environmental Commission, and sat as alternate on the Vermont Environmental Board (and reluctantly voted down Walmart's Vermont application). Divorced, he married a Colby Junior College lady he had met at Dartmouth before going to Vietnam. Tony sold his business in 1997 to Valero Energy and moved to Florida to enjoy both the weather and lack of state taxes.

Dartmuth Interruptus

Military and Maturity

LOCKWOOD (WOODY) BARR : U.S. ARMY

A t the end of my sophomore year in 1962, I found myself on academic probation with the very real prospect of experiencing Dean
Seymour's gentle propulsion out Dartmouth's door. As fall term
got under way, it became increasingly apparent that I was not
going to be able to salvage any usable parts from the academic wreckage
of my first two years. Dean Seymour sat me down in his office, and we
had a quick discussion about the obvious: I needed to get out of Dodge.
I remember him saying distinctly, "One year away isn't enough. Two is
better. Three or more even better still. The military is the best option for
students in your predicament." (He had been my second-term English
teacher, so knew all about my albatrosses.) This was 1962. If the war in
Vietnam had been on the radar at the time, I'm not sure what his advice
would have been.

I wandered somewhat befuddled back to my fraternity (Psi U) and sat
down with two brothers, who had just returned from "military sabbat-
icals" themselves. Bruce Cole and Wick Warrick both had served in the
Army Security Agency, and both spoke highly of this branch as an interesting option. Duty stations were appealing and very nontraditional,
and one might even be sent to Army Language School to learn another
language. At the end of our conversation Wick mentioned someone he
knew who was assigned to Army Intelligence. He said that this guy had
the most amazing experience, and perhaps I should inquire about that
option when I enlisted.

I took Wick's advice and asked the recruiting sergeant about the Army
Intelligence and Security branch (AIS). I was told to go to a different location in Boston, where I was interviewed by a couple of agents. After pass-

ing a battery of tests and an extensive background check (I learned later), I received the news that my AIS application had been accepted. I spent a harrowing eight or ten weeks at Fort Dix doing "basic" in early January 1963. In March, I was sent to Fort Holabird in Baltimore for Army Intelligence training. From there I boarded a troopship bound for Germany. My initial destination was Oberursel, on the outskirts of Frankfurt am Main, headquarters of the 513th Intelligence Corps Group. Five days later, I was told to put on civilian clothes, handed a duffle bag and a .38 Smith and Wesson detective special, and was hustled onto a train bound for Munich. At a young twenty, I was the epitome of the naïve American.

My duty station, a small field office of the 513th, was on the top floor of an old German military *Kaserne*. The unit operated under a cover name. My job was initially that of glorified clerk, working in support of others, called agent-handlers, whose job it was to recruit third-country individuals to gather information on military targets in various countries behind the Iron Curtain. Although it initially had the ring of a rejected James Bond manuscript, in fact it was tedious, routine work. It did become a shade more interesting when I spent my last year or so living in an apartment in downtown Munich under the pretext that I was an "international sales consultant." (My twenty-one- or twenty-two-year-old fresh-faced persona wouldn't have borne too much scrutiny, believe me!)

Sometime in 1964, Vietnam took on real shape for me. A young Bostonian named Stan was transferred to our unit from a yearlong stint in Army Intelligence working out of a village somewhere in the 'Nam boonies. The term "PTSD" had yet to be coined, but Stan was clearly its victim. He told hair-raising stories of what life and service were like "over there." He had developed several nervous tics he surely didn't pick up while studying at BU prior to enlistment. Our country's involvement in Vietnam was now undeniable. And so was the real possibility of my term of service being extended should things heat up even more over there.

In 1965 I got married and also applied for an early release from the military. Because my wife was "a foreign national," it was easier to grant my request than begin the cumbersome process of running background checks on her. I spent the next year working and studying in Germany. What I was actually doing was trying to muster the courage to reapply to the college. My service and the extra year away fit Dean Seymour's criteria for successful resumption of studies, so my application was accepted.

My marital and academic status, plus my nonessential Army MOS gave me first-tier protection from being recalled to service.

I was initially nervous about reentering the world of academe. After all, what had I done to prepare myself for a rigorous course of study? Gotten married? Worked a boring job in the Army? Read a few books? Well, the dean's words proved prophetic: time away, and "growing up," did indeed make a huge difference. I majored in German, was nominated for a Woodrow Wilson Fellowship, graduated "with distinction," and gained admission to Harvard for grad studies. Why the academic success all of a sudden? Upon reflection I think there were a number of contributing factors. Four years of added maturity, marriage, and the birth of our first child during my final Dartmouth terms certainly played a huge part. The friends I made in my unit also became important guides and role models for me. All my "comrades-in-arms" had graduated from college, most had done at least two years of graduate study, to a man they spoke fluent German and another language (Russian, Hungarian, Czech, Polish, etc.), and four of them were Woodrow Wilson Fellowship recipients, from Yale, UC Berkeley, Columbia, and the University of Pennsylvania. Conversations over our after-duty beer were about books and ideas rather than complaints about chow and the "first shirt," or senior noncommissioned officer. (We had to eat off-post, and some of these guys were already sergeants.)

Obviously, my time in the Army was markedly different from that of my classmates.[1] Not only in the nature of my duties, but in the timing. Leaving school midstream and returning married (with a child before graduation), living on the GI Bill and what my wife earned working for Professor John Kemeny in the Math Department, defined a much different "Dartmouth experience." My first years in Hanover had to do with the relationships I had with peers. My final years were defined much more by my course work and my professors—more than a few of whom were extraordinary teachers and scholars. My time in the Army certainly affected "my Dartmouth," but it also, directly and indirectly, set me firmly upon that other Frostian road, "the one not taken."

1. Especially that of my roommate, Bruce Nickerson, who perished while flying a combat mission in 1966.

After the Army, Woody Barr returned to Dartmouth, graduated in 1968, and went on to Harvard for a master of arts in teaching. He has since been a teacher and administrator in Boston; in West Berlin, Germany; several towns in New Hampshire and Maine; and in Vienna, Austria, from where he retired in 2005. He did further graduate work at UNH and again at Harvard. He currently resides in Portsmouth, New Hampshire, with his wife of forty-seven years and happily near his children and grandchildren. He volunteers in a local "alternative high school" and is a board member of Unlimited Possibilities, an education and service foundation.

Cold Wind for the Hanover Plain

NELSON CARMAN : U.S. NAVY

I t blew in off President Kennedy's lips the night of his T.V. address to the nation, October 22, 1962. For me, Homecoming 2012, and enjoying the fiftieth-anniversary celebration for our returning 1962 undefeated football lettermen, triggered a week of memories both stark and fuzzy, of concurrent joy and fear; it needed resolution.

Hark back to October 1962, when the day and the dates match up exactly with our 2012 calendar. On the evening of October 14, deep in the bowels of the CIA photo recon lab, very recent results of a U-2 spy plane overflight revealed a half dozen Soviet ballistic missile sites near completion in western Cuba. Blithely, on campus, under a glorious Indian summer canopy, a week of classes culminating with homecoming meant a showdown with the rated and hated Holy Cross Crusaders.

In total secrecy, President Kennedy and his top advisers were presented with the photo analysis and threat assessment on Tuesday morning, October 16. Kennedy was enraged. So began the absolute pinnacle of the Cold War, and history's closest whiff of nuclear Armageddon: the thirteen days known as the Cuban Missile Crisis.

The sold-out homecoming football showdown on October 20 went from tense anticipation to a monstrous burst of collective euphoria in the two-plus hours of gridiron collision; the fierce and imaginative secondary spider trap woven by Spangenberg and Madden, combined with the deCalesta-sizing of the Crusader running lanes, provided the statement shutout of the eastern power. Both stands emptied onto the field in frenzied release, and the Rollins Chapel bells pealed longest and loudest in a generation's recall. Celebrations raged on into Monday morning.

At the White House, Kennedy and his brain trust met behind very tight doors to ruminate over the military response offerings for Nikita

Nelson Carman, July 1965, Gitmo, Cuba

Khrushchev. The hawks (cowboys) wanted to bomb Cuba into oblivion. The cooler heads (doves) wanted a sober dialogue with the Soviets.

As I set off to Monday (October 22) classes immersed in homecoming glow, my hedonistic notions began forming for the coming weekend's great exodus to Cambridge, to witness our talent-laden team crush Harvard. Yet I cannot pull any memory of the lopsided pounding of the Crimson, because . . . I wasn't . . . I did not go! What?

The trigger to my memory banks became clear, recalling that Monday night of President Kennedy's television address to the nation revealing the crisis. He was up front and candid with us all. The Soviets had better remove all missiles in Cuba immediately, or face thermonuclear annihilation. Worst-case assessment: a few enemy missiles might sneak through, risking a maximum loss of only one-third of the U.S. population. Soviet R-14 nuclear missiles had a radius capability of Lima, Peru, to Hudson's Bay, Canada. So a free gift from Khrushchev to Hanover was a very unwanted plausibility. Like wildfire smoke, a palpable pall of gravity hung over the entire campus social week, as the high-stakes brinksmanship played out in plain sight on the U.N. floor and the TV networks. Indeed, undergraduates were glued into current events, openly discussing their fears, uncertain futures, and draft status from dorms to frat basements.

All Dartmouth ROTC unit totals neared three hundred—well over seventy-five per class, and in 1962 a very well accepted curriculum choice. The option paid for tuition in exchange for a second required minor involving at least four add-on extra courses, weekly drill, and summer military training assignments. All ROTC members were summoned by noon

Tuesday to their respective service department offices and were given a code alert and told "don't make any travel plans till further notice." Give us a list of communication chain of contacts, and, if you receive the alert, pack one suitcase and report to the basement of Alumni Gym. You will then be on active duty. The clarification confirmed—that's why I never made it to Cambridge.

Watching the wipeout of the Crimson on TV that October 27 was a welcome distraction, not knowing how close the globe came to the big launch through a number of small-scale hotheaded blunders. Ironically, the 1964 release of the Stanley Kubrick film *Dr. Strangelove* parodies the missile crisis, had the cowboys' desires prevailed. The crisis lifted Sunday morning, as the president and brother Bobby in their cool, collected, finest hour, got a secret deal done with Khrushchev, independent from the cowboy advisers. The missiles were removed from Cuba, and our entire military at DEFCON 2 (second-highest defense condition, one less than "nuclear war imminent") stood down. Whew! Tension released, a makeup road trip to Cornell ensued.

Upon graduation of the classes of the mid 1960s, the Vietnam War buildup steered heavily the initial military billet assignments after Dartmouth. Sadly, two close fraternity brothers, Steve Mac Vean, '65, and Eric Muller, '66, are memorialized on the Vietnam Wall.

In 2001 Nelson Carman returned home to the town that sent him to Dartmouth. Upon both parents' passing, he reverse-mortgaged the home he grew up in. Single, with no children, he spent twenty-five years teaching and coaching in public systems in the Rocky Mountain region and another twenty years as a field engineer rehabbing above-ground utility grids for telephone and power companies in forty-eight states. He became active for the alumni office in 1986, and is now on his third Dartmouth Club, running the Dartmouth book award program in Rochester, New York. Currently he works for the Town of Penfield, near Rochester, developing local history texts, as well as a special program coordinator for the Recreation Department in concerts, big band dances, and the town trail system development. He is always up for a "road trip" anywhere new where history and habitats intersect.

1964

U.S. Senate approves Tonkin Gulf Resolution authorizing the
president to "take all necessary measures" to repel attacks
against U.S. forces and to "prevent further aggression."

The Twenty-Fourth Amendment to the Constitution is adopted,
guaranteeing the right to vote in federal elections without
payment of any tax.

Three civil rights workers are murdered in Mississippi.

William Brewster Nickerson, '64

SAGE DUNLAP CHASE

L ieutenant (Junior Grade) William Brewster (Bruce) Nickerson, '64, U.S. Navy, was the first Dartmouth man to die in Vietnam. On April 22, 1966, he was bombardier/navigator on a Grumman A-6 Intruder off the aircraft carrier *Kitty Hawk* when his plane was presumably shot down by enemy fire over the Gulf of Tonkin, following an attack on the city of Vinh. His body and that of the pilot, Lieutenant Commander Robert F. Weimorts, were never recovered. Although initially he was listed as MIA, Bruce Nickerson's name is engraved on the Vietnam Wall. It was his sixty-second mission—he had just turned twenty-four.

Bruce was an only son, and his death devastated his father, E. Carleton Nickerson (of old Cape Cod lineage) and stepmother Shirley, and also his mother, Priscilla Carr, and stepfather Charles, of Naples, Florida. All are now deceased, but forty-six years later, his older sister still can't say his name without sobbing, and his younger half-sister regrets not having known him better because of being understandably preoccupied with her own teen life. His death left a huge hole in the lives of countless friends of all ages and all walks of life. For such a young man, he left a remarkably large legacy.

His parents divorced early on, and Bruce was raised by his mother in New Canaan and Stamford, Connecticut. He graduated from Deerfield Academy in 1960 and moved on to Hanover with a number of classmates. At Dartmouth he was a member of Psi Upsilon, on the Judiciary Committee, chairman of Cutter Hall, and head of Paleopitus. He was very active in St. Thomas Episcopal Church, serving as an acolyte and volunteering many hours at Edgerton House. Rev. Edward MacBurney and his

Lieutenant (JG) William Brewster
(Bruce) Nickerson

wife, Anne, were dear friends, and Chauncey Allen (longtime psychology professor) and his wife, Margaret, were almost surrogate parents.

Bruce was very conflicted about enlisting in the Navy. He was incredibly idealistic, patriotic, and moral— a truly "good" person who was sensitive and mature beyond his years. His life had been sheltered and privileged, yet he had incredible compassion for those who had less. Unquestionably scarred by divorce, he worried about doing the right thing. Not surprisingly, he chose to major in philosophy. In 1962, he spent time working as a Winant Volunteer doing settlement work in England, and spent the following two summers as a counselor for an Episcopal camp for inner-city children in northwest Connecticut—a job he loved. In his last year at Dartmouth he was seriously thinking of going into the ministry, or possibly doing graduate work in counseling or social services. Yet the Navy beckoned. It was a lonely, difficult decision for him, but as the war ramped up, patriotism won out.

Having made his decision, he put his all into his training at the Naval Air Station in Pensacola, Florida. He graduated first academically in his flight class and third when academic and physical factors were balanced. This allowed him to win an appeal against an earlier restriction on flying due to a minor physical disability. Although he was very excited about the opportunity to fly, as his deployment neared, the ethical conflict re-emerged. In 1965 he wrote:

> I am a living paradox or hypocrite, for I say I believe one thing, and do another. I love flying, Naval Aviation, and the Navy, but the part about dropping bombs fights with my heart and soul. I know I am doing what God wants me to and that I am here to sworchim, but to fathom the mysterious and seemingly incongruous ways he works leaves me totally perplexed.

Bruce as counselor
for inner-city
camp

"I am a living paradox or a hypocrite, for I say one thing, and do another. I love flying, Naval Aviation and the Navy, but the part about dropping bombs fights with my heart and soul. I know I am doing what God wants me to and I am here to serve him, but to fathom the mysterious and seemingly incongruous ways he works leaves me totally perplexed."

In a long letter written two days before he died, Bruce wrote of the beauty of Vietnam from the air—the lush vegetation and the "countless magic waterfalls and winding rivers," and how hard it was from the air to believe that there was a war going on. He was very aware of what a distanced and comfortable life those in the Navy experienced, compared to the Army and Marines on the ground. Yet their mission was cruel. "Many times I have made bombing runs and there has been a friendly

Bruce (standing fourth from left) on aircraft carrier

village within 500 yards of my target, or I've been asked to bomb every-thing in a village except the church. No war has been fought like this before, and it's a strange sensation to make runs so close to supposed friendlies."

There was an almost prophetic tone to this letter (received after his death). He spoke of his luck in surviving so far, and mentioned comrades rescued after being shot down the day before. He wrote of the pain of losing four friends, and of visiting the American-Philippine Memorial. "The beauty and silence of it [the memorial] was similar to what I saw at Ypres and Flanders Fields in Europe, and it helped to show me why I am over here, and why so many have given so much for our country. Words can't adequately portray how I felt standing in those places, for I was overcome by a sense of sacrifice and dedication to something I've never before experienced."

Those of us who loved him hope that he knows his name is on the Vietnam Wall, and that he was awarded the Distinguished Flying Cross, the Gold Star in lieu of the second Distinguished Flying Cross, the Air

Medal and Gold Stars in lieu of the second, third, fourth, and fifth Air Medals. He also received the Purple Heart, the Vietnam Service Medal, and three citations from the president of the United States for heroism and achievement. He would have been humbled, but proud.

For those of us less interested in posthumous awards, Bruce wrote some comforting words in that last letter. "The Navy has done an unbelievable amount of good for me so far, as I had hoped it would, and I don't regret my decision for one minute. It has made me realize so much about myself that I never would have admitted. . . . I now look at life much more positively than I did in June of '64, and I picture myself as standing in the small end of a cornucopia with all of life opening up before me, to be lived, loved and learned about. I may have just turned 24, but I feel younger and more excited about life and all that it has to offer than ever before." He was even entertaining the idea of becoming career Navy!

Bruce never resolved his ethical conflict, and because he was so hard on himself, his death may have spared him years of psychological and philosophical trauma. In April 1965 from Sanford, Florida, he wrote:

> Though the thought occurred to me before signing up, I now really developed it to any great extent, and that is the inextricable dichotomy of a Christian way of life and thought; and the human frailty and demon of war. Now that I'm being drawn closer to the heart of the concern the conflict has started to loom, for basically it can be said that I am being trained in part to be a professional killer, and I don't find this the most soul-satisfying of positions

"Though the thought occurred to me before signing up, I never really developed it to any great extent, and that is the inextricable dichotomy of a Christian way of life and thought, and the human frailty and demon of war. Now that I'm being drawn close to the heart of the concern, the conflict has started to loom, for basically it can be said that I am being trained in part to be a professional killer, and I don't find this the most soul-satisfying of positions to be in."

He was intrigued by a line from *The Varieties of Religious Experience* by William James, and posted the quote on his desk: "What we need now

Chauncey and Margaret Allen, Bruce, and Sage Dunlap
at graduation, June 1964

to discover in the social realm is the moral equivalent of war; something heroic that will speak to men as universally as war does, and yet will be as compatible with their spiritual selves as war has proved to be incompatible." Had Bruce lived, James's words might have influenced his life's work.

The world lost a very special person that long-ago day, and as we enjoy the careers, and children and grandchildren he never had, we must continue to remember and celebrate Bruce's short life.

Sage Dunlap Chase, Wheaton Class of '66, was Bruce's sweetheart during his last two years of college, and remained close, but uncommitted, until his death. Her Dartmouth roots are deep. Her father, David R. Dunlap Jr., '42, lost his life in World War II in the Pacific in 1945. Her twin brother, David R. Dunlap III, was Dartmouth '66 and Bruce's fraternity brother. Her husband of forty-two years is Richard H. Chase Jr., '60, Tuck '65.

Rolling Thunder
One Small Step to Enlightenment

ROBERT B. FIELD JR. : U.S. NAVY

R ather than easing into grad school, I was one of many fraternity brothers and members of our Class of 1964 who, immediately following graduation and often encouraged by an uncertain draft status and fathers who were veterans of World War II, opted to volunteer for three years plus of military service. For me, it all began with an "invitation" received from the Department of Defense to spend sixteen weeks from August to early December at the U.S. Navy Officer Candidate School in Newport, Rhode Island.

At the time, Newport was an all-Navy town, and its musty Thames Street waterfront and the Jamestown ferry teemed with sailors and Marines. The OCS facilities themselves were a patchwork of worn wooden barracks, temporary Quonset huts, and a few more-elegant buildings, some new, but mostly World War II and Naval War College surplus. Many officer candidates were fired up with the thought of becoming real, commissioned, one-gold-stripe, "black shoe" ensigns assigned to a hot, sexy, post–Korean War (*Mitscher* class) guided-missile destroyer. My aspirations were similar.

Most of us from Dartmouth performed very well with the academic elements of our training, and, more than likely "cumed out" (achieved a liberating cumulative grade-point average insuring graduation) at the end of the first two months of training. The military regime often presented a bit more of a challenge, but the abject fear of "bilging out" of the

"Rolling Thunder" was the operational code name used by U.S. forces (the Navy and Air Force) for the bombing campaign against North Vietnam, March 1965– November 1968.

Robert Field at commissioning

program, into a "boots-on-ground" status in Cam Ranh Bay, was palpable and served to bridle much of our suppressed individualism and recalcitrant enthusiasm.

Nevertheless, life was good, uniforms and all, and we had diversions the likes of Salve Regina College, the Tavern, and the America's Cup competition. The Class of 1965 (undefeated Ivy League champions in 1965) was still enrolled to ensure Dartmouth continued gridiron success, and the Harvard and Yale games, still played in Cambridge and New Haven respectively, were a convenient drive from Newport. It wasn't that bad—just no beer, tube time, and "Whales Tails" most evenings.

December came suddenly. The Tonkin Gulf was starting to boil, and we all separated and reported to new duty stations around the globe. I didn't get my "tin can." Rather, in the Navy's wisdom, and bearing the acute focus of a sociology/geography major, I was assigned to a new, Norfolk-based, ultra-sophisticated, nuclear-powered guided-missile cruiser, USS *Long Beach* (which, in 1995, after distinguished service, was decommissioned, and subsequently scrapped and sold to the South Koreans in 2012 for salvage value). Why such an assignment I'll never know. Rather than meeting my expectation of relief from academia, the Navy chose to send me for nine months more of training in computer and weapons systems (Naval Tactical Data Systems), Air Intercept Control and Combat Information Center (Surface Warfare), at Sea Island, Georgia, and Tidewater, Virginia.

Shortly after we concluded training, my ship was reassigned to Long Beach, California, for homeporting. En route we transited the Panama Canal. Thereafter, in short order we trained with the Seventh Fleet air groups for Vietnam carrier operations, and I was temporarily assigned as training liaison officer to the HMAS *Hobart*, a new guided-missile destroyer, one of three such vessels purchased by the Australian government. The Aussies were free spirits, their shipboard customs were more relaxed than ours, and "Fosters" flowed in the wardroom at appropriate hours.

However, the party soon ended. I returned to Long Beach and soon sailed to Hawaii, where numerous small automatic rapid-fire guns were mounted on the ship for surface defensive purposes. It was there in Pearl Harbor, in clear view of the USS *Arizona* Memorial, that I began to fully awaken to the realization that our lives were soon to be irrevocably altered.

During the holidays in 1965, we took up station in the Gulf of Tonkin just southeast of the North Vietnamese city of Haiphong, its major seaport. Our primary mission involved controlling, protecting, and refueling planes and helicopters. It also included assistance to aviators in distress, and rescue operations. Although attacking very similar targets with similar risks as their Air Force cousins, naval aviators, when in distress, sought only to go sufficiently "feet wet" into the gulf to await rescue by one of our "copters on station." In contrast, Air Force pilots, even when confronted with hostile civilians and enemy ground forces, primarily sought rescue by bailing out and hiding in the mountain jungles of Vietnam or Laos while awaiting the "Jolly Green Giants."

It was also obvious that war takes no holidays, and in late 1965 and the early days of 1966, we lost many pilots, radar intercept officers, and aircraft to very aggressive and effective surface-to-air cannon and missile batteries. One very sobering experience for me occurred shortly before Christmas Eve, when a pilot of an F-4 Phantom under my control visually tracked a surface-to-air missile launched at him. Just before his imminent destruction he pleaded on the squadron radio in words to the effect of "it's got me; take good care of Lucy and the kids." I still occasionally wonder about "Lucy and the kids." I wonder too about the chilling and brutal experiences of Senator John McCain and the other "Hanoi Hilton" prisoners. Certainly, Laura Hillenbrand's 2010 biography of the war experience of Louis S. Zamperini, *Unbroken*, makes patent the horrific circumstances and heroic survival that can accompany prisoner of war incarceration.

After a while, combat tactics were refined, and our aircraft and pilots became better adapted to missions flown in hostile airspace. While we were regularly involved with both the three-carrier task force positioned on Yankee Station and the Air Force, often for a full twenty-four hours a day, routine nevertheless settled in. To paraphrase Thomas Heggen, in the stage play *Mister Roberts*, we easily felt as though we were sailing between the islands of Tedium and Apathy, with side trips to Monotony. However, and as I have told my children, the heroes, unlike me, never came home.

The Vietnam War, as it was called, declared by Congress on the heels of a tenuous and somewhat "suspicious" North Vietnamese high-speed attack on the destroyers *Maddox* and *Turner Joy*, was a challenge to understand fully, and the beast that it became was compounded in scale, complexity, and mysteriousness throughout my tour of duty. Despite completely embracing our assignment, and fully committing to our task, for the few who dared to ask there always seemed to be a plethora of incomplete and obfuscated reactions and responses to issues of both tactical and strategic import. The politics of the engagement were never clear. The rules of engagement for the theater often seemed nonsensical, irrational, and unnecessarily force-debilitating and success-compromising. Abrupt commands, seemingly contrary to logic, often arrived in the Combat Information Center from secret "intelligence spooks" quartered in secure parts of the ship.

Revealed also was the enigmatic truth of the military review and advancement structure, and the essential need for many of the more senior officers to have records of combat service prominently made a part of their personnel files. I have since read and observed that the U.S. military "needs a war" every generation in order to identify and promote leadership, modernize and test assets of war, readiness, and strategies, and ensure ongoing congressional funding for weapons programs and research. It is interesting for me to note that the strengths of the naval officer corps in my time of service were arguably the junior OCS and ROTC officers, who, unlike the recent Naval Academy graduates, often viewed their service as temporary. As well, they were likely to be more original, questioning, and creative. Strength was also quite apparent at the senior officer level, where success had been achieved. Middle-level officers seemed to be the most self-doubting, insecure, indecisive, and, understandably, they were primarily committed to taking no risk that could potentially harm career advancement.

I served one tour in the Western Pacific and returned home safely to

Long Beach extremely proud of the successes and leadership opportunities I had experienced, yet aware of disappointments. Then, with the cooperation and support of my commanding officer, I enrolled at Boston University School of Law. The period from 1967 to 1970 was an undeniably tumultuous time in Boston and Cambridge for returning war veterans. We were scorned, sometimes ridiculed, and often isolated. Community ideals, ethics, and mores had changed. Women had been "liberated," and there was little effort made to accommodate and/or embrace the social "freaks" that were veterans.

There were, however, lots of us returning to civilian life, and in mutual support we found comfort. My law school class, in addition to having greater numbers of women, who enrolled while men were away, was made up of Army, Air Force, Marine, and Navy veterans. We often talked of and shared our experiences. We bonded, formed study groups, and from the sidelines observed the new culture. One must recall that at the time, the draft lottery had not yet been initiated, and those who could claim status as married men, teachers, graduate students in critical disciplines, medical trainees, drug users, along with others, were exempted from the draft. Fortunately, as people became aware of the potential and actual injustice that such a system wrought, the lottery was put into effect—though new devices, efforts, and ingenious means to avoid service were conceived.

Still, veterans kept coming home in ever-increasing numbers, and with the advancements of battlefield/trauma medicine, many returned home physically maimed and emotionally scarred. Publicly supported veterans' services were insufficient to address the demand, and society at large seemed not to be of a mind either to help or understand the breadth of the problem. As a country we turned our back on veterans. It wasn't until many years later and after the countless and tireless efforts of some, such as Senator James Webb, to awaken the public, that we hesitatingly and cumbersomely began to acknowledge their plight, reform our response mechanisms, and create objects of recognition and honor such as the Vietnam Memorial. We all know that the names of classmates are inscribed thereon. It is a somber and solemn experience to visit that memorial and to reflect upon the deeper national significance of the 58,228 names that are inscribed on the multiple panels of gabbro, also known as "black granite."

I received my law degree in due course and returned to the Granite State, where I have practiced law for over forty years. I continue to take pride in my naval service and do not regret the experience for a moment. But I recognize that I had it relatively easy and that I was lucky. I have my fingers, toes, legs, and arms, and (although my wife of forty-two years occasionally has doubts) I still have a reasonable capacity to think rationally, and can complete the *New York Times* crossword in spite of Will Shortz's best efforts, Monday through Thursday and most Sundays (Friday and Saturday are invariably unproductive experiences). I have family members who weren't as lucky. Over time, I have walked the streets of cities and small-town America, and I have observed the social, emotional, and physical cost of the Vietnam War. As is patently apparent, we still bear its cross of alcohol, drug abuse, homelessness, and suicide.

Perhaps I lacked a proper perspective in 1970. However, drugs and alcohol do not appear to be as debilitating today, and I don't recall there being as great a disruption in the lives, finances, and emotional health of young families, wives, children, and careers as we now observe in the aftermath of Desert Storm and in the Iraq and Afghanistan wind-down. About twenty years ago, a law partner, also serving as adjutant general to New Hampshire, discussed the recent emergence and growth of the role of the "citizen soldier/reservist," a force that serves side by side with, and composes more than half of, our regular armed forces manpower. He invited me to help deal with the developing social crisis by becoming involved with the New Hampshire Committee for the Guard and Reserve and accept an appointment to the committee, an arm of the Department of Defense, in the capacity of an ombudsman.

Since 2003, we as a country have witnessed an unrelenting dismantling of our active military, at a rate and to a degree that is unprecedented. What remains is a force many of whose members are periodically separated from their families and careers and deployed to foreign theaters of combat on repetitive eighteen-month cycles. This protocol is tragically disruptive to both family stability and careers, and also fosters a disruptive and adverse influence in the business community. Some predict a massive rift within the military as soldiers and sailors who thought they had careers are discharged into a jobless society. All threaten the once-held American dream of family, home, and career opportunity. These men and women serving in uniform, and their close friends and family, are also declining in number as a percentage of Americans having a connection with the military. Our servicemen and/or women are becoming "invisible," perhaps disposable, to an increasing number of Americans.

There are many more programs and services available now (a very good GI Education Bill, for example) to help address and assist the frustrations, disabilities, and needs of returning servicemen and women. In most instances the stigma of military service, as we saw post-Vietnam, is not as overtly present, but the cost of wrecked lives continues to be reflected in inordinately and unacceptably high suicide rates, which are predicted to accelerate. The practice of battlefield trauma medicine has, however, continued to improve, so fewer and fewer casualties of war result in death. However, the physical and emotional scars of war persist, and perhaps, even more tragically, such scars are frequently borne by family members at home who lack the support of a deployed parent or sibling. Those who deploy today with the reserve/Guard are typically older, have families, and are subject to the vagaries and swings of an imperiled economy, "underwater" mortgages, spiraling college tuition, and disgruntled employers and coworkers.

It is my role as ombudsman under the Uniformed Services Employment and Reemployment Rights Act to mediate and minimize conflict between employers and reservists/Guard members to ensure that they return home to their jobs and reposition themselves at a seniority level and with the institutional respect that they would have likely attained had they not been deployed. I also serve the employer by assuring him that the reservist/Guard member is meeting his or her obligation to provide adequate and timely notice of training and deployment schedules. By doing so, it is my hope that my efforts will help to preserve family units, maintain healthy labor relations, and maybe, just maybe, help some children get a better shake at life.

In summary, my short career in service with the Navy was one of the more important building blocks of my life. It was a time of maturing, discovering leadership potential, and determining career objectives. In retrospect I believe that it was also a time of societal awakening to the inevitably disruptive forces of war, and, extending over my lifetime, for observing portions of our society that have been stressed, or are being stressed today. The Vietnam period fostered the nearly unrestricted opportunity for political dissent and exposed the disruption it can wreak on a society that has very disparate forces residing within. I submit that the circumstances of the Vietnam War gave birth to, have challenged, and have possibly compromised our national agenda, mores, and previously shared values. Change is certainly inevitable, and those experiencing change are affected both positively and negatively. As we think about war, it must be viewed from a long-term perspective. War cannot be just turned on and off at will. Furthermore, it should not be employed as a political tool, as some of our politicians, past and present, may think. We will learn new but similar lessons from our Iraqi Freedom and Afghanistan experiences. Will our country, our government, and our fellow citizens be able to withstand both the challenge and the threat?

Robert Field still maintains a keen appreciation for our great country and the privileges and rule of law it provides. He believes that the ability to seamlessly transition our government in an evenly and philosophically divided electorate is a miraculous achievement that Americans seemingly pull off every four years—a political achievement well worth his sometimes unenlightened early personal effort to preserve it. For him, law has been both a career and a state of mind for almost forty-five years. Though often humbled, he says, he would not trade the experience.

Life aboard a U.S. Aircraft Carrier

PAUL T. (PETE) KOENIG : U.S. NAVY

I entered the U.S. Navy at Officer Candidate School in Newport, Rhode Island, in August 1964. That was a mere ten weeks after graduation and within days of the Gulf of Tonkin dust-up and resolution that released the "dogs of war" in Southeast Asia. None of us was aware of the significance of those events at the time. I had just escaped New Jersey Draft Board No. 29 by a whisker. I got my draft notice the same day I received my Dartmouth diploma, but that is another story.

I was commissioned as an ensign (or "en-swine," in salty sea slang) on December 16, 1964. The Navy ordered me to report aboard a carrier then under construction but not yet commissioned. I was part of the initial crew and thus became a plank owner of the USS *America* (CVA-66) when the ship was commissioned on January 23, 1965. I was present for and witnessed all the many first events that are duly recorded and chronicled according to Navy rules and regulations.

The flight deck of a U.S. Navy aircraft carrier conducting air operations at sea is a complex and potentially dangerous place. I have been told that Lloyd's of London has determined it to be the single most dangerous man-made work environment known. The noise, movement of planes, and violent forces at work can be frightening, particularly at night. Vigilance, care, and caution are always appropriate. Eventually you learn and get accustomed to it, and soon it takes on a routine like a ballet. That is, until something breaks, or someone messes up or miscalculates. Then suddenly, unexpectedly, all hell breaks loose. There could be fire, or possibly debris such as big pieces of metal flying around fast, injuring people and damaging planes and equipment. The idea is to do the best you can to minimize such incidents. This is especially true on a brand-new carrier, commencing service with a new crew that has never worked together before.

That is where I found myself in early 1965 during the shakedown cruises of the *America*. In order to safely begin training and operations, the Navy in its wisdom and according to long tradition makes sure that at least 10 percent of the initial crew has extensive experience in carrier air operations. So, while I was as new and inexperienced in these matters as I could possibly have been, I found myself alongside and under the wing of men with vast and diverse experience—literally giants in the world of naval aviation. The crew included ace fighter pilots, men who served on and were on carriers sunk in battle in World War II, and others with impressive histories. They brooked no nonsense when it came to implementing safe procedures to operate efficiently, which meant quickly and correctly. Over the course of my three years on board I became familiar and proficient with this complicated process. As I watch the history or military cable TV channels these days and see programs about air operations on carriers such as the *Ronald Reagan* and the *George H. W. Bush*, although the planes are different, I understand in minute detail everything the crew is doing.

I was first assigned to the Air Department. It operates the flight and hangar decks, the four catapults, the arresting gear, and maintains the aircraft maintenance facilities for the air wing. It is composed of squadrons of airplanes, all told about one hundred fighters, attack planes, tankers, photo-recon, electronic warfare types, and helicopters. I basically worked on the flight deck of the carrier in air operations when under way. First I was an assistant division officer in V-6 (aircraft maintenance). That division had 125 men. We maintained and provided the machinery and services to the embarked air wing needed to conduct air ops. I did that for about a year.

Then I was selected to be the ATO (air transportation officer) for the ship. My job included assignment as assistant division officer in the Operations Department. This division operated the Carrier Air Traffic Control Center—CATCC. The division had about twenty-five very senior and specialized enlisted men. They were all air controllers who handled the radars and radios for departure control, marshal control (stacking up of aircraft) for recovering aircraft, and final-approach control for all air traffic recovering aboard ship. During each launch cycle, every hour and a half, the ship would launch about twenty planes. This took about eight minutes, and as soon as the angle deck was clear, we would begin to recover (land) the planes from the previous launch. The whole process took about twenty minutes. The airspace around the ship was quite crowded, and critical events were occurring constantly. CATCC made sure that midair collisions were avoided and aircraft were landed quickly and nobody ran out of fuel—returning airplanes were low on fuel as a matter of routine.

As the ATO, I was also responsible for routing mail, passengers, and cargo arriving and departing the ship by air. We had a COD—carrier on-board delivery—plane and helicopters for this purpose. Mail was important for morale, as this was before e-mail and cell phones. The ship made two Mediterranean deployments, each of more than eight months. Also, we made several trips to Gitmo and the Caribbean for training. We spent much time in the Atlantic as a ready deck for any fliers needing to learn or practice how to land, take off, and operate in proximity to a carrier. The ship traveled over 120,000 miles while I was embarked.

I worked as air terminal officer in many airports overseas when the ship made port visits. This was detached and independent duty for me. It was basically the same duties moving mail, passengers, and cargo to and from the ship. We used C-130 and C-118 aircraft, as well as Pan Am and TWA flights. In port the scale of cargo moved was larger. With fifty-five hundred men aboard ship, people were coming and going all the time. In any ten-day port visit we would have several hundred men depart at end of enlistment or for transfer, and the same number arrive as replacements. That represented about one hundred thousand pounds of cargo each way—mostly aircraft parts (including engines), and tons of mail. I worked at airports in Valencia, Spain; Palma, Majorca; Beirut, Lebanon; Luqa, Malta; Toulon, Marseilles, and Nice, France; Genoa, Pisa, Naples, and Taranto, Italy; Athens and Thessalonica, Greece; and Istanbul, Turkey— more than once in most of them. Much of my service was outside the United States and was a busy time.

The Six-Day War erupted during my second cruise to the Mediterranean. My ship was the flagship for Carrier Division Two, along with the USS *Saratoga*. It was a busy and exciting time. We were constantly within sight of seventeen or so capital ships of the Soviet Black Sea Fleet, which entered the Mediterranean through the Bosporus for the first time to support Egypt and the UAR. The Israelis had lit them up pretty well the first day, your basic knockout punch, then moved their armor to the eastern edge of the Suez Canal. They didn't need us. We made a big show of doing nothing about two hundred miles off the Egyptian coast, no flying at all despite bogus Arab claims that we were attacking on Israel's behalf. I think the USAF did some U-2 surveillance, because I saw photos of the devastation on the Arab airfields. Not pretty.

We had a spy ship down off the coast, the USS *Liberty*, listening to all communications. We had tapped in by clandestine methods before the war began. *Liberty* would then retransmit its intercepts to the NSA (No Such Agency) in Washington. We were tasked to protect *Liberty*. Our admiral thought we could do this from over the horizon a hundred miles away. *Liberty* was attacked by Israeli planes and torpedo boats. Radios were gone with the first pass. *Liberty* suffered severe, nearly fatal damage during that deliberate and unprovoked attack. She nearly sank. Thirty-four U.S. sailors died, and I think about 175 others were wounded. That represented more than half her crew. We launched a strike to defend/retaliate, but our planes were recalled by those courageous leaders of the free world, Lyndon Baines Johnson and Robert Strange McNamara. *Liberty* limped up toward us, and we steamed to her, coming to within one hundred yards at first light. Visually unrecognizable, she was honeycombed with .50 mm machine gun, 20 mm cannon, and 2.75-inch rocket fire. She had also taken a torpedo amidships that made a huge hole above and below the water-line. We took off her casualties by helicopter as quickly as we could that morning. They were treated in our sick bay, which was busy and nearly overwhelmed. We also took the bodies that could be recovered and stored them in our morgue. *Liberty*'s captain got the Congressional Medal of Honor for his actions keeping the ship afloat. His exec was killed on the bridge during the attack. The captain was badly wounded but stayed on the bridge throughout. When the word of the Liberty being attacked reached us, about twenty minutes into the forty-five-minute attack, the *America* went to general quarters (GQ). This was the only time in my service that we went to GQ when it wasn't a drill. The Russian ships in company—cruiser, destroyers, frigates, and trawlers—fled in no partic-ular formation. They just turned tail and ran. There was no sea-theater such as pointing guns or lighting off fire control radars. In my view they were scared and confused and thus didn't know what to do.

Long after the event, the government of Israel paid many millions of dollars in claims to victims and their survivors. Israel claimed initially that the attack was made in error, that they thought the ship was Egyptian. Some people still believe this; however, this was our premier spy ship at the time, and nobody had anything that looked like it. Plus, we were listening to Israeli intercepts at the time of the attack, since they had overrun the points of intercept. Oh, and of course the ship was flying a huge American flag, and Israeli planes observed the ship for some lengthy time before commencing the forty-five-minute assault. It was as if they were checking and getting clearance for "weapons free." It wasn't a mistake, in my opinion, an opinion shared by most of the writers who have dug into this incident.

During the aftermath of the Six-Day War, I learned that the new GI Bill had been enacted, and I decided to apply to law school, despite my vow at our graduation that my schooling days were done. During my four-year military hiatus I met and married Pat Davis, and we had our first child, Kimberly. My service experience helped me to mature. My service companions included some truly great people who did important things during World War II, Korea, and Vietnam. Many went on to high rank and great accomplishments, long after I reentered civilian life. Four men I served with reached three-star rank. One went on to be the CNO—chief of naval operations. I am still in touch, through the magic of the Internet, with men who were sailors in my division. I attend reunions of the ship as often as I can. I got out of the Navy in December 1967 and entered Rutgers Law School in September 1968. I had been a lawyer for several years when I saw some of my friends return as former POWs from Hanoi.

I had great experiences in the service, not all of them pleasant; however, it was a great adventure for me and contributed mightily to my character. I value my time in the Navy without regret.

Pete Koenig graduated from Rutgers Law School in 1971. He practiced law in Mercer County, New Jersey, was the county's civil attorney, then county prosecutor, and was appointed to the Superior Court of New Jersey in 1992. He retired from that position in 2008.

His wife, Pat, retired from working as an internal auditor for the New

Jersey Housing and Mortgage Finance Agency in 2002. They left New Jersey in 2012 for Naples, Florida, where they now reside full time. Pete has two new knees. He and Pat play tennis almost daily, so the procedure was a success. He also enjoys skeet shooting, fishing, and watching baseball.

They have two children, Kimberly, the CFO of Good Samaritan Hospital in Palm Beach, and a son, PT, a family practice physician in Davis, California, who has two sons.

The Road from Dartmouth to Vietnam

JOHN T. LANE : U.S. ARMY

S ome things in life are controlled by our will. However, I have found that very often one small, unplanned event creates an impact many years later. My road to Vietnam started with freshman year at Dartmouth. A senior living across the hall was recruiting freshman to fill the ROTC training unit. At the time I had no particular interest in the military, and there was no economic incentive to join the Army ROTC unit. Nevertheless, when my hall-mate asked for help, I signed up.

Freshman year's commitment to the military was minimal. I made friends in the program, and consequently I continued with ROTC. I spent the summer of my junior year at officer basic training with students from all over the country. One name I never will forget is Cadet Mahar from the Citadel. He had a booming command voice and was the ultimate gung-ho cadet from a military school. I was to meet a much-changed Lieutenant Mahar in Vietnam.

Upon graduation I received my commission in the Army Medical Service Corps. My initial posting was with the Eighty-Second Airborne Division. Three months after I joined the division, the unit was deployed to the Dominican Republic. That nation was involved in a bloody civil conflict with significant Cuban involvement. Over one thousand people were killed or wounded before international forces arrived to stabilize the political situation.

Our division paid a high price. I vividly remember one aspect of the conflict. There was a temporary cease-fire in one sector of the city. At the time, our rules of engagement prohibited any firing, except in return of hostile activity. One platoon was stationed across from a rebel position. The rebels reinforced their position, adding a .50-caliber machine gun, and then opened fire. One American was virtually cut in half by the machine gun. Four others in the sector received fatal injuries before the rebel position was silenced. I saw the remains of the carnage as the soldiers were evacuated through our medical channel. It was a life-changing event for me.

During this deployment, my college roommate, Chuck Marsh, was stationed on a destroyer in the Santo Domingo harbor. Fate had drawn us together again.

Three months later I received orders to join a hospital convalescent unit that was being sent to Vietnam. For various reasons it was deemed highly preferable to keep relatively healthy sick and wounded soldiers in Vietnam for convalescence and return them to duty, rather than replacing all casualties with fresh troops. We were initially supposed to locate in Hue. Fortunately, wiser heads decided that Hue was too exposed, and consequently our hospital avoided the heaviest fighting in the Tet offensive. Instead we were sent to Cam Ranh Bay.

Prior to deployment I went home to Tennessee. I visited my old high school. Much to my surprise, one of my former teachers was very upset at my volunteering to serve in Vietnam. She was strongly antiwar and against violence. During our discussion, I could only remember the soldiers who were killed in the Dominican Republic while hoping the rebels would refrain from violent activity.

My initial duty with the Convalescent Center was to supervise the shipment of all equipment and supplies from the United States to Cam Ranh Bay. The transport was executed with a minimum of problems; however, when I arrived on station, we determined that we needed to obtain certain items from Saigon. I was sent to procure them, but when I arrived in Saigon there was no billet available.

My Dartmouth fate would take care of me. I decided to go to the U.S. Armed Forces radio station in Saigon. It was my wild hope that the Army had decided to use Al McKee's WDCR experience to good use in Vietnam. When I arrived at the station Al, an SAE fraternity brother, was broadcasting. He took me to his billet for the evening. All went well until 2 a.m., when a major explosive was detonated at the front of the billet. We were not harmed, but the lesson was clear. No place was safe in Vietnam.

When I returned to Cam Ranh Bay, work had begun on the site for the Convalescent Center. We were located on the ocean shore at the end

Convalescent center at Cam Ranh Bay

of the airport runway. This gave additional security for the airport, as a significant number of our patients at any time were almost ready to rejoin their combat unit. The Convalescent Center, however, was exposed to attack from the sea.

There are many stories of patients that came through our facility. I would like to share two. The first is my renewed acquaintance with Cadet Mahar from the Citadel. He had become a seasoned infantry officer. Gone were the visions of glory, the swagger and the confidence that America would easily prevail in Vietnam. His unit had seen extensive fighting in the highlands, where the enemy and malaria had hardened his soul. He still believed the cause he fought for was right, but he knew the price he and his men had paid was very high. Reading stories of antiwar demonstrations made his life much more difficult.

The second story is about PFC Battles. He was an inner-city school dropout from St. Louis. He had had a minor problem with the law and was given the option of going to jail or joining the Army. Battles joined the Army and went to Vietnam. He fought the Viet Cong and contracted malaria. I remember Battles because he was our first patient who acquired a serious drug addiction problem in Vietnam. We cured his malaria, but I feared drug addiction would ultimately destroy him.

After eight months in Vietnam, my tour of duty was up, and I rotated back to the United States. Two months after I left, the VC came to Cam Ranh Bay by sea. The Convalescent Center and my friends were hit.

John Lane is a retired managing director of JP Morgan. During his twenty-six-year career with Morgan, he served in leadership positions in Corporate Finance, Private Clients, Credit and Investor Services. He served as chairman of JP Morgan Florida. He was a director of JP Morgan California, Morgan Shareholder Services, Morgan Futures, and also served as a member of the firm's Credit Policy Committee. He has extensive international experience. He was chief executive of Morgan's Indonesian Investment Banking joint venture and regional manager for Southeast Asia.

Since retiring from Morgan, John has been an active private investor and consultant. He has also served on the boards of numerous for-profit and not-for-profit organizations. He is currently a director of the Healthcare Association of New York, the New York State Healthcare Foundation, HealthCare Trustees of New York, Winthrop University Hospital, the First National Bank of Long Island, the Cathedral Church of St. John the Divine, and ROTACARE.

The Green Lieutenant

HUGH SAVAGE : U.S. ARMY CORPS OF ENGINEERS

I am proud of my service in the United States Army Corps of Engineers as a combat engineering officer. I wish I could say the cause we fought for in Vietnam was glorious and honorable. Even when I was there, I had my doubts.

I was in Army ROTC at Dartmouth. My father and uncle had served in World War II, and I considered it my duty to serve; besides, I did not want to be drafted. I was commissioned a second lieutenant in the Army Corps of Engineers the day before we graduated. I went on active duty a month later, as I was uncertain as to what I wanted to do after graduation and wanted time to decompress and consider my options. Congress thought that perhaps ROTC graduates had enough training and might not need to go to officer training school before being assigned to their active-duty unit. So Congress tried an experiment. I volunteered to be a guinea pig in return for early entry to active duty. I went straight to my unit at Fort Campbell, Kentucky, and skipped four months of engineer officer's basic school at Fort Belvoir. (Had no one told me to never volunteer for anything in the service?) I could not have been greener. My first six months of active duty were a disaster. To begin with, I reported to my duty station in an obsolete uniform. My ill-fitting fatigues were hand-me-downs from a friend who had just completed his National Guard service. He was eight inches shorter and forty pounds heavier. It got worse.

Nevertheless, after a year of experience, I was considered fit for duty in Vietnam and shipped over as XO of HQ Company of the Seventieth Combat Engineer Battalion. After a few months I requested a demotion to platoon leader. My request was granted, and that began six months of one of the most satisfying periods of my life. My platoon built part of the First Air Cavalry Division base's perimeter defense. We put up the longest

Hugh Savage with
Vietnamese children

Bailey bridge in the country, repaired roads, and huddled in our bunker on nighttime alert to act as infantry if the base's perimeter defense was breached by attacking Viet Cong.

When I returned home, my two-year obligation complete, I found that my relationship with my father had changed. We had both commanded small units in a combat zone. I met him for lunch shortly after I returned. Our relationship had shifted from father and son toward one of coequals. In Dad's eyes my military service had been a rite of passage to full-fledged adulthood.

While on active duty I found that I enjoyed engineering as I experienced it in the Army. When I got home in July 1966 I enrolled in graduate school for a master's in engineering. My veteran status, at least in part, secured me a position as a head resident in a men's dorm at Tufts University, which included room and board. I also joined an active reserve unit in Boston, and I transferred to another one in Seattle when I went to the University of Washington for more graduate work. The income from reserve duty was a welcome supplement to a graduate student.

After a combined eight years of active duty and active reserve duty, I was nearly halfway to a pension. However, once I went to work, I would have been required to take my vacation time for reserve summer camp. This would not have been fair to my young family, so I resigned my commission as an Army captain.

As a platoon leader I learned to respect the wisdom and experience of the NCOs and specialists. I realized that I could not know all that they knew, but that my perspective as an officer was different and broader. That lesson carried over into civilian life. Once when interviewing for a supervisory job that was temporarily being filled by one of the waste-water plant technicians, I was asked what I expected my relationship to the technician might be. I reflected on my time as an officer and said that I would not supplant him, but strive for a cooperative relationship in which I would expect him to focus on the day-to-day issues and details of running the plant, while I would focus on the long-term issues. I was offered the job.

In a similar vein an incident formed a useful lesson in thinking out-side the box. On a training exercise, our company was tasked to assemble bridges mounted on pontoons to cross a river, and we were issued field manuals about pontoon bridges. Each platoon was to assemble a bridge. My platoon's morale had been low. Another platoon had a much more ex-perienced platoon sergeant, and in past exercises we had come off second-best. On a hunch I went to the company responsible for the maintenance and storage of the pontoon bridges and asked if they had a scale model. They did, and let me borrow it. With great secrecy I took it back to my pla-toon, and my sergeants assembled and disassembled the model until they could do it in their sleep. When it came time to assemble the real thing, my platoon looked like old pros, and we finished long before our rivals.

I encouraged our children to consider service in the military, even our daughters, but none entered. Perhaps it is just as well. The burden that has been placed on the active and reserve military in the last twenty years has been brutal. With the possible exception of our early campaign in Afghanistan, I have not been in favor of any of our military misadven-tures in the last forty or fifty years. Furthermore, the lack of support for damaged returning veterans has added to the tragedy and borders on the criminal.

While proud of my time in the service, I have not joined the Veterans of Foreign Wars or any other veterans organization, with one exception. I have joined online the Vietnam Veterans of Company A of the 70th Combat Engineer Battalion, and I attended their reunion in the summer of 2012. I was moved by the sense of camaraderie, even with those who served in the company after me. Several members have returned to Vietnam to build schools. They have been warmly welcomed. The final irony of the Vietnam War is that the fall of Vietnam to the Communists had a negligible effect on our national security, and today Vietnam is a thriving capitalist society.

Hugh Savage started Acorn Engineering to provide civil engineering services in Maine. It is now owned and operated by one of his five children. Two of his daughters are also civil engineers. Surely, at least one of his seven grandsons will be an engineer. To this day Hugh has a recurring dream that he is called up for active duty and shows up in an incomplete uniform.

Supporting Our Troops and Country

DERICK DENBY : U.S. ARMY

Prior to our June 14 (Flag Day) graduation and my commissioning as a second lieutenant, I selected the Army Security Agency as my preferred branch of the Army. Its mission sounded interesting, and headquarters were at Fort Devens, Massachusetts. I thought the latter meant I would not spend much time at Fort Benning, Georgia. Much to my surprise, the Army implemented a program where instead of having formal training, new lieutenants went directly to their unit for on-the-job training. Naturally I was assigned to Company C, 313th ASA Battalion, which was located at Kelly Hill, Fort Benning, Georgia.

Two weeks after graduation I reported for duty and learned that Company C was on maneuvers with the British army in Germany. They would not return until the end of the summer. Two other new lieutenants reported shortly thereafter. There was not much to do except work on improving our tennis skills. Because of our desire to be prepared to support the 82nd and 101st Airborne Divisions, and a need to earn extra jump pay, we signed up for jump school. After an airborne haircut, three or four weeks of training, and five jumps, I proudly received my wings.

When the main part of the company arrived back home in Georgia, I became a platoon leader, and my on-the-job training began. My main activities were managing a platoon, learning our mission, and understanding the purpose of our electronic equipment. We also did a lot of counting, cleaning, painting, and repairing in preparation for an IG inspection.

Another interesting responsibility came when I joined the duty officer rotation. On my first assignment I received a call notifying me that a member of my company was in jail for killing a man who was having an affair with his wife. On my second assignment I received a call to bail out our company commander, who had been arrested for DUI. From then on, everyone took note when I was the duty officer.

A trip to Coronado, California, for amphibious landing training was my next assignment. I learned how to cut templates and to simulate loading and unloading ships so that I would be prepared for the next amphibious assault. While in California I watched Navy SEALs train, enjoyed several visits to the San Diego Zoo, and experienced two or three hours in Tijuana, Mexico. On my way back to Georgia, I had a good time on Los Angeles's Sunset Strip with Johnny Rivers at the Whisky A Go-Go. Just like the Phi Psi basement!

One of my most memorable events was the U.S. occupation of the Dominican Republic in April 1965. The 313th ASA Battalion supported the Eighty-Second Airborne Division by monitoring the rebels' communications. Unfortunately, my closest Army friend, First Lieutenant Paul Semple, was shot and died in the Dominican Republic. While I lost a friend, his death was much harder on his fiancée and their families.

In the summer of 1965 in preparation for deployment to the jungles of Vietnam, the Second Division was transformed into the First Air Calvary. Helicopters were everywhere, with soldiers rappelling into parking lots. New equipment arrived every day. My company gave everyone leave to go home and spend time with family and friends; however, we were not allowed to tell anyone that we would soon leave for Vietnam. Upon my return to Fort Benning, I continued to prepare my platoon for deployment. Shortly thereafter my company commander asked me if I wanted to go to Vietnam. As I saw it, ever since I joined ROTC I had been preparing for this assignment, so I quickly said yes. Things are never so simple. My company commander said "Great. However, as you do not have enough time left in your enlistment, you will have to extend for six to nine months." As much as I wanted to go with my unit, an Army career was not my goal. I therefore declined the assignment.

With duffle bags and rifles over their shoulders, my company went off to war on an American Airlines 707, while I just watched. Being left behind was not fun. I spent the remainder of my tour of duty helping others get ready for deployment to Vietnam, cleaning up after their departure, and shipping matériel to Vietnam. I closed our Fort Benning facilities, then moved to Fort Bragg, where inventorying and receiving and shipping equipment filled the days. I quickly became an expert at loading trucks and vans onto railroad cars for shipment to units being deployed to Vietnam.

With the end of my enlistment in June 1966, I moved to Boston. In the summer of 1967, as part of summer camp, I finally spent time at Fort Devens, with a military police company from the New York City area. Several members' favorite activity was to use rocks to make peace signs ☮ in front of their barracks. Little did I know how much of an impact the peace movement would have on the U.S. involvement in Vietnam.

One or two years later I was notified that I had to take a physical at the Boston Army base. After taking my physical, I returned to my apartment and was pleasantly surprised to receive a notice in the mail that I had been promoted to the rank of captain. Thus ended my military career.

I very much enjoyed working with many outstanding, dedicated men. We had many good as well as some sad times. I learned a lot. I believe it is important that Dartmouth-educated ROTC officers play a role in the U.S. military services.

Derick Denby relocated from Fort Bragg, Nortrh Carolina, to the Boston area, and except for a year or two in Chicago, Green Bay, and Durham, North Carolina, he has maintained his roots there. Three daughters (one in San Francisco, one in Denver, and an eighteen-year-old at home) and a loving wife have kept him thriving. Only one remaining to get through college. When not doing financial and administrative work for organizations such as State Street Bank, Colgate Palmolive, Project Bread—the Walk for Hunger, Partners in Health, and Abt Associates, he has enjoyed family time around his Wellesley, Massachusetts, home, and on Nantucket (fishing for bluefish) and Cape Cod. In addition to not-frequent-enough trips to Hanover, Derick has continued to enjoy running. Four Boston Marathons and one race up Mount Washington are among his more memorable races.

Vietnam-Era Military Service

Some Good Memories

FRITZ CORRIGAN : U.S. ARMY

I signed up for Army ROTC during Freshman Week at Dartmouth because I couldn't get into any Navy programs and knew that I would be subject to the draft when I graduated. I was a sucker for the recruiting pitch: "Infantry officers ride and enlisted men walk." I also liked the prospect of future responsibility. It never entered my mind in 1960 that I would later get close to a shooting war. That wasn't part of the deal in my naïve mind.

Shortly after graduating and receiving my commission, I reported to Fort Benning, Georgia, for Infantry Officer Basic Training. I took one look at the jump towers and decided NOT to go Airborne/Ranger/special forces. I was pretty undistinguished in my academic performance at Dartmouth, and I resolved at graduation to try to do better as an Army officer. Things worked out pretty well. I enjoyed the infantry training and finished at the top of my class of two hundred newly minted officers.

I'll never forget the day we received our orders. They were posted on a bulletin board at infantry school. Like almost everyone else, I had requested a European assignment. Someone ran up to me and told me I was going to Korea. It was a real "Oh, s___!" moment. Ironically, it turned out to be one of the luckiest days of my life.

At that time career Army officers were encouraging us to volunteer for duty in Vietnam. It was a great way to "make your career," they said. I wasn't planning on a military career and didn't like the idea of getting shot at whatsoever. Shortly after I arrived in Korea, Vietnam was no longer a volunteer assignment, and most lieutenants like me were ordered there.

Fritz Corrigan at DMZ in Korea, summer 1965

While I served my country during the Vietnam era, I didn't serve in 'Nam. Nonetheless, I am proud to have served.

Having received infantry training, I reported to Fort Holabird in Baltimore for intelligence branch training before shipping out to Korea. Again, I did pretty well in class. The timing was good; August through September at Fort Benning was pretty hot, but fall in Baltimore gave me a chance to get back up to Hanover for a couple of football games and to New York City for Thanksgiving with Jim Hawkanson, Dartmouth '66, and others. I returned to Minneapolis for Christmas 1964 on leave after completing Intelligence School and before reporting to Travis Air Force Base outside San Francisco to fly to Korea. I brought my skis as far as Alta, Utah, for a few days of powder skiing in early '65 on the way but shipped them back to Minneapolis before heading to San Francisco. There were plenty of mountains and snow in South Korea, but no ski lifts!

Memories are really pretty special. As I write this I realize that, while I spent almost four hundred days in Korea, I remember vividly only about thirty of them. And the ones I remember were uniformly the good days. There were lots of days when I was just doing my job. I remember only the really special ones. Here they are:

Taking off from Travis AFB on a Northwest Airlines military charter full of other GIs like me was quite an experience. My imagination of the future extended to the forward bulkhead of the plane.
Beyond that was the unknown, an entirely new experience that I
couldn't know was out there in the dark sky ahead. When I arrived
in Seoul I was welcomed with open arms by the guy I was replacing.
He called me his "turtle" because it took so long for me to get there!

On my twenty-third birthday I played intercompany flag football.
We all took our fatigue shirts off but otherwise were in uniform—
couldn't tell rank that way. My assignment on most passing plays
(and they were almost all passing plays) was to block the defensive
end as he would rush the passer. In flag football, much like touch
football, nobody wears pads, and players can't leave their feet to
block. The opposing defensive end was killing me, play after play,
and our QB was getting figuratively sacked about half the time. I
decided to leave my feet to block this guy, which was very effective
until the referee blew his whistle and marched off fifteen yards
against us. A couple of plays later I did it again, hoping he wouldn't
see me. He did; another fifteen yards, but my QB wasn't sacked. In
the next quarter I did it again, and the defensive end had had enough.
We "dropped the gloves" (in hockey parlance) and were both ejected
from the game after the fight. On the sidelines I got to thinking: I'm
an officer, and here I am duking it out with an enlisted man whom I
don't know. How do I apologize? What do I say? When the game was
over and we had put on our fatigue shirts, I walked across the field to
make amends, only to discover the other guy was a second lieutenant
also! What a fine example we had set for our teammates.

That same fall of 1965, Dartmouth beat Princeton to win the Ivy
League championship. My CO and also Eighth Army G2 (head of
Intelligence) was a Dartmouth grad. I cannot remember his class,
but he was a full colonel and a really good guy. He had rotated back
to the States in time to see the game, and subsequently came back
on a fact-finding mission about the time I moved up to first lieutenant. While he pinned on my silver bars, he took great delight in
telling me all the gory details of that game. I wish I had been there
to see Dartmouth win.

Happy hours—beers cost ten cents, and mixed drinks were twenty-five cents. With five officers' clubs in Seoul, all with happy hours on different evenings, it didn't take much of our meager pay—$222 a month—to get a buzz on. It was cheaper than the Phi Delt basement!

"Getting short," or the "double digit fidgets," signified that you had fewer than one hundred days before returning stateside. By then we had made some lifelong friends; and the night before each left, those of us remaining would take him to the best officers' club in Seoul to buy him a steak (pretty rare in Seoul in '66) and share memories. He would then head for Kimpo Airport and the States the next day.

One not-so-great memory happened when I came through San Francisco on my way home from Seoul. I had applied to Stanford Business School for entrance in the fall of '66 and visited the admissions office on the Stanford campus for an interview—in uniform! I was proud to be serving my country, but in those days in the Bay Area, wearing a uniform wasn't very cool. I hadn't done my marketing homework very well and wasn't admitted. Still, I didn't like the disrespect with which I was treated. We have come a long way in the manner in which we treat those who serve. America is better for that.

I returned from Korea to the Fourth Military Intelligence Detachment supporting the Fourth Infantry Division, based in Fort Lewis, Washington. They were on orders to Vietnam and scheduled to deploy in early August. Luckily I was due to complete my two-year active duty commitment August 4. I put my friends on a troopship a few days before my discharge. While at Fort Lewis I reconnected with Steve Blecher, and sailed with him a time or two on Lake Washington in Seattle. I also shared an apartment off post with hockey great Jack Phelan, Dartmouth '63.

My Army Intelligence work was mostly classified top secret. I worked inside a windowless Quonset hut behind padlocked doors. By now lots of the work I did is either declassified or made obsolete by the passage of time and events. At the time I was in Korea, Communist China with

Mao, Zhou Enlai, and that crowd was off-limits to Americans. We studied China carefully but couldn't visit, so it was a big mystery. Since then I have been to China more than twenty times. I never thought in 1965 that I would ever be able to go there.

North Korea, on the other hand, hasn't changed much; but the passage of time makes what I knew and can still remember pretty irrelevant. We "knew" Kim Il Sung; now his grandson runs the place, and the North Korean people are no better off.

I do know a couple of things that I am pretty sure are still active and that I don't believe I can share. I choose not to out of fear that I would be breaking my commitment to the U.S. Army that I made in connection with receiving my top secret security clearance. This is a bit in contrast to the high-level leakers in the Obama administration.

My experiences with Koreans were of the everyday sort—normal interaction while in the street markets of Seoul, with wait staff at the officers' mess on Youngsan Compound (Eighth Army and U.N. Command HQ), and even alongside caddies on the small nine-hole golf course on the post. They were women complete with "coolie" hats tied down by white bandannas. They laughed with their gloved hands over their mouths when I hit a bad shot. I remember it well, because I hit lots of bad shots!

In broad terms, South Koreans were and are very industrious, hardworking people, quite happy and proud. They have built an amazing country since I was there in 1965. We returned to Busan (Pusan) this April for the first time since I was there over Labor Day 1965, and I couldn't recognize the place. It was a fishing village and small port then but is now a major Asian port city of over four million people. It is connected to Seoul by a bullet train that can make the trip in less than four hours. When I was there, I don't think I could have driven it in a jeep in twelve hours, and that would have been a very bumpy ride. These people have much of which to be proud.

Republic of Korea soldiers were and are pretty fierce fighters. Our classmates who served alongside them in Vietnam will attest to that—very tough. I don't worry much about what would happen if the North attacked the South today. It would be ugly for a few days, but the ROK troops would kick the butts of the North and send them packing pretty fast.

I visited the DMZ and the "negotiating center" at Panmunjom a couple of times in 1965, and it was pretty formal and tense. The DMZ was and is very fortified, probably as fortified as any border in the world. I'll bet it hasn't changed in the ensuing forty-two years.

Looking back, I really grew up during my two years in the Army. I expanded my understanding of the world and life, improved my ability to study and write, including top secret reports, and finally, I determined what I wanted to do after my Army service. I was much better prepared for the next step in my life, a career at Cargill.

I didn't serve in Vietnam like many of you who are also contributing your memories. I have huge respect for you, that you served our country, that you took unimaginable risks, and that you did a thankless task for which you received no credit at home. You did it with grace and courage. I salute you.

Fritz Corrigan completed his two years of active duty in August '66 and two weeks later began a forty-year career with Cargill. He continued his travels, including nine moves with his wife, Glenda, and their growing family in his first eighteen years, and global travel several times each year thereafter. He is still active on a variety of projects, family activities, and golf and skiing in retirement.

Two Souths Remembered

America and Vietnam in the Mid-'60s

JAMES P. STEWART : U.S. ARMY

Vietnam—the name still evokes a visceral response from veterans and those who lived through the era. Why was Vietnam different? There was virtually the same number of casualties in Korea, yet that is often referred to as the "forgotten" war. Both entailed use of the draft at home and enemy combatants from the north "in country." The only conclusion I can reach is that the length of the war in Vietnam was the factor that led to so much else. World War II encompassed less than four years of complete U.S. military involvement, Korea three years, while Vietnam dragged on in various forms for fifteen years, during which time almost nine million U.S. soldiers served. In my opinion the war, combined with the so-called Great Society program, also initiated by LBJ, led to "guns and butter" postwar inflation that changed our financial landscape in the late '60s and '70s. That partially led me to leave the financial business in Boston in 1974 and move to Florida and a career as a Johnson & Johnson orthopedic implant distributor. That was a good thing, and so was my military and South Vietnam experience. With the acute understanding that others have far different stories, here is mine.

The Stewart family could not be considered a military one in the conventional sense, yet several served. My mother was the family liberal. She had experienced three years of marriage and my birth alone as Dad served as an MIT-trained engineer and Army lieutenant colonel in Port Moresby, New Guinea, maintaining an air base for the Army Air Forces from the beginning of World War II. Her brother, my uncle, was killed and subsequently buried in France in 1945. He was nineteen years old. My younger brother went through Army ROTC and served in Vietnam as well. I chose the Army because it offered the shortest (two years) active-duty requirement, and I listed Military Intelligence first and the one obligatory combat branch, the Signal Corps, last for similar nonheroic reasons.

ROTC summer camp was at Fort Devens, Massachusetts, next to the town of Harvard, where I lived as a child. I had planned to work on Cape Cod the summer after college graduation. Uncle Sam had other plans and initially assigned me to Fort Meade, Maryland. We trained there with reserve soldiers and established a "newbie" officer group that largely stayed together through our subsequent assignments at Fort Bragg, North Carolina, and Vietnam itself. I was the Massachusetts guy. The other roommates were from New Jersey, South Carolina, and North Carolina. We had wonderful times together, and I enjoyed a great introduction to the South. Sure played a lot of golf.

We were attached to the gung-ho Eighty-Second Airborne Division during the year in Fort Bragg, but we worked independently. Because of a shoulder dislocation sustained while playing fraternity hockey at Dartmouth and a recurrence while taking karate lessons at Fort Meade, I ended up with surgery at Womack Army Hospital in Fort Bragg and never went to jump school. I roomed with a wounded Vietnam vet chopper pilot while in the hospital. His intense interest in the stock market probably led to my initial post-military career.

Many of my experiences thereafter were more out of *M*A*S*H* than *The Longest Day*. First, we went to Vietnam out of the Port of Charleston, South Carolina, on a World War II MSTS vessel (Liberty ship), through the Panama Canal and up the West Coast to Long Beach, California. Our ship started to take on water. Consequently we had almost two weeks of shore leave while a "new" ship came down from Seattle. Hollywood, Newport Beach, and Tijuana sure were fun places!

The trip across the Pacific was long, and we were certainly in no hurry. We played a lot of poker with chopper pilots. The ship made one stop at Guam and then headed up the Saigon River. We were kept inside for security reasons, only to emerge when at Saigon itself, where the first sight was water skiers zipping by—some war! We were initially assigned to "tent city" upon arrival in country on Christmas Eve 1965. The next day the now three of us headed out to the Bob Hope show. I ended up standing next to General Westmoreland, while watching Joey Heatherton onstage at Tan Son Nhut Air Base—that's wartime entertainment.

Initially we were assigned to individual field units, with mine being the

First Lieutenant Jim Stewart, Christmas morning 1965, tent city perimeter, Saigon

First Infantry Division or "the Big Red One." They were stationed just north of Saigon. In reality we all worked at the Central Intelligence Command, Vietnam (CICV), located on the air base. We lived near the Saigon racehorse track in a villa that ended up hosting many "social events." As officers we pretty much had the run of the city and were frequenters of Tu Do Street establishments of various flavors. We often headed up to the rooftop restaurant of the Rex Hotel for dinner while watching the fireworks (security flares) erupt on the northern horizon. Our villa landlady was French. I had my first taste of French onion soup the night she took us out. Another night I attended a Dartmouth Club of Saigon affair in Cholon, the Chinese district.

My responsibility at CICV was to track enemy troop strength and deployment. The North Vietnamese fighters consisted of the North Vietnamese Army (NVA) and the guerrilla troops, the Viet Cong or VC. We were supporting the weak Army of the Republic of Vietnam (ARVN) troops. You know the results. I recall the head of the Dartmouth Army ROTC faculty telling us one day that the military needs ten-to-one troop superiority to win a guerrilla war. That theory explains much about Vietnam then and Afghanistan now. We did have the Montagnards in Vietnam. They, however, did not have the territorial strength of the Kurds in Iraq.

My Scottish heritage led me to adopt an independent manner, although I was not alone in having a less than enthusiastic feeling about the war scenario in general. One West Point officer in particular took exception to my attitude. My assignment meant I gave occasional briefings to General Creighton Abrams (the Abrams tank namesake), who was Westy's number-two man and successor. Consequently I was fairly safe. Upon receiving a commendation from General Abrams, I was home free. Love that chain of command.

Rest and relaxation (R&R) meant a trip then to Hong Kong, Bangkok, or Hawaii—Australia was added later. Two of us headed to Hong Kong and did the usual tourist thing. I'll spare the details, exotic and otherwise. Later in country I played nine holes of golf at the Saigon Country Club, where play was limited to the front nine, as the VC controlled the back nine. Gives new meaning to the term "hazards."

In addition to my office job, I hitched copter rides out to the Big Red One on occasion to pick up reports firsthand. What a rush flying low over the city with our old warrant officer pilot friends from the transport ship. One night I was duty officer for our company at the enlisted men's compound. They had nightly movies we selected. A Vietnamese informant reported a boat of VC headed down the adjacent river, so I stopped the show and headed up a ladder to one of the lookout towers along the fence line built on the water's edge. A private was on duty manning an M60 machine gun. I asked him, as a precaution, if he knew how to use it. Thankfully he did, and we both squeezed off a few warning rounds for effect. The threat never materialized. C'est la guerre.

I had been dating a girl from Harvard, Massachusetts, and it was possible to have one-way conversations occasionally at the communication building. She was attending Connecticut College for Women in New London. The USO put on smaller shows for individual units in addition to the Bob Hope extravaganza. Wayne Newton and his brother gave a show for our unit one night from the back of a deuce and a half, or 2½ ton truck. After the show he announced that his next engagement was in Boston and that he would be happy to call any friends or relatives in the area. I gave him her home number, and later upon my return she confirmed that he did call—however, she confided she did not know who he was. We broke up soon thereafter. Guess that was before he made it big in Vegas.

By then I was becoming a short-timer. A fellow officer from Vermont was scheduled to head back stateside at the same time, so we hatched a plan that entailed finessing our return trip. We were supposed to be flying back through Okinawa to Fort Dix, New Jersey, for out-processing, since we both came from the East Coast. Instead we persuaded the clerk to fly us into Oakland, California. I still remember the roar of relief on board as the Continental Airlines plane made a rapid ascent from the airport to avoid potential enemy sniper fire. Our idea was to spend time in San Francisco and then find a transport agency that assigned drivers to deliver cars cross-country. We attended the 1966 U.S. Open at the Olympic Country Club and watched Billy Casper tie Arnold Palmer on Sunday, then win in a playoff. We were fortunate to find an agency that had a Ford Mustang a college student wished driven to her home outside Baltimore. Bingo! I still remember the silly movie *The Russians Are Coming* was all the comic rage at the time. The mood of the country changed dramatically soon thereafter. Only a few of us knew firsthand that the early stage colonial-style war was becoming a bloody mess. Timing is everything, and we were home, although certainly not as exalted veterans. At least no one spit on us; that came later. We were generally ignored.

The drive home went exceptionally well. I recall Yosemite, the Continental Divide, and the initial construction of a ski area called Vail. It appeared to have potential, located right off an interstate. I have been there a few times since! We eventually delivered the car to the girl in a fashionable suburb of Baltimore and enjoyed a dip in her family swimming pool. A pretty good plan, well executed, as perhaps can only occur when young. I spent that summer goofing off around New England while decompressing, and headed to Boston and the civilian workforce in the fall.

Military intelligence, the saying goes, is an oxymoron. That was not true in any respect. We filtered out the junk and gave good assessments to the "brass." They were under pressure from Washington to deliver, while the politicians in charge misled and withheld from the press and public. Once Tet occurred, and despite the fact that, like the Germans in World War I, we never lost a major battle in the field, it was all over domestically in terms of political and certainly public support. Had I passed along my ROTC ten-to-one ratio analysis to General Abrams, would it have made a difference? No, I was not on his staff, and he was destined to carry out the mission as assigned. That mission would later entail gradual withdrawal until the ARVN military collapsed.

Vietnam is a beautiful country with fabulous beaches. Its people are industrious and attractive, especially the women in those *ao dai* dresses. Saigon after all was then considered the Paris of the Orient. The weather is terrific, if tropical is your style. Now it is a unified, Communist country with a capitalist economic system and a U.S. trading partner. Many Vietnamese refugees live here and have helped make Asians the largest net immigrant group for several years. *Choy oy* and best wishes to all my fellow Dartmouth '64 Vietnam vets. Welcome home.

James Stewart returned to the civilian workforce as a stockbroker in Boston. He worked with a number of high-profile, interesting clients. The market debacle in the early seventies led him to a career as an orthopedic implant (total hips and knees) distributor in Florida. Ironically, he then worked in conjunction with several leading surgeons from Boston on new product initiatives. He is now retired and lives in Hypoluxo, Florida. His wife, Jane, is an IS/IT director at a hospital, his daughter Kristen is an emergency room nurse, and his dog Bischa is a standard schnauzer. He served as a VFW post commander and district commander (Palm Beach County), which reinforced his understanding of the commitments and sacrifices made by all veterans for their country.

"I Never to See You Again"

TIM BROOKS : U.S. ARMY

When I arrived at Dartmouth in the fall of 1960, the Republic of Vietnam was far from my, or anyone's, mind. I enrolled in ROTC because I assumed that otherwise I would have to enlist or be drafted, like my two brothers, and if I was going to serve somewhere, I wanted to do so as an officer. So when 1964 came I pinned on my gold bars, entered the Signal Corps, and spent a year with the 518th Signal Company at Fort Bragg, North Carolina. Then in June 1965 I was put on a large chartered commercial jet bound for Vietnam.

Seven out of eight American soldiers sent to Vietnam served in a support role, and I was one of those, so this won't be a story of combat. It is, rather, what it was like for the rest of us, a chance to see firsthand how America interacted with a very different part of the world.

After arriving at sprawling, chaotic Tan Son Nhut Air Base outside Saigon, I learned that I had been assigned to oversee the signal detachment at Vinh Long, a small helicopter base deep in the Mekong Delta, in the south of the country. It was a picturesque location, a cluster of small wood and cinder block buildings and Quonset huts sitting beside an airfield that was located in the middle of a vast expanse of rice paddies. Occasionally, Viet Cong shelled us with mortar fire, but their aim was terrible, and they mainly succeeded in blowing up the rice fields rather than the UH-1 helicopter gunships lined up along the side of the airstrip. Still, running toward a bunker as explosions went off around me was a reminder that this wasn't Hanover.

The detachment consisted of half a dozen enlisted men and myself, a cinder block building full of microwave communications equipment, and three hastily erected towers. None of us knew more than the rudiments of how to operate (much less service) this equipment. The Army in its haste to get troops into the field had put me into a program that skipped normal

Lieutenant Tim Brooks, 1965

technical training at Fort Monmouth (the Signal Corps school) and told me to "learn on the job." So we relied on the services of a civilian contractor from Texas, an older technician who was well paid and who lived in town. Lived well, we understood.

The story of how this bulky electronic and tower equipment got to the delta is interesting. Flying it in would have been expensive, and trucking it in would have required a heavily armed convoy capable of fighting off the inevitable Viet Cong ambush. So the Army hired a local Vietnamese trucking company and gave them money to pay off the enemy. Sure enough, the convoy was stopped en route, but the VC realized they had no use for such equipment, and if they blew it up the Americans would just bring it in another way and stop sending bribes. They took the money and let the trucks pass.

One is adventurous at age twenty-three, and running this little detachment didn't take much effort, so I soon volunteered to become pay officer for the company, which had detachments like mine all over South Vietnam. This involved shuttling around the entire country, once a month, dispensing piasters (the local currency) to soldiers on payday at bases large and small—sometimes very small, and very remote. Most of the travel was in small fixed-wing aircraft and UH-1 helicopters. The latter would lift off with sliding side doors wide open, and some passengers seated facing out, secured by just a seat belt, suspended precariously over open space as the chopper banked horizontally. Clutched tightly between my legs was a large satchel of money. One slip and there would have been piasters (or me) scattered all over the countryside below. Sometimes from the chopper we would see the tracer bullets of a firefight in the distance, or we would be warned of a possible ambush as we jumped into a jeep and raced up a lonely road to a small outpost in the hinterlands. Fortunately the action never got too close.

I had just obtained my first good camera, a Minolta SLR, and snapped hundreds of pictures in one exotic locale after another—Nha Trang, Qui Nhon, Hon Mot, Chu Lai, Quang Nai, Phu Bai, Pleiku, Ban Me Thuot, Kon Tum. What struck me was the surprising diversity, and often beauty, of this war-torn country, from the steamy delta to the cool, pine-forested highlands, to the beaches on the South China Sea. Saigon may have been the "Paris of the Orient," with tree-lined boulevards and shimmering white hotels, but it was largely Third World once you got out of the city center. It teemed with tiny blue-and-yellow taxis, but it was said that if the taxi stopped for any reason and the driver got out, you had better get out too, immediately. There might be a bomb. Other striking locations included the vast, sandy beaches of Cam Ranh Bay and Da Nang (the setting for the 1980s TV show *China Beach*), and the resort city of Dalat in the misty highlands, where I was billeted in the stately and almost deserted Dalat Palace Hotel. This was a holdover from French colonial days, a large ornate structure on a hilltop, with broad staircases that commanded a sweeping view of the surrounding forest and lakes. Its wealthy French patrons were long gone, and it was now empty, like an aging aristocrat abandoned by its servants. The imperial city of Hue in the north had gardens and the somewhat rundown palaces of the former Nguyen dynasty. American bombing during the Tet offensive in 1968 destroyed many of these.

One could see what a beautiful and elegant country this had been under French colonial rule, at least for the favored few. Now, after twenty years of war, it had gone to seed. The rich had fled, and the poor were still poor.

To entertain the American forces the military had established a radio station in Saigon, Armed Forces Radio. The Viet Cong had tried to blow it up, without success. Missing my radio days at WDCR, I informally wangled a Sunday morning show on the station, courtesy of classmate Alan McKee, who fortuitously (for me) had become assistant officer in charge of the station. It was easy to hop on a chopper for the thirty-minute ride from Vinh Long to Saigon Saturday afternoon, do my show Sunday morning, then catch a chopper back to the base in the afternoon. Nobody asks questions in a war zone. "Need a lift, Lieutenant?" It was the only station at which I ever worked that kept a loaded .45 caliber pistol next to the control board, in case the VC decided to storm the station.

The music was pretty sedate, meant to ease Sunday morning hangovers (Jo Stafford's *American Folk Songs*, that sort of thing), but I was happily back in radio. The gig lasted until one weekend when the detachment commanders were summoned to a Sunday morning meeting with the CO at company headquarters in Vung Tau. I recorded my show the week before. On the next weekend, as I walked past the company clerk's desk toward the meeting, I realized that he had his radio on, tuned to AFRS, and the voice on the radio was mine! My radio gig was totally unauthorized, and if anyone had noticed I would have been toast. That was the end of my Vietnam radio career.

None of this extracurricular activity seemed to detract from my assigned duties at Vinh Long. At the end of my tour I received a commendation for my management of the detachment. It seemed that the Army was largely wasting the talent it was harvesting from campuses across America.

Finally, there were the people. The Vietnamese that I encountered were quiet, hardworking, and weary of decades of war. They appeared to believe (at least in 1965) that the Americans had come to help them. At one point I volunteered to teach English to young soldiers at a Vietnamese army base in Vinh Long. This was somewhat ironic as I knew no Vietnamese, and they knew no English. However, the plan was to hand out small instruction books with Vietnamese text and the English translation side by side. I would read the English, slowly and clearly, and they would follow along, to learn pronunciation and perhaps pick up a few words along the way. I will never forget their faces, eager to learn so that they would be able to communicate with the Americans who had come to save their country.

The other unforgettable face was that of my "secretary," a shy young woman named Lieu Thi-Bé, known to all as "Cookie." The U.S. military was trying to help the Vietnamese economy by employing as many locals as possible, so I was given a secretary. There was practically nothing for her to do, and she sat quietly outside my "office" (a corner of our small cinder block equipment building) for most of the day. Whenever possible I would give her a bit of filing to do, or maybe a simple Army form to fill out (she spoke and wrote rudimentary English). Occasionally one of her friends would visit. We smiled at each other, and it was all perfectly pleasant, but it was an odd working relationship, to say the least.

When the time came for me to return to the United States in June 1966 and muster out, I waved goodbye to Cookie, smiled one last time, and thought little more of it. A few weeks later, to my great surprise, a package arrived at my home in New Hampshire. There was no return

Letter to Tim Brooks
from Lieu Thi-Bé

Lieu Thi-Bé

address, but inside was a beautiful seventeen-inch female doll, dressed in traditional Vietnamese attire, and a note carefully handwritten in broken English. They have been in storage for the past forty-six years, but I dug them out for this article. The note, on flimsy paper, has begun to deteriorate, and portions are now gone, like our memories of times long ago. I will transcribe it as best I can. It is, in a way, a surrogate for the relationship between America and Vietnam—good intentions, but a disappointing outcome, especially for the ordinary people of that tormented country. She wrote,

Dear Sir Brooks,
Some days later you'll come home. I want to offer you this small gift for the times you have been here, that is my country.
Sir Brooks, I have worked with you for months, but I feel to like you. You are very nice and serious. You were kind in daily business to me. For some time, I didn't understand, I think, if you liked me. I am very sorry, I can't write well.
When you go to home I am sad and sorrow after you. I am also worried if the new second lieutenant is as nice as you. I hope he'll be nice.
Before remember when you walking to the aircraft, good journey to you, and I wish you are happy.
I never to see you again.

Lieu Thi-Bé

- -

Tim Brooks remained in the National Guard for eight additional years and was eventually promoted to captain. He resigned in 1974. He has had a long career as a television executive, specializing in audience research, and a parallel career as an author. He has written seven books about television and the recording industry and is working on an eighth, about the history of student radio at Dartmouth.

Radio Days

ALAN MCKEE : U.S. ARMY

I hesitated to put anything on paper about working at Armed Forces
Radio in Saigon (AFRS) because it seemed trivial and almost insult-
ing, weighed against what real veterans faced, especially those who
became casualties of a tragic conflict. Besides, Robin Williams already
did the job. I didn't much like his take on events, however, and couldn't
resist the chance to put the record straight.

The whole thing started when I was back on the family farm in Iowa
during 1965 and got a call out of the blue from the Department of the
Army asking if I wouldn't like to be assistant officer in charge of AFRS.
That was bizarre, because it meant replacing Sturges Dorrance, Dartmouth '63, who had preceded me as WDCR manager at Dartmouth.
During those days I took things like that for granted as either the good
work of divine providence or evidence that folks in Washington were all-
knowing and wanted only the best for everybody. Proudly sporting my
second lieutenant's bars, thanks to Dartmouth's ROTC program, I found
myself supervising experienced enlisted personnel and draftees in Vietnam who had graduated from Penn, Cornell, and other elite schools and
were better broadcasters, but I assumed this kind of privilege was also just
in keeping with the natural order of things.

It is probably good I didn't arrive in Vietnam earlier, but it meant I
missed the best wisecrack of the war. AFRS studios were located in the
Brink Hotel in central Saigon, which was hit by a car bomb on Christmas
Eve 1964, just before Bob Hope and a bevy of starlets landed at Tan Son
Nhut for his annual holiday tour to entertain American troops. Hope
joked that he'd received the warmest welcome ever. "Why," he said, "my
entire hotel came out to the airport to meet me."

It is true that, even in Saigon, there was no sanctuary from random

Victoria Hotel BOQ in
Cholon after bombing,
April 1, 1966

violence. Favorite restaurants were blown up, regrettably including some with the best menus and most scenic settings. I stayed first in the Victoria Hotel officers' quarters in Saigon's Cholon district, which was unfortunately devastated by a terrorist bomb detonated just after I moved out. I relocated to the Brink Annex BOQ, a short block from the station. There I remember cowering under the bed at one point as the best available shelter from falling debris.

AFRS offered a good vantage point from which to take in the conflict, more as an observer than a participant. For one thing, we were part of Military Assistance Command, Vietnam (MACV) headquarters, which mainly meant we partied with the top brass and had direct contact with the military hierarchy from General Westmoreland down. (I called on him to record holiday messages for broadcast to the troops, which required quite a few "takes" before the message came out right; you'd be surprised how tangled your tongue can get trying to say "Happy Thanksgiving" into a shaky, hand-held mike.)

Ann-Margret at AFRS interview

There were plenty of MACV parties, sometimes brightly illuminated by flare ships hovering above potential infiltration routes at the edge of town. Of course, social arrangements got more complex after curfews were introduced from late evening until dawn, so companions had to consider the alternatives in advance to avoid any misunderstanding.

The Pentagon also made sure that in Saigon we were well entertained by professionals, ranging from an improbable *Hello, Dolly!* Broadway road show to individual personalities from Walt Kelly to Ann-Margret. Most stopped by the station for an interview. Kelly grabbed a felt-tipped marker in the studio to dash off a poster-size drawing of Pogo in full military uniform, captioned, "I didn't raise my boy to be no soldier."

We at AFRS liked to sit in on the so-called "Five O'Clock Follies" daily press briefings conducted by U.S. information officers, and noticed when big-name American journalists managed to cover the war by strolling over from the Caravelle Hotel bar, rarely taking the trouble to leave town. For his part, until he was reprimanded for unsanctioned moonlighting, my boss used to send voice feeds to U.S. networks every night. Sometimes hard news was really scarce. Once he helpfully advised listeners in the United States who wanted to get a feel for Vietnam's geography to contemplate a banana at arm's length.

What I wanted to say about *Good Morning, Vietnam* was that I didn't remember heavy-handed military censorship. I recall airing some pretty irreverent material without clearance from anyone and without repercussions. I'm not sure Adrian Cronauer was much like what Robin Williams portrayed, although my notes from 1965 rate Ade as a "top-notch DJ and production man." However, the producers could have showcased the felicitously named Don Busser, who did an earlier AFRS wake-up show called the *Dawn Buster*. Or even Tim Brooks, a particularly intrepid WDCR alumnus, who implausibly commuted to Saigon by helicopter from his field assignment to do AFRS programs as a volunteer. Turns out Cronauer eventually put himself through law school by successfully shopping the concept for *Good Morning, Vietnam*. Hard to fault a creative entrepreneur.

What I do remember, even from our peripheral vantage point, was the mind-numbing escalation of all elements of the U.S. presence. For a time, it seemed as if the powers-that-be had decided to assign two replacements for every departing AFRS staffer. That corresponds closely to the overall spike in U.S. forces from 184,000 to 385,000 in 1966. During that period we somehow felt it vital to start doing television broadcasts, which became such an urgent priority that they were launched from a military transport circling overhead with a chief warrant officer struggling to read the news from the back of the plane into an unsteady camera, while the whole jury-rigged setup bounced between air pockets. When we needed a high-end Uher tape recorder for remote field recordings, a crusty sergeant with years of experience insisted the only sure way to get one was to requisition a half dozen, so that's what we did. But, because this was the U.S. mission in Vietnam in the mid-'60s, we got all six.

The officers' mess on top of the Brink Hotel right above the AFRS studios represented another unique opportunity for us. Personnel dining there tended to be military advisers in from the field for a few days of R&R. They were, to a man, impressive and professional, and the protocol there was to join a table with one or two others to get their take on how things were going. Every such conversation for a year ran along the lines of, "Well, I can't see much progress where I'm assigned, but, with all the resources we're pouring in, it's hard to see how we won't prevail."

We did have the luxury in Saigon of plenty of time for reflection. I took a good extension course in Far East history under University of Maryland auspices, and, under my own steam, tackled Bernard Fall's *The Two Vietnams* and John Mecklin's *Mission in Torment*, which raised doubt both about the wisdom of our approach and our ability to make it work. There was also Graham Greene's *The Quiet American*, which turned out to be a parable of futile American intervention in Vietnam, unaccountably written a decade before the United States really got rolling. Seemed like pretty sobering stuff.

I found my niche in the war. Talk about being well situated. It turned out MACV needed a crackerjack drafter to ghost-write medal nominations for senior officers. Who better than a freshly minted English major, who had actually scanned a few major works of fiction the night before his comprehensive exams! Creative writing was a blast, and it represented a good dry run for quite similar work later in the Foreign Service.

Remarkable things happen with the passage of time. When I took a State Department course for newly named American ambassadors in 1996, a distinguished colleague turned out to be former congressman Pete Peterson, who had spent six harrowing years as a prisoner of war in North Vietnam and had just been designated by President Clinton as the first U.S. ambassador to the Socialist Republic of Vietnam in Hanoi. His palpable commitment to healing, reconciliation, and friendly relations was a powerful source of inspiration for all of us headed off to new assignments around the world.

Not long ago, my wife, Marty, and I got to visit Vietnam again. Everybody was nice. The country looked prosperous and peaceful. There was a swanky, new five-star hotel where the Brink BOQ had once stood. Unlike the resourceful but hard-pressed Cubans, the Vietnamese hadn't made any visible effort to keep driving the oversized old American vehicles we abandoned willy-nilly on departure. No high-finned, ex-military sedans in sight. Folks mostly had new Toyotas. The fiercest ongoing battle was the hard-fought Memorial Day soccer match between the Dragons from U.S. Embassy Hanoi and the Tigers from our consulate in Ho Chi Minh City. This year Hieu Trinh from the embassy's maintenance unit scored the winning goal.

By June 2012 Defense Secretary Panetta was visiting American sailors anchored in Cam Ranh Bay, regretting "blood spilled on both sides" in Indochina, talking warmly about prospects for closer bilateral military cooperation with "partners like Vietnam" and enthusiastically anticipating regular, stepped-up access to that former U.S. naval base and deep-water port.

Go figure. Makes me wonder who ended up with the Pogo poster, all those top-of-the line Uhers, and the wide-ranging AFRS record library. Fortunately, I spent a year duplicating pretty much the whole thing on a fine, seven-inch reel-to-reel Teac tape deck (we had really good PXs in Vietnam, too).

In what Alan McKee acknowledges must seem pretty improbable in retrospect, he was awarded a Bronze Star for service in Vietnam. He then served to the rank of captain in headquarters of the 197th Infantry Brigade at Fort Benning, Georgia, before hanging up his uniform for good in 1967 to begin graduate study at the Fletcher School of Law and Diplomacy, in preparation for a State Department career revolving around Africa, Canada, and Western Europe.

Vietnam and My Life

GEORGE MORROW : U.S. NAVY

I didn't join the military out of patriotic fervor; I was simply caught up
and carried into it by the flow of events that so powerfully affected my
generation. And though, at the time, I saw the experience as merely
something I had to go through, I now realize that the experience fun-
damentally shaped my understanding of myself and my country.

I served in the Navy as CIC officer on the USS *Duluth* (LPD-6), an amphibious ship that operated with the First Marine Division in the coastal
area north of Da Nang. Because the Vietnam War was not fought at sea,
and because very little fighting was going on in our area at the time (this
was prior to the Tet offensive), I never experienced the trials of combat
that so many others had to endure. Nevertheless, I was changed.

Being part of a relatively small ship's crew is to experience community
with a capital C. A Navy ship—particularly in time of war—is a community composed of individuals from every part of the United States
and every imaginable background. But it is also, like a living organism,
a community in which there are many, many different functions to be
performed, each equally important to the community's survival and success. Unlike many of the environments we experience in a lifetime, a ship
is a place where the importance of every man's role and contribution—
however modest—is often obvious. It is also a place where rank, degrees,
and social standing—the common credentials of civilian life—have little
to do with the value a man has in the eyes of his shipmates. I found that
many of the men I respected most came from social and educational backgrounds very different from my own. Only what one would expect, you
say? Yes, but it's one thing to believe in the theory and quite another to
have built this belief from actual experience.

I feel my Navy experience gave me a better sense of the composition of our country and the strengths of its people than I would have gained by simply going straight from college to the corporate world. I feel I am a better person and a better citizen for having served and am grateful for the experience. I am also now a strong proponent of some sort of required national service. It's important to our democracy that we citizens understand each other. Yet our different backgrounds, education, and interests tend naturally to send us off on different paths that give us little chance to live through a common experience, the kind of experience that builds real understanding. Required national service might be the answer.

After his three and a half years in the Navy, George Morrow spent most of his professional career in New York City creating tools to develop the business and technical skills of corporate professionals in banking and telecommunications. His favorite professional activity was the creation of computer-based trading and investment simulations, of which he developed several. His favorite nonprofessional activity was, and still is, choral singing.

Paradoxes of War

BUD McGRATH : U.S. ARMY

Freud tells us that if we keep track of our dreams over a period of time, provided our unconscious does not inhibit access to them, eventually a pattern will emerge that will tell us important truths about ourselves. The same may be true about the conscious stories that we tell repeatedly about ourselves to ourselves and to others. Heidegger, who said that we don't speak language but language speaks us,[1] viewed language and narratives not as referential primarily but as a kind of path breaking that creates its own truth and reality. Since serving in Vietnam I have told a number of stories repeatedly about my experience there. I never thought much about any pattern that emerged from these stories until my anxiety about writing them for this collection provoked a particularly violent dream one night from which I awoke with the outline for this essay full-blown in my head. The stories that follow have rattled around in my memory for the past forty-five years. I have occasionally told these stories to others, but more importantly they have persisted together in my memory. At this point I am not sure how accurate some of the details are or were in the first place. But that doesn't really matter. These stories have created a truth of their own for me. They are my metaphors for the Vietnam War.

When I graduated from Dartmouth and its ROTC program I took a regular Army commission, the same type of commission West Point graduates receive. Regular Army commissions differ from reserve commissions in that you serve "at the pleasure of the President" rather than for a specific time period. A regular commission also gave me more choice in

---

1. *Poetry, Language, Thought*, trans. Albert Hofstadter (New York: Harper & Row, 1971), 146, 215.

my branch and theater assignments. I got what I wanted—an artillery assignment in Germany; but few of us knew in 1964 what was going on in Vietnam, and my European tour was cut short after two years. Since I was serving "at the pleasure of the President," I wound up serving four years, the last of which was in Vietnam.

Let me begin, however, with a story about my experience in Germany, which sets a certain tone for my Vietnam experience. After serving for a year in a 155 mm self-propelled howitzer battalion, I was transferred to an Honest John rocket battalion, where I commanded a rocket platoon. The Honest John rocket was fired from a mobile truck launcher and had a nuclear capability. When I arrived at my new unit, I set about learning as much as I could about the weapon. The information manuals about the rocket were not classified, but the information about the warheads was classified, so the relevant manuals were in different locations. After reading the rocket manuals in my battery headquarters, I spent a few days in the office of the battalion S-2 (intelligence officer) learning about the warheads. One startling discovery stood out in my comparative research of rocket and warhead data—the kill zone of the largest nuclear warhead the rocket could fire exceeded the maximum range of the rocket. When I brought this fact to the attention of fellow officers, they responded to my "Did you know . . ." with "No, that can't be true," or they simply laughed or ignored me. I spent the next few weeks training my platoon to evacuate the launch site so efficiently that we could be two miles to the rear, just out of the kill zone, before the rocket reached its destination. The one weakness in our strategy was the trailer-mounted wind sensor that measured wind direction and velocity at the launch site. It operated hydraulically to a height of over twenty-five or thirty feet and descended very slowly after a launch. I decided that if we ever had to fire the largest nuclear warhead, we would sacrifice that piece of equipment.

In Vietnam I was part of a 105 mm howitzer battalion attached to the Ninth Infantry Division stationed at Bearcat, a huge base camp carved out of the jungle about fifteen miles northeast of what was then called Saigon. One day one of our soldiers heard a loud crack of breaking wood coming from the far side of our ammunition dump. When we investigated we discovered a box of explosives had been broken into, probably by a Viet Cong sapper, who, by the time we arrived at the scene, was long gone and left empty-handed thanks to the alertness of the soldier who heard the crack. We notified battalion headquarters, who in turn notified division headquarters. About a half hour later, while we were still standing at the scene of the crime, we heard artillery firing from the other end of the base camp, and a few seconds later a half dozen rounds landed a few hundred yards away, just outside the perimeter of our ammo dump. No further volleys followed. We had not called in any artillery. Needless to say, we left the ammo dump quickly.

Another much more serious sapper attack occurred at the ammunition dump at Long Binh, the largest U.S. supply depot in Vietnam, located near the Bien Hoa Air Base, a main entry and exit point for U.S. soldiers sent to South Vietnam. One night during the 1968 Tet offensive, piles of ammunition were blown up by Viet Cong sappers. Some of the sappers were caught. One of them, rumor has it, worked at the Long Binh officers' club as a barber. Daily he had a razor to the throat of generals. One of the strange features of this war was that we hired people we fought against at night to work in our base camps during the day, which may be one of the reasons Viet Cong intelligence often was better than U.S. military intelligence.

One night I was the OIC of one of the sectors of the perimeter guard at Bearcat. The base camp was approximately two miles long and a half mile wide, and the perimeter guard was divided into four sectors. Between the perimeter berm and the jungle was a cleared area of more than a hundred yards planted with mines and barbed wire. It was a hot steamy night, and my glasses were constantly fogging up. At one point in the early morning hours we heard an explosion in one of the adjacent sectors. Rifle and machine-gun fire, plus grenades coming from our perimeter guards, followed the explosion. Within minutes artillery began dropping into the area of the initial explosion; then helicopters and an AC-47 gunship poured fire into the area. Before the incident was over B-52 bombers on their way from Guam to North Vietnam were diverted and dropped their thunderous loads in the jungle just beyond the cleared area. Then all was quiet. When dawn broke, a patrol was sent out to investigate. All they found in the area of the initial explosion was a well-mutilated monkey. Apparently the initial explosion was from one of our own soldiers with a grenade launcher who had fired without permission at a sound he heard in the open area.

One month later the battalion headquarters and supply operation was moved to Xuan Loc, about fifteen miles northeast of Bearcat. After checking with the local MPs about road conditions between Bearcat and Xuan Loc, we were told that road conditions were green, meaning they were safe to travel. I departed in my jeep for Xuan Loc. With me was my driver and a machine gunner with an M60 mounted in the back of the jeep. We drove northwest to Bien Hoa and then headed east to Xuan Loc. About halfway between Bien Hoa and Xuan Loc we knew something was profoundly wrong. We were in the only vehicle on the normally well-traveled road, and we had not seen another vehicle, military or civilian, for the last several miles. Somehow others knew to stay off that road on that day. By the time we became aware of our vulnerability and exposure we were halfway to Xuan Loc. It was just as far back as it was forward. We continued on to Xuan Loc. When we arrived there we discovered there had been a battle the night before and the streets were still littered with the fly-covered bodies of NVA soldiers. The MPs in Xuan Loc told us that the road we had just traveled was code red—that is, extremely dangerous and should not be traveled without an armed convoy. What saved us? Any VC or NVA along the route probably thought it was not worth exposing their positions for the sake of destroying a single jeep and its passengers. At the end of the month when we returned to Bearcat, I did not rely on Army Intelligence about road conditions; I flew back by helicopter.

I was at Bearcat during the infamous 1968 Tet offensive. Army Intelligence warned of an impending attack. They said it was coming about a week before it actually came. With the first warning we slept, or I should say we lay on our bunks, in full combat gear. The attack did not come that night. We were told it would come the next night. Again we slept in full combat gear. No attack. It was sure to come the next night. By the third night, having found it difficult to snooze in my helmet and my hot sweaty flak vest with a weapon by my side, I was pretty well sleep deprived. After spending a fourth sleepless night in my gear I decided Army Intelligence was an oxymoron, and on the fifth night I shed my combat gear and slept soundly—that is, until a rocket landed on the road behind my hooch and rained shrapnel down on the metal roof. The hooch was protected up to three feet all around with sandbags, so I rolled on the floor, dressed, put on my gear as quickly as I could, and ran at a crouch out the door to the command bunker next door. In my haste I neglected to tie my bootlaces. At the top step of the bunker I tripped, tumbled into the bunker, and

Left to right: Captain McGrath, First Sergeant Chandler, Lieutenant Brocker, at Bearcat

landed flat on my back. My first sergeant snapped to attention, saluted, and greeted me with a cheery "Good evening, sir!" as I lay on the bunker floor looking up at him.

The night I left Vietnam I flew out of Bien Hoa Air Base, where I had flown in almost a year earlier. My inbound flight had been uneventful, but as we began our takeoff run on my homeward-bound flight the airport started receiving incoming rocket and mortar fire. To move troops into and out of Vietnam, the military chartered civilian aircraft, and I believe our pilot that night set records for shortest takeoff distance and steepest climb ever for a commercial aircraft. We all cheered in the plane's cabin as we left the war behind.

During my tour in Vietnam I saw no indication whatsoever of any kind of progress being made militarily or politically. For my service there I received a Bronze Star and an Army Commendation Medal. Why, I am not sure. I did my job, that's all. I can't say that I left Vietnam or the U.S. Army a better place. In fact, we devastated the country and impeded its progress into the modern world for more than a decade. As far as I could see, my major accomplishment was securing an air conditioner for the battalion officers' club; oh, and I learned to play pinochle with my warrant officers and my executive officer, our usual evening entertainment.

I realize that others had very different experiences in Vietnam. While I was at Fort Huachuca, Arizona, training GIs to go to Vietnam before I had been there myself, I had a young lieutenant working for me as a platoon leader. He was out of OCS, and he was one of the most reckless, impetuous, immature people I have ever known. One night he got drunk at the officers' club, and as he was leaving the base in his new Pontiac GTO he sideswiped several cars, nearly ran down the MP who tried to stop him at the gate, and then stopped at the gas station just outside the gate to refuel. I had to retrieve him the next morning from the post jail. He was infantry and due to be shipped out soon to Vietnam. I could not imagine how he could survive in combat. I never heard from him again after he left Fort Huachuca. I have always believed in Occam's Razor, and the simplicity of the Vietnam Wall in Washington, D.C., produced one of the most powerful monuments ever built. When I visited the Wall memorial, the first thing I did was look for the lieutenant's name. It took me a few minutes, but as I expected, his name was there. I have no idea how he died, but I can guess.

Toward the end of my tour in Vietnam my battalion commander encouraged me to pursue a career in the military. I politely declined. After four years in the military I was applying to graduate school to study English literature, where fiction made more sense than my military experience.

As an English professor I teach a course on Irish film (Irish literature and culture is my specialty). In my research I came across an enlightening essay by British film scholar John Hill, who points out that in most American films violence typically is the solution to social and personal problems, while in British and European films violence is usually the problem that destroys societies, families, and individuals.[2] (James Bond films muddy his thesis a bit, but one could argue that Hollywood is as much responsible for James Bond as the British.) We still live in a culture where World War II, with its clear sense of accomplishment and its clear

2. John Hill, "Images of Violence," in *Cinema and Ireland*, ed. Kevin Rockett, Luke Gibbons, and John Hill (London: Routledge, 1988), 147–93.

division between the good guys and the bad guys, constructs our paradigm for war, a war made for Hollywood and John Wayne. This paradigm has been reproduced by Hollywood over and over, not only in war films but in westerns and in the action films that have replaced them, where the solitary hero who lives on the edge of normal society preserves that society through acts of violence. All the wars since World War II—Korea, Vietnam, Iraq, Afghanistan—have not shaken the Hollywood paradigm. In the words of American singer-songwriter John Prine, "Some cowboy from Texas / Starts his own war in Iraq."[3] To preserve the Hollywood paradigm, the war in Iraq simply substituted "weapons of mass destruction" for the "domino theory."

To be sure, there have been counter-narratives—Joseph Heller's *Catch-22*, Michael Cimino's *The Deer Hunter*, Oliver Stone's *Platoon* and *Born on the Fourth of July*, Kathryn Bigelow's *The Hurt Locker*. But the Hollywood paradigm still persists; the dream factory rolls out one violent solution after another. Why are Europeans so much more reluctant to go to war to resolve problems? They could be criticized for ignoring atrocities that took place in Yugoslavia, in Rwanda, and now in Syria; but they have experienced the destruction of modern warfare. The United States has been fortunate that no modern war has been conducted on its own territory. Perhaps that is why we can still conceive of violence as the solution to problems rather than the problem to be solved.

After Vietnam, Bud McGrath went directly to graduate school at the University of Texas at Austin, where he received a PhD in English literature in 1973. Since then he has taught at the University of Pennsylvania, Rutgers University, and the University of Southern Maine, where he is currently a professor of English. His primary teaching and research focus has been Irish literature and culture. He has published a number of articles and two books, with a third book nearing completion. With his wife, Gena, he also owns a horse farm that offers boarding, training, and riding instruction. They have a farm website, www.springpointfarm.com.

3. "Some Humans Ain't Human," from the album *Fair and Square* (Oh Boy Records, 2005).

Ours Is Not to Reason Why,
Ours Is But to Sit and Wait

RICHARD MACK : U.S. AIR FORCE

My decision to make ROTC part of my college years was, as were many of my decisions at that time, not accompanied by a great deal of thought. Yet it shaped the rest of my life, perhaps with more impact than did many of my later and more contemplated choices. The military experience shaped my personal life, my career, and my guiding philosophies.

Although I was trained initially to be an airborne forward air controller, a position that only had function in Vietnam, I was never given a Vietnam assignment over my four-year commitment. At the time I felt invincible enough to crave such excitement. Instead, I served out my four years as a weapons controller, directing fighter aircraft intercepts from a radar screen during assignments in South Carolina, Taiwan, and Oklahoma. With the exception of the year in Taiwan, my assignments were with Tactical Air Command, a newly formed unit of the Air Force. We appeared to have no mission other than to train and prepare for the deployments that never occurred. We maligned Tennyson: Ours was not to reason why, ours was but to sit, wait, and hone a cynical sense of the comedy of our existence.

The remote Taiwan assignment was similarly an act of waiting. With two to four days of missions per month, the remainder of the time was spent reading, walking the beaches of our island in the Straits of Formosa, and traveling around Asia as "advisers."

What was the result of these years of limitless unassigned time? I regret that I was not sufficiently focused to take on a systematic study, although there was sufficient time and resources to develop a PhD level of understanding of an area of expertise. Instead, I read broadly, contemplated excessively, interacted with my fellows in waiting, and traveled extensively. The outcomes were very positive, as I:

» Developed a career directed toward the academic. This was a marked shift from my vague thoughts upon graduation of working for corporate America after the military commitment.

» Shifted my political and ethical stance from being a moderate Republican (we all can remember those now extinct beings, along with all the Nelson Rockefeller jokes) to that of a sometimes-Marxist lefty, a position that has moderated somewhat over the years.

» Learned to react to the ludicrousness of the military bureaucracy by viewing it as a great source of humorous story fabrication and retelling. This talent has served me well in coping with academic administration, the politics of the last forty years, and the vagaries of everyday life.

» Developed a love of Asian culture, which culminated in a career specialization in Asian regional economies. This specialization has afforded me many professional stints in China, Hong Kong, Malaysia, and Indonesia, as well as great adventures such as canoeing down the Mekong and sleeping in caves in China's Gansu and Shaanxi Provinces.

» Lived in parts of the United States to which my initial "game plan" would never have taken me. Living in the American South in the mid-sixties was a broadening experience that was a major influence upon my personal philosophy. It was the military that initially moved me off the East Coast to find a more suitable personal climate in the West.

» Made lifelong friends with whom I continue to share these experiences, the resulting values, and our continuing lives.

Above all, the military put me in a geographical position to meet Virginia, my love of forty-four years, and to enrich our relationship with our two daughters, Alexandra and Rachel. We have shared friends, extended families, academic careers, extensive travels, and all of those experiences that define life.

Although I pedantically explain to my young scholars that "On choisit le paysage de son âme—One chooses the landscape of one's soul," the role of the military in shaping my life was not initiated with thoughts of its consequential changes. Yet its influence has served me well.

After completing his military service, Richard Mack completed a PhD in economics at Colorado State University. He is now an emeritus professor of economics at Central Washington University, having retired in 2008 from thirty-six years of teaching, serving as dean, writing grants, and undertaking contract research. A resolute believer in a "real world" approach to learning, Mack has taken students to sites of economic activities and on research and learning experiences in China, Ireland, England, Scotland, and Morocco. By his estimate, he has graded 40,584 exams and told more than eighty-eight thousand jokes and puns while lecturing. Of these, only four jokes were censored by deans, provosts, or presidents.

Vietnam
A Defining Life Event

NEAL STANLEY : U.S. ARMY

I n each of our lives there are certain things that change our patterns of thought and modify our actions. For me Vietnam was one of those events.

I was twenty-five years old in 1967 when I received orders to become a military adviser to a Vietnamese combat unit. I had spent the three previous years in Germany as an officer in an armored cavalry regiment that patrolled the borders between West Germany, East Germany, and Czechoslovakia. I had tried to resign my commission, but the resignation was denied, and the orders to Vietnam came shortly thereafter.

I accepted the orders as a duty to be assumed. I was no patriot; I did not believe there was a strategic reason for our presence in Vietnam. We were involved in a civil war, and we had chosen a side to support. I wanted to survive my tour and get on with my life.

My unit was located in the Mekong Delta region of Vietnam, and I arrived during the first Tet offensive in 1968—replacing an officer who had been killed. We were besieged, but eventually we were able to secure a large enough area to allow our troops to begin offensive operations. We were affiliated with a special forces unit and spent considerable time on riverboats and helicopters, as well as infiltration missions into Cambodia. Friends died; we carried broken bodies to aid stations; and we lost troops to disease and injury. War for us was fighting to protect ourselves and those who were fighting with us. I have lots of stories—some frightening, some heartbreaking, and some perversely hysterically funny. But it was not the war that changed my life; rather it was people I met during my year in Vietnam.

I will relate a few stories and the lessons they taught me.

We were squatted along a road outside a small village. We were tired, dirty, and hungry. An old Vietnamese man came up beside me and held out a bowl of rice. I knew this was probably his food for the day, but he insisted I take it. I asked him why he was giving it to me. "So you will not kill me," was the reply. I asked, "Do the Viet Cong come at night, and do you give them rice?" "Yes," he said. Americans fight wars for political purposes, and civilians get swept up in the turmoil—all they want is survival and peace. The lesson for me: Don't be so focused on yourself or your mission that you miss what is really going on around you.

We thought we were going to be overrun. Two of us, both Americans and close friends, were in a foxhole, and there was a lull in the fighting as the enemy regrouped. The friend began talking. "I need to tell you this before I die," he said. "What?" I asked. "I fathered a child with another woman and never told my wife," he replied. At that moment "Puff the Magic Dragon" flew in and fired its machine guns on the enemy positions. We were rescued. Immediately after the incident my friend asked to be re-assigned, and he avoided all my attempts to talk with him. Lesson learned: It is not my duty on this earth to judge others. I will discover things that I would rather not know; I only need to discern if that knowledge is important for the relationship or mission. Leave judgment to God.

I spoke halting Vietnamese, but I had an interpreter who was my shadow when I was not in combat. Tran was the source of many amusing experiences, but he was also a budding entrepreneur. "*Dai uy* [captain], please loan me 500 piasters to buy two chickens," he asked. "What's the plan, Tran?" I replied. "I will put the chickens in a cage and put the cage over a small pond. The chickens will poop and feed the fish. I will catch the fish and sell them in the market. Then I will buy a baby pig and put it in the cage and feed it garbage. It will poop and the fish will be hungry and I will catch them and get more pigs," he said proudly. "When will I get my money back?" I asked. "When I sell the chickens," he replied. He returned the loan in one month, and by the time I left Vietnam Tran had three pigs; and he had slaughtered and sold at least two others. Lesson learned: Even in the worst of situations there are opportunities if you have the imagination and work ethic to make them a reality.

The old man, the frightened friend, and Tran have appeared again and again in my life. I met them and was blessed by their lessons because of Vietnam. The war changed our nation and etched a permanent mark on our political being. But personally it was a series of lessons that forced me to become acutely aware of the world around me and view it with a broader, deeper perspective.

Neal Stanley has more than forty years of experience in the management of insurance companies and insurance agencies. He served as president and CEO of three insurance companies. He was a partner in an insurance general agency. He developed a consulting firm that advised insurance companies and general agencies on business planning, product development, and captive management. He also is an attorney admitted to practice in California.

Neal is now the chief operating officer for a regional insurance brokerage with offices in California, Nevada, and Arizona. He and his wife, Mirella, reside in Fresno, California, and Mount Pleasant, South Carolina. Neal's daughter Chandra graduated from Dartmouth in 1996.

Vietnam
Before/During/After

DAVID W. KRUGER : U.S. ARMY

Before

n the early 1960s I do not remember that Vietnam got much attention on campus at Dartmouth. But for me at least, military service was a duty I was expected, by family and by myself, to fulfill.

Joining Army ROTC was an easy decision, as was staying with it for the four years. Participating in the mountain and winter warfare unit also sparked my interest in areas far away from the jungles of Southeast Asia. Commissioned as second lieutenant in Military Intelligence at our graduation, I went off to Infantry Officers Basic Course and was asked to stay on with Ranger and Airborne training, but declined. I applied for the Army's language training course in Serbo-Croatian in Monterey, California, and was accepted—but to learn Vietnamese—and also declined, still avoiding jungles. Then, with a stroke of good fortune, I was selected to join an elite intelligence unit, the Special Security Group (USASSG), and assigned to Washington, D.C. After two years and with my service obligation completed, I volunteered to go to Vietnam, contemplating an Army career.

During

Still assigned to USASSG, I was attached to the First Cavalry Division (Airmobile) in January 1967, working directly with the commanding general and his staff on sensitive intelligence matters. This was the time of our peak exposure in Vietnam, with about half a million of us on the ground. Morale was very good, and most of us thought we were there for all the right reasons. I traveled widely throughout South Vietnam that year, based at a forward landing zone (LZ Two Bits) up the coastal plain in

Binh Dinh Province north of Qui Nhon, and earned two air medals and two Bronze Stars for service, not gallantry. With frequent flying on reconnaissance, I was once in a helicopter that was shot down; three times I was in helicopters that crashed into rice paddies; and once during the monsoons I walked away from a fixed-wing plane that crashed going across the runway. Among the more vivid memories are two firepower incidents: watching an "Arc Light" B-52 carpet bombing strike, giving the ground an awesome shake even from six miles away; and seeing a fellow soldier at noon at the LZ reading his mail a hundred yards away totally disappear, the result of a direct hit by a "friendly fire" howitzer shell improperly charged.

Daily routine at the LZ was organized around defense against occasional rocket attack and whatever creature comforts one could manage. In spite of the oppressive heat, we had to sleep in a dug pit covered with steel culvert halves and fully sandbagged. Outdoor showers had water cans mounted high to be heated by the sun. Several soldiers had pet mongooses to effectively fend off snakes. Food was plentiful, but largely canned and centrally heated C-rations, much of it dating back to the Korean conflict, with very stale chocolate and cigarette four-packs. Weekly "horse pills" for malaria were a must. Cigarettes (most of us smoked) were ten cents a pack; beer (3.2 only) ten cents a can—in the heat it did not seem possible to get high on it. My unit had an old 2½-ton truck with trailer, shipped in from Korea with the C-rations. My sergeant and I drove it to the docks at Qui Nhon each month, armed with all of the beer ration cards from the LZ, including the general's, for that month's supply. On one trip we also liberated a new jeep for the fifty-kilometer drive up Route 1 to the LZ. Every month or so the sergeant missed duty on sick call, getting penicillin shots for venereal disease—he refused to use the condoms provided free. Immeasurably helping morale was "rest and relaxation" (R&R): at midyear my wife met me for a week in Hawaii; near the end of my tour I also got to Bangkok for five days.

After

Two weeks after I left the country in 1968 the Tet offensive exploded. While it was a great surprise, our reaction and counterstrikes returned a major tactical military victory, but the strategic political loss was profound, and eventually led to defeat through withdrawal. Reassigned again to Washington, I spent another very interesting year in the Army. Ten months back from Vietnam, I was quietly told that in two weeks I would be alerted to go back, and once alerted, I would have no choice but to go. I had and still have no regrets about volunteering and serving the first tour of duty, but once was enough. The next day I filed paperwork to leave active duty. I did remain in the reserves with two-week stints in each of the next five years, but all in the United States, including briefings to the secretary of defense on occasion.

Unexpectedly out of active duty, I cast about for what to do next. My good fortune continued, though, as my father-in-law called a family friend at a large Boston bank. I interviewed in the only suit I owned, my captain's uniform. Seven bank officers saw me that day—all Dartmouth graduates, and four of them World War II Navy pilots. They offered me a job, and I spent the rest of my for-profit working career with the company, almost thirty years.

By the 1980s I found myself back in Asia in charge of the bank's Eastern Hemisphere branch network for six years, based in Hong Kong. In 1988, remembering the physical beauty of Vietnam and its interesting people, I took advantage of the opportunity to be among the first Western tourists allowed back into the country. When my wife and I ventured into a street in Ho Chi Minh City / Saigon upon arrival, the locals began spitting at our feet—until they heard us converse in English. Profuse apologies were instant: "We thought you were Russians!" The word went out, and we were besieged by many Amerasians abandoned from the 1960s and 1970s: "You know Sergeant _____?" Rush hour saw the streets totally packed with commuters, but in contrast to the cacophonous traffic that I remember, everyone was on foot or bicycle and moved about in eerie silence. The omnipresent police routinely shook down impoverished hawkers selling individual cigarettes. Nightlife was largely attended by young men and women, apparently relations of the ruling cadre and obviously into alcohol and drugs without fear of arrest.

In 1993 as the country opened up further, we were invited to Hanoi to meet with the minister of finance to discuss opening a bank branch in the country. The minister's greeting to me in perfect English was "Welcome back to Vietnam, Mr. Kruger." I had the presence of mind to compliment him on his information about our 1988 visit, which led to, "Yes, but I was really referring to the year you spent with us in 1967." Included in his and his government's view of history and of pending relations was that more than half of the population was not even born in 1975, and "That was then, this is now." He commented that we in the United States had not yet in 1993 put the war behind us, as they had. Following a good two-hour discussion with him, we met with many functionaries that week, but we could not see how we could ever get an acceptable financial return on a branch there—and never opened one.

My wife and I have returned twice more, touring widely throughout the whole country—from Hanoi to China Beach to Hue and Da Nang to Ho Chi Minh City to the Mekong Delta. It is still a beautiful country with welcoming people, good accommodations, and excellent cuisine. The market economy, albeit with the politics under firm control, has brought an amazing relative prosperity to its people. The city streets are no longer eerily quiet, but raucous with civilian motorized transport of all descriptions. Our next trip there—in a year's time—is in active planning and again greatly anticipated.

David Kruger joined the credit training program at a large bank and rose to senior positions. Fed up with the stress, he managed retirement from the for-profit world in 1995 to devote his time to family, to not-for-profit board work, and to genealogy. He and his wife travel widely every year; his board positions have included a university chair and chair of the country's largest genealogical society; and he has researched and authored award-winning family histories.

Navy Days

PAUL E. HALE : U.S. NAVY

G raduation was approaching. My good friend Doc Davis and I hadn't a clue about what to do with the next phase of our lives. All we knew was that the draft loomed, and without any kind of defer- ment we figured our days were numbered. So rather than run the risk of becoming a soldier for two years, we decided that becoming an officer for three was a better bet. Having grown up on the water—Doc in San Francisco and I on Long Island—and liking the look of our roommate Barry Blackwell ('63) in his Navy ROTC uniform, we decided to apply for and were accepted to Navy OCS, both starting in October 1964. A good thing, too. Vietnam hadn't heated up yet, and a year or so later you prac- tically had to know a congressman to get in.

Doc turned out to be colorblind, so he went into the Supply Corps and was based in Naples, Italy. I put in for destroyer duty, deck or operations, because I'd never been out of the country, and the East Coast, because I wanted to see Europe before Asia. I got Mayport, Florida, but was assigned to an aircraft carrier—the USS *Shangri-La*, CVA-38—and to the engi- neering department as repair officer and assistant damage control officer. Go figure—this English major in engineering?

So two years later, when the public affairs officer billet on the ship opened up, I went to the executive officer, Commander Fred Carment, and begged for the position: "Commander, I was an English major—absolutely, this is the right job for me."

He said, "Paul, I'll do it, on one condition—you complete your engi- neering officer courses." So I did, and I got the job. Lesson learned.

Anyway, being repair officer was interesting work, except that most of the repair work got done whenever the ship was in port. So while my friends in CIC (Combat Information Center) and navigation had nothing to do but goof off or go on leave, I didn't get to do so much of that. This really culminated when the ship went into drydock in Philadelphia for a major refit, including installing air conditioning and better evaporators, which made for more regular showers. In addition, I ran a specially formed fire watch division, composed of sailors who had to man fire extinguishers wherever any welding was being done. I was pretty busy.

But not so my best friend on the ship, Ensign Jeffrey Pill, with whom I shared an apartment for those six months. He was in CIC—not much combat information work being done in drydock. So after a night of carousing we'd drag ourselves down to the ship for 8 a.m. quarters. Then I'd go to work, and Ensign Pill would go back to bed. This went on for the entire time there.

A year or so later, we were conducting night operations in the Mediterranean, when one of the eight destroyers surrounding the carrier became disoriented during a maneuver and plowed into the carrier's anchor locker. It is said that "a collision at sea can ruin your whole day." Try telling that to the OOD (officer of the deck) and the captain of the destroyer and the two sailors aboard who died.

We put into Naples, had a cofferdam installed over the hole in the ship's side, and had a steel plate welded in place. Then it was off to Norfolk Naval Shipyard for a proper repair.

Once there I soon got the call I expected—"The XO wants to see you." I went down to his stateroom.

Fred: "Well, Paul, it's time to set up another fire watch division."
Paul: " I figured that's what you wanted to see me about. But let me suggest something. I've got enough of a full-time job as repair officer, and it seems unfair to saddle me with the fire watch duties as well, when any junior officer could handle the job, and there are plenty of them in navigation and CIC who have nothing to do in port."
Fred: "Paul, you make a very reasonable point. Who would you suggest?"
Paul: "I think Lieutenant JG Pill would do an outstanding job."
Fred: "Good idea. I'll take care of it."

A few hours later, Jeff stormed into my stateroom bellowing "You sonofabitch!"

We're still great friends.

There are many other tales I could tell, but enough for now. The Navy was a great experience, and I'm very glad that I joined.

So, I served in the Vietnam era, not in Vietnam. Every day, my fellow junior officers would pick up the mail, hoping there were no orders to go "over there." Some got them; I never did. But some of us had to keep the shores of the Mediterranean safe for democracy.

Paul Hale has had a distinguished career as an investment banker and senior magazine publishing executive, and is presently working as an independent consultant and investment banker to the media industry, as well as serving as a senior adviser to A. Buchholtz & Company, a media advisory firm, and business manager for Robin Bell Design, a high-end interior design firm. His earlier sixteen-year publishing career included posts as president and publisher of American Heritage Publishing Company and executive vice president of *Esquire*. Paul has held several advertising and financial positions at Time Inc. and was part of the senior management team that launched both *People* and *Money* magazines. He is married to Robin Bell. They live in Salisbury, Connecticut, where they pursue their mutual passions for dogs, fly fishing, shooting, and downhill skiing.

Ready, Willing, and Able

Life as Helicopter Pilot aboard a
Frigate in the Gulf of Tonkin

ROBERT (BOB) PARKINSON : U.S. NAVY

Not exactly burning up academics at Dartmouth, I graduated with the class, but was unsuccessful with applications to graduate school. Reclassification to the front of the line in the draft and receipt of a notice to appear for a physical for the Army were sufficient for me to declare to Mom and Dad that I needed to join the Navy. On September 15, 1964, I asked for the keys to the family car because I was going to Seattle to join the Navy that day. Not knowing what the Navy would do with me, I suggested to Dad that he be prepared to come and get the car because I might not return home.

At the end of the day I was sworn in as an E-5. I reported to Officer Candidate School in Newport, Rhode Island, on November 15, 1964. I think we were paid about fifty dollars a month while at OCS. In the following four months I regained the discipline for time management, follow-through on assignments, and restoration of the athletic acumen that got me to Dartmouth in the first place. I finished high enough to be sent to Naval Aviation Training in Pensacola, Florida, arriving in March 1965.

Pensacola has been and still is the mecca for naval aviators. It was also the place where girls went to meet the finest male specimens that our country could provide. Most went through the flight training earning the wings of gold while remaining single. Not this one. Was I one of those specimens? Not sure, but two months into the year of flight training I proposed and in another two months was married to Trish on my birthday, July 10, 1965. This was done at a time when being married was an anathema—Corvettes were more attractive. However, you have not met Trish.

In June 1966 I received my gold naval aviator wings and was sent to

Helicopter Combat Squadron One in San Diego. Trish and I had arrived at the doorstep of a naval career. For you historians, recall that the Vietnam conflict was starting to escalate rapidly and that many of us who joined the armed services were destined to serve in and around Vietnam for many years.

Preparation

Arrival at Helicopter Combat Support Squadron One (HC-1) was relatively uneventful. I wanted to join the Navy Huey detachments in the Mekong Delta, but those slots had been filled. I asked to be a pilot on a Search and Rescue Detachment (CSAR Det.), flying off the Navy ships positioned to assist the Navy and Air Force combat missions going into North Vietnam. The flight training was centered on the UH-2 Sea Sprite, which was small enough to land on the decks of Navy frigates and cruisers at the time. In addition to the flight training, we received small-arms training with the Marines at Camp Pendleton and Survival Evasion Resistance and Escape (SERE) training in the foothills east of San Diego. In those days the SERE training was relatively realistic. I got a bloody nose from my obstinacies to the prison camp facilitators. I also learned that I had a strong will to survive.

Aircraft conversion, weapons familiarization, and SERE survival all completed by September, I was deployed with a senior pilot and twelve maintainers in October 1966. While there were jet passenger aircraft available at the time, the Navy chose to send us to the Philippines by C-118. Mind you, this was a proven aircraft, but it was slow. As I recall, the flight plan took three days to get from San Diego to NAS (Naval Air Station) Cubi Point in the Philippines. We took more than a week because we had a delay in Hawaii as a result of running off the end of the runway on takeoff for our second leg to Wake Island. Having a few extra days in Hawaii was not a bad deal.

We arrived in Cubi Point intact as a team to become familiar with our H-2 helicopter. We immediately set about training in the tropical environment and enjoyed the freedom of very few restrictions on our altitude above the terrain. At this time we knew of a few rescue missions that had required penetration inland into North Vietnam, all receiving small-arms hostile fire. We practiced flying with the helicopter fuselage below treetops—hard to call this a job. We also continued our familiarization with the self-defense weapons that we would carry on the helicopter—M60 floor-mounted machine guns, M79 grenade launchers, M16 automatic rifles, and Colt .45 pistols. We did the workups for about a month and then joined our frigate, the USS *Mahan*, in November 1966. We headed for the PIRAZ station in the Gulf of Tonkin.

Action

To set the scene, there were three Combat Search and Rescue (SAR) stations in the gulf: North SAR, PIRAZ, and South SAR, all north of the border between North and South Vietnam. PIRAZ was set up to be the center and the navigation point for flights in and out of North Vietnam. There was a CSAR helicopter on two of the three ships, depending on the target set that was directed from the targeting staff. We were on the PIRAZ ship, so in the center station. We would launch and be airborne when there was a strike directed into North Vietnam.

We were deployed to the gulf when the weather was particularly bad. A lot of rain, low visibility, and relatively heavy sea state limited our usefulness at this time of year. There were times when the ship was rolling and pitching to the extent that we could not launch the helicopter. This also affected the launching of strikes at enemy targets. As a result the number of opportunities to rescue was reduced, but we were there to perform when we could. We did pick up an Air Force pilot and a naval flight officer. We also launched on several alerts to rescue downed aircrew over land, but never executed an overland mission because the risk was deemed too high for us to be successful.

While our CSAR team was relatively limited in exposure, I can say that the potential was there for heroism. The pilot of one night rescue in North Vietnam was awarded the Medal of Honor for his successful rescue. There was also the loss of life in another overland mission that was unsuccessful. The helicopter was riddled with bullets. One round passed through the thin skin of the helicopter and struck and killed one of the crewmen. Miraculously, no rounds hit the flight controls or gearboxes, and the pilots were only slightly injured, still being able to fly the helicopter back to the ship.

We did two cycles of this action, the first on the USS *Mahan* and the second on the USS *King*. We returned to San Diego in the spring of 1967. My second deployment in late 1967 was aboard the aircraft carrier *Con-*

stellation for ten months. Our mission was to rescue pilots who had problems with the launch or recovery and ejected near the ship. It was not as exciting as working from the frigates in the northern part of the gulf.

Anecdotes

Trish and I met and married fairly quickly, even by standards in those days. However, Trish's father had been an aircraft mechanic at "bloody" Barren Field in World War II and had just retired from the civil service when we married. She had been around naval aviation many years, so had an attraction to those who participated. I was the lucky one.

When I arrived in HC-1 I was still an ensign, the only one in the squadron at the time. That made me the bull ensign, and I got to wear the bigger ensign bars. Not sure what this has to do with anything except to say that promotions were quick in those days, and it was an indicator that I got through the training pipeline faster than most.

Not given their due in this article are the enlisted troops with whom and by whom the aircraft I flew were kept safe for flying. The crew of twelve that maintained our helicopter on the ship and those that pushed the paper and ordered the parts are the unsung heroes of my part of naval aviation. Without a well-supplied, well-maintained helicopter, those two rescued air crewmen might not be here today.

I believe that the military would be about half as effective if members had to worry about family life back home. Trish and her peer spouses maintained a marvelous network of support for each other that on many occasions had to bear the agony and pain that comes from losing a loved one in combat or in training.

For all the losses we incurred in combat, the squadron I was in from July 1966 to August 1969 lost twenty-nine aircrew and forty-one people from training, maintenance, and material errors—far more than were lost in combat. I mentioned "bloody" Barren in my father-in-law's background. That title came from all the pilots that were killed in training at that field during World War II. The same issues were still rampant in HC-1 when I was there.

Reflections

My engagement with the enemy associated with the Vietnam War was relatively remote. We were kept in a holding pattern off the coast of North

Vietnam awaiting the call to go inland, but that call never came. However, my remembrance of the calls to man the aircraft for launch were real and like the butterflies in the belly before taking the field for a football game. Once in the helicopter and into the mission, all focus was on achieving success. No regrets, no misgivings, and no looking back. Had that call to go inland come, there would have been no hesitation. I knew that I was prepared and ready not only for success, but for a possible failure.

The discipline that I developed always to move forward in those first years in the Navy affected a lot of the actions that I took later in the Navy and in subsequent civilian life. One of the fallouts of the extremely high loss of life in HC-1 was my follow-on commitment to improving the equipment that we ask our Navy–Marine Corps aviators to operate. Subsequent to this CSAR mission I had many years in the test and evaluation of helicopters and their systems on U.S. Navy ships. I think that I have had an influence on the design, production, and maintenance of aircraft and their systems to prevent the loss of life in training and operations of our military aircraft.

My final reflection is on the family of military members. I think it is clear that I have utmost love, affection, and respect for my wife, Trish. She was left at home, first by herself, then with one boy and then with two boys for five separate long-term deployments, the longest of which was thirteen months. All in all it was one-third of our married life during the first fifteen years of service. Those boys are today an architect and a mechanical engineer, each with a wonderful wife and two children, our grandchildren. Trish is nearly single-handedly responsible for this. Am I proud of her? You bet!

Today our country appears to be very proud of how we treat our wounded warriors, in contrast to how we treated those returning from Vietnam. As you bask in that pride, I ask you to look at the woman that is at the veteran's side, the real hero of the successful return of that service member to productive use in our society. There is the power of a family. And men, get ready, there are now wounded women warriors. Watch the men at their sides. As our society seems to slip into immorality, I am proud to have been, and still am, with a sector of our society where morality, faith, and family support still prevail.

Bob Parkinson and Trish have been married forty-seven years. They (mostly Trish) have raised two boys, who married wonderful women and begat four super grandchildren, one of whom is from Ethiopia. Subsequent to the Vietnam tour, Bob, along with Trish, has been stationed at NAS Patuxent River, Maryland (three times—as test pilot, as test pilot school commander, and as vice commander of the Navy's flight test center); foreign exchange pilot with the British Royal Navy; squadron command of HS-8 in San Diego; Naval Air Systems Command program manager for the H-2 Sea Sprite, H-3 Sea King, and the president's helicopters, the VH-3 and VH-1. Post-Navy he has been with companies providing service to the naval acquisition business, including Bob's own company, RSBP, LLC. Going forward, Bob will be more focused on giving back though Rotary and running an oyster farm on the Chesapeake.

A Very Personal Experience

GLEN KENDALL : U.S. ARMY

I n my senior year of high school I narrowed down my choices of a college to either West Point or Dartmouth. From a very early age I believed my mission in life was "to help make the world free for democracy." I cannot discern where this came from. I recall that there was a strong and active anticommunist sentiment in my small, isolated community. I chose Dartmouth.

At Dartmouth I was in ROTC, graduating as a Distinguished Military Graduate with a regular Army commission in the infantry as a second lieutenant. I planned to be a career Army officer. After training I was assigned to Germany, where I spent most of my time in an airborne infantry battalion, jumping out of C-130s, guarding nuclear weapons compounds, and going on field exercises. Our mission was to prevent the Communist horde on the other side of the fence from overwhelming Western Europe. I felt I was doing my part. I was promoted to captain at age twenty-five and assigned to Vietnam. I still trusted my government to make the best decisions regarding use of military force, and I was willing to do my part, still with the idealistic mission in mind.

I arrived at Hill 59, outside Chu Lai, south of Hue, Second Battalion, First Infantry, 196th Light Infantry Brigade, and took command of Delta Company. The unit had been decimated, with only about six soldiers with combat experience remaining. All the officers and nearly all the NCOs had never been in combat. I had been given no training in the type of combat in Vietnam—heliborne assaults, search and destroy, adjusting close air support. . . .

Four days later we were making a "hot insertion"—going into a landing zone (LZ) under fire—ten helicopters, each with five of my men. The approach to the LZ was my baptism of fire. I was in the lead helicopter with the commander of the flight. The chaos was incredible. The machine guns on both sides of the helicopters were firing, artillery rounds were exploding along our route of approach, jet fighters were strafing the LZ and then dumping napalm. We could hear the pop of incoming small-arms fire. I was listening to the radio of the helicopters; the rear helicopter had been hit and was returning to base. Then the major said, "OK, Captain, it's up to us, do we go in or not?" I had no way of making such a decision; I didn't even know I was supposed to make it. That made me angry. We went in, jumping out of the choppers hovering a few feet off the ground, the LZ reeking of burned vegetation and napalm. I could see the incoming fire hitting the rice paddy dikes. After a day of sporadic combat and evacuating the casualties, we eliminated the resistance. More such insertions were to come, but we were now combat veterans.

I recall that Winston Churchill said something like "Nothing is so exhilarating in life as to be shot at with no result." It was not for me. As the choppers hovered over the LZ, I became another person—driven by my responsibilities of accomplishing the mission and protecting the 160 men under my command. I called in artillery fire and close air support to kill men I didn't know. I sent young American soldiers on patrols into very dangerous areas, knowing some of them would probably not come back alive. I loaded seriously wounded men onto medevac helicopters, their blood dripping through my hands. I became a very effective infantry company commander, devoid of human feeling, capable of very terrible things in the cause of "making the world free for democracy."

In Vietnam there was no front line. The enemy was everywhere and nowhere. The unit of combat was the company, sometimes isolated. The only outside contact was by radio. The only direct support was by helicopter, nearly always by day in decent weather. Sometimes we were ten miles or more from another military unit. As the company commander I was responsible for everything—navigating, medical care, access to clean water, deploying weapons, directing actions. It was a lonely job.

A few months and several heliborne assaults later, things were beginning to build up to what was a couple of months later the Tet offensive. We had slogged all day through rice paddies, looking for suspected enemy pockets, receiving sporadic incoming fire, nothing too serious. We settled in on a hill surrounded by jungle. I called for and adjusted the defensive artillery fire and sent out listening posts as an early warning system. It was very dark and raining. One of the listening posts was attacked. Only one of the three soldiers made it back to our line. And then another was attacked. I called for the defensive artillery fire. The attack continued. My artillery lieutenant called for more powerful defensive fire. The sky filled with the sounds of boxcars flying through the air. The naval ships off the coast were firing huge shells, which shook the earth when they exploded. For the first and only time, I was scared. There was the possibility we would not make it through the night. We did, but with serious causalities.

The next day, after the wounded and dead had been evacuated, a general came to the field to compliment us on a job well done. He told me we had spent more than $3 million on naval gunfire alone. Later that day we were transported back to a safe compound for a bit of R&R. I sat on the edge of the landing field, watching the men under my command, tattered by a night of intense combat, fatigued, dirty, dazed, waiting their turn for a shower and some clean clothes. Then it struck me. This was a stupid way to make the world free for democracy.

It had been a bunch of young men, trying to kill each other over a tiny piece of real estate of no consequence in the middle of the jungle, spending huge amounts of money with absolutely no result whatsoever. I submitted my resignation from the Army.

My tour as a company commander was over shortly after that incident. I spent the rest of my tour as a battalion staff officer. Perhaps I was morally weak at this point. I could have gone AWOL, joined the antiwar protesters, moved to Canada, but I was devastated, sick of violence, morally empty. I lost my soul.

There are many other parts to this story, too detailed for this forum.

I returned to the United States, spent some time in medical care at Fort Devens, Massachusetts. After that I went to Tuck for an MBA. Slowly I came to realize that the whole war had been unnecessary politically and poorly executed by the professional military. Perhaps worse, our political leaders learned no lesson from all this.

For years afterward I was haunted by nightmares in which I was in combat and was going to be killed just before I awoke. While the nightmares have gone, the scars remain. I had difficulties in relationships and in relating to other people. I find writing this extremely difficult.

Slowly I regained my humanity. I became a pacifist, actively campaigning against the Iraq War and others. I continue to campaign for and donate to veterans' causes, believing that if we don't take care of the wounded warriors we send to war, we lose a piece of our soul.

After graduating from Tuck, Glen Kendall worked in the Nixon White House, then the Environmental Protection Agency in Washington. He founded his own consulting firm in 1977, which changed into a software production company, Terrasciences, making software for earth sciences application, mostly for big oil companies. He traveled the world visiting clients. Later he was headhunted to manage a similar company in England, where he met and married his third wife. After retirement he volunteered to be the administrator of Calcutta Rescue, an Indian charity looking after the most needy people in Calcutta with medical care, education, and other services. He lived in the middle of a slum in Calcutta for a year in this job. He now lives half the time in England, half the time in France, with his Dutch wife, and continues to work for Calcutta Rescue.

Scooter Driver

NED MILLER : U.S. MARINES

After nine months of infantry officer training I made my first career change. Flying looked more interesting than being a "ground pounder," so I was off to Pensacola to become a naval aviator. It proved to be a good choice, but I often wonder where the path not taken might have led. From Navy ROTC at Dartmouth to flying to reentering the real world with graduate school at Stanford, those choices set the table for all that followed.

I was surprised to find Dartmouth classmates Ellery McClintock and Brad Evans in my preflight class at Pensacola. I recall a house on the beach and each of us taking different paths after that course ended. I moved on to the jet "pipeline," a series of stops in the Deep South culminating at Beeville, Texas. Twelve months in North Carolina, with lots of individual air travel and stays in Key West, Florida, and Yuma, Arizona, gave me a great view of the country. Every day was a test, with the final a tour in WestPac, Chu Lai specifically.

I was a "Scooter Driver," the affectionate name for an A-4 Skyhawk pilot. Our mission was close air support for ground forces. The Navy and Air Force shared the strategic mission, flying over the North—that's where most of the exciting encounters took place. We were subject to ground fire, and more dangerous operational hazards were ever present. "Cowboy," a fellow squadron pilot, was on hot-pad alert. Anxious to launch to an emergency strike, he took off downwind rather than taxi to the far end of the runway. With a full fuel and bomb load, short runway, and hot day, not much was recovered after he failed to get airborne.

After several months in Chu Lai (Vietnamese for the name of the Marine general who picked the spot to build the base), about seventy-five missions, and lots of excitement, our squadron was rotated back to

Ned Miller and his A-4 Skyhawk

Iwakuni, Japan. We continued training and preparing to return in country when the North Koreans captured the USS *Pueblo*. We immediately redirected our efforts toward a different war possibility. This was one of those life-altering events. After several months, things calmed down. The squadron prepared to return to Vietnam, but my five-year wingman, Dave, and I were kept in Japan.

Dave and I returned to Beeville, Texas, hard by the King Ranch. Aviators, as the Navy calls them, got their advanced training and wings in South Texas, where neither airliners nor people were in danger. It was peak pilot production time, so six- or seven-day work weeks were the norm. We flew a lot. A pilot's dream.

Along the way Dave and I married first cousins. Ginger Goodrich, wife of Dartmouth classmate Herb Goodrich, had introduced me to a housemate at Smith. Edie Kirk and I got engaged in Tokyo, and Dave met his bride, Edie's cousin, at our wedding.

In 1970 I became a civilian. You can be a pilot or you can grow up, but you can't do both! Time for another career change. I chose to go back to school in the Bay Area and then to stay. I was learning. Upon graduation I left an *American Graffiti* world, and it seemed like a *Coming Home* world I returned to. No Regrets. I learned a lot. The good memories are much clearer in my memory. The bad ones have faded. I saw a lot of places, met a lot of people, and learned from all of them. Flying jet planes was exhilarating, even the "exciting" (close calls) times. On a mundane basis I learned that checklists are very useful. I missed the whole Woodstock experience, and on reflection that was OK. Mankind continually learns that war is seldom the best choice. Not sure what to do about it. I wouldn't change much that happened to me. A Navy classmate said, "We went, did what we had to, and came back."

In 1970 Ned Miller left Texas for Stanford Business School, where class-mates included Chuck Marsh. He spent '72 to '81 at Wells Fargo in San Francisco in wholesale banking. He decided he didn't like travel, com-muting, and working for a big organization, and so became a partner in a local property and casualty insurance brokerage. The firm now has sixty employees in San Jose, California. He retired in 2008, traded tennis for golf, and got his handicap down to eleven. He and Edie have three sons: Kirk, '94, is an experimental physicist living in Santa Barbara with his wife and two sons. Jay, now a restaurateur, lives with his wife in Bend, Oregon, after ten years with Outward Bound. David and his wife and three children live in Palo Alto in his big childhood home after an inter-generational house swap. He is very successfully working for his dad's old firm without encouragement.

Vietnam War Experiences

CHARLES L. MARSH JR. : U.S. NAVY

n March 1960 I received my first telegram. The operator called my mother at our home in Arlington, Vermont, and read it to her and later mailed me a copy. Dartmouth was offering me admittance and the choice between a scholarship, loan, and job, or a Navy ROTC scholarship. They asked for an answer the next day. I enthusiastically accepted and began my twenty-five-year association with the U.S. Navy.

In the spring of our senior year the Navy asked us to complete our "dream sheets," setting forth our requests for type of ship and preferred homeports. My sweetheart, who had been my date for all twelve big weekends, was going to college in Rhode Island, so I asked for a small ship in Newport. I received orders to a destroyer, USS *Stickell* (DD-888). *Stickell* was visiting Scandinavian ports after a Mediterranean cruise when I was to report in June. Saving travel money, the Navy enrolled me in an eight-week Naval Justice School in Newport. Knowing I majored in sociology at Dartmouth, the Navy in its infinite wisdom assigned me to be the ship's electronic material officer (EMO). I was responsible for leading the technicians who maintained all of the ship's radars and communications equipment. The executive officer gave me the course book for naval electronics and said "go for it."

This job was more of a challenge for me, as the outgoing EMO had been a chief petty officer electronic technician whom the Navy sent to college to become an officer. He remained on the ship in his new job and ate at the senior officers' table, where he could criticize the condition of the ship's electronics to the captain. Perhaps the Navy knew what they were doing. I immediately assured my technicians that I was totally relying on them, would not be looking over their shoulders, and would support them in any way I could. We were successfully able to maintain the electronic

Ensign Charles Marsh

equipment for operations off the Atlantic coast and later on a Mediterranean cruise.

In January 1996 our destroyer squadron sailed for a seven-month deployment with the U.S. Seventh Fleet in operations in support of the conflict in Vietnam. We transited the Panama Canal, and after stops in San Diego and Pearl Harbor joined the Seventh Fleet in mid-February. During this cruise we supported search-and-rescue operations in the Gulf of Tonkin and were involved in several incidents assisting in the rescue of downed Air Force and Navy aircrews. During this time I was promoted to lieutenant (JG) and assigned as the ship's Combat Information Center officer. On the way home we continued the rest of the way around the world, and while en route to Malaysia we crossed the equator. I managed to survive initiation into the "Solemn Mysteries of the Ancient Order of the Shellback." We continued on with brief stops in India, Aden, Athens, Majorca, and Gibraltar, and returned to Newport after steaming over sixty thousand miles with fifty-five underway replenishments and visiting fifteen different ports.

Shortly after returning I was ordered to Destroyer School in Newport. This six-month school trained each of us to be an operations, engineering, or weapons department head on a destroyer. Over half of the course was focused on engineering and learning the steam plant on World War II–vintage destroyers. I found this section more challenging than almost all my courses at Dartmouth.

Destroyer School cleverly informed us on our first day that at the end of our course, our priority of choice for homeport, type of destroyer, and the department head job we sought would be matched with our class standing. My wife, Barbara, very much wanted to go San Diego, and I did not want to be an engineering officer on an old destroyer in Norfolk. So I worked hard and graduated third in a class of sixty-five and received my choice to be weapons officer on a remodeled destroyer in San Diego.

Soon after arriving on USS *Hamner* (DD-718), I again qualified as officer of the deck, underway, fleet operations, which made me the officer in charge on the bridge, for the safety and safe maneuvering of the ship and all other operational activities, during two watches of four hours each day.

In September 1967 we departed for Pearl Harbor and then Vietnam. By then I was a lieutenant. Our primary duties were providing gunfire support for U.S. Marines. We would stand by about five thousand yards off the coast and fire our five-inch guns at targets chosen by an airborne spotter. Our maximum range was eighteen thousand yards, or nine nautical miles. We totally depended on the spotter to identify the target and provide us with its geographical coordinates. We would plot them, enter our solution into a large World War II–vintage mechanical computer, and then begin firing. The spotter would adjust our fire with spots (right one hundred yards, drop one hundred yards, for example), to take into account inaccuracies in our navigation and our gunnery system (small errors, of course). We had several ten- to twenty-day periods of intense activity.

My role during firing was as the gunnery liaison officer (GLO), to coordinate between the airborne spotter, our guns, and the ship's captain. We had four guns—two in each mount—and could fire forty rounds a minute from each mount. During this period the other GLO and I stood what the Navy has called for years "port and starboard watches." We would be on duty six hours and off six hours around the clock. It was sleep disruptive, especially when you also had to administer your department (and eat) during the six hours off. We were young, and it was exciting. I was awarded a Navy Commendation Medal for actions during this period.

We also acted as a plane guard behind an aircraft carrier launching strikes against North Vietnam. On occasion a sailor would jump or fall off the flight deck, or a plane would crash in the water during takeoff or landing. Following a mile behind the carrier, we would pick up the survivors.

I had agreed to a one-year extension of my four-year obligation in order to attend Destroyer School. During our deployment in Vietnam, the Navy extended all Navy lieutenants one year, so I expected new orders when we returned to California. Soon I received a postcard saying my next duty would be in charge of my own little boat in the Mekong Delta of South Vietnam. By this time I had concluded, like so many others, that the war in Vietnam was not a worthwhile venture for our country and we should, as Vermont senator George Aiken suggested, declare victory and go home. I also had decided that the Navy was far too large an organization for me. I didn't want to stay in or work for a company (like IBM in those days) where I would be transferred from city to city.

For these two reasons I decided I did not want my own boat in the delta and asked my executive officer what type of assignment would take priority. He suggested that a job as an aide to an admiral would take priority. He kindly called the Bureau of Naval Personnel in Washington on my behalf. After an interview in Coronado, California, with Vice Admiral John Victor Smith, I received orders to be his aide and flag lieutenant. Admiral Smith, commander of the Pacific Fleet Amphibious Force, was very hardworking and demanding but a delightful person to work for. As his personal assistant I organized his schedule, provided assistance in a number of small ways, and was in charge of our Navy band, two boat crews, his administrative staff, and a Marine driver. I also oversaw the stewards and operated senior officers quarters for transient officers and the senior staff mess where we had breakfast and lunch every workday, including Saturday mornings.

The Pacific Fleet Amphibious Force included about fifty ships used to transport Marines to the beach, plus mobile riverine forces, other boat and beach support groups, and Navy SEALs and underwater demolition teams, all training to deploy to Vietnam in support of the war.

Our main thrust was to ensure that we were adequately training the personnel in the United States before they were sent to Vietnam. In order to evaluate our success firsthand we would go to Vietnam every six months and spend a few days on ships offshore, a few days in Saigon with the commander of the naval forces in Vietnam, and then travel to other locations in the Mekong Delta and along the coast up to Da Nang, meeting with naval commanders.

Because of the danger imposed by the poisoned punji sticks (very informative exhibit of this with tunnels now near Cu Chi, outside Ho Chi Minh City, formerly Saigon), which the Viet Cong would bury under paths, somebody declared that all in-country personnel would wear steel-bottomed leather boots with canvas uppers. I picked up a pair the day before we left Coronado and never had a chance to break them in. In Saigon we stayed with Admiral Elmo Zumwalt, who later became chief of naval operations. After dinner he mentioned to Admiral Smith that he and his aides ran five miles around the compound every morning at 5:30 and asked if he would like to join them. The admiral immediately responded "No, but Chuck would." The next morning I pulled on the steel-bottomed boots for only the second time and joined them. They, of course, had running shoes. After a mile and a half or so, Admiral Zumwalt noticed my footwear and said that I could stop if I wished, to which I replied a quick, hearty, "Aye, aye, sir."

My wife always asks me to tell another story about our four trips in country during my two-year tour. Although we never did this in Coronado, the admiral liked to take a swim before dinner in the large pool at the visiting officer quarters in Pearl Harbor, when we were there for briefings with Admiral John S. McCain Jr. (Senator John McCain's father). The admiral would stand at the edge of the pool, dive in, and swim underwater to the end of the pool. I would dive in next, swim as fast as I could, and pop up at about the one-third mark. During our second and third trips to Vietnam, I made it about halfway to the end of the pool. On our last trip, as we stood on the edge of the pool, the admiral said, "Chuck, swim slowly and conserve your breath." I did so and made it to the end of the pool.

I resigned my commission in the summer of 1970. The admiral awarded me a Navy Commendation Medal for my actions supporting the viewpoints of junior officers.

Although, as I have mentioned, I came to disagree with the war, I made a commitment to the Navy in the spring of 1960 and was comfortable honoring my obligations. I have generally positive memories of the many months on a destroyer during the war. The ship was generally safe, we had reasonably good food, a dry place to sleep, and a number of sharp sailors who had managed to get into the Navy to avoid the draft. Whenever we were in and around the coast of Vietnam, one could slack off a little bit on the normal officer's paperwork requirements and focus on the mission at hand. The Navy was great learning experience for me, and I'm glad I chose this path.

Chuck Marsh served for the next fifteen years in a variety of Naval Reserve jobs in the San Francisco Bay area and retired as a captain. Leaving the Navy in 1970, Chuck earned an MBA from the Stanford Graduate School of Business. He joined a small commercial real estate firm in

Cupertino, California. Chuck created and oversaw affiliated partnerships of the company, which developed neighborhood and community shopping centers in California, Arizona, and Oregon. Forty years later he still does some consulting and looks after one shopping center in Phoenix. His wife, Barbara, decided in 2000 she wanted to live in the San Juan Islands. This led to divorce in 2004. Chuck is now very happily married to Karla Eastling, with whom he enjoys traveling three months a year. In the fall of 2011 they enjoyed visiting Vietnam (including Hanoi this time), on a Dartmouth alumni trip.

Down to the Sea in Ships

ERNIE NOTAR : U.S. NAVY

Navy was the only choice for me. My father and uncles all served in the Navy in World War II, building airstrips in the Pacific islands. Growing up, as we all did, with the images and memories of the war, I latched onto the naval side of the story and was generally fascinated with the romance of the seas. "Join the Navy and see the world!" One of my shipmates who had grown up in an Air Force family told me he joined the Navy because "Air Force bases are always out in the middle of nowhere."

ROTC

I went to Dartmouth on a Navy ROTC scholarship and didn't mind the four-year commitment, even when extended to five years. It was peacetime military in 1960, and I was happy to wear the uniform and serve my country. I was then and still am a strong believer in universal and compulsory national service, including Peace Corps and other service agencies. Even as my politics have shifted from moderate Republican to liberal Democrat, I feel we lost something when the draft, for all its inequities, was discontinued.

Dartmouth campus life was exciting at first, but in time it seemed more and more like an extension of prep school: academically demanding, but a narrow all-male environment, even the same green and white school colors. Having grown up in Buffalo, New York—hardly the most exotic of places—I found Hanover by comparison to be very isolated at a time when I was desperate to explore a larger world. Summer midshipman cruises were like a breath of fresh air. The boot camp part was a little intimidating, but you figured it out. Beyond that we were exposed to all sorts of nifty new toys and experiences: shipboard life out on the Atlantic,

Lieutenant (JG) Ernie Notar

driving a landing barge up onto the beach in Norfolk, and flying in small planes in Texas.

I never contemplated a Navy career. It was a chance to do interesting things and gain useful experience. After a demo flight in one of the big planes that track hurricanes, flight training caught my fancy. Unfortunately I flunked the physical, owing to lack of color vision, the issue being the need to be able to read colored running lights on another ship or aircraft at night; this meant I was also ineligible for duty as a line officer. Thus I was shunted over to the Navy's Supply Corps, the repository for those who wore eyeglasses or were otherwise less-than-perfect specimens.

Supply Corps School

For those not familiar, Supply Corps is like the Army quartermasters, responsible for logistics. For the Navy this meant maintaining long supply lines and sealift capacity to be able to project power across the oceans with little or no support from local bases. This was provided by the service fleet, delivering food, ammunition, fuel, and general stores. It was not as glamorous as cruisers or aircraft carriers, but is an essential part of any military organization. Coincidentally, logistics duty also provided lots of analogues for a future business career. Twenty-five years later I noticed that MBA schools were offering programs in supply chain management.

My first assignment out of Dartmouth was to Supply Corps School in Athens, Georgia, for a six-month training course that was demanding but very dry. The main incentive for mastering the material came at completion, when a list of open billets for each class was released: new graduates were allowed to pick their next assignment in order of class rank. Everyone had a preferred destination: Boston Navy Yard, if the girlfriend was in New England; Charleston, South Carolina, or Norfolk for the Southeast; and San Diego if she was in California. Since I ranked seventh out of seventy, I was fairly assured of getting a good choice, which to me meant anything anywhere outside the continental United States. There was rumor of slots in Naples, Italy. I also had looked at icebreakers (based in Boston or Seattle) that steamed up and down both coasts of the Western Hemisphere all the way to Antarctica for rescue missions and scientific research.

When the list for our class arrived, it had three overseas billets: all on ships based in Japan. The first two went quickly, and I got the last one. The fellow next in line offered me $300 to pass it up. His wife was Japanese, and she wanted to be near family. Sorry about that.

WestPac

My orders were to the USS *Castor*, a general stores ship homeported in Sasebo, in southern Japan. By the time I caught up with her in early spring 1965, things were heating up in Vietnam, and the first combat troops were being sent to Da Nang. There were rumors that only unmarried officers were being sought for in-country duty because of the risk factor, leading to a rash of hastily scheduled marriages. Senior officers were also reminding juniors that combat zone assignments would benefit one's career.

I later learned that the other two Japan-based ships on our billet list had been permanently reassigned to Vietnam for coastal patrol duty, and the Navy's icebreakers had been turned over to the Coast Guard.

Castor had been originally launched as a commercial freighter in 1939 and repurposed by the Navy in 1940. It had survived Pearl Harbor and had been based in Japan since the Korean War. Its crew culture was like something out of a World War II novel. Many of the crew were old Asia hands, colorful and well-tattooed characters who had found ways to get repeat assignments to one of the few ships or shore-duty slots built into the Navy's permanent presence around the Pacific Rim. Many were Filipinos or had Filipino or Japanese wives. As *Castor* was part of the "working" fleet, discipline was more relaxed than on combat ships. Captains of service ships were often aviators, too old to fly, but trying to gain seamanship experience to become eligible for higher command. Our captain had been a jet fighter pilot in Korea; he was continually frustrated that the ship couldn't make more than twenty-two knots at flank speed.

As a general stores ship, *Castor* functioned much like a floating Home Depot. Bulk cargo came on commercial freighters to our warehouse in Sasebo, where the pallet-loads were broken down and staged for loading into racks and bins in *Castor*'s holds. We carried thirty thousand line items, everything except food, fuel, and ammunition. The inventory was kept on eighty-column punch cards in a room full of big IBM machines and staffed by about fifteen sailors at the keypunch machines.

After a brief stint in charge of the mess decks, I moved up to become stores officer, in charge of the holds and responsible for loading and distribution of payload, with the help of a large division of enlisted storekeepers. From Sasebo we alternated deployments with our sister ship *Pollux*, based in Yokosuka, near Tokyo. (Supply ships were often named for celestial bodies, so *Castor* and *Pollux*). Deployments, usually six to eight weeks, took us on a regular circuit, supplying ships in the Taiwan Straits, Subic Bay / Philippines and, of course, Vietnam, where we supplied aircraft carriers, coastal patrols, and various points up and down the coast, all the way to the Cambodian border.

Underway Replenishment

Most of our deliveries were carried out at sea, with two ships steaming alongside at close quarters, with booms and rigging strung between them. When servicing an aircraft carrier group, which might take a few hours, we would have three ships abreast: *Castor* in the middle, a carrier to starboard, and a succession of escort vessels to port.

Requisitions came in by message. My storekeepers would work around the clock to break out the requested items, load everything on pallets, and stage them on deck in the sequence that ships were expected alongside. We could transfer from as many as five deck stations simultaneously on each side and might also have helicopters picking up pallet loads off the stern helo deck.

Underway replenishment

Underway replenishment is inherently a risky maneuver. It requires precision ship handling, at speed, in close quarters, sometimes for a couple of hours at a time. As the ships roll, a cargo net transfer holding a half ton or more will bounce around like a tennis ball on a tether. There is ever-present risk of collision and serious injury. Fortunately we had no major accidents in my time, beyond losing some loads over the side.

Fortunately, we were not exposed to hostile engagement. Our explicit orders were to stay out of the way at all times. There was another supply ship, a newer vessel with its own helicopter and flight crew, plus a captain who was also a qualified helicopter pilot. As the ship happened to pass near an area where there was a firefight in progress on shore, that captain decided to take the bird out for a joyride to watch the action. He was se-verely reprimanded and very nearly lost his command.

This was all very hard, around-the-clock work, especially in Vietnam's waters. Like all ships, we would periodically get a few days of liberty in places like Hong Kong, Singapore, or Bangkok. In addition to the liberty ports, we also spent much time in the Philippines, the main staging area for Vietnam. One time in Subic Bay I was assigned to shore patrol, where at curfew we made a round of the bars with the paddy wagon to pick up drunken sailors. As the only officer assigned to this detail, my job was to approach any other officers found violating curfew, take information for reporting to their superiors, and encourage them to return to base immediately. Bingo! I caught two senior captains and a rear admiral and wrote 'em up.

Of course between deployments we spent extended periods in Japan to replenish our stock, which allowed me opportunities to travel about, pick up a bit of language, and meet locals, all of which just stoked my curiosity. I think many of us were captivated by exposure to the strangeness of it all. My future wife was a Peace Corps volunteer in Afghanistan during these same years, and we still talk about how these experiences shaped us.

Shore Duty

After two years at sea I was transferred to a more prosaic assignment: a joint-service procurement agency in New Jersey. I was one of a handful of uniformed officers working with a thousand civilian DOD employees. They were good people who were very kind to a lonely guy on a reentry curve. My job was to wear the uniform and go out with an audit team to inspect defense contractor sites. Since we were starting to encounter some antiwar protests, we were allowed to wear civilian clothes when not out on field audits. I lived on the civilian economy, and all my friends outside the office were civilians. They never saw me in uniform, and most never realized I was on active duty. This was essentially a holding pattern, but it gave me two years to adapt.

Civilian Life

As noted above, the logistics business was OK, but I just couldn't muster a passion for it. Had I stayed in the Navy, I would have spent the next ten years on shore duty working on procurement contracts and payrolls. Instead I was obsessed with an urge to further explore the Asia thing, without any idea of where it might take me. I looked about at grad schools and managed to get into Berkeley, where I completed a PhD in political science with focus on Japan. Though Southeast Asia was more appealing in some ways, I had more Japan experience to build upon, and Japanese studies as a field offered broader opportunities. I didn't focus on military issues; my dissertation was on Japanese labor policy and industrial organization, sort of a precursor to the literature on Japanese industrial policy and "the genius of Japanese management" that became so trendy a few years later.

Epilogue

What are my views on the war? That's a longer and more difficult conversation. I was OK with our involvement in the Vietnam project while in the midst of it and still feel I gained a lot on the personal level, despite the enormous cost to the country. As it dragged on I became increasingly disenchanted, but with hindsight have come to accept that there probably never was a "good" solution within reach, whatever that might mean. I see parallels in Afghanistan today and other likely cases on the horizon, especially in the Middle East, and I am not optimistic.

After leaving the Navy, Ernie Notar worked for several institutions: the Asia Foundation in San Francisco, the Asia Society in New York, UC Berkeley, and the University of Maryland were the main stops. Mostly he was involved in professional and scholarly exchanges, public education, research administration, and grant writing. Institutions like Berkeley and later Maryland inevitably began looking to the new wealth in Asia for support, first for Asian programs and then more broadly for all areas, including science and technology. Like many top universities, Berkeley has an incredible network of alumni at the highest levels in every county; building on those contacts quickly expanded into a full-time development role for Ernie, which meant a lot of travel and a lot of coaching of university officials for high-level meetings. International/cross-cultural fundraising became something of a growth industry, and Ernie gave numerous talks and gained a degree of visibility.

After all the years and all the trips, Ernie says that perhaps his obsession with Asia has run its course. No longer so mysterious, Asia became very familiar to him, even as it changed beyond recognition. Japan's glitter faded somewhat, to be superseded by China's. In recent years Ernie worked for an environmental organization, and now, fully retired, he does volunteer work for a social service agency. His reading interests have turned toward the history of Europe and the Middle East, all new territory for him. He is still married to the Afghanistan Peace Corps volunteer. They have one daughter, an inveterate traveler who has been to more countries than Ernie has. He is very proud of her.

Tet's Albatross

CHARLES G. WILLIAMS JR. : U.S. MARINE CORPS

When I was in the second grade, my father forced me to do two things—study math and memorize items (Catholic church). This had a profound effect on my future life. When I took the SAT test and an IQ test in high school, I did much better than expected. This performance enabled me to receive a scholarship offer from Dartmouth and one from the NROTC. I chose the NROTC, which I didn't like for the next eight years, but in the end it worked out.

With the NROTC I was scheduled to be a Navy officer. After two summers of Navy work I decided to become a Marine, because the Navy forced people to get up at night and do a four-hour meaningless schedule. I continue to be a person who doesn't mind missing food, but I can't miss sleep. When I went through my first summer with the Marines, I had to take a test. Since I was quick with numbers, my score was quite good. The Marines wanted to keep me in spite of the fact that my body and I were very un-Marine like.

I flew an F-4 Phantom in Vietnam. I had four or five interesting experiences there.

I was a good Ping-Pong player, so I was invited into town (Chulia) to play in a match. I did not do well, but learned something. The people in South Vietnam hated the North Vietnamese, and they hated the Americans even more. While flying I noticed that their farms had a large number of bomb craters, which affected their ability to provide food.

When I got to Vietnam, I stayed at a new, poorly built small cabin with eight other Marines. When the wind blew, sand would come in through the wooden sides. I also learned that the nicest bugs were spiders. You never removed their webs because they caught the bad insects.

One night I was awakened by a gunshot. There were no lights in the

Charles Williams after solo flight
(U.S. Navy official photograph)

cabin, but I saw somebody with a flashlight. He was a fellow cabin mate who had his flashlight on a rat that he had just killed. We always put any type of food in a locked storage site for a good reason.

Our cabin (not the right word for our living quarters) had no water inside, but there was a source of water outside. The previous residents had improvised an outdoor shower. Water passed through a metal hose, which was fixed to the top of the side of the cabin and sprayed water down. However, the metal hose coiled through a large, sand-filled barrel. When you wanted to take a warm shower, you poured a gallon of gasoline into the barrel and lit it. The water coming out of the showerhead went from 50 degrees to 140 degrees for about twenty seconds. That is when you took your shower.

One day I was walking to work. About one hundred yards ahead of me I saw another person walking in the same direction. I heard a gunshot. He fell to the ground, dead. He shot himself, but no one ever talked about it.

Albatross

Our cabin was right beside the runway. It was extremely noisy all the time. I often wondered if I would hear if we were being attacked. The Tet offensive began January 29, 1968, in the middle of the night. I heard the first rocket bomb explode. There was no question this was an attack. The nine of us ran out and climbed down into the bunker. It was completely dark, and as I was sitting, I heard this voice that I knew. I had just cut the speaker's hair earlier that day. I asked the man next to me to trade seats. I moved next to the guy whose voice I recognized. Three days later I awoke on a hospital ship. The man that I traded places with had been killed. He was married and had two young children. At that time I was married but had no children.

I was injured at the end of January 1968. When I awoke in the hospital ship, I got my second gift. The doctor told me that it was fifty-fifty whether they would remove my right arm. They elected not to. I still can't straighten the arm they saved. I stayed in the hospital until October, when I was released.

As a pilot in the service I always thought about being a commercial pilot after service in the Marines. With the injury to my arm, plus my severe head injury, I never would have been accepted by an airline.

Bearing this in mind, I decided to go to graduate school. Since I was in Pittsburgh and knew that I would be released from the Marine Corps soon, I started my graduate schooling in September while technically still in the service. I graduated nine months later from the University of Pittsburgh with an MBA.

I had many job offers but selected a bank in Pittsburgh, since it would be close to additional medical help and close to my family. I stayed with PNC for seven years and then went to work with a bank customer and developed a leasing company and a cable television company. In late 1984 I sold these companies and retired. I stayed retired until I lost all my money in the October 1987 stock market fall. My life was always about taking chances, and this one did not work out. So I started a group of four stores, which were like 7/11s but with my name. In 1994 I sold three of these stores and split the money with my ex-wife. I have essentially been retired since then. I now spend seven days a week playing bridge.

Dartmouth and ROTC

DONALD C. BROSS : U.S. NAVY

A s Dartmouth Professor Lew Stillwell said during one of his memorable Monday battle-night lectures, "History is a personal thing."
My personal history of military involvement is woven into my
experience at Dartmouth, as were three years of high school Army
ROTC, but in particular, NROTC at Dartmouth was part of my identity.
Everything that follows relates to personal reflections about Dartmouth,
military service, and the management of human conflict. I am not writing
what follows as an argument that only an ROTC experience is meaningful, nor that ROTC is the only way that officers and enlisted men from
very diverse backgrounds strengthen our country and the U.S. armed
forces. My point is rather that a visible and organized effort to incorporate
an understanding of the role that "legitimate force" plays in civilization
is necessary to a comprehensive liberal arts education.

I want to mention a trip to Washington, D.C., at the end of sophomore
year. At first this might not seem to connect with my overall story of military experience and what it might mean when military insight is acquired
in different settings. I carried a tape recorder for classmate Fred Eidlin
during spring break in 1962, as he interviewed ambassadors in Washington for his Dartmouth radio program *Meet the Ambassador.* As a
sophomore in NROTC, I was directly exposed to the work and thinking of
diplomats and international politics. My trip with Fred is a good example
of what can happen on an Ivy League campus when individuals preparing
for any career are exposed to a variety of fellow students who are interested in war and peace. During my time in Washington, I also encountered the broader and more encompassing challenge of resolving conflicts
in society and human culture as a whole. After Dartmouth, Fred became a
political scientist and an expert in the political cultures of Eastern Europe.

Donald C. Bross, PhD, JD, professor of pediatrics

Fred was still a student and living in Czechoslovakia when the Russians invaded during the "Prague Spring" of 1968. I learned about that episode through personal letters he wrote to a number of his friends. Fred's political science dissertation was wonderfully analytic and thoughtful. It was also, especially at that time, a counterintuitive thesis. He documented how the Russian invasion had changed the Russians and many within their military as much as it changed the Czechoslovaks. He showed that changes experienced by at least some Russians extended to the morale of their military and, for a few, changed some of their basic beliefs. These changes in attitude were as significant as the ways in which the invasion affected the Czechs. Fred's experience has benefited me as an important "case study" in understanding civilian and military morale and political culture.

This experience in Washington was important for staging what would happen in the fall of 1962. When we entered Dartmouth in 1960, many of us could not help but be interested in the conflict between communism and "the West." By sophomore year Lou Goodman and I began thinking that it would be good to understand the appeal of revolutionary movements in Latin America. Trusted enough by Professors Bob Russell (Romance languages), Frank Safford (history), Kal Silvert (political science), and Dean Thaddeus Seymour to experiment with junior year abroad in a non-European country, Lou and I went to Peru in the fall of 1962 to learn more Spanish and use our language for a number of practical applications. The Navy granted me a leave of absence to make this trip. One result was a paper I wrote for Professor Silvert titled "Institutional Attitudes of the Peruvian Military." Ten days before I arrived in Lima, just after my summer of NROTC Marine and naval aviation orientation courses, the Peruvian army drove a tank through the gates of the national palace (seat of government) in a classic *golpe* or coup d'état. I ended up doing a content analysis of publicly available writing by members of the Peruvian military about their own institutional beliefs. In November 1962, not long after the Cuban Missile Crisis, former Peruvian Army major Villanueva, who had participated in the failed *golpe* of 1948 in Callao, gave me an autographed copy of his new book *El militarismo en el Peru*. He documented a history of over one hundred years of military intervention in Peru. Each time the military's share of the national budget fell below a certain level, the military would revolt. Some months, but usually some years after increasing its share of the budget to as much as 40 percent, the military would respond to growing unrest and return the government to civilians. As I studied, it became clear that the military repeatedly allowed itself to revolt because military leaders saw themselves as the only true patriots in Peru, and that without them the country would be extinguished. There had been no George Washington to indelibly create a different tradition of military obedience to civilian authority. For whatever reasons, but perhaps because of the growing influence of the Centro de Avansados Estudios Militares (CAEM), Peru has since then achieved nearly fifty years without a coup. This is in contrast to Chile, Venezuela, and Argentina during the same period. CAEM was an innovative program to engage the Peruvian military with scholars, policy analysts, economists, and perhaps other disciplinary experts in a continuing exchange about the future of Peru.

In the spring of 1963, I was ordered to a destroyer in the Philippines for the summer of 1963, only to have my orders changed. Instead, I was sent as a midshipman to Colombia under the U.S. People to People program started by President Kennedy. I learned about the 1948 "Bogotazo" that seeded violence nationwide for generations. The Bogotazo refers to the years of extreme internecine political violence that erupted after the assassination of Colombian presidential candidate Jorge Eliécer Gaitán, on election eve.

The trip to Colombia was shared with three U.S. Naval Academy midshipmen, one a Colombian citizen who would return to his own military upon graduation. I had a remarkable opportunity to visit Colombia's coasts, the borders on the Amazon and the Putumayo Rivers, and the plains bordering Venezuela, as well as trips to all of Colombia's military academies and many of its bases. Even then, Colombia was responding to a mix of internal revolt and efforts from abroad to affect internal politics.

Midshipman Donald Bross
in Baranquilla, Colombia

What I observed and learned affected my approach to being a patrol officer a few years later in Vietnam. The importance of a military that remained democratic enough to help Colombia address its later problems of narco-terrorism has continued to interest me.

Returning in the fall of 1963, I was invited to join Bruce Nickerson in the "Cutter Hall Project," an effort to provide Dartmouth students with an interest in "things international," a place to exchange ideas. Thus began my all too brief friendship with Bruce, which also encompassed the time after we graduated when, to my surprise, Bruce called me to say he had joined the Navy. He was in training near Norfolk, my homeport at the time. In the light of what was happening in Vietnam, and given the danger of combat flying, I admired Bruce's bravery.

One important memory was that he believed in service and doing the right thing, which resonated with my own reasons for being in the military. Such a commitment is one of the primary motivations for a great many people who join the military (or police, fire departments, and rescue squads). I do not have the letter Bruce sent me in the spring of 1966, just before I received orders to command a PCF (patrol craft fast, or "swift boat") in Vietnam. I remember vividly my shock when I found out later that Bruce had been shot down over Haiphong. My recollection is that Bruce was concerned that we weren't involved in the right way or perhaps in the right war, but he did not specify why he felt this way. I sensed that he was sharing his doubts with me because I could understand his internal conflict. As for the details of Bruce's letter, I only remember that I thought if Bruce had doubts, knowing his patriotism, his courage, his caring personality and character, as well as his deep commitment to service, that we indeed had a difficult struggle on our hands.

My swift boat training began in early fall of 1966 and lasted two months. My impression was that instruction of the mechanical aspects of boat handling, radio communications, gunnery, inshore piloting, and tactics was reasonable for the time allotted. We received an introduction to Vietnamese language that was completely inadequate, unless a participant had a proclivity for foreign languages. More importantly, our briefing about the complexity of Vietnamese history, economy, ethnic groups, and national development, before and since the French and Japanese colonial eras, was very sparse, almost cartoonish. There was no insight offered about the insurgency versus invasion scenarios, the problems of corruption, and probably most importantly, no meaningful analysis of enemy strengths or weaknesses. I went through the small library at the Coronado training base and read through any book that seemed to offer insight into the motivations and conflicts that I would encounter as a patrol officer trying to interdict smuggling of weapons, transporting of documents, couriers, or other resources. I found very little that filled in the gaps of my knowledge. My experiences of thinking about the aspirations of people in emerging economies and societies in an environment in which the tension of "legitimate force" versus the forces of "insurrection" would be resolved made me feel acutely uncomfortable as to what I did not know about the people and contending combatants in Vietnam.

I sought a bookstore that might offer more sources of information to provide better background. At the Unicorn in La Jolla I bought a copy of Victor Pike's *Behind Viet Cong Lines* and Lucien Bodard's *The Quicksand War: Prelude to Vietnam* (1963). Pike took a pro-Communist approach and presented a gloss about the heroic struggles of the Vietnamese people for liberation. It was useful only for educating me more clearly as to how the other side was presenting itself, its assumptions, and, through inadvertence, how Viet Cong operations were conducted. I found Bodard's writing profoundly insightful and useful. He explained the cultural forces at play, the assumptions made by the French and by Ho Chi Minh and his generals, and how these assumptions played out. It should have been required reading for every military officer deployed there.

After a year operating from Cat Lo (1966 to 1967), in and near the Rung Sat Special Zone, I returned from Vietnam as an officer instructor for river patrol boats (PBR—patrol boats river), training both Navy and Army personnel for Vietnam duty. The location was Mare Island, California, and the Naval Inshore Operations Training Center. From my boss, Lieutenant Commander Roy Boehm, who had been the first enlisted SEAL, I gained a broader perspective of "special" warfare in countries struggling to develop. He had created eight weeks of more intensive training than I experienced at Coronado, and in particular a final week of realistic combat training for river patrol boat crews. The combat was "realistic" in the way that eighty pounds of TNT in one-half blocks can make training realistic. It was "realistic" because it took place in the Suisun Sloughs east of San Francisco Bay, at least geographically akin to the delta of Vietnam. In addition, all the officers and men doing the training had just come from either swift boat or PBR duty, some right after the Tet offensive, and had a sense of what would truly matter to the men going into combat. Fittingly, Roy Boehm made the training officer in charge act figuratively and literally as both the local Vietnamese army commander and the local Viet Cong chief. Similarly, the enlisted men acted as if they were ordinary soldiers and sailors during the time they were most visible to the students, but when it was not obvious or observable, they became "the enemy."

I had been designated the military intelligence officer for my squadron in Vietnam. When I arrived at Mare Island as a training officer, I eventually was made officer in charge of the reference and research library. In Vietnam I had prepared intelligence reports, and at Mare Island I saw those original reports and the way that each higher level of commander summarized or amended them. I noticed at each level that the admirable American trait that there is no obstacle or challenge we as a society cannot overcome played out. My experience was that very often each higher level of commander, confronted with daunting information about the enemy's support by the local population and its military strength, would subtly decrease the numbers of incidents, estimates of enemy capability, and trends toward greater potential, and would in this and other ways present the information in an optimistic manner. My thought was that our "can do" attitude meant that to imply the situation was more dire than it was understood to be was an admission that the individual in charge was not up to the task assigned. I've since come to realize how much downward pressure was being applied to represent the war as going well. I still remember my doubts that we really understood enough of what we were dealing with. Just over a month back from Vietnam, I recall seeing the statement by General Westmoreland that he could see the light at the end of the tunnel in Vietnam (if my memory serves it was published on approximately November 15, 1967), and I sold my few shares of stock shortly thereafter because I felt his judgment was incorrect. I had no confidence that we truly understood our enemy's capabilities or strengths. The Tet offensive began January 30, 1968.

In June 1969, following my wedding to Jodi earlier that year, we left for graduate school in Madison, Wisconsin, which, like Berkeley, was a center of opposition to the Vietnam War. In Madison my closest colleague also had a National Institutes of Mental Health traineeship in medical sociology. He was the son of a nuclear physicist father and a Quaker mother. His brother had taken the sailing ship *Phoenix* into Haiphong to deliver medicine as a protest. My friend's primary concern was (and continues to be) trying to prevent and treat serious mental illness. During my three years in Madison, four students blew up the mathematics building, killing a graduate student—because the four were "against violence." How could I understand human propensities to commit violence and the justifications for violence? Looking back, my early experiences at Dartmouth and through NROTC gave me a place to start.

During those same years in Madison, former naval officers who had been in my wedding and remained friends would sometimes call or write. Some came from very conservative backgrounds and remained conservative later in life. Others were, as officers and in life, more liberal. Some were completely comfortable with the war, and finished long, honorable naval careers. Others spoke out in various ways against the war, for example by meeting with congressional representatives. One particularly conservative friend, who became chief legal counsel for a major American corporation, was, I think, particularly effective right after Kent State in speaking against the war through meetings and letters in Washington, where he was attending law school. Inevitably, I heard about or met other individuals who had had no military experience. Some claimed patriotism but didn't volunteer, some were draft dodgers, while others were avowedly antiwar individuals who perhaps served as corpsmen, went to jail as a protest, or left for Canada. These latter nonviolent behaviors were an important contrast to those who used violence. It was also during that time that enough students and faculty at Dartmouth decided that a military presence on campus was not good, and that ROTC was no longer welcome at Dartmouth. I question removing the study of something we do not like from our educational experience, such as human violence or the military. We need the involvement of people who have direct experience with human violence and its management to assure that the topic is not ignored and seen only through academic lenses that distance the reality of these experiences. We must expend the time and energy necessary to address these important topics.

I did not participate in that debate at the time of NROTC expulsion. I was struggling to complete my education, and it seemed obvious that the passion of the time would rule. I could not help but think about the controversy, however. William Calley apparently came from a white-collar family, but had dropped out of school and was loading boxcars before he became a young second lieutenant in charge of the soldiers who committed the massacre in My Lai. The contrast between sending comprehensive leaders to a war as difficult as Vietnam, versus sending someone who was struggling to barely manage his own life, struck home. How many boys and men from the best schools and the best families served in Vietnam? Were they able to raise objections, argue policy, influence the country's direction, and be heard without violence through personal networks of political, cultural, educational, religious, and business associates? Political science professor Kalman Silvert taught us at Dartmouth that there are many ways that robust democracies tolerate, promote, and indeed endorse discourse. Did a Dartmouth purified of undergraduate participation in or exposure to military toxicity contribute to the end of the war? Or is it possible that removal of a military presence in liberal arts experience increases the odds that more isolated and militaristic cultures will be more prevalent in America's future? My experience in Peru, and since then watching events in countries like Idi Amin's Uganda of the 1970s, Argentina of the generals, Myanmar for decades, and the recent situation of many nations ranging from Africa to Pakistan and the Indian subcontinent, reveals country after country run by its military. History should

warn us that we do not want a military that does not include meaningful representation or participation from almost all elements of strength
in a society. If "war is only politics by other means," then how can a
fully diverse and competent liberal arts campus avoid the responsibility
of addressing authorized human violence as an ongoing issue of politics,
government, and, ultimately, civilization?

With the advent of the draft lottery, some of the most violent opposition to the war seemed to abate. A law school paper I wrote argues that
truly random processes for allocating scarce detriments and scarce benefits are perfectly arbitrary and hence fair, and "equality producing." They
are not the subjective form of arbitrary and capricious process Americans
reject, as in the packing of juries against the minorities of a given community. In any event, there must be a reason why the draft lottery made
such a difference in the country's willingness to talk more and be less
violent with each other. I assume it was the fundamental fairness of a
process that could touch equally the poor and rich, the man or woman of
every religion or none, and the son of a farmer or an inner-city mother
driving a bus.

But the point to be made is not only about sharing the burden and en-
suring that all parts of society understand the costs of war. The point is
also that those who will exercise legitimized violence on our behalf must
be provided the broad experience and capacities for reasoning, so that
all possible approaches to conflict are considered. There is an old Quaker
saying that "no one has won a fire . . . or a war." I do not want to lose a
war, but I take the point of inevitable loss and therefore the need not to ex-
haust a society, as perhaps the Soviets did. Only a few countries manage
prolonged national survival for centuries, and none has succeeded without
a commensurate ability to employ military resources well enough—but
not too much. Do we want to send uneducated officers and men to war?
Some will say that we shouldn't send anyone to war, but I think history
reveals that when confronted with violence at any level, most people want
to have someone who is prepared to address the violence in the best possible way. This is not a simple issue. For many, perhaps a majority, it is not
a topic they wish to address, at least not until violence confronts people
directly. In my first year in the Navy at firefighting school I learned that it
is a very bad idea to wait until a fire breaks out before you learn to fight it.

Finally, for those who will never go to war, who will never police a community, or who strive to prevent violence, their experience must be broad enough not to stigmatize or reject those willing to serve when the fire or war that no one wants is forced upon a country. In stating this I completely agree with the assessment that "we disapprove of the violence of others and approve of our own." It is because of the traps of using such phrases as "self-defense" disingenuously or even wickedly that those who receive the best educations must be challenged as well with such conundrums. Repeatedly for the half century since we graduated, wars in the regions of emerging economies and transitioning democracies have had an impact on our national life, and sometimes our national interests. In our freshman year, we were given books like Harrison Brown's *The Challenge of Man's Future*, presumably to encourage a broad appreciation of what needed to be addressed during our lives. Whether the problem is with a Manuel Noriega in Panama, Muammar Gadhafi in Libya, or Saddam Hussein in Iraq, the problem of national development and continuing challenges of nation states that do not have a military committed to civilian governance will not go away. Without a handle on the management of "legitimate" force, countries will struggle, and sometimes we will be pulled into those struggles. The absence of truly legitimate and noncorrupt coercion plagues east Africa, the Balkans, Asia, and exists as close as Mexico. If the work of policemen is seen as part of this problem, then corruption of "peace officers" can arise in every society on a continuing basis, including our own. It seems to me that Dartmouth has not been courageous in accepting the "challenge of humanity's future" by deciding not to be a place where the military role, or even the role of police, can be fully encompassed and improved where it is needed.

Serving in the military did not, owing to good fortune in war, prevent me from my work of nearly four decades, that is, trying to understand how violence and neglect of children can lead to subsequent tragedy, including more violence. Instead, the importance of how each child grows up, how well the women who mother children are cherished as daughters, wives, and colleagues, why it is important for men to be encouraged to learn about caregiving, and how all these elements play into the success or failure of society has been magnified for me by experiencing how wars begin, are fought, and are controlled or continue. For any of you who stayed with me during this reflection, my thanks as well for your support of Dartmouth. Finally, for your service, military or otherwise, my thanks.

In 1969 Don Bross left the Navy, received a NIMH traineeship in medical sociology at the University of Wisconsin, and for his PhD completed research on how to improve reporting of sexually transmitted diseases, just as HIV was being identified. He entered law school to understand how ethical and legal research with human subjects can be undertaken, and was clerking for the office of the university counsel when he was recruited to the faculty of the Pediatrics Department by Dr. C. Henry Kempe. Donald C. Bross, PhD, JD, is professor of pediatrics (family law), University of Colorado School of Medicine, and associate director for pediatric law, policy, and ethics at the Kempe Center for the Prevention and Treatment of Child Abuse and Neglect. During his faculty tenure, Don has represented maltreated children in court, served as parliamentarian for the International Society for the Prevention of Child Abuse, and founded the National Association of Counsel for Children. During the 1980s he helped the armed forces develop Family Advocacy Command Assistance Teams to respond to child maltreatment of military dependents. Don has just been appointed coeditor in chief of *Child Abuse & Neglect: The International Journal.*

Observe, Analyze, and Respond

STANLEY C. HERR : U.S. AIR FORCE

I selected this title because it is sometimes employed as a simple set of actions that a combat soldier should use as a checklist before firing his or her weapon. It is a reaction to the old "shoot first, then bother to find out what was going on around you" mentality of the Wild West gunslinger. But I never served in a combat zone. During my forty-four-year career of military-related efforts I worked in research laboratories and prototype systems development environments (R&D). That being noted, my entire career was also based on those three military activities: first I did reconnaissance, four years later I added intelligence analysis, and four years after that I moved on to the response phase by developing countermeasures.

But that is getting ahead of the story. My military-oriented career started as a freshman at Dartmouth when I joined Basic Air Force ROTC. My brother, five years my senior, had gone through Air Force ROTC while majoring in mechanical engineering. He was assigned as a heating and air conditioning engineer doing R&D at Wright Patterson Air Force Base (WPAFB) outside Dayton, Ohio. At the end of my freshman year I was able to visit him and toured several of the research laboratories there. When I returned to campus in the fall, I talked to the commandant about my visit to the Wright Field Laboratories. He said he could promise me a WPAFB laboratory assignment if I signed up for Advanced ROTC. Since I was majoring in physics, I was hooked.

Reconnaissance

I reported to the Optronics Branch, Reconnaissance Division, of the Air Force Avionics Laboratory on August 31, 1964, a day after my twenty-second birthday. I was told I would be part of a new group working on

Stan Herr and T-33 trainer

the use of infrared detector technology to detect and track ICBMs, either at Soviet test ranges or, eventually, as a part of a missile defense shield. This was all very new stuff, especially since semiconductor detector devices only became an operational reality in the mid-1950s. This office was clearly doing some very important and challenging programs. Looking back to a major aspect of my Dartmouth experience, I worked for three summers and two school years in solid state physics basic research funded by a National Science Foundation grant under Professor William Doyle. Thus, my first Air Force assignment looked like an ideal fit for my background and interests.

I had been in the laboratory less than a month when everything changed. On August 2, 1964, four weeks before I reported for active duty, a U.S. Navy destroyer had been attacked by three North Vietnamese patrol boats. While no real damage was done, it resulted in Congress's passing the Gulf of Tonkin Resolution. This act basically authorized President Johnson to enter and conduct a land war supporting South Vietnam against North Vietnam. By late September 1964 the Department of Defense initiated planning for moving hundreds of thousands of Army,

Navy, Marine Corps, and Air Force troops and weapons to Thailand, South Vietnam, and the South China Sea. It also initiated a large number of new R&D demands throughout the Air Force Laboratories. For the Reconnaissance Division this meant better reconnaissance cameras and film, but it also meant development of new solid-state infrared detector technology that would be needed to allow our forces to see enemy activity and targets at night.

Suddenly, I felt like I was part of the war effort and that I was going to be providing an important advantage to U.S. soldiers. Our team of new college graduates was enrolled in a multiweek, intensive training course about infrared technology, taught by a team of physicists and electrical engineers from the University of Michigan faculty. Their course material was so new it was provided as mimeographed notes, equations, and graphs in three-inch, three-ring binders, one for each week, three or four in all. This cadre of academics eventually produced the first infrared handbook, and its newer editions have been the bible of this specialized technology for decades.

Back in the lab we measured the performance of various detector chips, worked on bias circuits and amplifier stages, determined if we could get sufficient sensitivity from thermoelectrically cooled indium antimonide detectors, or whether we needed liquid-nitrogen-cooled mercury cadmium telluride detectors. Could we develop these systems into flight-worthy equipment? What could we see? Could we detect trucks with running engines? Could we even detect them after they were parked and turned off? Could we see antiaircraft batteries and radar sites? Could we possibly see a human being from a plane at ten thousand feet, flying at speeds of two hundred to four hundred miles per hour? The answer to all these questions eventually was yes, but it took several years to achieve the goals.

This capability was achieved with the development of the Forward-Looking Infrared (FLIR) system for the newly developed gunships. Since much of the development of these infrared systems resulted from close collaborations between government laboratories and contractors, I was fortunate to participate in a flight-test demonstration of one of the first successful infrared imaging systems, mounted in a hole cut in the belly of a Texas Instrument corporate aircraft. It swiftly moved from laboratory prototype into an operational combat system, and it then became the night eyes for the AC-47 "Puff the Magic Dragon" gunship. I was clearly making a contribution to the war effort, and it also gave me a great deal of satisfaction in my chosen career.

During four years as a lieutenant and then captain, I was the only person in my office on flight status, hence I regularly flew on test-wing aircraft acting as an aerial photographer or searching for targets on a monitor displaying infrared imagery. I logged more than two hundred hours running tests from the navigator/bombardier seat in the nose of test models of RB-47 reconnaissance aircraft, one of which is now in the National Museum of the United States Air Force. My most memorable flight, however, was on a Boeing 707/C-135 named "Weightless Wonder," where I assisted astronaut Gus Grissom, helping him learn how to climb through a hatch in a weightless environment. This weightless condition was created by repetitively putting the aircraft into a dive, executing a 2.0G pull-up, flying over a parabolic arc where everyone was floating for about thirty to forty seconds, and then going through a 2.5G pullout. Gus and two other astronauts, who were to be the first spaceflight crew of the Apollo program, were later killed in a command module fire during a ground test of the module that became known as Apollo 1. That number was never used for an actual launch during the Apollo program; and Gus had an Air Force base near Kokomo, Indiana, named in his honor.

Intelligence Analyst

With the Vietnam War going full bore in late August 1968, I opted to leave my blue suit behind and become an Air Force civil servant, employed by the deputy for foreign technology. This was a staff function for the three-star general who ran the Aeronautical Systems Division of the Air Force Systems Command. Once more it was entering on the ground floor of a new organization that was charged with a new mission. We would be developing the threat intelligence estimates needed to define design requirements of all new Air Force combat aircraft. While reconnaissance told us where the threat was located, we needed to assess the capability of those hostile weapons, and how much damage they could do to U.S. aircraft. What was their range, how large and efficient were their warheads, and how accurately could they target our aircraft?

My role was to characterize the optical performance data on the new threat weapon systems that used heat-seeking infrared trackers on air-to-air and surface-to-air missiles and optical fire control sensors on antiaircraft artillery (AAA) and surface-to-air missiles (SAM). These passive sensor systems were being used for initial detection and tracking of our aircraft. Because they were not active radar, they denied us warning and location information.

While we knew that the Viet Cong were being supplied primarily with Soviet-made weapons, we were not sure that they were receiving the latest technology. Confirmation that they were in fact quite capable had to await two events: first, our combat aircraft were being shot down, in spite of their sophisticated antiradar jamming systems; and second, we acquired pieces of hardware that allowed us to reverse engineer these weapons' characteristics and capabilities. When U.S. aircraft jammed the Viet Cong SAM battery radars, the VC would switch over to either a visual or TV-tracking system. Our challenge became to assess when they were able to do passive tracking and what we could do to negate it.

It was during this period in late 1969 or early 1970 that a new threat emerged in the Vietnam air war: the shoulder-fired, infrared-guided SA-7 missile. The shooter on the ground used a simple optical sight to align the missile seeker with the aircraft. When the target came within a range of three to four miles, the shooter would hear an audio tone that the seeker had acquired the aircraft's hot engine parts and had enough signal strength to target it successfully. Our challenge was to find out what kind of susceptibilities existed within these seekers.

Fortunately, we were eventually able to acquire complete weapon systems, either through intelligence channels or by capturing them in the field, and my task turned to running a major exploitation effort on these infrared seekers. I designed, developed, and conducted measurement and performance tests that allowed us to assess their capabilities and susceptibilities to decoys and active countermeasures. This exploitation or reverse engineering program became my major focus for the next two years. It also became an integral part of the research activities that would be my calling for the rest of my career.

Infrared and Electro-Optical Countermeasures

With the Vietnam War still raging and with our loss of major aircraft and aircrews to infrared-guided missiles, I finally turned my career toward the last of the three mission areas, countermeasures. In the spring of 1972 I left the Intelligence Directorate, moved back to the Avionics Laboratory, and began working on new infrared countermeasure systems for the Electronic Warfare Division. Hence, what Vietnam had taught me was that we still needed all three capabilities. We needed the reconnaissance systems to know where the threat was and when it was starting to attack. We also needed to analyze how effective and susceptible this threat was to our aircraft. Finally, we needed a response. If we couldn't do anything to defeat missile or gun attacks, the survival of U.S. aircraft was in jeopardy and the mission and aircrew could be lost. We had to develop those countermeasures and make them robust enough to defeat the next generation of infrared and/or optically guided weapons that was sure to come.

The first rudimentary missile detection systems, a simple threat warner, confirmed that a missile had been launched, and a few simple decoy and infrared lamp jammers were developed by the end of hostilities in 1975. They probably saved a few aircraft and aircrew lives. But this is not where the story ends of how Vietnam affected my life, or my subsequent career. From my position of developing countermeasures, I went on to run the first large airborne chemical laser development program that could defeat all types of infrared guided missiles. Then the challenge was to develop ever smaller lasers, detection systems and jamming techniques that would address ever-more sophisticated guidance systems.

I left government service in 1978, became a contractor, and continued working on the technical challenges of developing more-advanced and robust infrared countermeasures, as I have just outlined. It is a back-and-forth game of the enemy hardening his seeker, then we create a new way to confuse its guidance electronics. In the last thirty years of my career as an optical physicist, specializing in military R&D, I felt I had many very rewarding aspects to my work. Amid the daily challenges of developing new components, techniques, and systems, the most important accomplishment was that the U.S. Air Force has not lost an aircrew or major aircraft to an infrared-guided threat since Vietnam. I feel I was a small part of that success.

Stanley Herr's career as an optical physicist was broken up into three phases: fourteen years as an Air Force program manager and researcher; fourteen years working for a small engineering services firm supporting these government programs; and a final sixteen years working for one of the largest science and engineering support companies in the world, SAIC. Most of that career was spent in and around laboratories doing state-of-the-art research and system development. His roles would on occasion switch from issues regarding fundamental detector and laser research problems to system implementation and airborne system challenges. In the 1990s, he even spent a great deal of time working on the design and development of a digital infrared missile-engagement simulation that has become and remains the industry standard model.

In September 2008, a week before the financial markets fell apart, Stanley retired both formally and completely. Ann, his wife of forty-six years, had retired three years earlier from her twenty-year career as a stockbroker for Morgan Stanley. With their son in Denver and married daughter and grandson in Dayton, it was time for them to have some fun playing grandparents and traveling. They have a small condo on the Atlantic Intracoastal Waterway in South Carolina, and have enjoyed travels throughout Europe, the Middle East, and South America. They also enjoy spending several weeks at Drummond Island, Michigan, in the summer. They continue to be active volunteers serving on church, community, and arts organization boards in the Dayton area.

Vietnam in the Course of a Navy Career

MICHAEL W. PARKER : U.S. NAVY

G raduating from Dartmouth with a regular commission in the Navy in 1964, I was obligated to serve at the pleasure of the president for a minimum of four years after graduation. When I submitted my letter of resignation to attend dental school, having served four years, the president was not pleased. I was told that I could not resign until I had completed a one-year tour in Vietnam.

The prospect of serving in the war was a looming shadow almost from the time of my commissioning. We had sent advisers in country before I graduated, and it seemed likely that the U.S. role would escalate. It quickly did after the Gulf of Tonkin incident, which arguably was staged specifically for that purpose. I remember a poignant evening aboard my first ship in 1965 that brought the point home. Following a shipyard overhaul, our aging destroyer was undergoing a rigorous course of refresher training at Guantánamo Bay, Cuba. Exhausted after a long day of exercises and remediation, we were watching a movie on the weather deck beneath a starlit sky when a sister ship, USS *Bache*, unexpectedly got under way nearby. Word quickly spread that she had received sudden orders to deploy to the South China Sea for patrol duty off Vietnam. Our ship, USS *Waller*, would take her turn there, too, but only after I had left her to become executive officer of the coastal minesweeper *Frigatebird*. My experience aboard the minesweeper would dictate my assignment in Vietnam.

My orders in lieu of release were to report in May to Commander Naval Forces Vietnam (COMNAVFORV) as the mine countermeasures and swimmer defense officer. The '68 Tet offensive was making headlines as I headed to Coronado, California, for overseas indoctrination and SERE training. The Survival, Evasion, Resistance, and Escape course had the reputation of being a significant physical and mental challenge in preparation for falling into the hands of the Viet Cong. I like physical challenges, but I can't deny relief when I was told that only pilots would attend SERE. That policy reflects the relative safety of staff assignments (at headquarters). As a staff officer my capture was so unlikely that it was not cost effective to teach me how to escape. While my pilot friends underwent SERE training, I returned to Maine and saw my son take his first steps, then rejoined the SERE graduates for the charter flight to Tan Son Nhut Air Base in Saigon.

Residual fighting from the Tet offensive was prominently reported to be ongoing in the Cholon neighborhood of Saigon. Before leaving for my flight I assured my family that I would stay well clear of that, a promise I kept for about two hours. I was met at the airport by the man I was relieving at COMNAVFORV. He was an entertaining fellow, suffering severely from hemorrhoids and driving his own misappropriated Navy jeep, which would not be conveyed to me in his turnover of duties. He announced that we would check in at headquarters and then drive to the building where I would be billeted . . . in Cholon. The fighting there was not personally threatening. Tracer fire was visible from the rooftop, where we would often spend evenings writing home or reporting in with cassette tapes. I carried a sidearm, but it was little more than decoration.

My assignment was challenging and demanded my full attention. I made frequent forays into the field to evaluate our defenses and our countermeasures in sites up and down the country, but staff duty is not field duty. Staffs operate behind the scenes in relative safety. Those in the field often face bullets, explosives, and other harsh realities of war. For instance, I was not greeted upon arrival in my workplace by a medevac helicopter carrying the remains of my commanding officer, whose title I would immediately assume, as was my classmate, Jim Laughlin. I did not come under enemy fire, nor was I exposed to Agent Orange, nor did I fear for my safety in any particular way. I soon moved out of Cholon to a billet a block from my office in downtown Saigon and walked to work through a park. Excellent meals were served at a converted hotel dining room a couple of blocks away. After a painful two-month waiting period, my membership application was accepted at Cercle Sportif a block from the office. There, consistent with a work-hard, play-hard philosophy I had adopted at Dartmouth, I would play a set of tennis, shower, and then sip a tall glass of sweet tea in the noonday sun before returning to the challenges of coordinating mine and swimmer countermeasures. I don't mean to minimize my work there. I was challenged by it, and I devoted myself fully to it, but it was no more life-threatening than my previous tours aboard ship, and I suffer no aftereffects, beyond the burden of knowing the contrast with what my counterparts in the field endured.

Soon after I arrived on staff, freshly promoted Vice Admiral Elmo (Bud) Zumwalt Jr. assumed command of all naval forces in Vietnam. His predecessor had been a two-star admiral and, as such, carried little influence within the hierarchy of General Westmoreland's staff. Weakly represented, the Navy had become the illegitimate child in the military family. Not only was the Navy overlooked by the Army and Air Force brass—it was out of its element. The Vietnam War was a land war, apart from a wetland in the Mekong Delta. We were used to operating on deep-draft ships on the high seas. Here we were faced with muddy rivers and canals where smaller craft, supported by mother ships, were coming on-line with ill-defined roles. Bud Zumwalt, having three stars, gave shape to a new brown-water Navy, a term not used since the U.S. Civil War. Through his staff he developed tactics for the tiny PBRs (riverine patrol boats) and the somewhat larger and faster swift boats, never before tried. This modern brown-water Navy was born in our operations shop where I worked. Zumwalt directed our boats deep into the watery countryside and introduced the use of Agent Orange defoliant to unmask the jungle hideaways of our enemy. Army and Air Force brass took notice, and soon we were conducting joint exercises with our military colleagues, complete with air cover and support troops. These were heady times in the operations department, and the operators there would be rewarded later when Zumwalt left Vietnam to became the chief of naval operations.

As CNO, Admiral Zumwalt continued to devise visionary tactics. He established a squadron of ships called the Mod Squad, which he staffed with officers who were junior by one rank to their counterparts staffing conventional ships. A majority of these Mod Squad officers derived from his staff at COMNAVFORV.

As mine countermeasures and swimmer defense officer I was equipped to deal with conventional mine warfare by virtue of my minesweeper experience. The swimmer defense role dealt with unconventional mine warfare, which was much more prevalent and for which I was totally unprepared. I encountered conventional mines almost as soon as I arrived

Mike Parker being welcomed aboard a
supply ship on the Cua Viet River

in Saigon. In conjunction with the Tet offensive and just before my arrival in country, our forces had captured three very sophisticated Russian mines being transported along the Cua Viet River six miles south of the DMZ. These weapons posed a new and serious threat to our supply craft and support ships on the large rivers and to replenishment ships in the ports and harbors. Two fully functional mines were defused and sent to a Navy laboratory in Florida for analysis. Much of my time early in the tour was devoted to devising countermeasures to these sophisticated weapons. These mines could be programmed to detonate in response to three signatures left by passing ships: changes in the magnetic field, certain acoustical patterns, and/or a drop in hydrostatic pressure. Furthermore, they could ignore up to thirty ships before detonating, so they were potentially very hard to sweep. Fortunately, our only encounter with these advanced devices was the three we intercepted, and so I was able to turn my attention to unconventional mine warfare wearing my other hat, swimmer defense officer.

In this role I had little or no Navy experience. Viet Cong sappers along the shorelines were using the aquatic equivalent of today's IED (the improvised explosive devices used by insurgents in Iraq and other places). Sappers, either swimming or in a sampan, would plant an explosive device in a shipping lane and connect it by wire to a trigger-man along the shore. Or a swimmer would drift down on the tide to an anchored ship, where he could either attach a mine magnetically to the hull or tie it to the anchor chain for detonation.

Our anchored riverine support ships, where our sailors lived and maintained their boats, were particularly vulnerable to this form of attack, and it was my job to devise and promulgate countermeasures. We suffered many casualties before we learned to defend ourselves by simple measures such as changing location in order to minimize the vulnerability of a slack tide, tossing grenades into the water at erratic intervals to discourage reconnoitering swimmers, or running a metal ring up and down the anchor chain periodically to reveal and disarm attached mines or command wires. In my last month in Saigon I published a manual of lessons learned in the art of swimmer defense and mine countermeasures. I learned later from my successor that our newly minted brown-water Navy used this publication widely and effectively.

My views on the war were shaped by my preconceptions and observations, by available national news magazines such as *Time* and *Newsweek*, by the slanted view of *Stars and Stripes,* and by reports I was getting from my parents and my wife, Carolyn, who had returned with our son to Hanover for the duration of my tour. Up to the time of my arrival in Saigon, I was fully supportive of the domino theory, which postulated that if we didn't interfere, the Chinese were going to impose communism throughout Southeast Asia, one country after another, like falling dominoes. The view from my flight into Tan Son Nhut sparked my first cynicism toward the rightness of the war. It was not the domino theory that I questioned, but rather the cost of this now full-blown event. The staging area was a tribute to Secretary of Defense McNamara's ability to move matériel. The supplies and machinery built up for opposing unsophisticated Viet Cong guerrillas was appalling. I later learned that there were stockpiles like this all over the country. I now realize that such overwhelming matériel is the usual—and still ineffective—way to solve a political disagreement. If the accomplishments of war are its fruits, they have not changed much since Vietnam. They have remained consistently bitter and have provided little nourishment, in my opinion.

I found the mainstream news magazines to be at odds with information coming from military sources. There was a recurring theme of an imminent coup, which didn't materialize and about which we had no corroboration. It seemed like a make-news item, and I said so in an unpublished letter to *Time.*

From my wife I learned that the tone had changed in Hanover. ROTC, whose presence on campus had been well tolerated, if not fully accepted, in my tenure there, was now a pariah. Protesters spit on the husband of a neighbor of Carolyn's, an Army major teaching ROTC courses. Eventually, ROTC was banished from campus. I thought then that both Dartmouth and the military were losers in that decision, and my view on that has not changed. I was able to afford Dartmouth only because of my

NROTC scholarship, which paid for tuition, books, and a small stipend. In the course of my Navy career, which resumed after I completed dental school, I felt strongly that the Navy needed the contributions of liberal arts graduates to balance the preponderance of engineers and Naval Academy officers. In my experience we had much to learn from each other.

My arrival in dental school from Saigon coincided with an unrelenting surge of antiwar protest in Boston, which included my dental school colleagues. Many of them missed classes. Classroom respect for faculty was appallingly absent. My classmates perceived me as primarily an elder rather than a former naval officer. By virtue of five extra years of experience following college, my perspective differed markedly from many of theirs. I was single-mindedly on a quest for a dental degree. Unlike some of my military peers, I did not feel shunned or unappreciated when I returned from Saigon. I was not vilified, at least not until, fed up with classroom antics and a preoccupation with protest by my fellow students, I expressed in an article for the dental alumni newsletter my belief that many of my classmates lacked academic focus and were motivated more by a fear of the draft than by a desire for becoming professionals. Whatever our motivations, I have to admit that virtually all of us survived the war, the protests, the curriculum, and my musings, to become professionals worthy of our degree.

Admiral Zumwalt made such an impression on me that he deserves a special place in this account of my Vietnam experience. He was a visionary within an organization strongly resistant to change. As COMNAVFORV he revolutionized jungle warfare, creating a role for the Navy never before envisioned. During my four years of dental school he brought new meaning to the term "deep selection" by vaulting over thirty-three admirals senior to him to be selected the youngest ever chief of naval operations. In that role, using and promoting leadership skills that were beyond the pale of accepted Navy doctrine, he brought the Navy into the post-Vietnam era. If his tactics seemed extreme, it was for good reason. Many of his formerly senior subordinates were openly prepared to ride him out to restore the Navy to its former ways at the conclusion of his tenure. He needed not only to set the direction for change, but also to effect a new culture in four short years.

I spent my summer vacations on active duty supplementing the teaching staff at Officer Candidate School in Newport, Rhode Island. There

I kept tabs of changes that he was implementing through his famous Z-Grams. When I returned to active duty as a dental officer, after he had retired, I witnessed the changes he had achieved in Navy culture. Through his efforts, the Navy dealt effectively with the issues of racism, sexism, chain of command, and tactics, all well documented in his memoir, *On Watch.*

He paid a dreadful price for his decision to use Agent Orange along the waterways of Vietnam. Agent Orange turned out to be highly toxic, and many sailors, including his son, suffered eventually from its effects. Eleven years after my tour in Saigon, I reported to the Navy Graduate Dental School on the Bethesda Naval Hospital campus for a residency and later returned on staff. While there, I often encountered the admiral making visits for emergency treatment of his son's ultimately fatal blood cancer.

For his foresight as CNO and his ability to effect necessary cultural change, I hold Admiral Zuwalt in the highest esteem.

The Vietnam War has left scars on our veterans that I share only vicariously. If I had been a self-serving man with political influence, I could not have charted a course of duty in Vietnam any farther from harm's way than the one I experienced. I faced challenging and satisfying work with talented colleagues and I paid no price, compared to that of many of my Dartmouth classmates. Vietnam was a small part of my Navy career. It coalesces, however, with duty on three ships and choice assignments in my home state of Maine, Bethesda (Maryland), Scotland, and Bangor, Washington, to form a challenging and rewarding career. I would not rewrite much if I were to script it over.

Having grown up in the small town of Pittsfield, Maine, Mike Parker returned to his home state after his Navy retirement. He joined a thriving private practice in South Portland and continued dentistry for a dozen years. Now fully retired, he and his wife, Carolyn, a 1964 graduate of Mary Hitchcock School of Nursing, reside on the pristine shores of the Presumpscot River in Windham. They live active lives and are involved with a land trust, a church, massage therapy for cancer treatment patients, and, most recently, the study of beekeeping. They have three grown children and four grandchildren.

How Did I Miss Vietnam?

MICHAEL M. MACMURRAY : U.S. NAVY

I don't think I had really heard of Vietnam until I was at Supply Corps School in Athens, Georgia, in late 1964. One of my classmates there (who included Ernie Notar) got orders to Vietnam, and no one thought much of it. I went to a ship homeported in Guam and after a year became so bored that I asked to be sent to Vietnam in early 1966. I was quite taken aback when the Bureau of Navy Personnel said that there were no slots for Supply Corps officers of my grade at that moment (a situation that was soon to change). I asked if there was anything else available in the western Pacific. Well, they had just received a requirement for a JG to go to Penang, Malaysia, to run the rest and recuperation center for Vietnam troops, which I did for more than a year. My daily dealings were with men (no women, in my recollection) on their break from the war, helping them take respite from the battle, or—oh, hell, we all know that most of the troops in Vietnam were not actually in combat. Did I ever think about our Southeast Asia policies at the time? No, not even when I was slightly teargassed when LBJ visited Kuala Lumpur. I don't recall that anyone, expat or Malaysian, ever engaged me in a conversation about the war.

During my following tour in Newport, Rhode Island, I have to say that I was totally oblivious of the antiwar movement—I was in uniform, on a naval base, and protesters were invisible, if they existed. On a later tour afloat, I did encounter some antiwar opposition, a conscientious objector (CO). The CO thought that, as an Ivy Leaguer, I would somehow insulate him from criticism about how the case was handled; I recommended granting the young man's request and never heard of him or the case again.

When I next went to Harvard Business School (HBS), I was assigned to the MIT ROTC unit—Harvard's had been thrown off campus during the war protest. Our one concession was that we never wore our uniforms, but I think that might have been the case with or without the war. Haircuts got a bit shaggy, too! There was absolutely no antimilitary sentiment at HBS, and I don't recall anyone even mentioning the war there, either. The Cambridge side of the river was a different story, which is one reason why we didn't wear uniforms.

I spent the few remaining Vietnam years in Washington on assignments that had absolutely nothing to do with the war or Southeast Asian policy. I did encounter a few general antiwar protests, especially on December 28, the Feast of the Innocents, but they were pretty sparsely attended and largely ignored. You can bet they are kept pretty far away from the Pentagon these days.

As I read this over, I realize that I sound as if I were totally oblivious and insensitive to what should have been a defining moment of my life—except that it wasn't. The civil rights movement, yeah, but Vietnam just slipped by me, and, I suspect, most '64s, although I will let you speak for yourselves. The most defining moment for me came when I visited the Vietnam Memorial two decades ago and searched out Bruce Nickerson's name. I left in tears and will not go back again. It was just too painful.

But did Vietnam affect our lives in less direct, personal ways? I think without question. I have just finished reading Marvin and Deborah Kalb's *Haunting Legacy — Vietnam and the American Presidency from Ford to Obama*. While a bit overdrawn, the book makes it clear that the Vietnam experience is still with us in both domestic and foreign policy. Witness the subject of these essays.

Mike MacMurray retired from the Navy in 1985 and immediately became a civil servant in the Office of the Secretary of Defense as a foreign affairs specialist, where he focused at various times on the Middle East, South Asia, and the Western Hemisphere. He traveled extensively with several secretaries of defense and led multiple overseas delegations. Today, Mike is working on homeland defense strategy, which he finds less interesting than international relations. He says that retirement beckons. Mike's second wife died in 2001, and he lives alone in Northern Virginia.

1965

Marines land in Da Nang.

Entitled Elites and Exploited Expendables

The Privileged versus the Patriots

DAVID S. DECALESTA : U.S. ARMY

A Democrat is a Republican
who spent a night in jail.
—Anonymous

or

A Democrat is a Republican
who spent a year in Vietnam.

grew up in a wealthy suburb of Rochester, New York. The fabled Oak Hill Country Club was at the bottom of our street. Our fathers were doctors, lawyers, dentists, college professors, successful businessmen. Our moms mostly were stay-at-homes, and I guess a lot of them put in the hours at one or more of the four private country clubs. I thought I was upper middle class (and thus at least on the bottom edge of the elite class) because of where I lived, the public school I attended (in the top one hundred in the nation at the time), and the lifestyles of my friends and their parents. Rich, white, educated, and privileged. There wasn't a black, brown, or yellow face in my high school or town. There were a few other differences that slid by me: My parents didn't own the home we lived in—it belonged to my grandparents, who let us live there. My mom worked in a local gift store; I caddied at the country club rather than play the game; and I didn't have twenty-five pairs of shoes, thirty sweaters, or my own car. But off I went, like almost everyone else, to a prestigious college, where there were few (so few as to be token) black, brown, or yellow faces.

Four years later came Vietnam and the draft. They were not equaliz-
ers. Instead, I came to see them as definers of rank, class, and how things
worked in America. And they influenced how I looked at, and chose to
interact with, society. Prior to Vietnam I voted Republican, just like my
parents; that would change after a year of combat duty.

I was a draftee, receiving my draft notice a year after I graduated from
Dartmouth and the day my bride and I returned from our honeymoon.
We had been aware of the war brewing in Vietnam well before we were
married. Almost to a man, my high school male friends had found alternatives to service-via-the-draft: marriage; continued enrollment in
college as post-baccalaureates; divinity school; medical or law school;
cheesy medical exemptions discovered by friendly doctors; participation
in alternative-service programs like the Peace Corps or Vista; assisted
leapfrogging over hundreds of applicants to land in the National Guard
or Army Reserve; conscientious objection; or, a last resort, expatriation
to Canada.

We had planned a fall wedding, and ignored the dictum of then-
president Lyndon Johnson in midsummer of 1965 that men married (and
without children) after midnight, August 26, would no longer receive the
marriage exemption from the draft. We chose not to get married quietly
in a private civil ceremony prior to the Johnson cutoff date and then go
ahead with the planned public wedding after the date—for one thing, I
couldn't have looked my father-in-law in the eye, he who served in the
Navy during World War II. And when it was announced that married
men without children would be eligible for the draft after October 1967,
we did not frantically attempt to conceive a child to avail myself of that
exemption. So, two months and eight days after I was married, I reported
for my induction, much to the stupefied incredulity of my draft-exempted
friends.

Prior to my reporting date for the draft physical I explored the options for Officer Candidate School, figuring that as an officer I might
have a little more control over my fate if I went to Vietnam. I chose Army
OCS rather than Navy OCS because the Army required one fewer year
of commitment than the Navy. I rather thoughtlessly ignored the risks
of combat in the Army versus combat in the Navy. I was assigned to a
"special" OCS group comprising twenty-three recent college graduates.
As a group, we progressed through the prerequisite ten weeks of Basic

Combat Training and another ten weeks of Advanced Infantry Training with all the other noncollege draftees. It was during those twenty weeks of pre-OCS training that I was thrown into day-to-day, 24/7 contact with eighteen-plus-year-old boys who mostly were not white, not college educated, and not from wealthy families. In other words, non-elites who had no recourse to exemptions from the draft save marriage.

From day one of Basic Combat Training, we in the group of twenty-three were integrated with the non-elite noncollegians—we had no more or no less standing. In the eyes of the drill sergeants, we were all "goat-headed mother-fuckers." In the tent that was my ten-week home during basic training, I bunked with four African Americans, three Hispanics, and two really poor white guys from somewhere in Appalachia.

Along with those nine other Americans, I crawled through the same barbed-wire-covered trenches, pulled the same crappy KP, cleaned my rifle and made up my bunk, picked up countless cigarette butts, and took continual abuse from the drill sergeants. We answered the same mail call, read our letters from home under the same lights-out regulations, and collected the same pitifully small pay every month. We were them. They were us. No differences. There were no criminals, no fights, no stealing from each other. But in the conversations at night or during KP or breaks in training, I learned about what their young lives had been like and how different they had been from mine. None of them had tried to avoid the draft—but then how could they, without the wherewithal so easily available to my high school classmates and me? It did not escape my attention that these draftees took pride in what they were doing—they actually thought it was their patriotic duty to fight for their country when called.

As we progressed to Advanced Infantry Training, we learned how to work together in the basic infantry unit—the fire team. The five to six soldiers in the teams learned tactics and weaponry, but the foundation was always the same—cover your buddy's back and follow orders, or, in other words, maintain discipline. The officers, as we were later taught in OCS, gave the orders, which were followed under the implicit bargain between officers and enlisted—we'll follow your orders if they are well founded and do not put us at unrealistic risk.

Companies of OCS candidates (about sixty men) were divided into platoons of twenty or so, with each platoon being supervised by a combat-tested Army lieutenant. These lieutenants were to provide leadership training and evaluate our progress toward responsible and responsive junior officers. We learned more about weaponry, tactics, and leadership and were subjected to intense physical, mental, and psychological pressure designed to test whether we would "crack" under the pressures of combat. Those who couldn't take the heat were summarily dismissed. However, for the life of me, I cannot remember any training aimed at instilling in us basic respect or concern for those human beings we would order about and over whose lives we would have absolute control under combat conditions.

Once in Vietnam, I quickly learned that the men would follow you anywhere, and do anything for you, if you treated them fairly and never asked them to do anything you yourself would not do, especially if you proved it by habitually doing it. I earned their acceptance and respect by randomly taking the "point" position on combat patrols (the first man in a line of combat troops moving through the field was the point man, who often made first contact with the enemy). Every now and then I carried my radioman's field radio (those things were heavy—forty pounds—and I never figured out how they managed to carry them day in and day out without collapsing). And I had a policy that anyone who discovered a booby trap before it exploded got an instant R&R trip (one week respite from combat to one of a restricted number of locations such as Hawaii, or Hong Kong).

I also was exposed to the cavalier and naïve attitude of the brass (field-grade officers—majors and colonels) characterized by an almost complete lack of responsibility or concern they felt for the lives of men they ordered into combat situations they had planned. This was compounded by the fact that few of these officers had actually experienced combat under the conditions existing in Vietnam—the war was too young, and their (prior) company-grade experience as lieutenants and captains had been limited to peacetime posts in the continental United States, Europe, or maybe Korea. With few exceptions, these field-grade officers were elites—either graduating from the U.S. Military Academy at West Point or attending ROTC on some college campus. It was the untested elites directing (from safe firebases) the inexperienced but patriotic expendables who humped out ten or so klicks (kilometers) into the puckerbrush and back every day. Because of their inexperience with guerrilla warfare as practiced by the VC (local Viet Cong) and NVA (North Vietnamese Army regulars), it often happened that our elite planners would break the bargain and send us out on wildly naïve and dangerous missions that you could count on to fail. The men and noncoms (noncommissioned officers—sergeants) who actually had combat experience would try to explain to us green lieutenants why some of the particular orders were basically GI death traps. The smart lieutenants listened, and let the noncoms run the show until they—the lieutenants—obtained enough combat experience to "get it." Because their lives, and those of their men, were on the line, these lieutenants could not be the IKEs (I think I Know Everything, but I really know very little that is relevant) that the brass were. Unlike the brass, we lowly lieutenants did not consider ourselves (or our men) as expendables of little value. An example suffices:

For weeks our company had failed to pull off a successful ambush. We would dig our foxholes on line, in the L-shaped killing zone, and sit back and wait for the hapless VC to trot down the trail we were ambushing. Never happened. Then the "brass" had an inspiration. Figuring that the VC could not count, they developed a cuckoo scheme for setting up an ambush: A company of three platoons of men would mill around on the selected ambush site, and at random intervals a soldier from one of the platoons would sink down and stay in place. After a half-hour of milling and dropping, a platoon's worth of soldiers (twenty-five or so men) would be "secretly" emplaced along the ambush route. My sergeant was beside himself when I informed him that we were the platoon being secreted. Over his vehement misgivings, we went along with the plan.

All went well until about dusk, when my sergeant reported that there were sounds of digging along our flank, accompanied by the smell of marijuana. We had been found out, and the VC was setting up a counter ambush. When I radioed this information to the battalion headquarters, I was told to hold our position and give them our coordinates—suppressive 105 mm howitzer fire would be used to wipe out the VC (who, by our estimates, were less than fifty yards away). I had a whispered conference with my sergeant, and we decided the only way to save the day and our troops was to silently and slowly gather them up and sneak away. This we did, relocating to a slight depression five hundred meters away, at which point I dutifully radioed our previous location to the artillery boys, who proceeded to pulverize the area. Come dawn we went back to the devastated ambush site and found many blood trails where dead VC had been dragged away by the survivors. We also noted several large 105 mm craters in what had been our ambush line.

That was the day the men became "mine." It was also the day I began a lifetime of distrust of IKE elites, and developed an enduring empathy for the "little people." Thereafter our "search and destroy" missions became "search and avoid" exercises, as my main interest lay in bringing all my boys back home alive.

Someone "up there" smelled a rat, however, and I eventually found myself banished to a support company, where my main task was writing up "the brass" for fake awards, mostly Vietnam medals. The highest U.S. awards for supreme bravery and sacrifice were the Medal of Honor and Distinguished Service Cross. Those awards were almost always restricted to "the men," because they were the ones exposed to close-in combat with actual opportunities for heroism and self-sacrifice. I do remember being told to write up several colonels for the Silver Star (next medal down in terms of personal risk and bravery) and in particular the colonel who put himself in for a Silver Star because he hovered a half mile above a raging firefight in a helicopter, "heedlessly exposing himself to small-arms fire" (I'm not sure if small-arms rounds fired at the helicopter from the ground would even have penetrated it at that height) while directing the action. Ten or so years later I read with a belated sense of exoneration that the colonel, who had since been promoted to brigadier general, had had his Silver Star citation nullified as specious, been demoted to colonel, and essentially had ruined his career by claiming credit for a medal he clearly did not deserve.

It would be fair to say that my military experience, most of which occurred during training for and then service in Vietnam, instilled in me a distrust of IKE elites who in fact had little if any actual experience in the decisions they were entrusted to make on the behalf of the lives of the people they had control over. Likewise, because I had been a throwaway expendable, I identified with non-elite expendables who, because of race, economic status, or level of education were considered as second-class citizens and whose experience and advice were considered irrelevant.

Released from active duty after my stint in Vietnam was over, I enrolled in a graduate program in wildlife science. My employment experience prior to conscripted service in the Army had been as an insurance underwriter, and I had not cared for the subjective analysis I was trained to employ in determining who was worthy of insurance. I was also disturbed, again, by the casual attitude of those who made life decisions over insurance applicants—the decisions seemed based more on stereotypical race and economic status than on scientific analysis of risk. Hence my interest in a career based on objective analysis, which wildlife science exemplified.

Fortuitously, my first two positions as a PhD university professor involved conducting and publishing applied research (science!), translation of science into formats (leaflets, newsletters, brochures, workshops) that the non-elite publics (farmers, foresters, homeowners) needed to enhance and improve their personal and workaday lives, and training of future scientists/educators (graduate students). My last two positions, as a Forest Service scientist and as an independent consultant, also involved applied research and extension of scientific findings into formats that practitioners (forest landowners, forest managers, homeowners, recreationists) needed to enhance their livelihoods and personal lives.

In my forty-year career as a scientist, manager, and teacher in the natural resource field, I often encountered elites who, because of their wealth, political influence, education, and sense of entitlement, attempted to wrench decisions regarding management of natural resources to their benefit/philosophy, playing down or discrediting established scientific fact and relying instead on unsupported economic justifications or tactics that minimized ecological factors and played up to fears of the people they were exploiting and whose lives and livelihoods they considered irrelevant and of little value. Environmental elites and exploiters are no respecters of political party—environmentalists misrepresent safety and efficacy of pesticides to prevent their use by producers of the foods they eat (livestock and crops), and developers and businesspeople pooh-pooh adverse environmental impacts of their enterprises and instead promote economic returns to peoples whose lands and resources they wished to "develop." If the arguments they were pushing were not sufficient to win the day, they often bundled environmental concerns/promotions with hot-button issues such as gun control, abortion, and landowner rights. And their behavior (supercilious, IKE dismissal of science and empirical experience versus expedient and subjective treatment of class-affected issues) was deplorably consistent across a wide spectrum of issues.

This kind of behavior, of course, is not restricted to particular fields of study or human endeavor. An analogous example is a recent administration that ignored or made up facts to thrust us into the Iraq debacle, throwing into harm's way tens of thousands of expendable troops; that derided an established body of science to debunk global warming and foster unregulated extraction and use of fossil fuels mindless of the safety of the expendables who extracted and processed the fuels and the livelihoods of the small, irrelevant people who made their livings harvesting natural resources affected by deregulated extraction; and that enacted repressive legislation that denied or made difficult access to information / medical attention on birth control that disproportionately affected low-income women.

The bottom and telling line is who benefits and who suffers. The beneficiaries have always been the privileged elites, who send young men and women off to war at no risk to themselves or their offspring, and who wear their little American flags on their lapels as proof of their "patriotism," while cutting budgets that would assist the real patriots who return no longer sound in mind or body. Would that they read the definition of "patriot," which includes risking one's life in battle for one's country in addition to merely (and safely) loving and supporting that country.

The beneficiaries have been the wealthy and educated who don't have to live in the neighborhoods adjacent to the toxic extracting and refining industrial sites where their poorer, and exposed, brethren live and work to produce the fuels for the second homes and multiple fuel-inefficient vehicles of the more fortunate.

And because of the wealth of some elites, they do not need health insurance—with their immense resources they can afford to pay for any medical expenses they incur, and they are able to secure the very best medical care money can buy.

Beginning with my experience of how exploited expendables were treated in Vietnam and extending to my observations of how entitled elites game the "system" to favor their interests by buying and owning the arbitrators of the same system and by ignoring or profaning science and fairness, I have found it a waste of time to work with these thwarters of the American dream. Instead, I have focused on working with and trying to improve the lives of the "inconsequential" people disadvantaged by birthright and/or economic status. You know, the grunts, who do the actual work, often decried as menial, of producing the goods, foods, and services we all need, in addition to providing us security at home and abroad.

Dave deCalesta mustered out of the Army at the end of his Vietnam tour in 1968 and went directly to graduate school at Colorado State University, where he earned MS and PhD degrees in wildlife ecology. He spent the next fifteen years at North Carolina State and Oregon State University teaching, conducting research, and extending his research to natural resource publics. Jumping ship in 1988, he conducted research on forest/wildlife interactions with the Forest Service in a research laboratory in northwest Pennsylvania. Retiring from the Forest Service in 2001, he opened a consulting practice, primarily helping forest landowners manage wildlife species, chiefly deer. He recently closed his consulting practice and is publishing a backlog of scientific papers, in addition to writing technical books and novels.

The Police General's Horse

NEWELL GRANT : U.S. ARMY

S ergeant Brown of the Army ROTC staff said, "Well, if you don't
sign up for ROTC now, during Freshman Week, you can't sign up
later. But you can drop it anytime during freshman and sophomore
years. And you get thirty dollars per month."

Thirty bucks a month . . . beer money, I thought. Not bad.

"OK . . . where do I sign?"

And that led to two years in the Army as a second lieutenant—a casual
decision in that first New Hampshire fall, that last halcyon time. There
were courses, ostensibly academic, as part of the ROTC program, but they
weren't of significance. The military history course had more substance
and was taught by Louis Morton, who had helped compile the official
U.S. Army history of World War II. Roger Hull and I had a conversation,
which I vaguely remember, on whether military history was a valid academic topic; I don't remember if we came to any conclusion.

The summer camp after junior year took place at Fort Devens, Massachusetts, where we went up and down a hill, night and day, sunny and
rainy, through blueberries and poison ivy. Once, during a night orienteer-
ing exercise, we went through a cemetery, across a road, and were told,
"What are you guys doing? You're way off post—you're lost!" The lesson
that has stayed with me is that, no matter how badly you mess up, how
poor a job that you may do, there is always someone who is doing worse.
Keep at it, and do the best you can.

I served during 1965 and 1966, and my first assignment was in the
training command at Fort Ord, California, as the "dean" of a school to
train supply clerks. As part of assessing the new recruits who arrived periodically, I would try to determine their education—and was astounded
to come across a recruit who said he had just graduated from Dartmouth!

I talked to him once or twice—he couldn't avoid me—and he was non-committal and evasive. I came to realize he had never gone to the college —he just threw it out. Lesson two: not everything you see or hear is true.

Then I received orders to a supply depot in Korat, Thailand, about half-way between Bangkok and Vientiane, Laos. The theory was that if the Communists (or Red Chinese, or whoever) spilled across the Mekong River into Thailand, the United States would fly in troops, start up the tanks, and take care of the problem. This was 1966, and Thailand saw a huge U.S. military buildup, but it was largely Air Force; most of the North Vietnam bombing missions originated from Thai air bases. The Thais, adept at playing the middle game, acquiesced in the U.S. military presence but definitely did not officially acknowledge us.

The Army base was a couple of miles from the Air Force base, and we would go over to their officers' mess from time to time. It was a nice club, while the Army counterpart was just bare plywood walls. There were poker games all the time, with large piles of twenty-dollar bills as the pot. That was understandable, since the flight crews were very well paid, had virtually no expenses, and were dodging antiaircraft fire on a regular basis. The tension was evident. A couple of us were having dinner there once, and it seemed to be busier than usual when a pilot walked in with his hat on. The place absolutely erupted into a wild party—the pilot had just returned from a touch-and-go landing at the Hanoi airfield, braving missiles and antiaircraft fire both on the way in and on the way out. He was a gunslinger for sure.

I served as public information officer, replacing a major who was abruptly reassigned. My duty was to publish the unit newspaper, which involved periodic trips to Bangkok, and I wrote about Thai holidays and baseball games. Sometimes I parried with reporters, if they could find me. And from time to time I arranged briefings and protocol for the various military dignitaries who came through—General Creighton Abrams, Admiral U.S. Grant Sharp Jr., and General John K. Waters, to name a few. Lesson: keep your mouth shut, and let the colonels preen.

I accompanied the colonel to a festival in Korat once, to a formal gathering at the horse racetrack. The starting gate was a rope held by two attendants. I came to the realization that the Thai police general's horses always seemed to start about a length ahead of the rest of the field. And his horses won, too, by golly.

Thai army racetrack, Korat; getting ready to start the race

Lieutenant Newell Grant delivering water in northeast Thailand

Lieutenant Grant with a dark
Thai python

The job also had certain public relations and humanitarian aspects. The Korat plateau, while never wet, was in the middle of a severe drought, and the Army mounted a program to haul water to remote villages.

While the Thais were pleasant and genial, you never really knew if that was sincere. I walked past a village shop once and noticed a picture of Ho Chi Minh on the wall—time to leave. Children were often the key to the feelings of the elders.

A village carnival, where I was on some sort of goodwill endeavor, turned quickly from happy children getting free food into a food fight, then rocks— and into a near riot. Lesson: *Lord of the Flies* is a fundamental insight into human behavior.

My last assignment was as headquarters company commander. The lesson, as the most junior officer, was to live by your wits. There are no rules for dealing with lieutenant colonels or privates (or colonels) who preferred to be in the town with their Thai girlfriends, or an erratic supply line on the wrong side of Vietnam. Food supplies were often spoiled, or late or stolen. One could get the job done if there weren't any colonels around.

That year ended with Bob Hope coming through on his Christmas tour, then home for me to a late, snowy Christmas in Colorado and promptly starting graduate school in Philadelphia. The transition from roaring F-105s taking off day and night, to late-night study sessions, drunken undergraduate parties, and antiwar protests was not easy, but much easier and shorter in duration than for many. I will never forget those who came back hurt, or those I knew whose names are on the Wall.

In retrospect, those years gave me insights I would not have gotten anywhere else: Common sense is not the same as brains, and neither is related to education, background, or money. Nor is happiness. Nor is luck. Nor success. Nor is fairness.

And that is why the police general's horse always seems to win.

Newell Grant went to the Wharton graduate school after the Army but had to drop out when his father died suddenly. He worked for several years running a large ranch near Steamboat Springs, then made it to Wall Street, where he worked for Kidder Peabody in their real estate department for about five years. He and his wife, Judy, came back to Colorado in 1975, where he worked in real estate, water rights, and asset management. They have four children and two grandchildren.

1966

U.S. launches first B-52 raids on North Vietnam.

- - - - -

Viet Cong launch a rocket attack on Tan Son Nhut Air Base,
near Saigon.

- - - - -

Father and Son

GEORGE J. FESUS : U.S. ARMY

I was in Army ROTC at Dartmouth and was commissioned a second lieutenant, armor, at graduation in 1964. I deferred my entry into the Army to attend business school, so I didn't enter active service until the fall of 1966. I had signed up for armor because I thought I would prefer riding to walking, because I had seen the movie *The Desert Fox: The Story of Rommel,* and because I spoke German and figured I would end up with a duty assignment somewhere near the Alps and skiing. However, by 1967, when my first assignment as a training officer at Fort Knox ended, the Vietnam War had really heated up, and new assignments were thrown into disarray. Consequently, I volunteered for Vietnam and was sent to Civil Affairs School and to Vietnamese Language School. To do this, I had to extend my duty commitment by three months, but that all worked out for the good in the long run.

I arrived in country in December 1967, assigned to an advisory team of about fifteen working with the provincial government and army in Go Cong Province, a rich, arable province about thirty-five miles south of Saigon in the Mekong Delta. I spent a year working with the local officials, supporting them in the construction and improvement of medical facilities, primary schools, and local marketplaces. I spoke as much in French as Vietnamese because many of the educated Vietnamese had learned fluent French during the French colonial era.

In addition to my regular jobs, I was also able to meet with my father, an eye surgeon, sixty-seven years old at the time. He had given up his practice in Baltimore for three months and served in the regional Vietnamese hospital in Can Tho, the largest city in the Mekong Delta. At the time he was the oldest doctor to volunteer to go to Vietnam, and won outstanding recognition for his service and his treatment of Vietnamese civilians with eye problems.

Things got a little tense for our team during the Tet attacks in 1968, but we did not experience the same major onslaughts as other areas saw. The province survived quite successfully, and I was convinced that the people there wanted nothing to do with North Vietnamese invasion or with Viet Cong sympathizers.

I was quite sorry to leave after the year. I was also aware of the fact that, unlike my predecessors in World War II, I had the privilege of being rotated out of an unfinished war, which, when all was said and done, was not vital to the survival of the United States, as victory in World War II had been. I was also eager to get on with the rest of my life.

The fact that I had extended my duty period by three months meant that I got out of the Army in December 1968. That gave me time to go to Austria to ski for three months before the start of corporate recruiting at business schools. It was during those three months that I met my wife, Susan, who was from San Francisco and also happened to be skiing in St. Anton, Austria.

I found my tour in Go Cong significant and satisfying. I confess to being a lifelong, resolute anticommunist. My parents escaped Hungary just as communism was taking hold in the late 1940s, so I have always known communism to be the most repressive and suffocating form of government ever forced on people. Every form of government is imperfect. Churchill is reputed to have said: "Democracy is the worst form of government, except for all the others." Communism is surely the vilest. Even dictatorships have had benevolent dictators. And, in my view, there was no doubt that, at least in Go Cong, the population did not want this North Vietnamese invasion and did not support the Viet Cong cadres. The 1.5 million South Vietnamese refugees who got into boats and tried to flee Vietnam after the fall of Saigon seem to have borne that out. I believe that all Americans and I were sent to Vietnam to help the people of South Vietnam improve their lot, withstand the false promises of a Communist dictatorship, and keep their individual freedom. Vietnam was a very different war from Afghanistan and Iraq. We went into Afghanistan and Iraq to protect and further direct U.S. interests.

We went into Afghanistan to achieve a U.S. objective: to hunt down and neutralize al-Qaida and prevent the safe haven that had been provided them by the Taliban government.

We went into Iraq to remove a dictator who we, and the Western world, believed was a growing threat to Middle East and world peace, and to America's safety, through the potential use and proliferation of weapons of mass destruction.

In Vietnam, there were no direct threats to America, no interests to protect, and no direct benefits. We went in to help South Vietnam fight off an invasion from the North and subjugation by a Communist government.

I am sorry we were not able to do that, but in the end I think we accomplished a lot, and Vietnam will get there. Communist states of the twentieth century did not want to have free societies at their borders. Had the Vietnam War not delayed and weakened the export of communism from China, I do believe that the neighboring dominoes would also have fallen. And now I believe the shortcomings and lies of communism are more obvious, and the tide of philosophy is turning back toward individual initiative, freedom, and democracy. The societal progress China and Vietnam have been making in this century are due to the returning entrepreneurship and initiative of their citizens, and to the easing of control and tyranny of their governments. One day, Vietnam will be a free society, and just as Leningrad again became St. Petersburg, so Ho Chi Minh City will one day again become Saigon.

Would that have eventually happened anyway, without intervention by the United States in the '60s and '70s . . . as it is slowly happening in China? Who knows. But the U.S. effort certainly didn't hurt the cause of freedom, in Vietnam or in the rest of Asia.

George Fesus completed his military service with the Vietnam posting, got married, and went to work in New York. He had a seventeen-year career in credit card marketing and management at American Express and MasterCard International, with postings in Australia, the UK, and New York. In 1984 he moved to Boston to join State Street Bank and retired in 1995 as CFO. He and Susan moved west to spend half the year in Aspen and half in San Francisco. Skiing is still their number-one hobby.

A Life Saved

WILLARD COOK : U.S. NAVY

The first six months of my year in Vietnam (July 1967–July 1968) were spent stationed at the White Elephant in Da Nang working for Rear Admiral Paul Lacey Jr. The last half of my tour was served as a supply officer in the huge Naval Support Activity supply depot in Da Nang. This supply depot supported all allied activities in I Corps, the northernmost sector of South Vietnam. Our customers were Korean, Australian, and British troops, as well as all U.S. troops.

As a customer service supply officer in the supply depot, I was in charge of expediting strategic matériel. The Tet offensive began in January 1968 and created a great deal of pressure on "supply types" to get the proper and adequate material needed in the field.

Some of our most important customers were the U.S. Marines stationed up north at Khe Sanh and other villages next to the demilitarized zone (DMZ). When the Tet offensive started, I was besieged with requests for concertina wire for camps to strengthen their perimeters.

We obviously had not anticipated this surprise offensive, so had not stocked enough concertina wire to meet the demand. I immediately placed several orders to get as much as I could from multiple sources. I tried hard to raise the purchase order priority designation so that the concertina wire would be shipped immediately. I tried all the routine and acceptable methods I knew to expedite such supplies, but I couldn't get it shipped . . . and I had fierce pressure exerted on me from the Marines who needed it.

One day my creative juices kicked in, and I simply signed the purchase order with the name of my commanding officer—his name and rank would expedite those supplies! And, lo and behold, the concertina wire was received expeditiously.

A couple of weeks after the precious concertina wire was received, I was called into the commander's office. He asked me about those particular orders and told me that he himself had not placed that order. I immediately admitted to signing his name "in order to get the materials," as my own efforts had been futile.

He explained to me very kindly, but very clearly, that there was a reason he had three bars on his shirt collar and why I had only one. He had years of experience and could be trusted to make those kinds of decisions, while I had very limited experience. He appreciated my efforts but explained that I should never do that again. I remembered that conversation and lesson for many years when I was frustrated with the way "my superiors" handled my ideas and requests. I have even used the same language and example to employees junior to me, when circumstances warranted it, now that I am a seasoned senior citizen!

My most memorable experience in Vietnam, however, is much more personal.

The Saved Life

One night in February 1968, during the Tet offensive, I was lying on my cot in the bachelor officers' quarters of Camp Tien Sha, where most Navy personnel were billeted while serving shore duty in Da Nang. I was friends with fellow officers who served on the security staff of the camp, and recently I had overheard them talk about "evacuation drills" when they would sound a siren and monitor us as we headed into the sandbagged bunkers strategically placed throughout the camp.

When the siren sounded this night I was just too tired to treat it seriously; I decided it was strictly a drill. I would simply wait it out there on my cot.

Unfortunately, I became scared to death when I heard several explosions. This was the Tet offensive, after all! It was too late to make a run to the bunker, because I would expose myself to shrapnel and other explosives, so I hid under my cot in the corner of my room, all curled up.

It was here that I confessed my belief in and allegiance to Jesus Christ. I became a "foxhole Christian," although not literally in a foxhole.

The Back Story

In junior high I attended a church camp at the First Presbyterian Church in Sheridan, Wyoming. One day our teacher, Mabel Johnston, told us the story of the crucifixion of Christ in the company of the two thieves. She explained how the second thief confessed his belief that Jesus was the Christ and was being punished unjustly while they, the thieves, deserved their punishment. In response to this confession of belief, Jesus told this second thief, "Today you will be with me in paradise" (Luke 23:40–43).

Well, as I listened to this account from the Bible, I started thinking, "Hmmm, all I need to do is to confess to Christ before I die and I can go to heaven. . . . I won't have to worry about all the Christian restrictions on the 'good life,' here and now." Yes, I thought that I was a pretty smart young man.

From that time on I developed several variations of the "deathbed confession," which I learned to recite in about two minutes. After I learned to drive I drove back and forth from Wyoming to Detroit ferrying cars for my father's Ford dealership, and I figured out that I might not actually have two minutes to get right with God. A car accident might happen suddenly, so I compressed my confession into less than sixty seconds.

Then, as I attended Dartmouth and flew back and forth across the United States, I realized that I might not even have sixty seconds to complete this safety net of getting into heaven. I compressed my confession into some fifteen seconds.

Of course, I did not want to deal with the thought that I could be snuffed out at any moment while stationed in Da Nang.

"Presumption" is the word that best describes my attitude toward God. As smart as I thought I was, I had not preconceived a scenario where I might not have even fifteen seconds to make myself right with the Creator. Now, reflecting back on this whole life-changing episode, I am not certain that one of my prefabricated confessions would have sufficed. I now understand that this one-sided discussion with God is not like presenting a "get out of jail free card," which I had carefully tucked under my pillow. I was acknowledging and confessing allegiance to the Creator of the Universe. This was worthy of serious consideration.

I am humbled that my Lord chose to get my attention and gave me time to make the correct decision that night in Da Nang. I have served him since.

Upon rereading this account I am inclined to point out the similarities between these two events—both challenging authority—which have, to this day, affected my life. The comparison, of course, is strictly superficial.

It is the same as comparing one's whistle to call a dog with the full symphony playing Beethoven's Fifth. Although these two events both brought me face to face with yielding to authority, the one was temporal and limited, the second is bowing down to the Creator.

After Dartmouth Willard Cook earned an MBA from Northwestern University and then went on to Officer Candidate School in Newport, Rhode Island. While at Newport he met Sarah Francis from Cody, Wyoming, through another OCS candidate, who was also from Wyoming. He and Sarah were married in June 1969.

In the fall of 1969, they moved back to Willard's hometown of Sheridan, and he went into business with his father as a dealer principal in a Ford, Lincoln-Mercury dealership. Over the years he served as a dealer representative in many local, state, and national automotive organizations, including as a director for the National Automobile Dealers' Association. He sold the business in 1998 and moved to the Boston area to be able to enjoy its many cultural offerings.

The Cooks have two daughters and two grandchildren.

The Maturing of a Dartmouth Marine

LEE A. CHILCOTE : U.S. MARINE CORPS

n June 2012 I participated in Marine Week in Cleveland, Ohio. Other than an early viewing of the Vietnam Memorial in Washington, D.C., I had not joined in any Vietnam-era event since retiring as a Marine Corps captain in December 1968. As I watched the Marine Corps Drill Team, the Marine Corps Band, and a mock invasion by the Marines of 3/25 across the tarmac of Burke Lakefront Airfield in downtown Cleveland, my mind flashed back fifty years to my first training as a platoon leader candidate in Quantico, Virginia, in June 1962.

As I walked among the crowd of nearly one hundred thousand veterans, widows, family members, and other Marine Corps supporters, I was struck by the juxtaposition of the young Marines and the older crowd. The Marines were mesmerizing the crowd with their skill and discipline, while many of us were realizing how long ago we served. I suddenly remembered that as a young Marine Corps captain, I was part of similar exercises in 1968 in Washington, D.C., as a part of what was then called the Defense Orientation Conference Association (an earlier goodwill effort by the Marine Corps to maintain and develop support among the civilian business leaders).

Except for the officers, none of the Marines I saw on that hot summer day in June 2012 was older than twenty-five. I met the commanding officer, Michael Branigan, a lieutenant general with thirty years' experience, only to realize, as we talked, that he was not yet fifty years old, and although a high-ranking officer, he was more than twenty years my junior. How old was I when I served? Could I have just been twenty-five? My God, I was!

My mind flashed back to my first days at Dartmouth. When I arrived in September 1960, I can recall that I was somewhat intimidated by the pros-

Lee Chilcote

pect of being in college and was somewhat afraid to jump into extracurricular activities. Other than sports and outdoor activities, which I had done in high school (including soccer, swimming, skiing, and canoeing), I could not conceive of doing anything outside of studies. So I played freshman soccer, participated in the Dartmouth Outing Club, joined the Ledyard Canoe Club, and skied, all activities I had done all of my life up until then. However, as life would have it, I met some classmates who were signing up for Navy and Army ROTC. After listening to them and receiving encouragement from my father (Dartmouth '30), I enlisted in the U.S. Naval Reserve and immediately began to understand and believe that serving one's country was a duty and a privilege.

I took a tortuous route to the Marine Corps. I started out in NROTC and convinced myself that I was Navy all the way. As a Dartmouth freshman in 1960, I signed up for the NROTC rifle team. I had learned marksmanship during my days as a camper and had earned the National Rifle Association's expert riflemen badge with eight bars by the time I was fifteen and was a pretty accurate rifleman. We shot competitively against a few other NROTC teams and generally won.

During my first Dartmouth spring vacation in March 1961, at the suggestion of the then NROTC commander, I qualified for and attended a preflight training program in Pensacola, Florida. At that point, I had 20/20 vision and was a good candidate to become a Navy pilot. What an exciting time! We were schooled as pilots in an intensive three-day class setting, tested psychologically and physically, and then asked to fly second position in a T-34 jet trainer, both off a landing field and an aircraft carrier. I was mesmerized by the prospect of becoming a pilot. When we were catapulted off the World War II small carrier, I found the experience exhilarating. When we experienced 8G of force coming out of a dive, I was surprised that I did not black out and was able to keep control of the plane. I felt as if flying could be for me.

During my second Dartmouth spring vacation, I had the privilege to attend submarine training at New London, Connecticut. The purpose was twofold. First, I was being considered for an appointment by the secretary of the Navy to become a regular NROTC candidate, and second, I was interested in whether I could become a submariner. I went to New London that spring with high hopes, but after the experience realized that a Navy life was not for me. That was the turning point.

At Dartmouth we were required to take Navy technical classes and military history. Our professor was our NROTC commander. We had a Navy man for 1960 and 1961. In 1962, a new commander, Major Philip Frazier, was appointed. Major Frazier was a veteran Marine Corps officer, whose father was a Marine colonel who had served in World War II and in China. Philip was born and raised in China. Major Frazier had served in Korea and had just served as the senior Marine aboard ships in the Bay of Pigs invasion in April 1961. He came to Dartmouth shortly thereafter with his wife, whom he had met and married in China.

I met Major Frazier almost as he arrived at Dartmouth, fresh from his experience at the Bay of Pigs. Coming off my negative experience at New London, I was ready to consider a change from a pathway leading to a commission as a regular Navy officer to a commitment to the Marine Corps. I can remember spending several sessions with Major Frazier, listening to his warnings to me against making a decision before truly understanding what a complete commitment to the Marine Corps required. He told me that most Marines came from military families whose members had served in the Corps; that I would need to do well at one or two summers at Platoon Leaders Class (PLC) in Quantico; and that just because I was in good shape and a good athlete was no guarantee that I would be selected. He said that more than half of those who attended summer camp would not be selected. His warnings only made me more determined to convert my opportunity for a four-year regular Navy commission to a Marine Corps commission. I clearly did not understand what lay in store for me, nor did I understand that Major Frazier was truly concerned that I would not make it.

I had my first PLC experience in Quantico in the summer of 1962. I was shocked. I rolled into Quantico on an early July evening. In less than thirty minutes, I was under the gaze of a drill instructor from Parris Island, South Carolina, who was describing me as the scum of the earth, a silver-spoon-fed Ivy Leaguer who would never make it in the Corps that the drill instructor had known and loved for his thirty-five years. I suddenly realized that despite my heavy involvement in athletics, I had no background or experience for the rigors I was about to face.

That summer was the most difficult of my life up to that point. While I did well on all the runs, marches, and other physical requirements, I did not do well in mastering the leadership development skills that the Marine Corps was trying to inculcate. I thought my physical prowess was enough and partially sloughed off the heavy criticism of my performance and potential to be a Marine officer. To my utter horror, I was told at the end of the summer that I would not be recommended for a commission as a Marine Corps officer. I remember a young lieutenant telling me that he did not think I had what it took to be a Marine. That hurt.

For the first time in my life, something did not come easy. I had been rejected. I went back to Dartmouth and was afraid to talk to anyone about what had happened and was confused about what I should do.

I finally sat down with Major Frazier, who reminded me of his warnings earlier that year. I begged for his support and stated that I wanted another shot at the Marine Corps. He said he would think about it and get back to me. By January 1963, Major Frazier had somehow persuaded himself and the Marine Corps to allow me to attend a second summer at Quantico. His support was life changing. I now knew that I was willing to put every ounce of my physical and mental energy into the second opportunity.

To be sure that I was ready, I constantly sought advice from Major Frazier, read and studied Marine Corps history voraciously, and kept in top shape during the winter months by running inside the old field house that preceded Leverone Field House. I even trained for and fought my way to the finals of the Dartmouth wrestling intramurals, mainly as a way of maintaining my conditioning. Word that military advisers were being sent to Vietnam was beginning to surface in the media, but there was no talk of sending troops.

The summer of 1963 was a repeat experience in terms of requirements, but entirely different in terms of my attitude. I was determined to finish first among platoon leader candidates. After two weeks of the six weeks, I was beginning to gain the respect of the drill inspectors. They could see how badly I wanted to be a Marine Corps officer.

During the third week, a make-or-break incident occurred. While we were running on what was known as the Hill Trail, with sixty-pound packs on our back, a candidate collapsed directly in front of me. At that moment, no drill instructor was around, and I could see that the candidate was suffering from extreme heat exhaustion. We had already had one candidate die that summer, so I knew I had to make a choice as to whether to go on or stay with the candidate. However, we had been advised not to stop in the event one of our fellow candidates ran into trouble. Despite the admonition, I chose to stay with the candidate, which meant I would not likely be first in the Hill Trail run and would probably be disciplined. I immediately took my canteen and poured all the water I had on him. Just then, the drill instructor came up, saw what I was doing, and ordered me to get back on the Hill Trail. I did so immediately and ultimately ended up finishing the trail run first. I wasn't sure what reaction I would get.

Later that evening, I was thoroughly chewed out by the drill instructor for not staying on the trail. However, for the first time in my Marine Corps experience, I could tell that the drill instructor was really proud of me for evidencing the leadership skills of an officer. At that moment, I knew I would be a Marine Corps officer. Sure enough, at the end the summer, I was recommended as the top candidate within my company. Two times was the charm.

The remainder of my Dartmouth experience was inconsequential insofar as the Marine Corps was concerned. I dropped the Navy rifle team activity, attended mandatory NROTC drill sessions, and completed eight history classes with Major Frazier, which I thoroughly enjoyed. I graduated in June 1964 with the rest of our class, but stayed at Dartmouth that summer and for my fifth year at Thayer School of Engineering.

In June 1965, I graduated from the Thayer School, was commissioned as a Marine Corps second lieutenant, and immediately received orders to report to Officer Candidate School in Quantico. Although President Lyndon Johnson began to raise the troop level in Vietnam in June 1965, I could have requested and would have been granted a service deferral to attend my second year at Tuck School (I had completed one year in conjunction with my Thayer program). I chose not to request a deferral and was actually eager to report for duty.

As in the case of my PLC experience, I was determined to finish near the top in OCS. Having had two difficult PLC summers was a distinct advantage.

Many of the officer candidates came from prominent Marine Corps families. One significant example was Lewis B. Puller Jr., who was in the candidate class that reported to Quantico just after us. His father was the legendary Lewis (Chesty) Puller Sr., whose heroism in the Pacific during World War II made him the most decorated Marine in the history of the Corps. The younger Puller went to Vietnam in late 1967 as a Marine first lieutenant. After a land mine explosion on October 11, 1968, that riddled his body with shrapnel, he lingered near death for days, and his weight dropped to fifty-five pounds. He had lost his legs and parts of both hands. According to his own account in a book he wrote, entitled *Fortunate Son*, and to the accounts of friends and associates, he survived primarily because of his iron will and his stubborn refusal to die, a trait he had clearly inherited from his father. After he returned to reasonably sound physical condition, he served for years as a lawyer at the Pentagon. He remained a prominent veterans activist until his death. But it was his harrowing experience in Vietnam that defined his life. Though he had a law degree and had mounted an unsuccessful campaign for Congress in eastern Virginia, he battled black periods of despondency. He drank heavily until 1981, when he underwent treatment for alcoholism. He shot and killed himself in 1994.

My experience at OCS was outstanding. Many of the candidates who were sons of prominent Marines simply underestimated my determination. By this time, I had learned to keep quiet and not get too close to my competition. I ultimately finished second in my class.

The six months of OCS were very competitive and were at times life challenging. We took numerous courses in weaponry, map reading, leadership, and counterinsurgency. As I look back, the counterinsurgency training was the most curious. At that time, the United Sates had no recent experience fighting nonconventional wars. Apparently not knowing what to teach young Marine officers, the Marine Corps chose to teach the tactics of Che Guevara, an Argentine-born Marxist revolutionary, who was prominent first in the Cuban Revolution and later in Bolivia, where he was captured and executed in 1967. The intent was to expose us, as young lieutenants, to the psychological and physical methods used by Che in Cuba and Latin America as a means to create a better understanding of what we would face in Vietnam. At that time, troops were just arriving in Vietnam, and very few of our commanders had served in combat, and none in a counterinsurgency.

Despite the apparent incongruity of using the methods and tactics of an experienced Marxist leader, the training was helpful for what we would face in Vietnam. It focused on physical fitness, reflex firing techniques, and tactics. The training was practical, with discussions, case studies, model and outdoor exercises. Live situations were created during the outdoor exercises to judge the reaction of the officer candidates at the spur of the moment. We were taught to traverse difficult and hostile terrain, and eat and sleep like the guerrillas of Che's own forces. Unfortunately, however, as far as I recall, none of the drill instructors had had any experience in fighting insurgents or terrorists.

As the months wore on, it became apparent to me that I would finish high in my officer candidate class. Each week was more difficult than the previous one, but I did well. About two weeks before the end of the school, a few of the candidates had dropped out or were asked to leave; yet we knew that more than 20 percent of the class would not make it. The moment of truth came in late November 1965.

As a test of our stamina and mental fortitude, the entire class was taken on a rigorous physical course that concluded with a thirty-mile march. Prior to the march, each of us had to traverse several obstacle courses, climb ropes, and complete push-ups, pull-ups, and sit-ups. It was evident to all of us that if you exhausted yourself excelling at the obstacle courses, ropes, and calisthenics, you might not finish the march, so you had to conserve your energy. The pressure was enormous. As I recall, I completed 150 push-ups, 50 pull-ups, and 200 sit-ups in order to ensure that I would be in the running for winning the entire course. As soon as we completed the first portion of the exercise, we were sent off on the march. I wondered whether I had expended too much energy on the first portion of the exercise.

The march was grueling. We each had to carry sixty-pound packs. The march was continuous and was designed to break those who were not ready. At one point, when more than three-quarters into the march, I was walking in my sleep but had no recognition that I was asleep. I did not even know that it was possible for a human to carry a sixty-pound pack and keep a pace while sleeping—I assure you that you can. You will yourself to do it. However, many of the candidates did not remain standing and fell off the march. At the end of the march, about three-quarters of us had completed the course. Those who did knew that they would finish the school with a high ranking and that in all likelihood they would have their choice of MOS (military occupation code) and duty. For me, it was infantry officer (0302) and Vietnam. It was well-known that those in the top ten would automatically have their choice.

During the last week, they announced the rankings: I had finished second out of 150 and received my requested MOS of 0302 and orders to Camp Pendleton, California, in preparation for duty in Vietnam. We finished school in late November 1965. Two battalions of the Ninth Marine Regiment of the Third Marine Division had been deployed to Vietnam between June and December 1965. My orders were to join the rear elements of the division in Camp Pendleton for further infantry training and deployment to Vietnam. Marine Corps officers are trained in the same way as the enlisted Marines, and therefore it was expected that new officers coming from OCS would go through the same infantry training schools as Marines coming from boot camp at Parris Island.

After a brief leave at home, I traveled to California to report at Camp Pendleton. My mother, who feared it might be the last time that she would see me, asked whether she could accompany me to California by car. I readily accepted.

We had a great trip traveling the southwest route from Cleveland, where I lived, through St. Louis and then west through Oklahoma, Texas, New Mexico, Arizona, and to San Diego. In traveling through New Mexico, we were able to visit a ranch property, known as Heart Bar Ranch, that had been acquired by my father, Lee A. Chilcote, '30, and seven other Dartmouth alumni, including Charles M. French, '26. When we arrived in San Diego, we transferred the car in which we were traveling to Charles French so my mother could fly back to Cleveland.

I reported for duty in December 1965 at Camp Pendleton and was immediately assigned to a week of live-firing infantry exercises. As soon as I completed those exercises, my orders were modified to ship out to Vietnam—before Christmas. Ultimately, these orders were delayed, and we did not fly out of Coronado, California, until the third week of January 1966. We flew for twenty-six hours, refueling in Hawaii and landing briefly in Guam, before arriving in Okinawa in the Ryuku Islands. We spent four days there, and I had a chance to meet mostly elderly Japanese. I was struck by the lack of emotion, other than laughter, that was shown. It seemed to me at the time that the elderly people still bore the memories and tragedy of World War II on their thin faces, but maybe I was imagining what I wanted to believe. On February 23, 1966, I wrote: "Okinawans are hard and cold people, scratching the earth to find their livelihood."

I arrived in Da Nang, Vietnam, on February 24, 1966, and reported to Colonel Simmons, then commanding officer, Ninth Marine Regiment, Third Marine Division, and Lieutenant Colonel Dolan, commanding officer, First Battalion. I was immediately assigned to lead Second Platoon, A/19 Company, known in Marine jargon as A 1/9. The company commander was Captain Christy.

Staff Sergeant Thompson had commanded the platoon. The prior second lieutenant had been killed in action a month earlier. For the first few days, the platoon was positioned on the perimeter of the base and undertook only limited patrols. The limited activity allowed me to familiarize myself with my platoon.

In early March, I led three so-called "civic action" patrols. On one of the patrols, as we approached a small village known as Ap Moi, a slow drumbeat started. We could not tell whether this was to warn the Viet Cong (also known as the National Liberation Front, or NLF). As we walked through the village, we could feel genuine friendship from some of the villagers, but were also wary—who were the Viet Cong, and who were not? As we exited the village, we approached the Cam Le Bridge. A firefight was taking place across the river in which a unit from Second Battalion, Third Marines, was engaged. At the same time we could see NBC interviewing troops from another unit that was behind us. A bit later, as we entered another village, I met a Vietnamese man who spoke clear French. I was somewhat fluent in French, so I attempted to talk to him. He was elderly, and I knew he would recall the French colonization of Vietnam, so I asked him about the French occupation. We had difficulty communicating, because his French was such a mixture of dialects, and my French was not as strong as I had thought. After some exchanges about the withdrawal of the French after the battle of Dien Bien Phu in 1954 (First Indochina War), he wrote the following for me on a piece of paper: "L'homme sans amour est comme les fleurs sans odeur"—A man without love is like flowers without a smell. This was this Vietnamese man's way of expressing his hatred for the French, and a warning to me to not make the same mistake in handling the Vietnamese people. What a juxtaposition of events: a firefight, a media interview, and a warning from an old French-speaking Vietnamese, all in the same afternoon.

I spent the rest of March, and all of April 1966, conducting patrols around Da Nang. Places such Hill 55 and Hill 22 became familiar to me, and we learned where all the spider holes, tunnels, and escape routes were located. It was a constant effort to set up ambushes on both sides. Land mines and surprise Viet Cong mortar attacks were our greatest threat. I lost two Marines during this period, both by well-aimed mortar rounds. Many units did not fare as well as we did, mainly as a result of mines laid by the Viet Cong along village paths and other access points to the villages that we patrolled. Because of the open nature of rice paddies, which made troops traversing them an easy target for the Viet Cong, it was difficult not to follow the tree-lined pathways through the village. I was fortunate that I had very experienced Marines who could uncover booby traps.

Beginning in May 1966, our battalion left the Da Nang area and moved into An Hoa and then to Phu An, at the beginning of an operation known as Operation Georgia. Upon arriving at Phu An, we were immediately put on alert and very quickly loaded into LVTs and moved out in replacement of L Company (I later found out that L Company had four killed in action and thirty-four wounded and had killed eighteen Viet Cong.)

As we moved into position I could see the men that L Company had lost (they had been carried to LVTs and covered with ponchos), as well as several Viet Cong that were lying dead nearby. Suddenly, just as we were getting into position, a mortar round landed a few feet from me in the middle of one of my squads. In the midst of the smoke and confusion, one of the men yelled out "Sergeant Sewell is dead, and they got the lieutenant." I assured everyone that I was alive and still in the lead. However, I quickly discovered that Sergeant Sewell, one of my best squad leaders, had received a direct hit and been killed instantly. Lance Corporal Shipko instinctively took control of the squad, but then hit a mine just down the path from where the mortar round had landed. I could see that Shipko had lost a leg, and I ordered the corpsman to give him morphine, but I also knew that he had lost too much blood to survive. Another man had been hit by a piece of shrapnel that had traveled through his left cheek. Another trooper, Corporal Derritt, lay dying, and I knew it. At this point, my men were panicked, and it took all I could muster to keep them moving and calm. I knew that the most important thing was to keep moving toward the enemy, which is exactly what we did. It worked. We flushed out and killed a number of Viet Cong and captured 81 mm mortars and other equipment. After the firefight ended, two of my troops went into shock and became nonresponsive. I tried to work with them, but as each mortar round exploded, they went into deeper shock. In all, we had received twenty mortar rounds from two different directions and had lost three killed and four wounded. We counted more than thirty Viet Cong either killed (ten) or captured (twenty), found large, recently used Viet Cong tunnels, and uncovered and detonated several Russian mines.

Operation Georgia went on for several more weeks, and our experiences in firefights were similar to what is described above. The day-in and day-out stress of anticipating a firefight for more than four weeks was one of the most intense times of my Vietnam experience. I learned later that my work in Operation Georgia (and Operations Hastings and Prairie, discussed later) earned me a Bronze Star with a Combat V. I was able to support one of my men for a Silver Star, which was awarded posthumously.

In May 1966, I was taken out of the field and assigned to the Headquarters and Service Company of 1/9, pending reassignment to the northern area of South Vietnam. The North Vietnamese Army was known to be moving south, and the word was that the Marines would be moving north to interdict the movement south.

I spent about two weeks at 1/9 headquarters and was assigned to conduct interrogations. For the first few interrogations, I watched other officers and enlisted men conduct them, and then finally, on May 31, 1966, I conducted my own. We traveled to a nearby village known as La Tho Bac. The village was thought to be friendly, but was likely controlled by Viet Cong at night. Interrogations involved asking control questions to which we knew the answers and then intertwining questions designed to elicit information that would establish whether the interrogated person was telling the truth. The villagers were now used to seeing and conversing with Marine patrols, and there had been no snipers, mines, or other signs of Viet Cong for many weeks, so it was good opportunity to test the sentiments of the village.

I interrogated a younger Vietnamese woman. Some of the more than fifty questions and answers that we recorded provide a flavor for what was going on at the time:

Question: "Why don't you leave with all the fighting around your village?" Answer: "Our family has always lived here, and we do not have anywhere to go." (See question about relatives, below.)

Question: "Do the Viet Cong force you to pay taxes?" Answer: No, she would not pay. (We had captured Viet Cong who admitted that they had extracted monies from the villagers.)

Question: "Do you have relatives living elsewhere?" Answer: "Yes, we have an aunt and uncle in Saigon." (Because of her answer above, we later became convinced that she was very likely a Viet Cong supporter.)

Question: "Do you see the Viet Cong at night?" Answer: "No. They stay in their spider holes." (We knew that the opposite was true, and the Viet Cong were in their spider holes during the day—she was likely misleading us so we would not come into the villages at night.)

Question: "Where are the men of the village?" Answer: "Most of them work in Da Nang." (Many of the village men were likely Viet Cong and would actually stay in the village with their families when they could.)

Question: "When did you last have a school for the villagers?" Answer: "The French were here seven years ago, and I learned French and many things about France then. The Viet Cong never came here then." (This was an honest answer.)

Question: "When did the village last have a chief?" Answer: "Six years ago before the French left. He was killed, and no one will take the job." (This was an honest answer.)

Through this interrogation process, I began to realize that South Vietnam was extremely weak as a country and that the departure of the French years earlier had left a huge vacuum, which was being filled by the Viet Cong. I began to wonder: How would the United States be able to bolster the South Vietnamese when we could not even establish rapport with nearby supposedly "friendly" villagers?

In June 1966, I was reassigned to G 2/9 and flown to Phu Bai. From there, we were helicoptered into a new area near a town known as Đông Hà. It was the northernmost town in South Vietnam and was ultimately the location of the most strategically important combat base maintained by the United Sates at the time. The Marines of 2/9 were outposted to Đông Hà to provide surveillance and interdiction of North Vietnamese troop movements across the DMZ. Đông Hà is the capital of Quang Tri Province and is situated at the crossroads of what is known today as National Highway 1A and Route 9.

The Marine Corps base at Đông Hà was established during the summer months of 1966. The 2/9 was the first unit to be outposted there since the arrival of the Marines in Vietnam in June 1965. Many other units from the Ninth Marines and several Army artillery units soon joined us. At that time, the 3,900-foot airstrip had not been built, and Đông Hà was one of the most remote outposts in Vietnam. Our assignment was to establish a perimeter and provide protection for the development of the airstrip. I remained based there until March 1967, although our unit also conducted operations between Đông Hà and Khe Sanh, about sixty-five kilometers to the southeast.

It is those operations that (most?) stir my memory. Khe Sanh is located a few thousand yards south of the Roa Quan River dividing South Vietnam from North Vietnam and just east of the border with Laos. Most will recall Khe Sanh from the Tet offensive of 1968, without question the finest hour of the Marine Corps in Vietnam. In the first days of that offensive, no activity occurred at Khe Sanh. However, the North Vietnamese Army (NVA) had lodged large artillery batteries around the hills surrounding Khe Sanh, and beginning in late February 1968, the NVA attacked several of the strategic hills around Khe Sanh. The battle of Khe Sanh went on for nearly half a year. The 2/9 Marines were heroic in that fight.

Our time in the area between Đông Hà and Khe Sanh in late 1966 and early 1967 was nothing like what 2/9 faced in Khe Sanh during 1968. However, there was one encounter I will never forget. In November 1966, I was field-promoted to the rank of first lieutenant. At the time, I was conducting company-size patrols in the jungle area around Đông Hà. We had not seen any heavy action, although there were sightings of NVA regulars in the area and a number of empty encampments containing AK-47s and other Russian weapons had been found. Intelligence reported that significant troop movements had been spotted to the west along the Ho Chi Minh Trail. Shortly thereafter, we received orders to form a regimental-size unit and to move west to the area in an effort to interdict the North Vietnamese Army regulars as they traversed into South Vietnam. As the senior platoon leader within the regiment, I was assigned to lead the point company (our company commander had been killed in action, and I was appointed as acting company commander of G 2/9).

The operation, known as Operation Hastings (sometimes called Prairie), lasted from the beginning of October to the end of November 1966.

As we left the relatively open terrain of the Đông Hà base, the terrain quickly became impenetrable jungle. Here I was, leading nearly a thousand Marines through an area that could only be traversed by using a good machete.

As any good infantry commander knows, if you are leading a large contingent of Marines, it is critical to keep small scouting patrols on the flanks of the main unit. Imagine trying to do this in steep jungle terrain. As we traveled farther from Đông Hà toward the Ho Chi Minh Trail, the terrain became filled with deep ravines and steep hillsides. We were literally funneled down the steep ravines and would find ourselves walking single file down a stream. I would periodically stop the column and re-establish the flanks, but then would almost immediately receive an order from the regimental commander to move forward more rapidly.

One of the smaller incidents of the operation comes to mind. At one point when my unit had been largely funneled into a single column in the middle of a small river and seemed particularly vulnerable, we came to an open sunny spot, and I ordered the troops to set a perimeter and rest. No sooner had I given the order that a shot rang out, clearly from one of my troops. I moved toward the sound of the shot, only to find one of my squad leaders standing over a fourteen-foot python. The squad leader had completely forgotten that we were near the Ho Chi Minh Trail trying to preserve an element of surprise.

Within a few days, we came upon the Ho Chi Minh Trail. As we traversed in parallel just off both sides of the trail, we found triangular trenched areas that had obviously recently been occupied by North Vietnamese regulars. We were fearful that these would be prime areas for ambush and were hesitant to go into them, but soon learned that these entrenched areas were merely stopovers for the North Vietnamese regulars as they completed another day's travel south. We tried to post a few troops in these areas in the late afternoon, thinking we would have advance warning of arriving units stopping over.

A few nights later, we spotted a regular North Vietnamese unit, probably a company, moving toward us. We spread out on both sides of the Ho Chi Minh Trail and waited. The sun had set, and the light was fading. Our company was quite far forward from the regiment, so I called for backup Marines to join us. Apparently thinking that there was time to helicopter in additional troops before the North Vietnamese regulars got close, the regimental commander ordered a helicopter to land at our location. Although I am certain that everyone understood that the sound of the helicopter would pinpoint our location, being the Marines that we were, we believed that this was a positive. We actually took up positions in one of triangular trenched encampment areas, thereby inviting an attack. The North Vietnamese regulars did not fall into our trap. Although I will never be certain, it seemed likely that the North Vietnamese spotted our location while traveling south, veered to the west, and occupied positions on the west, north, and south of our unit. We were partly surrounded and outnumbered. At the time, we thought that the North Vietnamese unit was considerably northwest of our location.

Within a few minutes of my call for backup, a helicopter came over a nearby hillside and began to land in the middle of the triangular trenched areas where we were positioned. All hell broke loose. Before we could react, the helicopter had been hit, was spiraling down to the ground, and crashed. To our amazement, the North Vietnamese apparently did not realize that we had many men on the ground and immediately moved in to capture the pilot and the troops who had crawled out of the helicopter.

Imagine the situation: It was night, and the only light was from the burning helicopter. The Marines who had been faced outward from the triangular trenched area were now turned inward and started firing on the North Vietnamese who were approaching the helicopter and its pilot. From the light of the burning helicopter, we could see that the pilot had been killed and the only troops inside the perimeter were North Vietnamese. I do not recall whether or not I called for a cease-fire, but in any event, the initial panic firing quickly subsided, and I could see Marine figures moving in and capturing the North Vietnamese who had ventured inside the perimeter of the trenched area. Then, all hell broke loose again. The bulk of the North Vietnamese who had remained outside the perimeter opened up. The battle raged all night. I can remember feeling so fatigued that I was not sure I could keep my head up, even though tracer bullets were flying all around us. At one particularly desperate moment as I lay behind a tree, I could feel the pounding of the bullets hitting the other side of the tree, just a few inches from my head. The North Vietnamese had a bead on me. At that very moment, I saw a white light and was sure that I had died. Over the years, as I thought about what that experience

Lee Chilcote on Operation Georgia

meant, I have become convinced that God was present with all of us and meant for all of us to live and be on this earth.

Somehow, our unit kept its position, and we prevailed without losing any of our men. We actually captured most of the North Vietnamese, including the commander and his woman companion. We did not know it at the time, but later learned that many of the North Vietnamese units traveled with prostitutes who serviced the troops as they moved down the Ho Chi Minh Trail.

Unquestionably, this was the most harrowing experience of the Vietnam War for me. As I reflect back on all of the experiences related in this writing, I realize that not only did the maturing of a Dartmouth Marine occur, but those experiences made me who I am today. None of the losses, hardships, misfortunes, and other happenings of life since Vietnam have seemed difficult when compared to my Marine Corps experiences. For that, I am forever grateful. Semper Fi!

- - - - -

Editor's Note: Lee Chilcote's Bronze Star citation, given for combat service in 1966, reads in part: "First Lieutenant Chilcote participated in seven major operations and courageously led his platoon on Operation Georgia in Quang Nam Province from 23 February to 15 May 1966 . . . [and] on five major operations, including Operations Hastings and Prairie, in Quang Tri Province from 16 May to 21 November 1966. During periods of intense enemy fire [during these operations], he repeatedly exposed himself to hostile enemy fire to effectively direct and control his platoon. His aggressiveness, sound judgment and tactical knowledge inspired his men and contributed significantly to the success of [Operation Georgia]. Deploying his unit against North Vietnamese regular troops [in Operations Hastings and Prairie], First Lieutenant Chilcote displayed outstanding knowledge of tactics and exceptional presence of mind." [Signed V. H. Krulak, Lieutenant General, U.S. Marine Corps, Commanding.]

After his Marine Corps service, for the last forty years Lee Chilcote has served the Cleveland community in a wide variety of public, private nonprofit, and philanthropic leadership positions while also actively serving clients as a lawyer in firms and companies. He is known for dedication and service to his community and his clients, traits he learned, in part, from his experiences at Dartmouth and in the Marine Corps.

Winning Hearts and Minds

IVARS BEMBERIS : U.S. ARMY

I thought I would paint a mural of my war experience, but what emerged is a mosaic. When I was in country, there were more than five hundred thousand soldiers in Vietnam, of which fifty thousand were ground combat troops. Everyone saw a different war; most did not fight, but served in a massive, essential, rear echelon supporting those chosen few. Support came in all forms; mine would be in refugee relief and civic action to "win the hearts and minds" of the civilian population.

World War II utterly devastated my youth and preconditioned me to serve in the military. Separated at age three from a father and a land I was never to know and tossed around Europe until age nine, I finally arrived in the United States to find an identity, sense of home, and nation. My love of American history drew me to rife examples of volunteer warriors prompted to serve in the spirit of "my country right or wrong!" So at Dartmouth, I made a conscious decision to serve in the military by joining the ROTC. Commissioned Saturday, graduated Dartmouth and married Sunday; in the space of thirty hours my life was decided. By the time I finished grad school, Vietnam service was almost a certainty. Before reporting to active duty, in October '67, I set out with my wife, Jeannette, to "see the USA, in a Chevrolet" (Corvair Monza convertible). Our trip of eight weeks took us from Hanover to Seattle, down the coast to SoCal, and then back east.

Following officer's basic at Fort Belvoir, Virginia, I was assigned to the Ninety-Fifth Civil Affairs Group at Fort Gordon, in Augusta, Georgia (we even went to the Masters in April '67). I graduated second in my class at the Civil Affairs School and was promoted to first lieutenant. My wife was asked to attend the ceremony to pin on my silver bars. She said she did not have transportation—the company exec offered to send a jeep, but she de-

Ivars Bemberis near Song Mao

clined. She arrived dressed in a Navy-style blouse and had our son, Scott, dressed in an outfit decorated with anchors, in her arms. This was her silent protest against my service. Her dad had served in the Navy during World War II and then was recalled for the Korean conflict. Jeannette reasoned his service was sufficient for our family.

Rotation to Vietnam was very hard because orders were cut in February for an August deployment. Living with those orders for six months was difficult. Though I would have to leave my wife and baby son, my expectation was that I would survive and return. This also was my wife's prayer. I was leaving from Fort Lewis, Washington, but we decided to say our goodbye in a favorite place, San Francisco. We had a good time there.

When the plane door opened, the hot, humid air of the Cam Ranh Bay airport welcomed us to Vietnam. I was assigned to the Forty-First Civil Affairs Company in Nha Trang, which had teams scattered all over II Corps. I was to be the engineering officer for Team 9, at the Edap Enang Resettlement Camp. EERC was created to house people moved out of free-fire zones along the Cambodian border in the vicinity of the Ia Drang Valley. Forty-seven Jarai Montagnard villages were forcibly moved to EERC. By adviser account, 7,200 people were moved into the eight-square-kilometer area. Actually, the population varied between 3,000 and 7,000, depending on how the Vietnamese bureaucracy treated them.

After a flight to Pleiku, I traveled west by jeep to Edap Enang on highway QL 19. The driver casually informed me that the road was often mined and there was sporadic sniper activity. The comment was upsetting enough until I saw our compound, cordoned by concertina wire on the edge of QL 19. In the best military sense, it was a bivouac. An ARVN company and a 105 mm howitzer battery provided security. Across the road were the lines of tin-roofed, thatched huts of the Edap Enang encampment.

Quarters initially were a cot in a multiperson tent. Sleep did not come easily. In the dark, shadows appeared to move; VC were preparing to overrun the compound. I thought sleeping with a loaded .45 would help; it didn't, but I continued the practice during my time in country. As the shadows moved, my thoughts were not of dying, but rather of being taken prisoner. Both my father and stepfather had been POWs during World War II. In my father's case, he was a Latvian conscript in a German uniform captured by the Russians. He was sent to a gulag for twelve years. I could not imagine his life there, but got a glimpse of it when I read Solzhenitsyn's *One Day in the Life of Ivan Denisovich* during my senior year.

At the time of my arrival, the Civil Affairs (CA) team hadn't even been issued M16s. Paranoia led me to select an M79 (grenade launcher) for my personal weapon. The M79 with buckshot rounds was an excellent choice for close combat. To augment the persona, I also started to "smoke" cigars. They served as a "Guard All Shield" and underscored my adopted mantra: "Yea though I walk through the Valley of the Shadow of Death I shall fear no evil because I'm the toughest mother x@#@X in the valley."

I spent six months with a team of three officers and four enlisted men, subsisting in the boonies. I learned a lot about team building through balancing our personal needs while assisting the camp. As a small, detached unit we had to fend for ourselves. There was no mess hall, no PX, no refrigeration. Because of our isolation, satisfying our own daily needs consumed a significant portion of our time. Luckily, my NCOs were oldschool master scroungers, so we ate well most days. When I became team leader, I christened my jeep "the Big Green."

This assignment was full of déjà vu. As a child I lived in displaced persons' camps for six years in Germany before emigrating to the United States. Over that period, I experienced want, privation, hunger, forced relocation, and more. The Montagnards in "Tin City," as some described EERC, faced all those miseries. The Vietnamese authorities regularly overestimated the population and then under-delivered provisions of rice and dried fish. A U.S. Army Engineer battalion had cleared land for these nomadic farmers, but the Vietnamese government failed to provide seeds.

Through Med Caps (Medical Civic Action Program) we learned from time to time that villagers were not receiving their rice or dried fish rations for weeks on end. They subsisted on bamboo shoots and leaves.

A school and dispensary had been built, but they were being used to house local military. There were no local doctors, nurses, or teachers. The Montagnards are Vietnam's largest ethnic minority, and the Vietnamese government mistreated them like the American Indians in the Old West. The villagers had many needs. My approach to civic action was to enable the indigenous populations to help themselves. Civic action is effective when a local need is met by marshaling unavailable (to local populations) resources for use by local manpower. I had a degree in civil engineering from the Thayer School, which allowed me to undertake civil works: drainage, market and school construction, and water diversion for spillways to provide easy access to water for drinking and bathing.

To define the essential needs of the villagers, we had to get agreement on basic needs and build rapport between the local authorities. Many meetings with village elders and Vietnamese officials produced prioritized project lists. We built personal "bridges" by sharing humble meals with the villagers. The local cuisine was very basic. Sometimes meat was on the menu; frequently it was dog charred on an open fire. And as culture required, food was washed down with rice wine sipped through a thin bamboo tube from a clay crock.

Our roadside bivouac was vulnerable to attack. As team leader I was responsible for our safety, with virtually no support from our military. We fortified with sandbags and concertina wire as best we could and slept in bunkers, but ultimately we were reliant on an ARVN company for security. I was comforted that they patrolled at night; I was pissed that they played their portable radios while on patrol to avoid VC contact! Although we were located in a "safe" area, our daily schedule had to be unpredictable to avoid ambush. We were most vulnerable on Medical Civic Action Program missions carried out in outlying areas.

Our medics found no lack of work—each morning many patients lined up outside the compound awaiting treatment. We also provided health care for a leper colony. The Montagnards preferred U.S. medics to ARVN medics, mostly because the Vietnamese medics lacked medical supplies. I had a superb medic with outstanding medical skills. I was astounded by his medical knowledge and expertise. His accurate, early diagnosis of a junior officer's bacterial meningitis no doubt saved the officer's life. He could painlessly insert a hypodermic needle into a small child. Equally, he could make the needle burn when giving an "off-record" injection to a GI to control venereal disease.

I learned some animal husbandry at EERC. One of the villages had a prized baby elephant that became ill. With nighttime temperatures in the fifties, we suspected pneumonia. Our medic had no clue, but we had access to resources and flew in a vet. Even with this expert assistance, the elephant could not be saved. I know we lost face in the eyes of the village elder.

Next came pigs. By a fluke, 160 piglets were sent to EERC for a ceremonial meal. The male piglets should have arrived castrated, but my Georgia pig farmer NCO saw that their organs were intact. He proposed to negotiate with the village elders to save the piglets for breeding, and the EERC "pig farm" was born. Pens were built, arrangements were made for pickup of kitchen slop from military units in Pleiku (fifteen miles away over mined roads), and donations of breeding boars and sows were obtained. The harsh winter took a small toll on the piglets, but the project was sustained long enough to convince the villagers that the delayed meal of 160 piglets was amply surpassed with a long-term, renewable food source.

Vietnam service was also a "theater of the absurd." When serving in remote areas, you soon realized that your weapon was your best friend. But contradictions popped up everywhere. As needed, we could access the Air Force PX for supplies essential to carrying out our mission—beer and whiskey. We ate by bartering our liquor allotment for mess supplies. We would not dare travel without weapons, but I had to leave my driver with my M79 at the air base gate; grenade shells were not allowed on base!

Even though our daily activities were geared to assisting civilian populations, Military Intelligence (MI) officers with translators were attached to our teams. Often nightly MI "interrogations" subverted the hearts and minds we won by daytime humanitarian activities. We worked to win trust, while MI created distrust.

EERC was on the "map" as an example of a successful resettlement program. Quickly I started to ask myself whether we were fighting a war or conducting VIP tours. Visits required some two thousand villagers to arrive early in the morning, rehearse "spontaneous" welcomes, and then wait till midafternoon for the honored guests to arrive and spend, at best, less than forty-five minutes at the camp. The Montagnards viewed these proceedings with confusion, because the guests' remarks were translated into Vietnamese, which they did not speak, much less understand. It was all to show that the government of Vietnam was doing wondrous things for their minorities, yet with total disregard for the comfort of these people. The "Notable Visitors List" included Senator Ted Kennedy of Massachusetts, Congressman Alphonzo Bell of California, Charlton Heston, actress Ann B. Davis, and countless Vietnamese VIPs. To be always available to host visitors, I was told to drink beer half diluted with tomato juice to mask any hint of alcohol on my breath. I learned to like it.

Even in war, training is important to the military. The Forty-First used "buddy" training by holding quarterly team leader conferences to exchange success/failure stories. In December '67 I was sent to Saigon for a MACV/CORDS orientation (Civil Operations and Revolutionary Development Support) introducing the newly centralized CA program. The orders read "weapon not authorized." In a war of insurgency, with VC everywhere, including Saigon, I had to travel without a sidearm! Since I normally carried a .45 in a shoulder holster, in Saigon I simply wore it under my fatigue shirt. I could not imagine sleeping in Saigon without it under my pillow. Only one month later, there was fighting in the streets during the Tet offensive.

The MACV/CORDS course became a Christmas present. I was able to call home from the Red Cross phone station, unthinkable in the boonies of Edap Enang. One evening, I went to an officers' club (OC) on top of some nondescript Saigon office building. Shortly after walking in, I was sitting in a group with four AXA brothers and some half dozen more Dartmouth grads. Being our age and on active duty, we inevitably had to be in Vietnam. Why not in Saigon and why not in this OC?

"Off duty" hours moved slowly. We had a generator, so there was light in our hooch where we played cards, read out-of-date *Army Times*, books, and listened to tape recordings of *Laugh-In* that my wife sent. I read most of what James Michener had written because the books were long. The cool evenings were eased by coffee laced with Rémy Martin Cognac (one dollar per bottle). Comforting sound-effects were provided by the whistle of 175 mm artillery shells (M107 self-propelled gun) heading for the free-fire zones to the west. In my daybook I noted that one day I had written eighteen letters to friends and family. Jeannette was teaching and caring for our infant son, yet she wrote frequently. Letters and photos were great, but the real treasure was voice tapes, which provided emotional, personal moments with family stateside. I managed two phone calls home, the first before Christmas '67 while in Saigon. The other was from Hong Kong, where I took a second R&R in June '68. (Compare this with the multiple communications channels available to our troops today.)

In late January '68, the Viet Cong and NVA launched a massive offensive during the Tet holiday. It was a concerted, coordinated surprise attack on major cities. We were actually ignored in the boonies. The savage attacks took a great toll on the civilian population. In the aftermath, CA teams concentrated on refugee relief and public health, most notably providing for burial of the identified victims. We assisted in Pleiku, and indelible images of trench graves dug by D-9 dozers continue to linger.

In February '68 I was reassigned as team leader at Song Mao, north of Saigon on the coast. The change of station had its protocols. Hand receipts were executed transferring equipment and relief funds to the next commander. Citations were written to recognize outstanding service of team members, using appropriate phraseology to ensure acceptance of the commendations. Awards for team leaders were a different matter. The practice in the Forty-First was to draft your own and submit it to the CO. Little did I realize that this was expert training for the corporate world, where I would frequently execute my own performance ratings for the boss's countersignature.

I did not know what to expect in Song Mao. I did make a cryptic entry in my daybook: arrive "Paradise." Unlike the bivouac atmosphere of Edap Enang, my team had its own villa in an old French agricultural compound occupied by an MACV advisory team. My first impression reminded me of the French military in Vietnam, sallying forth in the day to work and then to retreat to their villas at night. Song Mao also was in an isolated area. Our contact with the outside world came courtesy of the Australian Air Force "Wallaby Air Lines." "Wallabies" were what they called the two-engine C-147 cargo aircraft. The Aussies were awesome. I was told they even flew in resupply on Christmas Day. One day while I was on board, they decided to prop wash their plane, flying very low over the South China Sea. That was really scary fun.

In a capsule, Song Mao was about hydraulics and psy ops. The hydraulics part involved repair and maintenance of the water distribution pipelines from the water tower to the town (and our villa). The local military units surrendered the countryside to the VC at night, allowing the pipeline to be constantly sabotaged. Repair teams were sent out daily, along with sentries to ward off sniper attack. Maintenance of a piped water supply was critical to demonstrate that the local government was in control, not the VC.

The psy ops part of the story was the "weekend wars." The VC often attacked local army installations Friday nights. Whether the intent was to disrupt local calendar events or the leisure moments of the MACV advisers was unclear. When VC contact was sustained, we could call for naval gunfire support from destroyer escorts patrolling offshore. A gunnery ensign often came ashore on a launch and set up a fire direction center. I have a surreal memory of sitting in a cemetery at sunset atop a burial mound directing fire by radio. During the spring of '68, VC activity was frequent in the area, and casualty rates for Vietnamese "local forces" (LF) soldiers mounted.

One of the MACV lieutenants was scheduled for R&R, but because of the tactical situation the MACV team leader refused to let him go. The looie was crushed. In a moment of insanity, I talked the major into allowing me to fill in while the lieutenant went on R&R. I went on patrol as the adviser to local forces. I learned a lot about their fighting attitudes and a lot about myself during the hours on patrol. The LF soldiers frequently cautioned me to stay down because the VC were firing, but no gunfire was heard, and the bullets were silent.

Time for my R&R also came in Song Mao. I chose Hawaii and stayed at the more remote Kahala Hilton. Jeannette made the reservations and "bought a memory." We decided to leave our fifteen-month-old son with her mom and dad, who had taken them in while I was in Vietnam. My father-in-law had become my son's father figure. Scott was fortunate to have the doting attention of this kind, gentle man. But, on arrival in Hawaii, I was met at the airport by Jeannette *and* Scott, and the surprise was absolute! We spent a glorious time living well in a beach resort with a porpoise pool and other amenities. R&R is a time warp to the normalcy that you leave behind to go to war. Yet you are keenly aware that all too soon you'll be going back. It was hard to say good-bye in San Francisco; now we did it again with the same anxiety that it could be the last.

For a third time, I was reassigned, now to company headquarters in

Nha Trang, as "special projects" officer. I brought it on myself by filing an after-action report for Team 9. It was not required, but it seemed appropriate to summarize the team actions under my leadership. The CO thought so, too. My report was subsequently published in an obscure military magazine. My job was to initiate such reporting for all teams. These reports also became a focus for quarterly team leader meetings.

I left Vietnam exactly one year after arriving. Since 1968 was a leap year, the Army exacted an additional day to make my count 366! My initial flight to 'Nam had been filled with anxiety; the return flight was strangely sober and oddly quiet. I got off the plane at SeaTac, changed to civilian clothes, went to the ticket counter, and bought a first-class ticket to La Guardia. I did not want to risk missing the first available flight. I had earned "combat leader tabs" and was proud to wear them while in company of comrades, but I was advised to shed the uniform to avoid possible confrontation with protesters before reaching home. This is a stark contrast to the warm welcomes extended to returning soldiers today! It was only recently that, for the first time, a stranger who overheard that I had served in Vietnam thanked me for my service.

After my return, Jeannette confessed that her worst fear was coming home from school every day. She was afraid of turning the corner and seeing a strange car with two uniformed soldiers in front of the house. A second nagging fear came during the evening news. There was war footage every night showing the cruelty of the war framed in beautiful landscapes with wild flowers. Every Friday night the news ended with an "honor roll" listing local KIAs. She was convinced that if I were to become a casualty, she would see it on the honor roll before being notified. Facing those fears on a daily basis just wasn't fair.

Now, forty-four years later, I still don't understand the emotional drain its remembrance places on me. I saw very little combat, so I really don't appreciate what GIs faced daily in the jungles and rice paddies, but it frightened me that my wife remarked that it took me eight years to become "normal." For me, Vietnam service was a zero-sum event; I was not killed, and I killed no one. Yet it was more than that; I now appreciate life and family more than ever. I was also not in a hurry to visit the Vietnam Memorial. When I did, I was surprised by my visceral reaction. Its simplicity and power are awesome. It is personal and intimate in encouraging visitors to touch the celebrated names.

As a postscript, I was never comfortable with the security of my team locations. Fortunately we did not come under direct attack. However, shortly after I left Vietnam, both Edap Enang and Song Mao were over-run. Recently I got a call from a team member who told me he was glad to learn that I was alive. He had found my address on the Forty-First CA Company website and called to reconnect. He thought I had been killed in the attack on Edap Enang.

Ivars Bemberis left the military after discharging his ROTC obligation. He entered industry, where he had a career in commercializing state-of-the-art technologies in advanced wastewater treatment, ultrafiltration, and chromatographic purification. After continuous employment for thirty-five years, which included six mergers, he took early retirement, but still consults on business development for a Japanese fine chemical company.

1967

U.S. initiates bombing of Haiphong harbor.

A Quiet War, a Damped Conscience

ROBERT J. (WOODY) WOODRUFF : U.S. ARMY

I went to great lengths never to set foot in Vietnam, and failed, mostly miserably.

I can't remember a time when I thought that U.S. intervention in the decades-long, postcolonial conflict was a positive idea. In 1965, as a graduate student in New York City, I was not among many superpatriots. Even in 1965, informed criticism of the war was widespread. Anyone who has ever been to the West End Bar on upper Broadway will testify I was not likely to find many superpatriots ranged along the sticky length of the great U-shaped, stool-strewn bar.

"Deciding" (more like discovering) that a PhD in English literature was not compatible with my current dedication or intellectual heft had that predictable bad consequence, however—it converted my draft status to 1-A. Acquaintance with Bellow's *The Dangling Man* may well have sharpened a fatalistic sense of being in the rapids of someone else's river. A brief interval followed in which I trained for, and then flunked out of, Peace Corps training for Thailand. The feeling of being in those rapids grew stronger. I went down to NYC's Whitehall Street, later made famous by Arlo Guthrie, and enlisted in the U.S. Army a few days before my drop-dead reporting date for the draft at Jefferson Barracks in Missouri, still my home state of record.

But I had an ace up my sleeve. The recruiting sergeant with whom I discussed attending the military language school assured me that the Army Security Agency (ASA), my likely employer should I learn a language through Army schooling, did not have installations in combat zones like Vietnam. In July 1966 I signed up for four years.

For a nascent left-winger who responded strongly to the still low-key rumble of protest against the conflict, this would be a win-win that would keep me out of jail and my conscience somewhat unsullied, I thought.

I can hear other Army veterans of the era chuckling already. You may think you have it figured out and greased yourself for an easy wriggle through the obstacles, but that's just what you think.

Though I found basic training a pit of terror, there were enough guys in my company who were even sadder sacks than I that I didn't draw enough attention to merit complete crushing. I remember being aware of, almost appreciating, the military's basic training strategy of removing all the props that held up your identity and sense of self, and then, while you teetered, offering exotic concepts—like unit cohesion, adherence to norms, and the freedom to hate and assault someone officially designated an enemy—as new props.

The Defense Language Institute at Monterey was way different, though enervating in its own fashion. Just as old-timers predicted, I had my first dream in Mandarin about three and a half weeks into the Mandarin 1 curriculum. I learned to wear a big, floppy hat on weekends to Berkeley and the "Summer of Love" to hide my GI haircut, having already incurred one Article 15 (nonjudicial punishment) for incautious grooming.

After the structured terror of basic, a school command is where you find out just how firm and broad your military friendships can be, and that seems to make the uniform fit less poorly somehow. Monterey's language school was full of college-boy dissidents. Eccentricity was as well distributed among the students as the number of languages studied. My everyday class included a majority of Navy and Marines, my first encounter with other services. Air Force Mandarin studies, which had been the first model for the speak-learn method by which we learned the four-toned national language, still remained aloof from the rest of us, studying more intensively in their own separate facility and producing tightly wrapped, wild-eyed "lingies."

The tone of my class was set by Chief (Petty Officer) Partee, whose easygoing ways made me and the Navy enlisted comfortable with learning. The Marines were different yet, letting the rest of us know without a lot of talk that we were—compared to them—amateurs at making war and would probably remain so. They struggled with Mandarin; they seemed to accept that as the natural course of things.

Monterey was great duty and a hugely pleasant place to be, my first extended stay in Northern California. The candy-blue color of the kelp-haunted surf at Pacific Grove, just a walk down the hill from the Presidio, was unlike anything I, an East Coast boy, had ever experienced. Weekends I saw live concerts by the Dead, Big Brother, Quicksilver. But I crashed with Dartmouth friends who were securely in grad school in Berkeley, and for whom this whole military and war thing was a specter outside the door. So there was seldom a day I didn't anticipate, long for, my resumption of civilian life in 1970.

Thus, when I landed at Tan Son Nhut Air Base in September 1967 during the VC celebration (with mortar attacks) of Ho Chi Minh's birthday, I was pretty flawed goods—only so-so at Mandarin and not very good at either the U.S. Army way or a positive in-country attitude. I still felt opposed to the intervention project and its costs, and I still felt guilty just for being there instead of taking my stand and going to jail.

Saigon—where we had to lie on the bus floor as a precaution on the way from the airport to the holding barracks—was a sweaty hell, soon left behind. White Elephant Landing in Da Nang was just a stop on my voyage to the heart of I Corps, but looked more to me like the Vietnam I was hoping to find, a place that was somehow suspended outside the war.

How did I wind up at Phu Bai (just about fifteen clicks south of Hue) despite the recruiting sergeant's assurances about ASA and combat zones? Simple—the Eighth Radio Research Field Station (RRFS) had the ostensible mission of investigating the effect of radio waves on the atmosphere. Followers of James Bamford's excavations into the workings of the National Security Agency will not be surprised to hear that this innocuous-sounding scientific research station was swarming with Army Security Agency personnel, including me.

My time at Phu Bai was a blur, tempered only by my relief at the secure surroundings. We were right across the main highway from "Divvy," the HQ of the Marine division that ran I Corps at that time. Nobody messed with Divvy, and we were safe in the penumbra. Until Tet 1968, a few months after my departure, no hostile action broke into the Eighth RRFS's peaceable pursuit of collecting and transmitting various communications of both the NVA and the local VC—much of it in Morse code. Did I use my Mandarin skills at work? No—a tiny enclave of Mandarin linguists had just been laid off when I arrived, the "voice" activity having proved to yield little information from the few Chinese railway battalions busily repairing the tracks and bridges that were being routinely demolished by U.S. bomb raids.

Along with the other orphan Mandarin specialists, I got another job, fairly menial and mindless, and the machinery of ASA ground slowly to work, preparing to send me and the other deportee linguists on to posts where our skills might bear COMINT (communications intelligence) fruit. Our training had been expensive, and ASA chafed at having pricey linguists and other communication specialists working as clerks. My Chinese skills were used mostly to sweet-talk barmaids at the service club in very bad Vietnamese pidgin, because at least both languages were tonal.

Our lives were spent at the club and in air-conditioned trailers, which we were uncomfortably aware were far better digs than the combat soldiers enjoyed. I settled in among jovial, underemployed Mandarin linguists who had come out of Monterey ahead of me. They could already see their exit papers from the Bad Place being laboriously typed by a clerk somewhere, and were good company.

I had spent a typical new guy's few days with dysentery, pinwheeling in a latrine toilet stall trying to get both my vomit and diarrhea where they were supposed to go. That may have had more effect on me than I thought at the time, because of all my attenuated memories of Phu Bai, the flimsiest are those concerning food—what there was to eat and which sort of fare I looked forward to, where was the mess hall, etc. For most periods of my life, my memory of the food (usually expressed quantitatively) associated with any place and time has otherwise not failed me, to the persistent astonishment of my wife. But I have no recollection of eating in Vietnam, other than a plate of fries with my beer and endless plays of the Box Tops' "The Letter" at the club.

Like many travelers to a foreign land, I had hoped to meet, and find out about, Vietnamese. It became clear quickly (and the evidence had been available to me before I arrived) that I was not a standard traveler to a foreign land, and that such encounters were potentially lethal, at least outside the confines of our secure compound. Those Vietnamese who worked inside the compound, it seemed to me, knew they were under perpetual suspicion and were understandably resentful and not inclined to make friends with the occupying force. Interpersonal skills have never been my long suit in any case, but I never got to know any Vietnamese.

In country, though, I found reinforced in myself some traits and practices that I may not have liked but which comforted me: a sureness that I would do just about anything to support my enlisted comrades; a skill at distinguishing pro-GI NCOs from irredeemable lifers; the knowledge that officers were sometimes smart but never to be trusted.

What I didn't do was allow any pangs of conscience I had about the U.S. policy in Vietnam to emerge from solitary confinement while I was on that country's soil. Fear and peers, I suppose, helped keep that sensibility in the lockup. Many of my fellow soldiers were scornful of the conduct of the war and the pronouncements of those in charge—but there was little overt, fundamental questioning of the motives and agenda that might be in play. Shamefully, I stayed mute.

When I and some other superfluous ASA types left RVN for other parts—in my case, Korea—the four months in country seemed like a fleeting dream, mostly spent inside fortresslike and windowless buildings. My rare tours of night guard duty had afforded views across the mountainous, narrow neck of the country toward Laos and the flicker and flash of aerial bombardment.

When I called my family from Japan right before Christmas, indicating I was really, really not in Vietnam anymore, I remember my mother bursting into tears of relief.

What stuck with me most about my time in Vietnam was the serenity and beauty of the old imperial capital, Hue, where I had traveled several times as part of a chaplain-led group providing exemplary (we hoped) native speakers of English for students at Quoc Hoc School—a school that was unashamed to say it was Ho Chi Minh's alma mater. Hue's monuments of old imperial governance, which seemed 100 percent red-and-gold lacquer and filigree and altogether beautiful, marked an earlier, proud, and independent country that had stood off invaders since the Trung sisters fought the Chinese (AD 12–43)—but seemed above the current battle, at least to me.

But battle caught up with Hue during the 1968 Tet offensive just a few months later, when many of its treasures were devastated or destroyed. By then I was on a remote island ASA facility in the Han-Imjin delta on the west coast of Korea, as close to the PRK as the ROK and within earshot of giant North Korean loudspeakers blaring propaganda at our island province. The news of Tet's devastation of Hue fell on me there like a collapsing building, fueled by a sorrower's binge in the NCO club before going to swing-shift duty at 4 p.m. The shift boss sent me, useless and sobbing, back down the hill to bed. I said goodbye to Vietnam without ever really having said hello.

Robert J. (Woody) Woodruff returned from his year in the Republic of Korea on New Year's Day 1969, as Broadway Joe on a snowy TV in Kimpo Airport established the AFL's bona fides. In due course Woody was cast out of the Army Security Agency for good for participating in antiwar activities in Washington, D.C., and exiled from Fort Meade to Fort Bragg, North Carolina. Returning to Fayetteville a year after his discharge, he was a founder of the Vietnam Veterans against the War chapter, uh, "serving" Fort Bragg. A life earnestly misspent practicing and teaching journalism in Florida, Washington, D.C., and Maryland has followed. He is now a superannuated doctoral student, ABD in media history, at the University of Maryland, College Park.

My WestPac Tour

STEPHEN M. THOMPSON : U.S. NAVY

I arrived in Vietnam waters in October 1968. I had attended Navy Officer Candidate School in Newport, Rhode Island, and served on the destroyer *Marshall* (DD-676) homeported in Tacoma, Washington, on a mission to train reservists. I had requested a western Pacific (WestPac) tour in order to experience our front-line Navy in action. The result was assignment to the destroyer *Rupertus* (DD-851) homeported in Yokosuka, Japan.

When I reported aboard, *Rupertus* was engaged in hostile-fire operations off Vietnam. This was shortly after the May mini-Tet offensive, and while we were still bombing North Vietnam.

During my tour on *Rupertus* our missions included (1) PIRAZ, or providing antiaircraft and missile screening protection in the Gulf of Tonkin for aircraft carriers conducting bombing missions over North Vietnam; (2) Market Time, intercepting attempts by North Vietnam to resupply its ground forces via the sea; (3) SAR, search-and-rescue for aircrew downed at sea while *Rupertus* was operating independently; and (4) plane guard, similar to SAR except assigned to a specific carrier and positioned off her stern during aircraft launch and recovery operations. We even found time to rig and practice for recovery of both the Apollo 7 and 8 capsules, had they been forced to land at an alternate site near our WestPac station.

Our most frequent mission was gunfire support for land operations along the coast from Da Nang in the north to the Mekong Delta in the south. During her two-year WestPac deployment, *Rupertus* fired over twenty thousand 5-inch, 38-caliber projectiles out of her pair of two-gun mounts. Each gun had an extended range of about twelve miles and, if the barrel was not past its useful life, could be accurate to within fifty yards of the designated target. We could achieve this accuracy despite

USS Rupertus (DD-851)

difficult sea and weather conditions through the use of an analog gunfire control computer that used inputs such as course and speed of our target, wind direction and velocity, set and drift of the ocean currents, course and speed of our ship, and our pitch, heel, and yaw (inputs from our ship's gyroscope). The effect of this control was to keep the guns steady even though the ship might be moving substantially. In fact, if you could stand on a weather deck and watch the guns, they would be absolutely steady relative to the horizon, while the ship itself would roll around the guns.

In my experience the most intense gunfire missions were when we were providing support to our troops engaged in close combat. Especially challenging was when our troops were between us and the enemy, requiring us to fire over our troops but land the projectiles close enough to successfully impact the enemy.

Usually these operations were supported by airborne spotters, who would give us live fire range and bearing adjustments until we were on target and released to "fire for effect." Unfortunately the casualty rate for these low- and slow-flying spotters was quite high. To try to reduce spot-

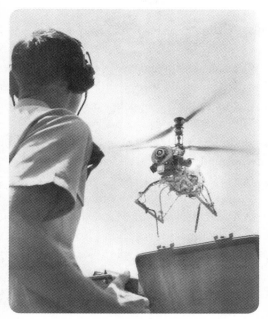

Snoopy returns to Rupertus

ter deaths and to increase our ability to respond quickly and accurately to requests for help without waiting for a spotter to get on station, we experimented with drone aircraft to spot our own missions.

This drone was not the type of high-flying, silent drones used in the Iraq and Afghanistan conflicts. We converted our drone antisubmarine helicopter (DASH) weapon by replacing the torpedo-mounting apparatus on the drone with a television camera and transmitter. We also added television receivers and monitors on our drone flight deck and in our Combat Information Center (CIC) in order to see the drone's live video. This converted and classified drone, code-named Snoopy, was remotely controlled from *Rupertus* by our personnel.

While the concept was terrific, and we actually had some success using the system, Snoopy ultimately proved too unreliable for close troop support. The main problem was that as a helicopter it vibrated the camera so much that we did not always have a good view of the target—especially a moving one. Also, Snoopy was a relatively noisy and low-flying aircraft, which made it a worthwhile target for enemy fire. In fact our last operational Snoopy was shot down and required a difficult in-country recovery using various military and quasi-military for recovery. The Snoopy system was deactivated shortly thereafter.

On *Rupertus* my underway watch responsibility was officer of the deck—fleet qualified (OOD-F). That meant I was qualified by the commanding officer (CO) to manage his ship to achieve her mission in close operating formations with other ships, including underway replenishment and full darkened ship conditions at night. These conditions could be the most difficult and dangerous under which to operate. To get an idea of these challenges, consider the fate of the destroyer *Evans* (DD-754). At the same time *Rupertus* was on the gun line off Vietnam, *Evans* was engaged in a joint Southeast Asia Treaty Organization (SEATO) naval exercise in another part of the South China Sea with ships from other nations. Because of procedural and judgmental errors by bridge personnel on June 3, 1969, *Evans* was hit amidships by the Australian aircraft carrier *Melbourne* (R-21). The result: *Evans* was split in two, her forward section, including the bridge, sank, and seventy-four men perished. The Navy made a combination documentary and training film about the incident, and it is still in use. It is very well done, and you can watch it on YouTube: search "The Melbourne-Evans Incident." It is a sobering viewing for any prospective OOD-F.

My professional responsibility on *Rupertus* was her main propulsion systems, including four boilers and two steam-driven turbine engines. Reporting to me were about forty men. Together we were responsible for operating the plant, as well as doing both preventative and corrective maintenance. The working conditions were challenging: at least four four-hour watches *each day* for each man in his workplace, seven days a week, for as many as eighteen straight weeks between liberty stops ashore. In the warm waters of the South China Sea, the main propulsion workplace temperatures regularly reached 115–120 degrees in high humidity. Because of the underway watch and maintenance responsibilities, my men and I averaged about four hours sleep per night.

Given these conditions, I was not surprised that maintenance activities had sometimes slipped. When I reported aboard I saw how clean the work spaces appeared to be, including the clean-painted insulation covering the steam piping and equipment. But the plant was not operating well, and it was becoming less reliable. It was as if the main propulsion motto was:

Mary Soo's team paints the ship's hull

"Paint it white, shine it bright, and hope to hell it runs all night." That unreliability was totally unacceptable. It took about seven months of attitude adjustment and hard repair work under difficult conditions (like repairing the main condenser while outrunning a typhoon) to change the motto to a proud: "Paint it white, shine it bright, and know it *will* run well all night."

After up to eighteen straight weeks of heavy action at sea, all hands eagerly anticipated liberty. During the time we operated in a hostile-fire zone, we received two financial benefits from the federal government: ordinary military pay earned during that time was exempt from income taxes; and we each received an additional tax-free hostile-fire bonus. Since there was virtually no way to spend that money on a destroyer while at sea, the men had plenty of money to spend when they finally got ashore.

If the liberty port was going to be Hong Kong, there were unusual preparations to be made. After each gunfire mission, men would scramble over the main deck gathering the empty brass powder casings that had been used to fire fused projectiles from our guns. This brass would then be stored until we reached Hong Kong. There the ship's supply officer negotiated with an institution called Mary Soo. The currency from the *Rupertus* was the stored brass casings, in return for which Mary Soo provided the labor to remove the ship's garbage and to perform other ship's work while we rode at anchor. For example, her people (mostly women) washed and painted *Rupertus*'s hull with paint provided by the ship.

Other WestPac-deployed destroyers shared most of the experiences described above, except for Snoopy. One additional experience that was unique to *Rupertus* occurred in late April 1969. A U.S. intelligence-gathering aircraft, an EC-121M, was shot down by the North Koreans in the Sea of Japan. None of the thirty-one personnel on board survived.

The North Koreans contended the plane invaded their airspace, while the United States claimed the plane was over international waters. In quick response to the incident, the United States decided to mount an extensive military exercise to demonstrate its resolve to protect future flights over international waters. Consequently Task Force 71, a huge group of ships including *Rupertus*, was dispatched to the Sea of Japan to conduct the exercises while being observed by both U.S. and South Korean officials.

Rupertus was positioned as an outside screening ship for the formation, which had several aircraft carriers at its strategic center. Soon after *Rupertus* was on station, a Russian frigate began to shadow (follow) the formation. Since it was sometimes the intent of this Cold War adversary to attempt to penetrate and disrupt the formation, *Rupertus* was assigned the task of steaming independently to keep the Russians from penetrating the formation and also to avoid a collision either with the Russian or other U.S. ships. Essentially it was if we were playing basketball. The center of our formation was the Russian's goal. She was the offensive player trying to reach the goal, and *Rupertus* was the defender trying to deny her that success. As it turned out, though she kept pace with the formation through several maneuvers during a long day and night, she never actually tried to penetrate the formation.

On the morning of the major battle exercise, the plan called for the formation to steam over the horizon and then launch aircraft as well as surface-to-surface and air-to-surface missiles in a remote location relative to the formation's position. Oddly, that same morning the Russian stopped following the formation and came to a full halt. *Rupertus*, per her orders to stay with the Russian, came to a full halt as well. At one point we were within a few hundred yards of each other, and each ship's personnel on her weather decks were clearly visible from the other vessel. While in this halt state, we were overflown by a Russian Bear aircraft. Its mission was probably reconnaissance. In fact it was at such a low altitude that we easily could make out the profile of one of the aircraft's crew members.

As we monitored the progress of the battle exercise by secure radio and plotted the planned attack, we realized that the Russian and *Rupertus* were standing in what was to become the target area for the missile launch. After reviewing the matter with the officer in tactical command of the exercise, we decided to try to contact the Russian to warn her of the imminent danger. However, no one on board *Rupertus* could speak

Lieutenant (JG) Stephen Thompson

Russian. So we decided to try encoding a flag signal following a rarely used International Code of Signals publication. Of course we had no idea whether the Russians had the same publication or would understand our methods of sending and acknowledging signals. Despite these unknowns, we encoded and sent a signal that said: "Danger. Explosive Ordinance Disposal Area." After several tense minutes, the Russian returned a signal that read: "I understand Captain, I will follow you." Together we immediately steamed out of the area to a safe distance of several miles, just before the exercises were executed as planned. There must have been some reaction on the Russian ship when the sea where we had both just been literally exploded from all the exercise ordinance shots. Importantly, we had no further issues with the Russian after that incident, and we returned to our ship's normal routine.

In September 1969, President Nixon approved the withdrawal of thirty-five thousand men and women from the military forces in Vietnam. I was surprised to learn that my name was on the list. That meant that my military duty would not be completed in March 1970 at the end of my three-year commissioned officer commitment; instead, in October 1969 I left Vietnam, returned to the States, and was released from active duty.

On reflection, when I decided to serve in the Navy, I swore to protect and defend the Unites States and to fulfill my duties to the best of my abilities. I did that. And if I were back in 1968 faced with the same circumstances, I would make the same decision again . . . in a heartbeat.

After an MBA at Stanford and three years' Navy service, in 1970 Stephen Thompson joined Boise Cascade's office products distribution unit with annual sales of $79 million. By 1976 he became region manager officed in San Francisco, with P&L responsibility for, in different combinations, fifteen western operations and the headquarters unit in Chicago. He also had such diverse assignments as lobbying for the forest products industry (Washington, D.C.); facilitating the integration of a major Canadian acquisition (Toronto); managing the conversion from a centralized mainframe to a distributed, fully integrated data-processing system (Chicago); conducting the study to divest successful wholesale operations; and evaluating expansion opportunities (Shanghai). By his retirement as a senior VP in 2005, the unit had achieved annual sales of $8.6 billion.

Vietnam—Accelerating My Maturity

PETER E. LUITWIELER : U.S. ARMY

Yes, I wanted to be in the military. I signed up for ROTC, but after my freshman year at Dartmouth the staff sergeant in charge of ROTC was pleased when I handed in my resignation. The reason for my decision was that I had an excellent summer job running a caddy camp at Lake Sunapee Country Club in New London, New Hampshire. My earnings were critical to pay for school, and the job was a great experience. I even got to know Red Rolfe, the Dartmouth athletic director with whom I needed to work as captain of the Dartmouth Rugby Club.

The staff sergeant was happy because he felt I did not have the talent to complete the four years—partially based on my performance in the drill team exercises. He was trying to teach us a "Queen Anne Salute" (I think), and as I spun the rifle and went down on bended knee, the rifle came apart. I had the trigger housing on my finger, and the rest of the rifle was scattered on the ground! He had never seen anyone do that. After graduating from Dartmouth and Tuck School of Business in June 1965, I went off to the corporate world with an excellent job with Gulf Oil in Pittsburgh. They had given me a complete scholarship for my final year at Tuck and had been very active in recruiting me during 1965. Like many a newly minted MBA, I was very immature and stepped on a few toes during my first year. I was filled with total confidence and only learned ten years later some of the stupid mistakes I made in my initial years at Gulf Oil. It was a great company to work for, and they "overlooked" some of these events because they must have seen something that showed management potential.

About a year later, my mother called me and said the Selective Service head in my hometown, Winchester, Massachusetts, had contacted her. He mentioned that "my number" was coming up in the next few months.

Upon learning this I opted to enlist. I was rejected by the Navy because of a ruptured disc in my back, which I got playing intrafraternity hockey, making me a 4F or 1Y, the same classification as world champion boxer Muhammad Ali. As the Vietnam War heated up, classifications changed, and suddenly I was eligible—just not for the Navy.

I talked to the Army recruiter about a new program called College Graduate Officer Plan (or something like that). It required sixteen weeks of basic and advanced infantry training and then six months of Officer Candidate School at Fort Benning, Georgia.

Marlene Frederick, my future wife, and I discussed the options and decided the OCS route was the best option. In May 1966 I got on a bus in Pittsburgh and went to Fort Jackson in South Carolina. For the next sixteen weeks I worked hard, slept little, toughened up, and learned what life was like as an infantryman. I lost weight, learned how to handle weapons, and was determined to become an Army officer. Next stop was Fort Benning, where I began to understand what military discipline meant. My eyes were about to be opened at OCS! There were ninety recent college graduates in our company. When we were in formation the first night, our tactical officer (TO), Captain Paris, made a few comments and then shouted, "Any Ivy Leaguers, step forward, NOW!" At that moment I wished I had been a graduate of the University of New Hampshire or Colgate, but I double-timed to the front of the formation with a Harvard graduate. We were told to drop and "give me thirty push-ups." When we finished, we jumped back up to attention, and the TO proceeded to tell all of us, "These two Ivy grads will have to do more physically than everyone else for the next six months. When you do twenty push-ups, they will do thirty; when you run three miles, they will run three and a half miles." In retrospect, that turned out to be a good thing for both of us. We were both plenty smart and athletic, so we excelled throughout OCS and eventually graduated in the top 5 percent. It made us better prepared for Vietnam, but it was a long six months.

Halfway through OCS I was able to return to Pittsburgh to get married to Marlene. Our honeymoon was driving our used Opel station wagon through some snowstorms back to Fort Benning. When we got there, we unloaded her items and very few of mine into her apartment, which she shared with another OCS wife—two bedrooms with "very thin walls." We got to see each other occasionally on Saturdays, if our company performed well—difficult to begin a marriage that way, but at least we were together.

After OCS graduation, we spent three months together in Baltimore near Fort Holabird. There I was learning specialized talents to use as a Military Intelligence officer in Vietnam or elsewhere. I did complete a "dream sheet" of places I wanted to be assigned, but it was obvious we were headed to Vietnam. At least Marlene and I got to live together for those three months before I shipped off from San Francisco to Saigon via chartered airline.

In Saigon it did not feel like a war zone—lots of people doing regular jobs, streets crowded with bikes and buses, restaurants and bars full and no sense of urgency or fear. That changed before I left Vietnam.

I met with the commanding officer, and his first question was, "Do you speak Vietnamese?" I responded, "No, sir, but as you will see from my language ability testing, I have a knack for learning languages." I asked several people if I could go to the Presidio in Monterey, California, to learn Vietnamese and sign up for another year. They all said no. They needed us in Vietnam! My CO vented about the stupid SOBs in the Pentagon and what a waste of time and talent this was. So he assigned me to I Corp, just south of the demilitarized zone. I had assumed I would be working with computers and analysis of intel in Saigon. On my records it was stamped in large letters "Unfit for Combat" because of my ruptured disc. The CO basically told me to talk to my congressman but in the meantime get repacked and fly to Quang Tri the next day.

The government, then and now, has a lot of waste. I did not complain, but proceeded ahead to my assignment. I worked as a civilian in Quang Tri for about five months, living in a three-bedroom house with two other MI agents. We had a jeep and a motorcycle. We ran agents behind enemy lines—not very successfully. The three of us never had any combat or close calls. It was not a difficult life, except I was living in a strange country and could have been shot any day. It was obvious to anyone watching our activities that we were into some kind of undercover operation.

I did mingle with other military people at the Quang Tri Military Assistance Command Compound. There were about seventy-five military personnel, mainly Army and Marines. They had Jolly Green Giant rescue helicopters, a small PX, a small mess hall for meals, and a chaplain. It was a nice change of scenery from our Vietnamese house and neighborhood.

Our activities as an intelligence-gathering post were limited—basically a waste of resources, in my humble opinion. In this regard I was not surprised or disappointed when the decision was made to close many of these small outposts. When the Army brass closed a lot of these Military Intelligence offices, they unveiled the Phoenix Program. This was a program to coordinate all the intelligence units in different regions in an effort to identify and eliminate or capture Viet Cong and North Vietnamese leaders and infrastructure. I was selected to undergo one week of training in Saigon to establish a Phoenix field office. When I stepped off the bus in Saigon to start my training, a friend who had gone through MI training with me at Fort Holabird recognized me and was shocked. He came over to me and said, "I heard you had been killed a few weeks ago. Glad to see it was just a bad rumor." I found out later that one of the other wives called my wife to express her condolences. Luckily Marlene knew that the Army would have contacted her to relay bad news; but without the Internet, rumors spread and were hard to verify. Sure glad that Marlene and I exchanged a letter or tape three to four times per week.

When I completed my Phoenix indoctrination, the Army wanted to send me to the Cambodian border. I requested an assignment in the Quang Tri area so that my past five months would not have been wasted. They actually listened to me and sent me to the Trieu Phong district about thirty minutes north of Quang Tri. This time I lived with about eighty Vietnamese soldiers, like National Guard troops, and four Americans and one Aussie, all advisers to the Vietnamese. I had a small office inside the compound where we lived and coordinated about seven or eight different Vietnamese and U.S. intelligence efforts and worked with the CIA chief in the province. From that point onward I went on numerous operations to search for Viet Cong or North Vietnamese leaders. I had frequent contact with U.S. troops throughout I Corps and sent weekly reports to Saigon. I was much more active than in the prior five months. We were never under heavy fire on these raids, but one time my Vietnamese radioman stepped on a land mine and lost a leg—a very difficult moment for us. I called in a helicopter and had him medevaced fairly quickly.

My biggest challenge came during the Tet offensive in January 1968. Our intelligence agents were indicating that large North Vietnamese forces were headed to South Vietnam and would be heavy in the Đông Hà area of Quang Tri Province near the DMZ. The Army command moved

Pete Luitwieler receiving
Medal of Gallantry from
Lieutenant Colonel Nguyen
An, Quang Tri Province

the First Cavalry Mobile Division with lots of helicopters and firepower
to a location about five miles away. Previously, only Marine combat units
were in that region. We had a wonderful Tet / New Year celebration with
the local community inside our compound, with probably 250 people
being permitted inside our walls to eat, drink, and be merry. Lots of liq-
uid that was like sake, but not as smooth! No security checking of those
who came in or left, just visual controls.

Very early in the morning after the holiday, we found that North
Vietnamese surrounded our entire compound, our electric generators
had been sabotaged, and we were being shelled with mortars. We started
returning fire. The South Vietnamese were manning our machine-gun
nests, which were surrounded by sandbags on top of one of the compound
buildings. Their job was to keep the NVA from advancing. Suddenly, two
of these soldiers came running down the steps because the NVA had shot
a rocket-propelled grenade that exploded right behind them. A Marine
lieutenant and I ran up the stairs and remanned the machine gun and
started firing back at the NVA. Was that a courageous or stupid thing to
do? Looking back, it was not smart, since the NVA had already fired one

RPG right there. The two of us did not think, we just responded to the situation, as we had been trained. Our actions gave others courage, and we were able to hold off the advancing NVA for about thirty minutes, by which time a First Cavalry helicopter gunships arrived. It was important that the First Cav had been relocated only five miles away; otherwise we might have been overrun by the NVA. Once the gunships started wreaking havoc on the NVA, they retreated rapidly. A few months after that attack, we were both decorated with the Vietnamese equivalent of a Bronze Star for valor. That one event had a major impact on my life and my maturity. I stepped up to the line with my life to save others. I did not think about it—I reacted!

Thereafter, I became much more involved with the First Cavalry, planning Phoenix-type missions and making many helicopter trips, either for an operation or for a meeting to discuss intelligence and options. Riding a bubble helicopter with a pilot and a machine gun in front of me as we skimmed over fields to avoid being shot at—this too matured me much faster than many of my classmates and people I had worked with at Gulf Oil. We also did a lot of work for the local community. I taught English three days a week at a nearby school. Three or four times a month our medic took a team of us out to a village to give the people some basics like using soap, medicines, etc. The other attached picture shows what I normally wore when not on missions. In the background is the building we lived in. It had a kitchen/eating area, a bedroom with four double bunks and small closets, and an office area with military communication gear. After the Tet offensive I noticed holes in my closet where mortar fragments had come through the wall and damaged a uniform or two!

I did not find my time in Vietnam to be a rewarding part of my life, but I was thankful that I made it through without injury. I also feel strongly that that one year strengthened the strong bond I already had with my wife. We communicated in-depth most every day. We covered a wide spectrum of topics—probably topics we might not have discussed if we were just sitting around the kitchen table. I also reread her letters and listened to her tapes when I had free time. Distance really did make our hearts grow stronger. We understood each other much better, and our life priorities changed. Yes, that is part of my accelerated maturing from service in Vietnam!

When eventually I got out of the service in May 1969, I did return to

Pete Luitwieler in Trieu Phong

work for Gulf Oil in a new position in Houston. About two weeks before being relocated from Pittsburgh to Houston, we had our first child, Mark. As I write this in August 2012, he and his family have also just relocated to Houston, working for an energy company.

My whole outlook on life had changed during my three-year stint in the military—primarily during my 365 days in Vietnam. I was only twenty-six, but I probably acted like I was thirty-six. My wife and I stayed close during that year by writing and exchanging letters almost daily—no e-mails or phones. We were also fortunate to spend five days in Honolulu on R&R after my first seven or eight months. I can remember distinctly one of the nights we were fast asleep in our hotel bed and there was some loud noise. I quickly rolled out of bed onto the floor and started yelling "Incoming"—a response we learned when our compound was being shelled by mortars. That shook up both of us. After talking about what happened, Marlene and I laughed, and I think we went for a walk on the beach, as I could not go back to sleep.

In retrospect, I am proud I was able to serve with distinction. I am glad I had a wife at home to share my thoughts and concerns. I wish that more people had been happy to see me return to the United States, but I knew quickly that no one wanted to hear about my year in Vietnam. I avoided political discussions and just forged ahead with our family and my career. It is so wonderful today to see how Americans acknowledge soldiers. My present wife, Jane, and I always reach out to thank those in uniform.

One interesting side note—my commanding officer for my final three months in Trieu Phong was a very talented Army major named John Shalikashvili, who became the chairman of the Joint Chiefs of Staff during the Clinton years. He was an excellent leader and mentor for me. When he was elevated to his position, I sent him a congratulatory note that he answered very promptly. Sadly, he died in 2011.

Pete Luitwieler was in the U.S. Army for a three-year hitch, which included OCS at Fort Devens, Massachusetts, conveniently close to family. After the service, he rejoined Gulf Oil in Pittsburgh for a short time but was transferred to Houston, where he and Marlene spent the next eighteen years. In 1984, Gulf was bought by Chevron, and after working on the corporate merger, Pete and his family moved to Tulsa, to begin a wonderful fifteen-year career as an executive with CITGO Petroleum. In 2000 he retired and has been an industry consultant and participant of several boards. Marlene died in 2005, and he is now married to Jane (Swearingen) Luitwieler. They reside in Tulsa. Pete has three children.

Life in a Jungle Base Camp

CARL DUREI : U.S. ARMY

We arrived at Tan Son Nhut Air Base in March 1967 on a chartered commercial airliner. We stepped off the plane on a pitch-dark night into what seemed like a hot, wet blanket. We had flown for fourteen hours and were very jet-lagged because of the twelve-hour time-zone difference from home. After a day of processing at the Long Binh replacement center, I was transported to my unit, the Aerial Surveillance Unit of the Ninth Infantry Division headquarters at Bearcat, about twenty-five miles northeast of Saigon.

Bearcat was a base camp for two battalions of infantry and several support units. It was a rectangular-shaped tent city surrounded by ten-foot-high earth berms with machine gun entrenchments every one hundred yards. The berms were about a half mile by a quarter mile long and had been built by Army engineers who bulldozed a large clearing in the middle of a jungle. Artillery batteries occupied two opposing corners, and we soon learned the difference between the sound of friendly outgoing artillery fire and incoming Viet Cong mortar rounds. On several nights we would be roused from sleep to head to our protective underground bunkers.

Life at Bearcat was not particularly pleasant, but I was happy to be stationed near the division commanding general and felt reasonably safe. We worked six days a week, twelve hours per day, and had Sunday off. We lived in medium olive-drab tents that accommodated six bunks set on a floor of shipping pallets to keep us out of the mud during the six-month rainy season. The pallets also served as walkways to the mess hall and our community shower. The tents kept us dry at night but were too hot to be in during the day. The food was OK, but most days we were longing for a normal, solid bowel movement. The smell of burning shit was everywhere, as that was the preferred method of dealing with our out-house latrine waste.

Communication with my wife, Amy, was accomplished through a combination of snail-mail letters and recorded audiotapes. Personal computers, cell phones, and the Internet were not available back then. Amy and I were able to meet in Honolulu, Hawaii, for the one week of R&R (rest and relaxation) the Army provided each soldier at approximately mid-tour. We had a wonderful time at the *Hawaii Five-O* famous Ilikai Hotel. It was difficult to go back to living in a tent after that week.

Occasionally on our Sunday off, another lieutenant and I would make a trip to Saigon in our quarter-ton jeep. It gave us a chance to see the incredible poverty in the rural areas and the extremely heavy traffic in the city. We would visit the officers' club at Tan Son Nhut for a good meal and then head to the huge military post exchange in the Cholon district of the city. There we could buy electronics, cameras, clothing, and all sorts of consumer goods at really low, subsidized prices.

My workday consisted of supervising a group of fifteen men who studied aerial photography that had been ordered by our boss, the division G-2 (deputy chief of staff for intelligence), for surveillance of areas of suspected enemy activity. The men used stereoscopes to get 3-D images. They would identify enemy bunkers, bridges that had been blown, new trails in the jungle, and so on. We would then update maps with this information and provide them to the company commanders who were conducting search-and-destroy missions. We also gathered intelligence reports from other sources such as POW interrogations and radio intercepts and would update the maps with this data as well.

The company commanders would also request recent photos of helicopter landing zones for their upcoming missions. We accommodated them by shooting pictures with a handheld 70 mm camera from a small observation helicopter. The pilot sits in the middle with a passenger on each side. You are strapped in, but there are no doors, so you are very exposed to any snipers on the ground.

One day the warrant officer who normally took the pictures talked me into coming along with him on the LZ photo mission. He said the day before he had seen a herd of cattle in enemy territory and that after we had taken the photos we could have some fun and destroy an enemy food

First Lieutenant Carl DuRei

source. He knew the pilot well. He said to bring my M-16 and that he would get us a bag of grenades. At first we couldn't find the cattle, but we did see something moving in a water-filled artillery shell hole below. We swooped down with our guns blazing to discover as we got closer that we were attacking a warthog that was taking a bath! Then, a few minutes later, we did spot the cattle moving into the jungle for cover. We hovered at treetop level, and the warrant officer and I heaved grenades down to where we thought the cattle were. We have no idea whether we killed any, and looking back, hovering at treetop level in VC territory probably wasn't very smart. But that was the only time in my Vietnam tour that I ever fired my weapon, and we did make it back safely.

My unit also participated in "people sniffer" missions. The Army had a device that was supposed to be able to detect the odor of large groups of humans as they perspired in the jungle. Unfortunately, it also detected smoke. The probe of the people sniffer was mounted on the front skid of a Huey helicopter, and a technician passenger monitored the instrument screen for positive readings. At treetop level, the copter flew back and forth in 0.5-kilometer passes over a predetermined area of suspected enemy activity. When he had a positive reading, the technician radioed the reading to one of my personnel who was flying at fifteen hundred feet above in a single-engine observation plane and tracking the copter's location. My guy would mark the reading on the map only if it was not just smoke or a friendly village. He would then radio the coordinates to the artillery branch, who would shell the area. I chose to ride in the Huey during two of these missions. It was quite a thrill to be soaring over the trees at 125 mph.

At the end of my Vietnam tour, I was awarded the Bronze Star for meritorious service. I flew home in January 1968, ten days before the Viet Cong launched the Tet offensive. I was twenty pounds lighter, but in good health and happy to be getting back to civilian life.

Following active duty in the Army, Carl DuRei returned to work on the audit staff of the Arthur Andersen Boston office in 1967 and was promoted to partner in 1978 when he transferred to Andersen's Chicago world headquarters. In 1981 he returned to the Boston office to lead audits of clients in a wide variety of industries. He became the office expert in mergers and acquisitions and worked on several client SEC registration statements, and he was responsible for quality control of Boston office audit reports. He retired in August 2000 and now spends seven months in Bonita Springs, Florida, in a golf and tennis retirement community. The other five months he splits between Boston and a Lake Winnipesaukee house in New Hampshire.

LST-912 on the Rocks

ALAN S. WOODBERRY : U.S. NAVY

Early days

I joined NROTC at Dartmouth with a commitment to serve two years on active duty and four years in the reserves. My father was a naval officer in World War II and encouraged me to join NROTC. The eight Dartmouth NROTC courses were taught by naval officers and did not address what one might expect to encounter in Vietnam.

In June 1965 upon graduation from Tuck School I was commissioned as an ensign. At the beginning of July, Jerry O'Brien ('64 and Tuck '65) and I reported to the Navy Supply School in Athens, Georgia, for six months of training. We learned that the Navy had a supply system reputedly designed by geniuses, which anyone could manage.

After graduation from supply school, I reported as the supply officer to the *Mahnomen County* (LST-912). An LST (landing ship tank) has a relatively flat bottom to allow landing on sandy beaches, vertical doors at the bow that open up, and a ramp that comes down to allow discharge of cargo and vehicles. She (ships are referenced in the feminine) had many water tanks, which could be partially filled with seawater for the ship to ride lower in the open sea, or emptied to ride higher for beach landings. She had an anchor on the bow and another on the stern, which was primarily used to help winch her off the beach while the engines were in reverse after unloading her cargo and closing the bow doors.

Her aft part had quarters for a crew of about one hundred, mess hall, storage compartments, and more. At the top of the superstructure she had a bridge from which the ship was driven. Personnel on the bridge gave commands to the engineers belowdecks who operated the engines that drove two propellers, one rudder, and other ship machines. She was built during World War II and had seen action in the Pacific. World War II LSTs

Alan S. Woodberry

Ensign Woodberry with Supply Department

were desirable for Vietnam because they could navigate shallower rivers than larger LSTs built during the 1950s and 1960s.

One-Way Voyage

In January 1966 the newly assigned crew of some rookies and some experienced seamen assembled in Norfolk, Virginia, to outfit *Mahnomen* for a voyage to Vietnam. In late January she sailed south along the East Coast, through the Caribbean and Panama Canal, to Hawaii for extensive repairs, and then to Okinawa to load cargo. She finally arrived in Vietnam in May 1966. Her top speed was nine knots, and equipment failures were common on the old ship.

Her mission was to supply U.S. military bases in Vung Tau, Saigon, Phan Rang, and Chu Lai, Vietnam, with cargo from Kaohsiung in Taiwan, the Philippines, and Okinawa. The principal cargo was cement for building airfields in Vietnam.

While at sea we learned that a typhoon was nearing. All the water compartments were filled with seawater, causing *Mahnomen* to ride as low in the waves as possible. Fortunately we had a full cargo tightly tied down in the hold to help lower her even more. In howling winds and high waves she keeled over about thirty degrees to port and then about thirty degrees to starboard, while the bow and stern alternated between slowly plunging into and rising from huge waves. For a couple of days she survived this turbulent ride with most of the crew tied in their racks. Had she rolled over, she and we would have been toast. After that experience, an effort was made to avoid encountering typhoons at sea.

When *Mahnomen* was in Vietnamese waters we heard guns shooting and bombs exploding and saw the night sky illuminated by explosions. We were never a target of attack.

A U.S. Army officer escorted a few of us to tour a local village near Vung Tau. We asked how he knew whether the villagers were friendly or Viet Cong. He said the Army only visited the village in the daytime, when the villagers seemed happy to see visitors who offered snacks and toys. He said he did not know what happened in the village at night.

On the evening of December 31, 1966, I was showing the movie *Bad Day at Black Rock* in the wardroom. The supply officer showed movies in the wardroom because he did not stand watch on the bridge. Watch was an around-the-clock exercise in four-hour segments. *Mahnomen* was anchored by only the bow anchor near shore at Chu Lai, waiting for an opening on the beach to offload cargo.

A typhoon hit that evening. *Mahnomen* was driven onto the rocky beach by waves and winds before the officer of the deck (OOD) realized that the World War II bow anchor chain had broken. She was impaled on the rocks, and efforts to refloat her were to no avail. At low tide the crew could scramble down cargo nets on her side and walk on dry beach and rocks. The Marines were not happy about her resting half on shore and half in the water very near their helicopter pad.

In late January I flew to Sasebo, Japan, where our squadron had a small headquarters staff to complete paperwork to write off the ship and its contents. The CO, XO, and OOD attended a board of inquiry and court-martial in Sasebo.

Shore Duty

In February 1967 I was assigned to the Boston Naval Shipyard, which was near where I was raised in Lexington, Massachusetts. I recall several people quizzing me at length about the war—should we be in the war, was the war good or bad, when would the war end, and how? Some question-ers had given these subjects much more thought than I had. I remember being confused about the big-picture issues of the war.

At the Boston Naval Shipyard in Charlestown, I worked with visiting crews from our allies Germany and Taiwan. These crews were in Boston to pick up World War II ships donated by the United States.

I was released from active duty June 30, 1967. In late August I moved to San Francisco and joined a Naval Reserve unit. I stayed in the reserves for about ten years and retired as a lieutenant commander. My most interesting reserve activity was in a reserve unit that acted as consultants to the Navy. The members generally had MBAs or PhDs, and we conducted monthlong consulting projects for the active Navy at bases in Guam, Hawaii, and elsewhere.

Reflections

My naval duties provided several positive experiences and lessons.

I learned to respect the weather even more than I had in Hanover.

The Navy introduced me to the Pacific Ocean and Asian countries. In September 1967 I joined Price Waterhouse (now PricewaterhouseCoopers) in San Francisco. Most of my time was spent doing international tax planning, and much of that work involved Asian countries.

The Supply Corps is a staff function in the Navy that supports naval personnel pursuing the Navy's primary missions. I learned that it is better to be in the mainstream of an organization than a support or peripheral function. In my civilian career I always tried to work on the most vital aspects of a project.

The Navy provided my first significant experience working full time with a large team, motivating the team, keeping the bosses happy, and building relationships. This was valuable people-experience for working at Price Waterhouse.

While I generally enjoyed and respected the Navy, the Vietnam War was a confusing, costly, losing war. As most books on the Vietnam War chronicle, the war was a mistake driven by misunderstandings, communication failures, overconfidence, and overzealous military leaders and politicians.

For the first time since leaving Chu Lai in January 1967, I visited Vietnam about five years ago with a tour group led by the Vietnamese wife of a friend. The country has rebounded economically. Ho Chi Minh–style propaganda still thrives, as one would expect from the winning side. The Vietnamese people do not seem to hold a grudge and also appear to be relatively happy. The United States continues to learn the lessons of participation in foreign civil wars.

After active duty in the Navy, Alan Woodberry moved to San Francisco to begin a thirty-five-year career with Price Waterhouse. In 1974 he married Molly Tritschler, whom he had met in San Francisco. They have two wonderful children, Sara and Andrew, '02, who live in California. Last year Sara married Colin Lauver. Andrew is engaged to his Dartmouth classmate Amy Grubb, '02.

1968

Tet offensive

My Lai massacre

From Lawyer to Aerial Recon Commander

JAMES LAUGHLIN III : U.S. ARMY

I t was probable that eventually I would be drafted into the armed forces. I felt that I would be better off serving on active military duty as an officer as opposed to a draftee or enlistee, so I joined the Army ROTC upon my matriculation at Dartmouth in September 1960. I completed the four-year program and was designated as a Distinguished Military Graduate, with an "exceptional aptitude for military service." As a result, I was offered a commission in the regular Army. Although I may have had the aptitude for it, I did not intend to make the military a career, so I declined the offer, opting instead for a commission as a second lieutenant in the Army Reserve, intelligence branch, which only required a two-year stint on active duty. I thus became an OBV-2, a volunteer obligated to serve that two-year term.

I made the decision to take a three-year delay in fulfilling my active-duty obligation after graduation to attend law school at the University of Michigan. Little did I know that the Vietnam War would explode during that time span. In 1964, I don't think anyone knew much about the place or the armed conflict that was beginning to boil up there.

After graduation from Michigan Law in 1967, I was ordered to active duty and sent to Fort Benning, Georgia, for a ten-week course at the infantry platoon leader school (along with six other attorneys). As a result of having been in the Army Reserve for three years, I was promoted to first lieutenant after my first day on active duty. During our third week there, prior orders for those of us assigned to Military Intelligence were canceled, and we were informed that all of us were going to Vietnam. You could have heard a pin drop in the assembly room when that announcement was made. Stunned disbelief was followed by anger and not a little self-pity. Why were we law school grads being misused by being

James Laughlin III

sent halfway around the world to serve as line officers in what by then had become a vicious war for which I and many of my peers had no enthusiasm?

We might as well have railed against the ebb and flow of the tide, which is inexorable, so we completed the infantry phase of our training around the middle of October 1967. During that time the movie *The Green Berets*, starring John Wayne, was being filmed at the infantry school. Toward the end of September, the foliage turned a decidedly untropical color, so it was spray-painted green for movie realism (just like the roses were painted red in the Queen of Hearts' croquet ground). Paradoxically, at the same time, the Army and Air Force were doing their level best to defoliate huge swaths of territory in Vietnam to deny the cover of vegetation to the enemy.

After Benning, I was sent to Fort Holabird, in Baltimore, for a four-week crash course in combat intelligence, then on to Vietnam on December 7. My wife, Pam (Michigan, '66), whom I married during the summer after my second year of law school, went back to Michigan to stay with her parents for the ensuing year, much to her dismay. After having been out on our own, she was less than enthusiastic about having her mother looking over her shoulder again, sixteen short months after our wedding. It was a tremendously dislocating experience for both of us.

Initially I was assigned to the 219th Military Intelligence Detachment, Second Field Force, near Bien Hoa, approximately fifteen miles north of Saigon. The Tet offensive broke out on January 30, 1968, and we came under attack by elements of the 275th VC Regiment, more familiarly known to us as the Dong Nai Regiment. A heavy rocket barrage initiated their assault at around 0300 hours (3 a.m.), a very harrowing experience. Simultaneously, sappers infiltrated and blew up the huge, nearby ammo dump at Long Binh. It looked like a mini nuke going off. We hit the ground in our bunkers, as the blast wave leveled everything in its path. Fortunately the ground assault was mistimed and didn't commence until daylight, by which time we had helicopter gunship cover, which, together with our defensive fire, inflicted heavy casualties on the attackers. In general, this action represented in a microcosm that the Tet offensive, while a military disaster for the Viet Cong and North Vietnamese, struck a strong psychological blow that had a major impact in the United States. I think this was a turning point in the war, which eventually led to our disengagement over a period of time, and ultimately the fall of South Vietnam in 1975.

After Tet I was transferred to Advisory Team 96, Military Assistance Command, Vietnam (MACV), based in Can Tho, Phong Dinh Province, smack in the middle of the Mekong Delta (now a major attraction on the standard Vietnam tour route). With no special qualifications other than that I was there, I was assigned as assistant G-2 Air, IV Corps. The G-2 Air section was responsible for planning and implementing all aerial reconnaissance missions flown both by the Army and Air Force over the southernmost quarter of the country. In addition, all the officers in our section occupied aircrew slots. We rotated flying on low-altitude visual and spot photo missions in light planes and helicopters. Spot photo missions were directed at small areas where detailed low oblique photos were required and could only be obtained by a low and fairly slow approach, and were generally flown in O-1 Bird Dog aircraft (no, we didn't have drones). During these missions, we had to deal with hostile ground fire, bad weather, mechanical problems, and our own errors in judgment. In order not to dwell on what might have happened, I convinced myself I was invincible.

At the end of my second week there, our section commander, a captain, was killed on just such a mission. As the next-highest-ranking officer, I immediately became the de facto G-2 Air. Fortunately, we had a great sergeant who was on his fifth tour in Vietnam, and we didn't miss a beat. I was promoted to captain in June 1968. By the time I returned to the States in December, I had flown on seventy-seven missions all over the delta, from the South China Sea to the Gulf of Thailand, and along the Cambodian border.

My first civilian job, which I started after my release from active duty in June 1969, was as assistant legal counsel to Princeton University. The manner in which the university administration handled the violent antiwar protests and building fire-bombings in 1970–71, and our views and opinions regarding those actions, cost both the head counsel and me our positions. That's another story for another time.

It's hard for me to believe that forty-four years have elapsed since I served in Vietnam. The events of that yearlong tour of duty remain crystal clear in my memory. The passage of time has had an ameliorating effect, and Viet vets no longer are reviled as monsters for participating in that conflict (as if most of us had a choice). People now thank us for our service, which is both surprising and gratifying. I believe that the Vietnam Memorial in Washington, D.C., has had a healing and unifying effect on our population, which was torn apart by that conflict. The Wall, with its over fifty-eight thousand names, is a powerful, emotion-evoking monument. I cannot adequately put its impact into words.

In a strange twist of fate, Vietnam resurfaced in my life within the last two years. In 2006 I was diagnosed as having Parkinson's disease. Late in 2009, the Department of Veterans Affairs (VA) added that condition to the list of disorders it automatically considers to be service connected, presumptively caused by exposure to the defoliant Agent Orange while in Vietnam. So, in April 2010, I filed a disability claim with the VA. After many months of gathering records (medical and military), neurological exams at two VA hospitals, and an interim determination, the VA issued its final decision March 2, 2012, finding that I have a permanent service-connected disability evaluated at 100 percent.

I finally received my honorable discharge from the armed forces on October 31, 1974. When I received my commission upon our graduation in 1964, I never even remotely imagined that, despite OBV-2 status, I would be wedded to the Army, in one capacity or another, for ten years, or that events would unfold as they did during my active military duty, or afterward as a result of it. I'll wager that a lot of my classmates who served in the armed forces will say the same thing.

After completion of his active military service, Jim Laughlin worked for two years as assistant legal counsel to Princeton University. He then embarked upon a career in the private practice of law as a principal in a small firm in western Morris County, New Jersey, from which he retired in

2006. Since 1980, he also has served as the managing principal in a partnership, which owns and operates a forty-eight-unit low-income senior citizens housing project in Hunterdon County, New Jersey.

Following retirement, he and his wife, Pam, who taught school for twenty-five years, moved to northern Florida, where they both remain active in a number of volunteer organizations. They have been married since 1966 and have three sons and three grandchildren.

The War at Home

KARL F. WINKLER : U.S. ARMY

A fter 9/11, I was in the Atlanta airport with time to dawdle before my flight. Instead of taking the airport train to concourse D, I was meandering down the corridor. Along with several others, I was admiring the statuary in the corridor when a door opened to our right. National Guard troops walked out single file, dressed in desert camos, boots, and soft caps, and carrying identical duffles. A master sergeant, who was roughly my age, watched them file down the corridor to another door.

"Bless you for your service," came from the passengers. Applause, approving noises, thumbs-up, and salutes followed as the uniformed men and women continued their walk—a little taller, a little bouncier—toward their assignment in Iraq.

I was right about the sergeant. "Not like 'Nam, Sarge." He glanced at me, his eyebrows raised. "Officer?" he said. "Captain," I said. "A lot better than 'Nam," he said. We both watched. Shook hands and parted.

November 5, 1968, was election eve, Humphrey versus Nixon. It was 2 a.m., and I was in the flight service station at Norton AFB near Redlands, California. I was hitching rides on military flights to see my parents in Auburn, Alabama. I wore Army greens with combat tabs under my recently received captain's bars.

The police riot in Chicago, Lyndon Johnson's one-term presidency, college demonstrations, and sit-ins all preceded the election. I assumed my next set of orders would be for Vietnam. This could be my last trip home. As I left, the TV indicated Mayor Daley had still not released the Chicago vote.

The duty officer told me the flight was ready. It was a huge C-141 Starlifter, built to deliver troops, vehicles, and supplies to a debarkation for combat. I climbed the ladder into the huge fuselage of the transport. It

First Lieutenant Karl Winkler,
battery commander

was like entering the foyer of a deserted Sears Tower. I was alone. No equipment. No troops. A canvas seat along the fuselage with at least sixty other seats and floor space big enough for tracked vehicles. I could imagine myself and the company I would command lining the sides of the plane in those seats as we headed for Da Nang or some other exotic place in Vietnam. The huge, hollow aircraft jumped and roared with all its power into the midnight sky.

By false dawn I was in another flight service center. This one in San Antonio. I was waiting for the medevac flight to Montgomery. Mayor Daley had still not released the Chicago vote, but it looked like Nixon was winning.

A tired, faded DC-8 rested about fifty yards from the service center. Long shadows streaked behind it as it faced the rays of the rising sun.

I entered a door in the middle of the fuselage, ducking to avoid banging my head and gold-banded cap. It was dim inside. And quiet. I couldn't quite stand up in the aisle without hitting my head. Tucked into shadow were cots and the young men on them. As my eyes adjusted to the light, I could see bandages and missing limbs while I walked to the front of the plane, carrying my bag.

The boys in the beds were looking at me. One raised his hand. "Sir, captain," he said softly. Half his face was covered in bandages, the arm on that side hidden by a blanket pulled under his chin. I thought to myself that it must have been a mine; that he had lost his eye and his arm, maybe his leg.

"Yes, soldier," I said.

"We are right, aren't we?" he said.

I didn't want this conversation. The other boys, who were conscious, were looking and listening. I thought, What can I say to them? They've given so much of themselves when so few have. They were the boys without college or graduate school or political pull or a huge metropolitan draft pool. This war never made sense to me or my fellow trainees from officer's basic course. We proudly served. We didn't have to believe. But what to say?

"You were right, soldier," I said as I shuffled forward to the passenger section, thinking of the price each of them had paid.

The slow plane ride took a long time. Corpsmen moved back and forth in the section among the wounded and maimed. Eventually we landed in Montgomery, and I left the plane after the boys had been evacuated.

I was directed to a building next to a fence. That was where my parents would be sent to pick me up. I walked toward the building.

There was a crowd at the fence. They had signs. "Murderers," said a sign. "Shame," said another. A guy with a megaphone was yelling. The signs and screaming were directed at the boys on stretchers, who were being loaded into military ambulances. The crowd gathered by the gate as it opened and the procession of ambulances moved through. The guy with the megaphone and his followers spat at those boys who had given all they had. No "We honor your service," no applause, no salutes or kind attention or thumbs-up.

That was Vietnam at home to me. The treatment of our combat troops —often black, Hispanic, country boys—by others not serving their country appalled me then and appalls me now. I was lucky and never got orders for Vietnam, partially because my twin brother was in country.

This experience at Maxwell Air Force Base was seared into my memory and still smokes and gives off acrid fumes today. It is a microcosm of everything the Vietnam War meant and still means to me. Thank you for asking me to share it.

Before separating from active duty in 1969, Karl Winkler was asked to commit to another four years to train to be a military judge and declined. Since separation he has practiced law in Rockford, Illinois, chiefly as a trial lawyer, and is certified as a mediator in state and federal courts as well as the U.S. Postal Service. Karl has served on a variety of boards, earned his pilot's license in 1979, traveled to more than a dozen foreign countries, and has written for legal publications. He and his wife were married while he was in law school. Their twin sons live in San Francisco and Austin, Texas.

Lawyering in the Army—
Vietnam and Stateside

PHILIP McFERRIN : U.S. ARMY

L ooking back at my experience in the Army, I naturally have mixed
feelings. Forty years or so after the end of my active duty, I somewhat grudgingly concede that my service was a positive experience, although I did not want my sons to serve. Perhaps it is
because of the total absence of any recognition from the public of that
service. Only within the last few months has anyone said, "Thank you
for your service," and that was from a call center employee at USAA. I
am grateful that the returning veterans from Iraq and Afghanistan are
being recognized in their local communities (at least it is happening in
my town), but I have not seen that recognition extended to the veterans
of Vietnam.

When I graduated from Dartmouth and even more so when I received
my law degree from Virginia, I sensed that my professional career would
be in the corporate world. And it was, almost entirely. This rarefied seg-
ment of society provided me comfort, but it did not expose me to the
world at large. Only my military service did that, and that is what I would
like to explore in this writing.

I was only a mediocre ROTC cadet at Dartmouth, and the staff at Fort
Jay, New York (headquarters, First U.S. Army), saw no reason to assign
me to anything other than a combat branch; accordingly I was assigned to
the field artillery. In my heart of hearts, I did not want to go to Vietnam
in the artillery, and I especially did not want to be a forward observer. (I
later learned that officers assigned to the combat branches sometimes do
entirely unrelated activities. As I was entering Vietnam, I ran into classmate Richard Neely, an artillery officer, who was on his way out. He told

me he had been assigned to set up savings and loan associations in South Vietnam.)

So, against the advice of some, I decided to transfer from the field artillery to the Judge Advocate General's Corps, even though it doubled my active duty obligation to four years.

The Army's JAG School was located next to the University of Virginia Law School in Charlottesville and shared some of its classrooms. I noticed that many of the students in the advanced course at the JAG school had recently returned from duty in Vietnam. I thought that I might avoid that, but, as it turned out, I could not.

After completing my basic officer training at the JAG School in Charlottesville, I was off to my first duty station. I was to go to Fort Knox, Kentucky, but I soon learned nearly everyone's initial orders would be changed, and so were mine. I ended up at Fort Wolters, Texas, a facility in Mineral Wells, two counties west of Fort Worth. The sole purpose for the base was to grind out helicopter pilots for the conflict in Vietnam.

While there were a few commissioned officers among the students, most of them were enlisted men, kids, fresh out of high school. The Army had (and perhaps still has) a warrant officer candidate (WOC) program, and it was a much better assignment than being an infantry rifleman. I was, of course, assigned to the post judge advocate office, and all we did was "legal assistance." The cadre would order the students to go to the post JAG office and get a will. (Along with the dangers in combat, occasionally students would be killed learning how to fly.) In addition to providing assembly-line estate planning, we tried to help our clients with financial problems. Typically, a young WOC would get his first flight pay, make a down payment on a car (a Mustang or maybe even a Corvette), wash out of the program, lose his flight pay, and be unable to make payments. Our office would write a letter to the finance company knowing full well that there was not much to be done.

Housing at Fort Wolters was a joke. If you were a bachelor, as I was, you lived off-base, probably in a trailer. I stayed in the BOQ (bachelor officers' quarters) for about one week. A young infantry lieutenant back from 'Nam was also staying in the BOQ, and we decided to rent a trailer in town. My trailer-mate wanted to make the Army his career, but he knew that would entail another tour of duty in Vietnam, and he did not want to go against the wishes of his widowed mother.

Our neighbors were a hoot. One was a salty, older chief warrant officer who had successfully escaped being killed or wounded as he piloted his Huey Cobra over the jungle canopy. His trailer-mate was a captain, also a pilot, who may have been wounded. Purple Hearts were common among the cadre at Fort Wolters. I had never known men quite like this, but as I think about it, they run through the history of our nation, unrecognized but essential. These guys decided, as a lark, to buy a used pontoon boat. The Army maintained a recreation area on a lake formed by a dam on the Brazos River (with the wonderful name "Possum Kingdom"). On weekends, the four of us would go up to the lake, put the boat in, and start drinking beer.

After two or three months at Fort Wolters, I received orders for Vietnam, for the First Infantry Division, "the Big Red One." After being issued the necessary clothing and getting all the shots (plague, yellow fever, etc.), I was off to Asia early in July 1968. Before I left, however, I received one of the biggest breaks in my life. My orders were changed. I was assigned to Headquarters, U.S. Army, Vietnam, with duty station in Saigon (Ho Chi Minh City for you politically correct readers). My job was to be a member of the Foreign Claims Commission, the office that receives and adjudicates claims against the United States for noncombat-related injuries and property damage. Our offices were in the heart of Saigon, across the street from the Rex Hotel that housed an officers' club, complete with a rooftop swimming pool. I lived in an apartment building in Cholon, the Chinese section of Saigon, across the street from Hotel Victoria, an establishment best known for its hookers.

Before moving to my quarters in Cholon, I lived for a few months in another BOQ and had a remarkable roommate. He was either a very senior captain or a major—I don't remember because he never wore a uniform. He was assigned to a clandestine group that carried out missions in parts of Indochina where the United States officially was not present. He was an infantry paratrooper and looked with scorn on any soldier who did not make jumps. He showed me photographs of himself riding an elephant, somewhere in Laos, after he had delivered gold to a village chief to keep him loyal to our forces. I do not know why, but he chose to leave the Army after his tour ended in Vietnam.

I worked for Major Jack Mullins, clearly one of the most dedicated JAG officers in the Corps. He worked seven days a week (we worked six), but he faithfully attended Mass each Sunday at the Catholic cathedral a block or two away from our offices. I don't know if his superiors particularly liked him, but when he left Vietnam, he was awarded the Legion of Merit. He retired from the Army as a lieutenant colonel and practices law in Victoria, Texas.

Major Mullins reported to Colonel John Jay Douglass, the staff judge advocate for U.S. Army, Vietnam. He was a most impressive leader and typified all that is admirable in our military. He left Vietnam shortly before I did, and I encountered him in Charlottesville about a year later. He had been made commandant of the JAG School and, I believe, retired from the Army in Charlottesville. He later moved to Texas and became dean of the National College of District Attorneys. He is now on the faculty of the University of Houston Law School.

I worked with several other junior officers, all captains, but I will mention only two. Frank was a scholar, and he had extended his tour of duty in Vietnam. Frank introduced me to the more pleasant parts of Saigon, including the U.S. Embassy, the military public library, and the city zoo. Frank went on to do graduate work in criminal law at the University of Texas and later became clerk of the U.S. Court of Military Appeals in Washington. He is a retired colonel in the Army Reserve.

Ken was, like me, a native Floridian. At lunchtime, we would often go across the street and grab a sandwich and then go lie by the rooftop pool at the Rex Hotel. He tanned; I burned. Ken went to work in the corporate law department of Coca-Cola and is now a principal in a commercial real estate firm in Atlanta. He is also a retired colonel in the Army Reserve.

We had a number of Vietnamese working in our office, mostly translating documents. Vietnam had been, for many years, a French colony, and the Vietnamese preserved the French tradition of having a written document for most events and transactions. One woman I remember in particular. Nguyen Thi Thanh (we called her Win-Tee) was the classic Vietnamese young lady—always smiling, wearing her *ao dai*, and being so terribly polite and demure.

The Vietnamese women in our office took naps each afternoon after lunch. I suppose local law or custom required this, and it caused us no problems.

After four months in Saigon, I was transferred to Da Nang to run the Foreign Claims Commission that served I Corps, the northern quadrant of South Vietnam. I Corps was predominantly under the control of the Marine Corps rather than the Army. I was quartered on the east side of the Da Nang River at Camp Horne, the headquarters for the Third Marine Amphibious Force (III MAF). I was treated very kindly by the Marines and especially by the officers attached to the III MAF legal office.

My office was on the west side of the river in the middle of the commercial district. I had three enlisted men helping two Vietnamese translators and me. My senior enlisted man was very able and dearly wanted to be a commissioned officer, but he had not graduated from high school, and the Army rejected his application. My two junior enlisted men were ordinary guys that were grateful to be working in a JAG office and not assigned to an infantry platoon. The two Vietnamese were among the best persons that I have ever known. One was Buddhist and the other Catholic. Each celebrated his own and the other's religious holidays. I did not care; they were both fine workers and fine persons.

The claimants were a mixed bag. Some were so uneducated that they could not count money. Some were very sophisticated. There was a Vietnamese army major who owned a fish hatchery in Da Nang that was damaged, allegedly by U.S. negligence. He continually tried to bribe me to render a favorable opinion, but the proof was just not there. Another claimant was a clerk at the local French consulate. A U.S. Army jeep had struck the consulate's vehicle, but we had the most difficult time trying to determine which unit owned the jeep so we could obtain an accident report. We finally determined that it was a jeep operated by a special forces unit that was trying to keep its existence and location confidential. We paid the claim on the damaged French vehicle, earned the gratitude of the clerk, and, most importantly, received an invitation to the going-away party for the French consul in Da Nang, complete with champagne and French pastries.

The most interesting group of claimants were the owners and tenant-farmers of a rice paddy that was damaged when a pipeline carrying jet fuel at the Da Nang Air Force Base sprung a leak and the fuel seeped all over the paddy. After reviewing the claims, we drove out to the paddy and paid the claimants under the watchful eye of the village chief.

One day when I was walking back to the launch that took me across the Da Nang River to Camp Horne, I looked up in the sky and saw what I had only seen before in old newsreels showing atom bomb explosions:

shock waves radiating out across the sky followed by a tremendously loud boom. We later learned that the Vietnamese had set a controlled burn to kill some grass on the berm surrounding the Marine Corps ammunition dump on the edge of Da Nang. When it became apparent that the fire was getting out of control, the local fire department was called to extinguish the flames. The hoses could not reach the flames, so the fire entered the dump and BOOM!

I found Da Nang to be a wonderful assignment. It has a beautiful setting, with a broad river separating the commercial area on the west from the beach area on the east. As in the Caribbean, mountains come down to the sea. My first impression on seeing it was that it could be a first-rate resort area, were it not for the war. Now it is a regular stop for cruise ships.

When Saigon fell to the North Vietnamese Army, I worried that these loyal Vietnamese who had helped me, and their counterparts who had helped other Americans and allied forces, would be "reeducated," imprisoned, tortured, or worse.

I returned to the United States from Asia on July 4, 1969. I had informed the judge advocate general that I did not want to make the Army my career. Even though my tour in Vietnam was far better than most, I wanted to be a civilian.

I was assigned to Fort George G. Meade, Maryland, for the remainder of my active-duty obligation, about two years and two months. This is an old post located between Washington and Baltimore. It is the site of the National Security Agency and had assorted combat and support units assigned to the base. For me, the most important of these units was a "Special Processing Unit," the place where apprehended AWOL soldiers, many of them returnees from Vietnam, stayed awaiting trial by courts-martial. At this time, the Army was made up of a large number of draftees, and unfortunately many went AWOL, and many used narcotics. There was an especially serious narcotics problem in both Washington and Baltimore, so Fort Meade kept busy trying heroin cases as well as other assorted infractions.

I had the great fortune to be associated with outstanding soldier-lawyers at Fort Meade. My closest friend was Wayne, a tough trial lawyer from Mexico, Missouri. He had served a year in Vietnam as a prosecutor with the First Infantry Division. Wayne was assigned to the group of lawyers at Fort Meade that investigated the cover-up of the My Lai massacre. He was worked very hard by his superiors and had absolutely no interest in making the Army a career, although he would have been an outstanding staff judge advocate.

I completed my four-year active-duty obligation and went on with my life as a civilian. Two years in Washington, D.C., as a clerk with the Tax Court, three years with a law firm in Memphis, and the remainder of my working career, in and around Chicago, with three years in the middle in Denver, all focused in some way on employee benefit plans and trusts.

As I try to keep from slipping into senility, I fondly remember the people I served with in the Army. I am glad that, for some reason I have yet to understand, I signed up for Army ROTC at Dartmouth.

Phil McFerrin married Thea Coulis in 1979, and they have two sons, John, a financial engineer in Chicago, and Peter, an economist in San Francisco. Phil and Thea have two grandchildren, Madeline and James.

Vietnam
Once in a Lifetime

CURT LITTLE : U.S. ARMY

O n a hot day in September 1967 I was sitting in bleachers at Fort Benning, Georgia, with about a hundred other first and second lieutenants (mostly recent college, graduate school, or law school graduates), learning the fundamentals of being an infantry officer in Vietnam during a twelve-week course. The Army officer lecturing the group made a point of saying that for nearly all the young men sent to Vietnam, this was their first experience outside the United States, and probably would be their only experience abroad. While we have definitely become a more global society since that day at Fort Benning, I have often thought of that comment. We were young and inexperienced, with limited training for what we were expected to do in Vietnam, and had no knowledge of the Vietnamese people or culture. We had no idea what was in store for us. Vietnam would be a once-in-a-lifetime experience that stayed with many of us the rest of our lives.

I left for Vietnam on Mother's Day 1968. I had attended Army ROTC at Dartmouth and was commissioned a second lieutenant upon graduation. After a three-year deferment for law school, I began active duty in the fall of 1967, training at the Army Intelligence School, Fort Holabird in Baltimore, in counterintelligence. If I had actually been assigned to a counterintelligence unit, I would have been wearing civilian clothes, doing background investigations, and tracking people suspected of spying on the United States.

My class at Fort Holabird (about thirty) was originally scheduled to go to Korea, but when the *Pueblo* incident occurred midway during our training, we were reassigned to Vietnam. As a result, five months of training was largely irrelevant to what I actually did in Vietnam. Since most of us who went to Fort Holabird, having been assigned to intelligence, had not taken the infantry training at Fort Benning very seriously, I suspect that when we actually wound up in Vietnam we were haunted by the constant refrain we had heard from the instructors at Fort Benning: "What you learn today may save your life someday in Vietnam."

As I look back on my going to Vietnam, I am surprised by how little I thought about what my parents might be going through prior to my departure. I knew it was difficult for them, but I was much more focused on what lay ahead. That my father called me several times during the days before I left should have been an obvious clue. I do not recall what their thinking about the war was at the time, but having since become a parent who has worried about far less traumatic issues than a son going to Vietnam, I am sure it was much tougher for them than I ever imagined.

Once I arrived in Vietnam, I was assigned to the Military Assistance Command, Vietnam (MACV) and an advisory team in the village of Can Giuoc in the northern part of the Mekong Delta, a few miles south of Saigon. My team varied from six to eight military advisers, and for part of the year a civilian adviser from USAID was assigned to us. The basic task was to work with local Vietnamese militia forces in fighting the local VC, as well as civic action focusing on improving the quality of life in the district. The civic action usually involved improving the local marketplace and re-building schools and bridges destroyed by the VC. The overall mission was to "win the hearts and minds" of the local Vietnamese population.

My assignment was a far cry from doing the background investigations and counterspy activities for which I had been trained. The training at Fort Benning was far more relevant. I was supposed to work with my Vietnamese counterpart in identifying and capturing members of the local VC political infrastructure (I never ascertained whether there was in fact such a political infrastructure in my district, other than the VC "tax collectors" who kept meticulous records showing from whom they collected money and how much). While my assignment relied on both Vietnamese and, to a limited extent, American intelligence-gathering efforts, the job boiled down to countless military operations in the rice paddies and hamlets in the district of Can Giuoc (equivalent to a small county) searching for VC operatives. Most of the time, no contact was made with the VC. If made, it involved a very small group of VC who usually disappeared after a short firefight.

My Vietnamese counterpart and I had our own intelligence office with a couple of secretaries and an intelligence squad that reported to him. Occasionally, we would go on combined operations with U.S. units. They were usually no more productive than when we went out on our own, but were more exciting in that we frequently traveled by river assault group boats, armored personnel carriers, and helicopters.

My counterpart, who spoke broken English, was a lieutenant in the ARVN. The troops we worked with were local militia living with their families, but the leadership had been ARVN trained. Initially, I had an interpreter who had previously worked with U.S. special forces and was experienced in military operations. Unfortunately, he had a habit of criticizing and second-guessing my counterpart and the local Vietnamese military leadership. Once we had word that his life was in danger he was replaced by a less-aggressive interpreter. Allegedly, this interpreter was a law student in Saigon, but as far as I know, he never attended any classes while he worked with me, and I never had any discussions with him about the law, even though he knew I had graduated from law school. In any event, going on operations was not something he cared to do or for which he was well suited. He wound up working in my intelligence office translating Vietnamese materials and serving as an interpreter at meetings in our district headquarters. Fortunately my counterpart and I developed an effective means of communicating with one another and worked well together without an interpreter.

Our district was divided by a river that ran north–south. We conducted most of our operations on the western side. The eastern side was much more of a no-man's-land, probably more under VC control than ARVN. We could generally tell if we were in an unfriendly hamlet when none of the children came out to ask for candy and the local residents pretty much stayed in their thatched huts unless working in the rice paddies.

As advisers, we lived in a military compound with the Vietnamese. We relied on rain for our water. During the dry season a water truck would sporadically come to our village from Saigon. Our 10K generator provided basic electricity except when the more well-to-do villagers (the district chief and his family) wired their televisions into the generator at night, causing it to die. We would dutifully respond by cutting their wiring.

Life in Can Giuoc was pretty quiet. We did not have to deal with terrorists and generally were not particularly concerned about being attacked in the village. Occasional mortar barrages at night were more of a nuisance than an attack and rarely caused any damage or injuries. We often ate at Vietnamese "restaurants" in the village (great "Chinese soup," steamed clams, and boiled crabs) and occasionally bought produce in the village market. While in theory we were supposed to "live off the land," we relied heavily on provisions from the Long Binh commissary outside Saigon, or bargained for supplies from neighboring U.S. units (VC flags and weapons were usually great trading items).

Occasionally events occurred that uniquely captured certain aspects of my Vietnam experience. The following vignettes are based on such events. In reading these stories, however, please bear in mind that they are based on recollections filtered through a forty-year-plus prism of time. I do not have a diary or other written record upon which to rely. For example, distances that I thought were ten to twenty miles turned out to be much shorter when I checked a map. The wartime condition of roads and bridges (often partially destroyed) clearly affected my recollection.

Arrival at Tan Son Nhut Air Base

Other than entire units being inserted into a combat zone, most of us flew to Vietnam on a commercial airline. In my case, it was a Braniff 707 with an experienced group of flight attendants who were great at keeping everyone calm during the steep descent into Saigon. On disembarking from the plane, we faced one of the most depressing moments of the entire year in Vietnam. Those arriving in Vietnam had to pass by those who had completed their tour of duty and were lined up to get on the plane just vacated by the new arrivals. After hearing some of their comments, I believe most of us felt that our greatest joy in life would be lining up to get on the plane leaving Vietnam. At that moment twelve months seemed like an eternity.

The anxiety level of arriving at Tan Son Nhut was heightened by a siren going off shortly after our arrival. Assuming we were ready to be attacked with rockets, many of us looked for cover, only to be advised that it was simply a siren sounding the noon hour.

The first few days in Vietnam involved briefings on being "in country." My Fort Holabird classmates and I were lodged in the Rex Hotel in Saigon. Nights were spent at the bar on the roof of the Rex, watching the tracer bullets from the gunships that were firing on suspected North Vietnamese locations within the Cholon area of Saigon. It was hard to believe that only a couple of days earlier we had been in the United States, totally removed from the Vietnam conflict. Basically we were still civilians and much like a group of first-year associates at a large law firm suddenly transported to the rooftop of the Rex Hotel, watching gunships in action.

After briefings we were given assignments to specific advisory teams throughout South Vietnam. The trip from Saigon to the capital of Long An Province, in which my district was located, was my first adventure in a Huey helicopter with a pilot, copilot, and a pair of door gunners. Probably few jobs in Vietnam were riskier than being a door gunner (one of the most popular and sought-after jobs), and virtually every door gunner had his share of near-death experiences, which he could describe in graphic detail to his passengers. The door gunners on my first trip were no exception, and before we took off I knew all about the "hot LZs" they had recently encountered in and around Long An Province. Between their stories and the cracking noise of the helicopter's blades sounding like gunfire, I was convinced that at any moment we would be shot down by the VC.

After a couple of weeks at the provincial capital, I was sent to the district of Can Giuoc. When I ultimately reached Can Giuoc by helicopter, I was met at the landing pad in the middle of nowhere by a staff sergeant who drove me to the compound where I lived for the remainder of my year in Vietnam. Arriving at the compound, I saw a shrapnel-ventilated wall-locker dumped in the courtyard. Upon learning that that would have been my wall locker, but for a mortar attack a few nights earlier, I was quickly introduced to the riskier side of life as a military adviser in a small town in the Mekong Delta.

The Ten-Most-Wanted List

When my Fort Holabird classmates and I arrived in Vietnam, one of our first briefings was by an FBI agent on how to find and capture VC operatives in our respective districts. The key to his presentation was developing a "ten-most-wanted" list. This meant finding the names of ten suspected VC whom we thought we had a reasonable chance of capturing, identifying them to the community as the top ten VC, and announcing that we were going to capture them. He emphasized "catchability." What we did not want to do was simply name the top ten in the area without knowing if we could actually catch them. Once one was captured, we were then to generate maximum publicity. He also promoted fingerprinting VC suspects.

Once I was in my district, I met with my new counterpart and explained the "ten-most-wanted" list to him. He patiently listened and then asked a very good question. "If I think I can capture someone, why would I want to alert him? Wouldn't that make the job harder?" With that, we pretty much put away the "list" and only came up with it on those moments when visited by high-ranking military and civilian officials who asked our progress. Usually we included the name of someone we had actually captured. On one occasion an assistant to the secretary of the Army visited us. After listening to our presentation on what we were doing and our successes, he concluded that if all the districts in South Vietnam were as successful as we were, the Americans and the South Vietnamese would be winning the war. (If he only knew.)

We also gave the fingerprinting operation a one-day trial. A U.S. instructor came to our village and spent a day training our local police in fingerprinting. After he left, the police started fingerprinting everyone in sight, including themselves. Upon discovering how tough it was to remove the ink from their hands, let alone meaningfully index the fingerprints, they gave up the project.

The HES Report

The Vietnam War was the first major war undertaken by the United States that heavily involved computers. One of the nightmarish projects of every MACV advisory team was preparing the monthly Hamlet Evaluation System (HES) report, which took very subjective information and formulated through the use of computers an apparently objective analysis of how effectively each hamlet and village in the district was being won over to the side of the Republic of South Vietnam. This evaluation included a variety of subjects (for example, incidence of VC attacks, whether there was a school or marketplace, any known affiliations with the VC, whether there was an "elected" village chief), which were rated by number as to how far along the village or hamlet had moved to pacification. Since the leader of each advisory team was rated on how well his team was doing in the area of pacification, it was incumbent on the leader to show progress in each hamlet. This process resulted in a "pacified" rating for a hamlet in our district that was well off the beaten path—that is, in a dangerous area, and which neither my advisory team nor any of our Vietnamese counterparts had visited recently. The officials in Saigon who were in charge of pacification were so pleased that such a hamlet had been pacified that they decided to hold a major ceremony in the hamlet to honor its new status as a "pacified hamlet." When the day came for the ceremony (an individual had been designated "hamlet chief" shortly before the ceremony), a substantial contingent of militia soldiers from the district (perhaps all of them) and our advisory team (as security for the visiting dignitaries) made the trek to the pacified hamlet. Noticing that the troops were speaking in very hushed tones as we approached the hamlet (usually there was a lot of boisterous chatter among the Vietnamese soldiers on an operation), I asked an interpreter why they were so quiet, and his response was "They are afraid they are going to die." Fortunately, the ceremony was held without incident, and we never returned to that hamlet.

Delivery of the M14s

When I arrived in Vietnam the members of my intelligence squad were armed with M1 carbines. These were small rifles, which had been used by ranger and paratroop units during World War II. While lightweight, they were not particularly powerful weapons. After I had been with the advisory team a few months, we were notified that the squad members were to receive M14 semiautomatic rifles to replace the M1 carbines. The catch was that we had to go to the provincial capital to pick up the rifles. My counterpart and I, along with a couple of Vietnamese soldiers, took one of our advisory team's jeeps one morning and headed to the capital a few miles away. Once there, we loaded up a dozen or so M14s, along with the basic load of ammunition for each rifle, which I recall was about seven magazines of twenty-two rounds. The Army sergeant in charge of delivering the M14s warned me as we were leaving that the VC would love to get their hands on these weapons and that we would be wise to take a different route back to our district.

Having taken the well-traveled route to the capital, I was stuck with the "road less traveled," which had a couple of stretches that were deeply rutted, narrow, and overhung with dense vegetation—perfect for ambushes. The fact that we were traveling during the noon hour, when the Vietnamese forces were usually taking a two-hour break, was not particularly comforting. I did not know whether the VC also took two-hour breaks at noon. The trip went smoothly until we reached the narrow, winding stretch. The VC had constructed a roadblock as a nuisance to travelers. When we got there it had been partially knocked down and in effect had become a ramp. We hit the ramp full throttle, and for a brief moment or two were airborne. When we hit the ground, the rifles and ammunition in the back seat of the jeep scattered onto the road. The two Vietnamese soldiers who had been sitting on the gunnels of the jeep were definitely hurting (the jeep had no shock absorbers to speak of), and we had to stop and pick up the rifles and ammunition. The trip was otherwise uneventful, but our team's senior adviser noted a couple of days later that the jeep was not driving quite right. The Vietnamese never took another jeep ride with me.

The Whorehouse

The Vietnamese and my advisory team enjoyed American movies that we brought back from Long Binh. We had a screen set up in the courtyard of our compound, and we all watched flicks at night. One evening we were watching a Vietnamese favorite, *The Green Berets*, starring John Wayne. There was something about John Wayne that they loved, particularly when he tried to speak Vietnamese. They wanted to watch the movie over and over again, especially the ending when John Wayne is speaking to a young Vietnamese boy about what a great future awaited him as the sun set over the South China Sea. The Vietnamese noticed, much more quickly than did the advisers, that the sun does not set over the South China Sea if you live in Vietnam. They thought that minor instance of "cinematic license" was great comedy.

About halfway through the movie, we were visited by an Army colonel who was upset that, as he put it, "prostitutes were inside his perimeter and were intermingling with his troops." He wanted the police chief (a movie regular) and my counterpart to go out, locate, and remove the prostitutes. We looked at each other (intent on watching John Wayne and his Green Berets) and realized that we really had no choice. When we got to the middle of an open area where the Army unit was located, the colonel proceeded to light up the entire area with a flare. No prostitutes were sighted, and the U.S. troops who were securing the perimeter immediately commenced yelling obscenities at whoever was stupid enough to light a flare.

The colonel decided we should proceed to another spot where troops were located to look for the prostitutes. We had to pass through an area where the unit's "tiger scouts" lived. They were allegedly highly trained, specialized Vietnamese soldiers who worked with U.S. units, particularly in conducting patrols and locating the VC. As we proceeded to the tiger scout living quarters, the colonel cautioned us to be respectful of the privacy of the tiger scouts, since they lived with their families. As we started to go through their living quarters, one thing became immediately apparent to the police chief, my counterpart, and me: we were in the veritable den of iniquity being sought by the colonel. No Vietnamese wife would have dressed the way the women with the tiger scouts were dressed. We grinned at each other, moved on without saying a word and without finding any prostitutes, and returned to John Wayne and his Green Berets.

General Death

Combined operations between Vietnamese and U.S. units were generally unsuccessful, with one exception. One day we were visited by a young couple who had worked with the VC tending to wounded soldiers, but who had become disenchanted with the VC and defected. They were willing to lead us to where the VC were tending to injured soldiers. In conjunction with a U.S. Army unit, and using armored personnel carriers, we went to the suspected location in a swampy area heavily vegetated with nipa palm trees. We searched the area. Other than a cooking fire and some rice and tea that were being heated, there was no sign of the VC. The U.S. unit gave up the search, but my intelligence unit and the other Vietnamese soldiers kept looking. Eventually, they located an underground shelter and captured several VC without a shot being fired. Most of the VC soldiers' wounds were from booby traps set by the VC, who did not keep records or mark where they had placed explosives.

As a result of this operation, the U.S. unit decided to award Bronze Stars to several members of my intelligence unit who had found the VC. The district chief was also to receive a Bronze Star as a matter of protocol, although I do not recall that he accompanied the operation. Shortly after the operation, a U.S. Army general came to our compound and awarded the Bronze Stars. As fate would have it, within two weeks most of the recipients of the medals had been either killed or seriously wounded in action. The general became known among the Vietnamese as "General Death," and no one after that was particularly eager to receive any U.S. military honors.

The Chicken Leg

During operations, we ate "off the land." Somehow, out of nowhere, chickens and ducks were produced and cooked at noontime when we were in the field. It was never clear if the owners of the chickens and ducks ever received payment. The Vietnamese method of cooking was to chop up the bird, put it into a pot with vegetables, and boil it. Everyone else would take chopsticks and enjoy a good meal. I still struggle with chopsticks and was really ineffective with them in Vietnam. I usually wound up grabbing a foot or neck out of the pot, rarely anything that I could actually eat. One of my great moments in Vietnam came late in my tour of duty when the leg and thigh of a chicken were boiled intact and given to me. I was most appreciative.

The Short Rounds

An artillery base was located in Can Giuoc for part of my year in Vietnam. The artillery fired on suspected VC and North Vietnamese locations, and occasionally a round landed without exploding (a "short round"). Usually a team of specialists was called in to detonate the short rounds. Once a couple of short rounds fell in a local hamlet. As often was the case in incidents like this, the only people who seemed to be concerned and wanted to rectify the situation were the advisers. The artillery unit sent a two-man team one Sunday afternoon to detonate the shells. On this particular day there were neither advisers nor soldiers available to lead the team to the site where the short rounds had landed. Since the hamlet was in a fairly secure area, I went with the explosives team to show them the location of the shells. After wrapping the shells in detonation cord, embedding them in the muddy bank of the river, and lighting the detonation cord, the team dropped back to a secure area to await the explosion. After dropping back, they noticed an old man in a sampan cruising down the river not far from the shells that were about to explode. Both ran to the riverbank shouting and waving their arms. The old man turned around and sailed off in the other direction, no doubt wondering about the two gesticulating Americans. He soon found out, and no one was harmed. I will always remember the courage of those two Americans, who may well have saved the life of a total stranger.

Departure

One of the saddest days of my life was leaving the village of Can Giuoc, which had been my home for a year. Close relationships invariably develop in such circumstances, not only with fellow advisers but also the local people. While my Vietnamese counterpart and I initially had difficulties relating, by the end we got along well, and I had no need of an interpreter. When I got into the jeep for the last time and left the compound, there were probably twenty or so advisers and Vietnamese waving goodbye. Emotionally it was a tough experience. While I could not predict the ultimate North Vietnamese victory in the South, I knew that, whatever the outcome, life for most of the Vietnamese with whom I had worked and lived would be filled with inevitable hardships with little or no future. While I was able to leave and return to what we all called "the world," the Vietnamese had nowhere to go.

The night before I left Vietnam, I got together with those classmates from Fort Benning and Fort Holabird with whom I had flown to Vietnam. No one in our group was injured, and most of us flew home together, but there was not much celebration. Everyone was glad to have survived, and we talked a little bit about our experiences, but the focus had already shifted to returning home.

The Army had redesigned the entering and exiting procedures at the air terminal. I don't recall seeing any incoming troops. Once in the United States, life picked up pretty much where it had left off. I interviewed at law firms in San Francisco on the way back to Baltimore, where I served the remaining four months of my active duty at the National Agency Check Center (a centralized data collection station for all intelligence information gathered about American citizens by the armed services). People wore their hair longer, sideburns were in fashion, and clothing styles had changed. Vietnam quickly became a faraway place, constituting an interlude in my life, which frankly I did not talk much about. While I might have reminisced in general terms about the experience, and described some of the more humorous moments of my year in Vietnam, there was no one I could talk to who could relate to my experience. Within a few months, I was an associate at a large law firm in Rochester, New York, far removed from Vietnam. Eventually I was joined in the firm by a couple of young lawyers, who had flown over North Vietnam as Navy and Air Force fighter pilots, and another who had served in the Navy commanding a river gunboat. There were not many lawyers, friends, or neighbors in Rochester who had served in Vietnam. Only when I came to New Hampshire in 1981 did I meet an attorney with my new law firm who had served in the Army in Vietnam in a similar capacity.

Two events occurred shortly after I returned home that brought back into focus the tragic side of my experience. Two weeks after my return, I received a letter notifying me that my Vietnamese counterpart had been wounded by a booby trap and died while being flown by a medevac helicopter to the U.S. Army hospital in Saigon. His wife, who had been told that he was still alive when he had been placed on the medevac helicopter, had come to our compound looking for me to find out his condition. My replacement, who was a complete stranger to her, had to give her the sad news.

At about the same time, I read a story on the front page of a Sunday edition of the *Baltimore Sun* about Colonel Asa Gray, who had been the senior adviser for Long An Province during my tour of duty. While trying to persuade a U.S. Army artillery unit not to shell a hamlet from which it was receiving small-arms fire, Colonel Gray had been killed by a sniper's bullet. Colonel Gray had been an Army engineer who was serving as an adviser to get his "ticket punched" for service in Vietnam. He had also become a friend of mine and a man I greatly admired. Several years later I made a point of finding his name on the Vietnam War Memorial in Washington, D.C.

Afterthoughts

In reading the above stories, it is important to keep in mind that they took place over the course of a year. Most of the time, life as an adviser was extremely routine, broken up with occasional trips to Saigon and the Army base at Long Binh for supplies. One could get up at four o'clock in the morning for an operation searching for VC in rice paddies and small hamlets where people lived much as they did in biblical times, and by the afternoon be headed to Saigon for drinks at the Continental Hotel and an opportunity to read the international edition of the *New York Herald Tribune*. The toughest part of such days was to make sure you got back to Can Giuoc before dark.

As odd as it may seem today, when I returned from Vietnam I had not developed any particular view for or against the war. I knew that whichever side prevailed, life in Can Giuoc probably would not be much different, although those who had fought for the Republic of South Vietnam and did not escape no doubt would risk execution or relocation into some sort of detention center. I accepted my year in Vietnam as a "life experience," with no lasting adverse effects. It was an opportunity to have participated in the first major event of my generation (other than the civil rights movement). I also recognized, particularly with the passage of time, that I had learned a lot during my time in the Army, including my approach to judging and dealing with people. I still have clear memories of the Infantry School at Fort Benning, and the lessons learned there by a group of very young men.

I returned to South Vietnam with my wife, Alice, in 2000. We arranged with our guide for an afternoon trip to my village. After assurances from both our guide and the driver that they knew where Can Giuoc was located, we pretty quickly got lost once outside Ho Chi Minh City. When they started to ask me for directions, I knew we were in trouble. After several stops asking for directions, we arrived in Can Giuoc in the late afternoon. The village was basically unchanged, except for telephone and power lines. The marketplace looked somewhat ramshackle. The compound we had lived in was still used by the military, and looked the same, except that windows had been installed where previously there were only wooden shutters. Despite the efforts of our guide to persuade the guards at the compound to let us in, after some discussion among themselves the guards concluded that it was not a good idea to allow an American in the compound. We quickly became the center of attention in the village, particularly among the children. Unfortunately, since we arrived late in the afternoon, we did not have much time to walk around. After visiting the marketplace, we headed back to Ho Chi Minh City. By that time, it had gotten dark, and for a moment when leaving the village I had a knee-jerk reaction that we should not be traveling in the countryside at night.

Curt Little joined a law firm in Rochester, New York, after completing active duty with the Army in September 1969. He later served as corporate counsel to the Lake Placid Olympic Organizing Committee in Lake Placid, New York. Following Lake Placid, he joined a law firm in Manchester, New Hampshire. He currently practices corporate law with a law firm that he formed with three other attorneys in 1996. He lives in Bedford, New Hampshire, with his wife, Alice.

"I Guess You Can Learn Something Anywhere"

WALTON SMITH : U.S. ARMY

July 1967 to January 1968

When I graduated from law school, as Dean Griswold shook my hand, he asked what I would be doing next. I told him that I was in JAG and would be going directly to Vietnam. He was silent for a few seconds and did not release my hand. Finally he said, "Well, I guess you can learn something anywhere." I took that as a very ambiguous blessing and set out to "learn something." Maybe I did.

My first six months in Vietnam were relatively uneventful and better than law school, which I had not enjoyed. The work was not demanding. I was getting paid. The beer was good and cold. The French had left numerous good restaurants in Saigon and good recipes for both bread and coffee.

Lieutenant Colonel Ralph Murray, head of the Foreign Claims Unit (FCU), was a Boston Irishman, who had been enlisted during World War II and joined JAG when Korea came along to avoid being enlisted in World War III, which he thought was coming. He had been passed over and was working toward retirement as quietly as possible, a task made difficult by the animosity of Colonel Ivey, the MACV staff judge advocate, who thought Murray had "jumped down the gin bottle." Murray did keep a pitcher of vodka in the freezer in his BOQ room and invited the younger officers over from time to time for drinks and dinner at the field-grade mess. The four or five action officers (all JAG captains) were relatively fresh out of law school.

The enlisted men in our office were a varied lot. Specialist Schaeffer was a German who went from being a very young member of the Wehrmacht to being a translator for the Americans in 1945 and was still in the Army twenty-three years later. Specialist Soares had been an MP but could no longer pass the MP physical, so transferred to JAG as an investigator. We had a former RAF (Royal Air Force) enlisted man who had seen air-conditioned enlisted barracks at a U.S. Air Force base in North Africa and changed allegiance as quickly as possible. One specialist was a member of the New York bar, one a coal miner/politician from West Virginia, and the whole lot was presided over by an amiable Tex-Mex sergeant.

All in all I considered my situation better in Saigon than it had been in law school, except that the work was totally futile. The job was to adjudicate claims made by noncombatants for injuries done them by U.S. personnel. Under the Foreign Claims Act of 1943, enacted when U.S. personnel were involved with foreigners in the UK, Australia, and a few ports around the world, we were required to apply "the common law of the United States," as if that were something one could easily determine in an office in Saigon that had no law books. The claimants were used to local customary law, to the Vietnamese version of Chinese customary law, and perhaps to some colonial version of French civil law, but certainly not to the common law of the United States, so whatever we did would appear foolish to them.

After much agonizing, we figured out that moving files was what the Army wanted us to do, and the easiest way to move a file along without complaint was to pay something, regardless of the facts, which we could not know, or the law, which only confused the matter. Years later, I read an article that indicated that some VC villages got along on payments coming out of the FCU, with the help of our senior investigator/translator who would write up a good claim for anyone for a price.

The FCU had countrywide jurisdiction, so I went to Pleiku, Da Nang, and other beauty spots in Vietnam. On a trip to Pleiku toward the end of 1967, I went out with a civil affairs officer to a village we had threatened to offend by agreeing to pay a poor widow woman a small sum as the result of the death of her son. That payment would have made her the richest person in the village, thus harming the status of the local headman. The solution to the problem was for someone from MACV (me) to take the money in an envelope to the village and give it to the headman and for him to give it and all (or some) of the money to the widow. A small convoy of us rode out from Pleiku through the coffee plantations to the village. The civil affairs officer and I had an awkward conference with the village elders and drank the black drink with long straws from the bottom of a long hollow vessel. I took as little as possible while still appearing to be polite.

I went on from there to Da Nang to help out in the FCU branch office there, which had recently been damaged by the bombing of the building in which it was located. The official version of the bombing was that the VC had attacked the MP station in the same building. The JAG people were annoyed because the real cause of the blast, they thought, was that some of the MPs had patronized a local brothel and had failed to pay their debts before rotating home. The unpaid girls used the bombing as a way to indicate to the remaining MPs that payment was expected before leaving. Whatever the cause, the JAG office was still dealing with files filled with ceiling plaster and window glass when things got much more serious a few weeks later.

After spending several nights in a Marine BOQ at Third Marine Amphibious Force (3MAF) headquarters outside Da Nang running to the sandbagged bunker every time there was a mortar alert, I returned to Saigon, where the city was being decorated for the Tet holiday with yellow and pink flowers. The translator, who turned out to be selling claims, invited the officers to his house for a celebration including little cakes, hot rice wine, and firecrackers.

February 1968 and After

The next day, I was in the office and got a call from Specialist Schaeffer, who was at the fire department out at Tan Son Nhut investigating a claim. While there he overheard radio calls from all over the country that towns, cities, and U.S. installations were under attack. He asked whether he could "pick up" some weapons for us at the office. (As we were located in the middle of the city, carrying weapons was forbidden.) I said, "Do what you think best" and got off the phone. A little while later there was Schaeffer down on the street hollering up to the office for us to send some of the boys to help him carry up what he had "procured." He had gotten several rifles, some pistols, several boxes of small-arms ammunition, and three or four crates of hand grenades. I had all that stuff put in the vault in the office and began worrying about how I was going to explain its presence.

The famous Five O'Clock Follies press briefings were held across Le Loi Street from my office in a theater on the ground level of the Rex Hotel, a BOQ for senior officers. Colonel Murray frequently let himself into the briefings and came back and told us what was being said about the war. In his absence, I took myself across the street to try to find out more. I found a place at the back of the room and watched as the briefer tried to convince a restive press corps that nothing was going on and what was going on was just fine. An older journalist near me punched his younger associate before the briefing broke up, and said, "Let's get out of here and go find out what's really happening." Relations between the MACV briefers and the press were sour well before the Tet offensive had started, no matter what recent books on the subject say.

At the end of the day, the British specialist asked whether he could distribute the weapons to the men and have them take them to their quarters, as more attacks had been reported and there were no weapons in the hotel that served as barracks for twelve hundred enlisted men. Wanting the things out of the office and thinking that they would be easier to secure scattered with individuals, I said, "Get them out of here!"

That night the VC made a hit-and-run attack on that hotel, and the only responding fire was from the Marine guard at the entrance and a few JAG clerks on the roof. MACV had given no warning of a potential attack and had not provided any additional troops or weapons to protect those unarmed men, except the ones Specialist Schaeffer had procured for us.

For the next several weeks, we were in an island in the middle of the city with little or no communications with MACV at Tan Son Nhut. For a few nights, I was issued a double-barreled shotgun and stood guard duty inside the TAX Building with an Australian army major. There was a large set of stairs from the office floors down to shops on the ground level. The Aussie and I sat at the top of those steps and listened for any sign of activity on the surrounding streets. Fortunately, no one showed up to test my skill with the blunderbuss. When you've got your JAG officers standing guard, things are pretty messed up.

The FCU did, however, get along quite well during Tet. Specialist Soares joined up with some of his MP buddies and did night patrols in downtown Saigon for several weeks. Among the places they checked was the U.S. Embassy, especially its food storage facility. They liberated steaks, which we grilled for lunch on the roof outside the office, and fifty-pound bags of rice, from which we doled out a couple of pounds a day to pay the Vietnamese employees when the normal payroll could not be brought into Saigon from MACV headquarters.

Later that spring, I had to go to Nha Trang on a claim resulting from a shoot-out at the Vietnamese National Railroad maintenance facility during Tet. There was no way I could pay the claim, which was clearly combat related and did not involve U.S. personnel, but I could make it appear that the U.S. took the matter seriously by actually going and listening gravely to the explanation of what happened. A brand-new diesel switching locomotive had just arrived from the United States and was being fitted out for service on a repair track with a maintenance trough under it. The attacking VC had been chased into the rail yard by South Korean troops (called ROKs) whose headquarters was in Nha Trang. The VC took refuge in the repair trough, using it and the new locomotive as a very substantial bunker. The ROKs fired rocket grenades and machine guns into the locomotive until a lucky shot ricocheted into the trough and exploded, ending opposition and the useful life of the locomotive. Driving from the U.S. air base to the rail yard, I was struck by the thought that Nha Trang was one of the most beautiful seaside cities I had ever seen and that it would be a wonderful resort but for the existing unpleasantness. On that trip I passed through Pleiku and learned that the civil affairs officer and some of the others with whom I had gone out to the village the prior fall had been killed when the VC had attacked the camp.

What struck me about the U.S. effort in Vietnam was how bad we were at it. We did the individual things well enough, I suppose; but the overall strategy was just not something we could pull off. It was not one of Queen Victoria's "glorious little wars" in which a few thousand solders led by an eccentric brigadier wander off into the jungle and come out a few months later with a new colony. We expected to go in, do something quickly, leave everyone happy that we had come, and go home. On the other side, still fighting, was Uncle Ho, who had paraphrased Jefferson in 1945 when he had declared Vietnam's independence from France. His horizon and ours were completely different. I do not mean that the United States cannot fight a long struggle—we opposed the Soviet Union for forty-five years before it collapsed—but in this case we were not prepared to do so. In this case most Americans who went to Vietnam did so for twelve months, never learned much about the country, the people, their history, their language, or why they fought. Even those who ran the American war and did stay "in country" for over a year generally did not leave American bases, officers clubs, or golf courses, other than for the occasional venture to the French colonial cocoon of the Cercle Sportif.

January 2009

I returned to Vietnam in January 2009 on a standard tour of the country: Hanoi, Ha Long Bay, Hue, Da Nang, Hoi An, Nha Trang, Dalat, Saigon, My Tho. I took great pleasure in seeing places I had been and visiting some I had not been able to get to forty years earlier and in the great advances the people of Vietnam had made for themselves.

In Saigon, the TAX Building is now an upscale shopping arcade. Where my office was located is now a fancy children's boutique. At the base of the stairs from which I had watched for VC was a statue of a boy riding a water buffalo where children could be photographed as they would be with Santa in this country. The officers' club on the roof of the Rex Hotel now is an open-air restaurant and bar. The Saigon Saigon Bar in the Hotel Caravelle remains, but no frantic war correspondents hustle for a story. Tu Do Street is now Dong Khoi (from "Freedom" to "General Uprising"). Its bars and bar girls are mostly gone now, but the little shops selling Vietnamese artwork remain.

Nha Trang has become the beautiful seaside resort that its location indicated it could become. Its airport, the former Cam Ranh Bay U.S. Air Force Base, was—like many others in Vietnam—built by the American taxpayer at the cost of many billions of dollars and no few lives.

A small portion of the 3MAF base outside Da Nang is now a Vietnamese military post. The rest is falling into disrepair. The seafront opposite was being built out as vacation homes for golfers and sun seekers from Japan, Korea, and China.

Learning Something Anywhere

In my time in Vietnam, I think I did learn something, but probably not what Dean Griswold may have had in mind. I became more cynical about U.S. policy makers and their agents in the field and more sympathetic to those—both Vietnamese and American—who were mere pawns in their games. I learned to be more humble regarding the real motivation of people who appear to be opposed to what we want. The United States in Vietnam was fixated on its real, global conflict with the Soviet Union. The

Vietnamese wanted to complete the recovery of their independence from all outside domination—French, American, Chinese, or other. They had their own motives and objectives in mind, and we were merely another in a long series of obstacles to be overcome on the way to achieving them.

- -

Walton Smith remained in Army JAG at the Pentagon for three years after returning from Vietnam. He then joined the legal department of Amtrak, which was just forming. In 1975 he joined Lord, Bissell & Brook, with which he practiced law in Washington, Chicago, and Atlanta until he retired in 2004. He now resides in Clarkesville, Georgia, where with his wife and son he owns Soque ArtWorks, a gallery of regionally made art and craft.

Thoughts on Vietnam

JIM HARRIS : U.S. NAVY

Fittingly, I am writing this on Memorial Day. Surprisingly, thinking about Vietnam is harder than I imagined. First, a bit of history. When we were boys, World War II was not a distant memory; nearly every man, it seemed, was a veteran.

My father rode a destroyer for four years in the Solomon Islands. I grew up knowing that I would join the Navy when the right time came. That time came in 1966, about halfway through law school, when I volunteered for the Navy's JAG program. After I graduated and passed the bar in 1967, I went on active duty.

Vietnam was a growing, ominous spectacle for us in law school, but it was still a world away and surely would not amount to much. I opposed the war simply because I thought it was an arrogant use of America's power devoted to no good end. Neither the war nor my opposition to it played any part in my commitment to serve.

What I did not understand at the time was that the North Vietnamese were just as devoted to the freedom and union of their nation as the people of America had ever been. Before partition into North and South in 1954, the Vietnamese had a thousand-year history of independence. They had fought the forces of colonialism since the middle of the nineteenth century and had utterly defeated the French at the battle of Dien Bien Phu in 1954.

As British military historian Martin Windrow writes on page 42 of *The Last Valley: Dien Bien Phu and the French Defeat in Vietnam*, Dien Bien Phu was "the first time that a non-European colonial independence movement had evolved through all the stages from guerrilla bands to a conventionally organized and equipped army able to defeat a modern Western occupier in pitched battle."

Jim Harris

America's bellicose policy wonks ignored this lesson. America *chose* to fight in Vietnam.

Our adopted classmate, Jim Wright, has written a new book called *Those Who Have Borne the Battle*. In it, he refers not to Vietnam but to the war in Korea as "the missing chapter, the absent lesson in American military history." We did not learn.

In his review of Wright's book in the *New York Times Book Review* of May 27, 2012, Andrew J. Bacevich concludes that "war was becoming amorphous—undeclared, lacking clear objectives, with victory as such no longer the goal." Clearly, Korea was but a dire portent of Vietnam.

The Vietnamese, of course, were not at all impressed by even so powerful a nation as America. They had suffered under French rule, first as a protectorate and then as a colony for almost a hundred years, from 1859 until the Vietnamese victory in 1954.

A young Vietnamese nationalist, later known as Ho Chi Minh, began soliciting help for the independence of his people at least as early as 1920 in a letter to Secretary of State Robert Lansing. After the declaration of Vietnam's independence in 1945, he wrote to President Truman, to no effect. He later exchanged letters with Presidents Johnson and Nixon, again apparently to no effect.

Beginning in 1950, American military advisers arrived in what was then French Indochina. U.S. involvement escalated in the early 1960s, with troop levels tripling in 1961 and again in 1962. U.S. combat units were deployed beginning in 1965. America's role ended with our defeat in 1975. Vietnam remains Communist to this day.

Early in my active-duty years, 1967–71, I was legal counsel to the Physical Disability Review Board at St. Albans Naval Hospital in New York. The board's purpose was to meet with wounded sailors and Marines and to evaluate and pass judgment on the degree of their disabilities. There,

I witnessed wheelchair races in the halls among young men with one or both legs missing.

I remember learned discussions among the medicos as to exactly how much a twenty-year-old with only half a right hand or no legs below his knee would be worth the rest of his life. One young man had his forehead blown away, an involuntary prefrontal lobotomy. He seemed only vaguely amused at the proceedings. Later, I was assigned to the trial team at Brooklyn Naval Station, where I both prosecuted and defended errant sailors and Marines. One such Marine had run afoul of the Uniform Code of Military Justice shortly after being awarded the Silver Star for charging an enemy position using guns he had retrieved from dead enemy soldiers after his own weapon had run out of ammunition.

As the war increased in intensity, I felt increasingly betrayed. For the first time, I realized that my government would lie to its citizens.

There was General Westmoreland with his absurd search-and-destroy missions that turned out to be far more destroy than search. There was Calley's slaughter of 104 civilians in a ditch at My Lai.

There was Johnson, who at first I thought was just a Texas rube, misled by a cadre of Walter Mittys. Now, Robert Caro notwithstanding, I think he was just a Texas rube.

There was McNamara, who now admits, with blood on his hands, "I was so wrong. God, I was wrong."

There was Nixon, invading Laos, first with carpet bombing by B-52s and other aircraft. Then, he crossed the frontier of Laos with an invasion force of six hundred thousand U.S. and South Vietnamese troops, all the while loudly proclaiming, "This is not an invasion of Laos."

This same Nixon also loudly proclaimed, "I am not a crook" as he decamped from the White House one step away from impeachment.

There was the unholy alliance of Nixon and Kissinger, who during peace talks conspired to bargain away men's lives for the hope of political advantage.

When the war ended in 1975, after ten years and more than 58,000 American deaths, plus another 350,000 wounded, I took comfort in one thought: at least we will never fight such a stupid war again. But that was before Iraq and Afghanistan.

Jim Harris was released from active duty in the Navy in 1972 and returned to Nashville to begin his law practice, which he continues to this day. Upon his return to civilian life, he affiliated with the Naval Reserve, and remained an active, drilling reservist for the next nineteen years. He rose to the rank of captain and retired in 1989. He served as pro bono co-legal counsel for the Nashville Music Association for eighteen years and as a member and chairman of the Music City Tennis Tournament, a benefit for Vanderbilt's Children's Hospital, for more than twenty years. He currently serves as chair of the KeyBoard, an advisory board to the Blair School of Music at Vanderbilt University.

Duty and Service in the Cold War Era

EDMUND B. FROST : U.S. ARMY

My first memory of Americans being called to war is hearing on the radio in the summer of 1950 that North Korea had invaded South Korea and that we were at war against the Communists. From then on, through graduation from Denver's South High School in 1960, the Cold War and the threats coming from Russian and Chinese Communists and their puppet states became vividly present in my understanding of the world.

As I grew older in the 1950s I learned about patriotism, duty, courage, sacrifice, and military service, as well as the need to defend America and its values in a world still plagued by totalitarian states.

During high school I was very active in competitive skiing in Colorado. Many veterans of the Tenth Mountain Division were active in the skiing industry and served as coaches and mentors. I started to see these past warriors as heroes and potential role models.

When I was getting ready to leave for Hanover in September 1960, my father told me that one of my tasks at college was to figure out how I would fulfill my duty to serve my country. It was easy, then, for me to decide to join Army ROTC with its mountain and winter warfare program run by veteran Tenth Mountain Division master sergeant William Brown. In my freshman and sophomore years I made many friends and greatly enjoyed this program.

By 1962 the Cold War was heating up, and the draft was a reality. Addition of a monthly stipend made it easy under the circumstances to make a commitment to the Advanced ROTC program and to service as an Army officer.

During junior and senior years, ROTC provided a valuable part of my Dartmouth education—especially in the military history course taught by Professor Morton and in practical information about human organizations, governance, and leadership. At the time, military presence and acknowledgment of authority were not very visible in my personality. At graduation from Dartmouth I was commissioned into the Adjutant General's Corps (administration and personnel) instead of a combat arms branch.

I received a deferment from active duty and headed to law school at the University of Michigan in Ann Arbor. There I was more focused academically and was able to reach almost the top of my class. In June 1966 I married Molly Spitzer (Wellesley, '66).

In my last year of law school I applied for an honors clerkship position with the general counsel of the Army. One position was available each year. It required a three-year commitment, but would have fulfilled my active-duty obligation. In January 1967, after my interview at the Pentagon, the general counsel informed me that I had been provisionally selected. The hitch turned out to be that the man who interviewed me resigned. The new general counsel, Robert Jordan, passed over me and selected a well-qualified man who was graduating from Georgetown Law School and who also worked for Senator Edward Kennedy I learned this in a phone call from Jordan. He also told me that I could keep in touch and that he would see if he could find me something else challenging in Washington.

After law school I had time to take the bar exam and work for a law firm in Denver. I reported for active duty October 17, 1967, at the Army Adjutant General School at Fort Benjamin Harrison in Indianapolis.

In late November orders came down from the Department of the Army assigning me to the staff and faculty of the Officers Advanced Course at the Army Intelligence School at Fort Holabird in Baltimore. I reported there January 2, 1968. My duties involved security and administrative matters. I was also working on constitutional and human rights issues relevant to military intelligence and national security matters. My assignment at Holabird was supposed to last for the rest of my active-duty tour.

My wife, Molly, got a job teaching high school English at the Maret School in northwest Washington near the National Cathedral. We oriented our lives toward Washington and have been living there ever since.

My work at Holabird was interesting but uneventful, with one exception. I was appointed to be the lawyer for a student at Holabird—a young second lieutenant who suffered a mental breakdown and, without a hearing, was being forced out of the Army with less than an honorable discharge. I developed an argument that he had a constitutional due process right to a hearing, and I petitioned for a hearing at successively higher levels of command until I reached the secretary of the Army. I filed a written appeal with the secretary of the Army. Then, based on my earlier conversation with Robert Jordan, and being a zealous advocate as required by the canons of ethics, I called the office of the general counsel of the Army to see if I could get some help. I talked to one of the "honors clerks" (I think it was the one from Senator Kennedy's office). He was interested in my argument and said he thought he could help. A few days later, in late May, an order came down from the secretary of the Army granting my client a hearing. A couple of days later I got orders for Vietnam. This whole chain of events was scary and sobering—especially in the context of the Tet offensive and the political chaos in the United States in the spring of 1968.

Protesting my Vietnam orders did not seem to be sensible, or honorable, for that matter. I did, however, visit the Adjutant General's Corps career branch at the Office of Personnel Operations, Department of the Army, to see what I could do about getting an interesting and challenging job in Vietnam. Not long after this visit, orders came down changing my new assignment to Headquarters Eighth Army, Office of the Adjutant General, Seoul, Korea. By this time I was starting to learn something about keeping my head down. I never asked and never knew how this change in assignment came about. In any event, the Army really did not want a hearing, so my Holabird client got an honorable discharge, and I got a fascinating tour of duty in Korea.

Upon arrival at Eighth Army headquarters in Seoul I reported to my new boss, Colonel Robert W. Franz. He had grown up on an Iowa farm and graduated from Iowa State with an Army ROTC commission. He had served as a tank commander in Patton's Third Army in World War II, married a girl from Paris, made the Army his career after he was called back for the Korean War, and was sent by the Army to Harvard for an MBA.

Colonel Franz was smart, capable, wise, ethical, and tough. He also had a wry sense of humor. He expected a lot from his junior officers. At our first meeting he told me that I would often be a little over my head in a lieutenant colonel's job, and that I would undoubtedly make mistakes. Nevertheless, he told me to make my own decisions rather than coming to him for advice all the time. He added that I should be on the lookout for my mistakes and that when I saw one, it was time to let him know so that he could help me, if fixing it was needed. I was truly fortunate to have the experience of working for Colonel Franz—one of the finest men I have ever worked with.

My job at Eighth Army HQ turned out to be interesting and challenging. I started as the deputy to Captain Harry Ruppenthal, the chief of the Adjutant General's Officer Personnel Branch (known in Army jargon as HQ Eighth Army—AGPO). This office was in charge of all officer requisitions, in-country assignments, and personnel actions for Army officers from second lieutenant through lieutenant colonel. When Ruppenthal's tour ended in April 1969, I became the branch chief.

AGPO had two officers, a master sergeant, about twenty other enlisted men, and an equal number of Korean civilian employees. It was constantly filled with the press of routine assignment orders and personnel actions. There was also a steady stream of interesting problems. From time to time there were issues relating to needs in the field for specially trained officers and for company-grade infantry officers. There were also problems regarding officers sent to Korea who had lingering difficulties arising from previous combat tours in Vietnam. We worked closely with the surgeon general's office and the chaplain's office to help these men with counseling and medical support so that they could make it through their thirteen-month tour in Korea.

There was also a custom of paying special attention to the needs and wishes of the medical doctors who were assigned to Korea. My contribution was to figure out how, consistent with the joint travel regulations, to send the docs home at the end of their tours going west through South Asia, the Middle East, and Europe.

I filled my off-duty time working with Korean college students. Through an introduction from my international law professor at Michigan, I taught a weekly seminar in comparative constitutional law at the Seoul National University Law School. I was also, as successor to Captain Ruppenthal, the English-speaking adviser to the Orient Club, a group of students from top colleges who met Wednesday nights at the Seoul YMCA to practice spoken English. This Orient Club connection also led to many other informal social occasions and club outings. It also helped me gain a basic facility with the spoken Korean language.

My wife, Molly, was able to join me in Seoul in May 1969 after her teaching year in Washington ended. She got a job teaching English at Yonsei University, which expanded our involvement with college students. We both thought highly of our students' abilities, enthusiasm, and idealism. We were fortunate indeed to be able to work with these students who, with their peers, courageously brought South Korea from an era of hardship and authoritarianism into its modern era of democracy and prosperity.

As my time in Korea and my two-year tour of active duty drew to a close, Molly and I made plans to return to the States. Using the returning doctors' itineraries as a precedent, I was able to arrange for a twenty-five-day terminal leave and a travel route that went west through Japan, the Philippines, Hong Kong, Thailand, India, Israel, Greece, Italy, France, and England, to New Jersey. We got back to Washington just in time for me to start my law career at Steptoe & Johnson on December 1, 1969.

The experience gained during my active duty was undoubtedly valuable in my future law career. Colonel Franz was a great mentor in the basic skills of dealing with all sorts of people, carrying responsibility, and working out the real-world meaning of good ethics. Our Korean experience gave us an abiding interest in Asia and knowledge of how people with greatly different backgrounds and culture could share the same values and aspirations. We had been spared the horrors and injuries of war, and we enjoyed fantastic travels. We had also cemented our own relationship and felt ready to take up purposeful roles in society. We knew that we were very lucky.

Looking back to that time long ago I have a bit of survivor's guilt knowing I did not have to share in the burdens of fellow soldiers who made real sacrifices in their service. I am still proud that I answered the call to serve and that I served as a citizen soldier.

Edmund and Molly Frost stayed in Washington and still live in the Cleveland Park neighborhood, where they raised four children. He practiced law there for forty years (mostly federal litigation). Now he and his older brother are managing a family natural gas wildcat operating and production company in Fort Worth, Texas. Molly earned a PhD in Chinese linguistics from Georgetown University and is teaching Chinese culture and history at George Washington University.

The Past as Prologue

ALAN E. FERRIS : U.S. ARMY

The date was February 8, 1967. While driving to Fort Benning, Georgia, in my 1954 Chevrolet convertible to begin my two-year tour of duty in Army Intelligence, I could not help but hear on the radio, my only companion on the trip, news commentary describing the importance of our country's involvement in Vietnam and the need to stop the surge of communism. Yet, just a short while earlier, while working in New York City at 30 Rockefeller Plaza, I had seen a huge crowd demonstrating vociferously against the war in Vietnam. As I was observing, someone in front of me said "Alan?" He was young, had a long beard and wild hair, and his attire was unkempt. At first I did not recognize him, but then he said "I'm Mike, Howard's brother, from Manhasset." Yes, it was indeed! My recollection of him was as a likable, bright, respectful, quiet but intelligent boy, three years my junior. He had looked up to me as a basketball player on our high school team but did not seem like someone who would morph into an angry young man who was about to tell me that the United States was evil or that Communist China was the principled savior of society. Nor someone who upon hearing I was soon to go on active duty hoped I would be killed in action. Sadly his transformation reflected the division in our country at the time, which was characterized by a growing and deepening schism between conservatives and liberals that was characterized by hard and fast, uncompromising viewpoints. On the one hand, many young people thought the United States was evil and needed to extricate itself from foreign entanglements. On the other hand, liberals were oft seen as idealists, soft on communism and devoid of patriotism. That was the thought of many who went through the experience of World War II and/or Korea.

Although the specifics of the philosophical debate at the time were different from what they are today, there are numerous parallels in the sense of the respective viewpoints having hard-and-fast opinions about a variety of subjects. Just as in the era of my youth, the country is, again, heavily polarized, with conservatives unable to understand how liberals do not see the "truth," while liberals have the same feeling about conservatives. And, with evolving technology, twenty-four-hour news cycles, bloggers, etc., the polarization seems to be even more intense than in the past. Such polarization interferes with the ability of our government and our society to discuss critical issues of the day in a civil and productive way. That fact is evidenced by a national government that has been frozen into inaction on many important issues.

Now, as I have this occasion to sit back, think about and briefly document my military experience, I relish the opportunity to relate some portion of that time in my life for my children. That is especially true for my grandchildren and other loved ones. Not only to reflect upon what my military experience meant to me, how it touched me, and what some of the values it inculcated in me were, but also to see if I can extrapolate some learning experiences into guidance for them.

Early in my freshman year at Dartmouth, I joined the Army ROTC with the expectation that my military service, which I believed was inevitable because of the draft, would be best served by becoming an officer. This included the likely prospect of an assignment to the Intelligence Corps and a tour of duty in Germany. Looking back, I realize that my thought process at the time was superficial, limiting my consideration to the fact that the Intelligence Corps was both a safer branch of service and also more exotic than a combat branch. In addition the assignment would be more suited to my personal strengths, which were more cerebral than physical. In retrospect, I wish I had also considered such things as the greater potential for leadership training and personal development, which would be advantages more related to the combat branches.

At the end of sophomore year we all had to decide whether to commit to completing the ROTC program or to drop out. We all knew that electing to finish the program meant that we would have to serve two years in the military and that such service could be in one of the combat branches, with no certainty of being assigned to the Intelligence Corps. Therefore, my decision to proceed with the program and become an officer seemed axiomatic and wise. If I had to serve, I preferred to do so as an officer and with a greater prospect of being in the Intelligence Corps as opposed to a combat branch. Although my mother was desperately hoping that I would be excused from military duty and would somehow be lucky enough to fail my physical examination, I recognized that this was just a mother's hope. More to the point, I did not object to military service. On the contrary, I loved my country and thought I had a moral obligation to participate in service.

By the time I graduated in 1964 and was commissioned a second lieutenant in the U.S. Army Intelligence Corps, the Vietnam War was escalating. That became clear after my deferment to attend business school between 1964 and 1966. For those who had elected to become officers and were assigned to the Intelligence Corps, our path was obvious. We would first be assigned to Fort Benning, Georgia, to attend IOBC (Infantry Officer Basic Course), where we would learn the functions of an infantry officer in a Vietnamese setting, after which we would attend the U.S. Army Intelligence School, located at Fort Holabird, Maryland, where we would learn the basics of the various intelligence functions, ranging from photo intelligence to prisoner-of-war interrogation. Then we would be assigned to a tour of duty in Vietnam, where we would be given specific assignments. Following commissioning in 1964 and graduating from business school, I took a job in venture capital while waiting for my active-duty notice. I served from February 1967 to February 1969.

I participated for thirteen weeks in the IOBC course at Fort Benning, where we trained for a combat tour in Vietnam. We went through multiple exercises, with training often ending in the early morning hours and beginning again in the early morning hours. This led to a highly developed skill of sleeping through daytime lectures. I remember clearly many elements of that training, most of which were what one would expect, such as learning to fire multiple types of weapons (which was fun), throw grenades (they were heavy), march in formation (boring), engage in physical exercise (not fun, but healthy), read maps (important for many Army skills), organize and run a platoon (leadership training), etc.

Notwithstanding the more mundane elements of IOBC, there were many special moments that have left a lasting impression. I vividly recall that within the first few days, we assembled at a firing field at night and saw a striking display of the firepower an infantry company could produce. Tracer bullets filled the night sky, first from one solitary gun, then a second, then a machine gun, then a platoon, and finally a company, all with cascading blankets of red and the attendant din. How could anyone survive such an onslaught? I thought, and how horrible it would have been to be on the receiving end of such fire. Then there was the day we divided into groups of four and engaged in a series of exercises, rotating leadership positions so that we each led 25 percent of the exercises, which included such things as finding a map on the ground (was there a booby trap beneath the stone holding the map?), leading a reconnaissance squad and hearing the enemy approach (should we kill the enemy or let them pass without seeing us?), and deciding the best path to traverse. Where was the explosive device most likely to be? Failure to make the right decision in each teaching example could lead to death, either for ourselves or those we were leading, and also to failure of the mission. During that day we each died multiple times, but these exercises also must have saved countless lives on the real battlefield. Then, there was the night of "escape and evasion," when at around 5 p.m., having not eaten all day, our company was divided into about twenty groups of ten individuals each, given a live rabbit and a full canteen of water, and were told that we were behind enemy lines and had to get to a specific site to avoid capture and interrogation. Our mission, obviously, was to kill and cook the rabbit, which would be our only food, and escape capture by regular infantry enlisted men who had an incentive of "days off" for each officer they captured. I was the only member of my group who avoided capture and interrogation, but it was a frightful night spent escaping one capture attempt after another, worrying about snakes, and trying to figure out how to navigate through the night back to the safe haven. There was also the cold and rainy night I was sent on reconnaissance with another soldier to ascertain the location and strength of the enemy. I vividly recall, huddled next to my companion, being totally focused on preserving body heat until daylight, so that we could complete our mission.

Finally, I recall the commencement speech after I completed IOBC at Fort Benning. The commanding officer asked all of us seated to "look to [the person on] our right, look to our left, look to our front, and look to our back," after which he told us that in one year, two of the four people we looked at would have been killed, and one would be wounded. I was not shaken with personal fear, primarily I think because I knew he was talking about infantry officers and not intelligence officers. However, having watched numerous World War II movies with my brother while growing up, there was invariably an individual who predicted he would not survive the war. When a young infantry officer from Brooklyn, just recently married, proclaimed he did not think he would survive his service, I did feel a powerful sense of the personal risks being taken. I learned later that he did not survive. There is no question in my mind that my infantry training experience profoundly influenced me in a variety of ways.

Leaving Fort Benning, I traveled to Fort Holabird for four weeks of intelligence training. Nothing exceptional happened there, as our training was merely a perfunctory introduction to the many kinds of specialties we could encounter in Vietnam. The only thing of real importance was waiting for the four weeks to end, at which point we were to receive our assignment in Vietnam, where our real training would commence.

My orders were a major surprise, as I was already mentally and emotionally adjusted to spending my next year in Vietnam. As it turned out, even though the practice had been that 100 percent of the graduating intelligence class from Fort Holabird was assigned to Vietnam, two of the fifty officers in our group were assigned to Washington, D.C. I was assigned to the Defense Intelligence Agency (DIA), headquartered in Arlington, Virginia. The other individual, a Yale Law School graduate and head of the Young Americans for Freedom, was assigned to the Defense Department, where he became a player in the Nixon/Hoover scandal involving spying on Americans by opening their mail. My assignment to the DIA, I learned, was the result of my having spent two years at business school with classes in organizational behavior and analytical thinking involving management information systems. This was an expertise the Army thought could be useful in helping the DIA introduce computer systems into the intelligence process. I had not realized that Army personnel actually read and studied my background and attempted to match individual capabilities with assignments.

My principal assignment at the DIA was to be a systems analyst. Before I was involved in that activity, one unusual, seemingly mundane and irrelevant event occurred. This event, I believe, had positive and unintended consequences, which had a bearing on my entire experience at the DIA in terms of the image it created of me in the mind of my commanding officer. Specifically, my body had reacted to the sleep deprivation I had experienced at IOBC. I developed mononucleosis, which was diagnosed just as I arrived at the DIA. The doctor told my commanding officer, a colonel, that I did not have to come to work until the disease had resolved, but I went on time every day and worked the full day, before returning to my apartment and collapsing in sleep. The colonel seemingly interpreted my actions as reflecting a sense of duty and responsibility and honor. I think the mental image he formed of me influenced his perception of all my subsequent activities, which always seemed to meet with his approval and thus greater responsibility. Ultimately, they contributed to his recommending that I receive a Joint Service Commendation Medal, a special honor. In addition he recommended that I be promoted early to captain and put on a fast track through the Intelligence Corps. When I turned that promotion down, he invited me to join him in starting a new software company, a vote of confidence that I truly appreciated. Again I did not accept. Instead, my wife, the former Madeleine Sherman, whom I met while she was finishing her MA in government at Georgetown University, and I decided to move in a different direction.

Upon arriving at the DIA, I was not even allowed into its offices until my security clearance was approved. While waiting, I spent my time learning about computers and programming. After receiving my clearance, my job was to act as a liaison between programmers and analysts. For example, when working with those responsible for photo intelligence, I had to understand their entire thinking and analytical process related to photo intelligence: what they were looking for in the photographs; how they documented what they saw; how they used the information; how they saved the information. In effect, I had to become a photo intelligence analyst. Similarly, I had to become a specialist in every other type of intelligence analysis, whether it related to information obtained from interrogations, or captured documents. Then, I had to learn exactly what the computer programmers could technically do. Once knowing the needs of the analysts and the limitations of the programming, I had to go back and forth between the two to arrive at a construct that could usefully serve the needs of the intelligence analyst, but which could also be developed by the programmer in a timely manner. I also had to use my behavioral skills to persuade analysts who had worked under a system without computers for their entire careers to work with this new technology, something they were reluctant to do. In short, I learned the skill of listening.

I also handled other functions for my commanding officer. He used me as a DIA liaison for certain national security intelligence activities, mainly by attending NSA meetings at the DOD, an experience that gave me insight into organizational politics, "turf" wars, and the dysfunction resulting from disparate entities, each harboring a proprietary interest in gaining credit for success. Though I was totally prepared to go to Vietnam, I never served a day in that theater of operations, something I often felt was unfair, given all the others who had served there.

What went wrong in the 1960s was a war in Vietnam that was corrected by popular activism. What went right in the 1960s was a social agenda that produced major breakthroughs in civil rights, women's rights, and voting rights, and major entitlement protections. An activist government was involved in both areas. What has gone wrong in the early part of the twenty-first century has been a miscalculated war, a monumental economic decline, and a retreat into a battle of fiercely uncompromising positions on social issues and entitlements. Even now we do not know what has gone "right," as the Left and the Right, conservatives and liberals, battle for their respective positions. Partisanship has been the order of the day, often cloaked in adherence to principles. What is needed today, what was needed in the 1960s and the 1970s, and what will always be needed in a society that intends to remain viable and prosperous is some driving force that can lead to an honest and intelligent discussion of issues so powerfully done as to foster new decisions, removed from the shackles of old clichés. Discussion based on thinking through each issue beyond the superficiality of sound bites, and then having the leadership move the country in the right direction. Does our populace have the educational capacity to understand fully and process micro- and macroeconomics? No, but does it have the capacity to engage in a deeper discussion of the issues than it has? I hope the answer is yes.

So, nearly forty-five years after completing my military service, I can reflect back and still be learning from my experiences. On the self-evident side, I learned what it really meant to be a soldier at war, something one could never comprehend from watching every war movie possible. Importantly, I learned to think more carefully about the arguments for and against going to war, including how war will be conducted. While I thought we should have gone to war in Vietnam, I did not fully consider the arguments against U.S. involvement in Indochina based on such elements as the French experience, the difficulties inherent in fighting an indigenous and nationalistic insurgency, or the capabilities of the South Vietnamese government and people. Thus, when the decisions involving Iraq faced us, I viewed that situation more intelligently than I did the Vietnamese war.

I learned something about bureaucracy, something that has helped me in our family business, where interpersonal relationships and human dynamics play such an important role. Next, I gained personal experience in making decisions in the midst of crises, whether the crises were the incredibly real-life simulations of training, where simulation emulated reality and one could immediately see how someone could live or die based on a decision I made, or whether they involved real-life decisions relevant to creating the best possible intelligence system that could save the lives of my fellow soldiers in Vietnam, or shorten the war. The comfort gained in making decisions has proven useful in my business as well as my personal experience, as, for example, being able to say no to a business transaction even if money would be lost, or saying yes to one, even if risk were involved. In a personal context, we have had to deal with life-and-death situations where decisions had to be made quickly, and I felt comfortable making those decisions, and living with the results. I also learned about self-reliance, about the limits my body, and mind, could take, about organizational conflict and inertia, about "company" politics, about taking personal responsibility and always trying to give my best effort at whatever I undertook. Translating these elements into evaluating myself, I admire that I have always given my full effort, just as I did when I worked through illness, and that I have always tried to live up to the goal of doing the honorable thing, such as protecting investors who have trusted in us.

Having lived through the events I have, what advice would I give my grandchildren? First, educate yourselves about the issues of the day and make sure you study opposing points of view, because life is often more "gray" than "black and white." Never close your mind to opposing arguments, and be logical in how you analyze and interpret facts. Do not be afraid to ask questions or take unpopular views if you think they are right and they are based on serious intellectual thought. Second, learn to be a good listener. Listen carefully to each argument you hear, paying attention to the assumptions inherent in each argument as well as to presumed "facts." If assumptions, or facts, are incorrect, then the conclusions are likely to be incorrect. Third, always stand up for what you believe is right, and always put yourself in a position where you have thought in advance about issues, whether they are personal, business, or societal in nature. Further, do not be afraid to make decisions once you have armed yourself with good information. Fourth, *get involved* in all aspects of life, and get involved in as many things as you can reasonably do. Be involved with your spouse, be involved with your children, be involved with your business, be involved with your society, and always strive to do the right thing, and to do it well. Never let yourself be in a position where you did not commit yourself to your fullest capability in matters of importance. Next, always pay attention to the "big picture." In personal matters, always err on the side of achieving the right outcome rather than succumbing to petty issues, even where you think you are right. Just always "do the right thing." Never look back and focus on regrets for things you did not do, or did not do well, but focus on the future and how you can do things better. Finally, realize that the more you attempt to do, the more globally you need to think, paying more attention to big principles, and less to every small detail. Our country, your country, indeed the world, is changing at a more rapid pace than ever, and your responsibility is to do what you can to play as constructive a role as possible. Following these principals can, I believe, lead to a happier and more fulfilling life.

Following military duty, Alan Ferris worked for Exxon for three years in its newly formed venture capital operation. There he gained valuable entrepreneurial experience, which facilitated his forming, along with his wife, father, and brother, Arruth Associates Inc., a boutique real estate management and development company. Arruth specializes in multifamily residential communities including rental apartments, "for sale" condominiums, and mixed-use elements. Arruth's projects are located in multiple states, including Arizona, Alabama, and the Carolinas, as well as the Ferrises' home state of Texas. While he and his wife have worked very hard at Arruth, the center of their personal universe revolves around family, namely their two children, Greg and Katie, their spouses, and three grandchildren. Arruth is headquartered in Houston, where they reside. Madeleine and Alan are together literally 24/7 and can honestly report that they love it that way!

Vietnam Remembered

ROBERT HAGER : NEWS CORRESPONDENT

didn't want to go to Vietnam. It was 1969, I was nine years out of Dartmouth (a history major) and well beyond the draft age. Furthermore, I was married with three children, and the youngest was still an infant—all good reasons to stay away from a war zone.

But the problem is that I was a journalist and the war was far and away the most dominant story of the time. Even though I already had a good job as a reporter on a local television station in Washington, D.C., I really wanted to move up to cover national or international news for one of the big networks—NBC, ABC, or CBS. Executives at all three said they were familiar with my work and would take me on. But, alas, each set out a similar condition: that I would have to start in Vietnam. They explained that they had run through their cast of older correspondents—most had already served one or more tours out of Saigon—so now they were counting on their new hires to fill the gap. Finally, after a year of saying no, I realized that I had to give in. If I wanted to move on from local news anytime soon, there was only one way. I chose NBC and reluctantly told the people there that I would go.

Later, I was glad I did. As it turned out, it led to a thirty-five-year career reporting for this network. But more to the point was the eventual importance of Vietnam to the history of my chosen profession—television news. I would not have wanted to miss that. It marked the first time that combat was brought directly into the intimate setting of American living rooms by a still relatively new medium that featured video as well as verbal reporting. To some viewers it was shocking. Over time, this had an impact on the public's perception of the war and on national policy. I was also glad that I went because of what it taught me about the value of witnessing events firsthand—of making up one's own mind about what

Robert Hager northeast of Saigon with 199th Infantry, 1969

is true and what is not. Finally, it left me with many haunting memories —small snapshots of the fighting and the people it affected.

I went out to Vietnam as a "hawk." I was in favor of the war. By the time I returned, six months later, I was a "dove"—against it. As a reporter, I knew that I should keep my feelings from interfering with objectivity in covering the story. But I also felt I had a journalistic obligation to portray events as they really were unfolding. When I say that I began as a hawk, it's because I was a product of my generation. After college, I had been a huge admirer of President John F. Kennedy. He told us that we must draw a line in the sand against the spread of communism worldwide and more particularly in Asia. But now Kennedy was dead, and his successors, Lyndon Johnson and then Richard Nixon, had inherited the war. After I had been in Vietnam for several months and observed for myself what was happening, it seemed apparent to me that the policy wasn't working. I felt that we, the Americans, were not winning, in spite of casualties that sometimes amounted to as many as three hundred U.S. lives a week. It also seemed to me that in this divided Asian nation our allies, the non-communist South Vietnamese, seemed to have no passion for the fight, while the other side, the invading North Vietnamese and their guerrilla supporters in the South, the Viet Cong, gave every impression that they *were* motivated—willing to hide all day in small, underground tunnels before emerging at night to launch attacks—willing to spend months working their way down from the North via forbidding conditions along the jungle-shrouded path called the Ho Chi Minh Trail.

That was the big picture. But the scenes that haunt me the most, all these decades later, have to do with innocent victims caught in the middle. What follows is just one of many.

It was about halfway through my time in the country. I was slogging through the knee-deep muck of rice paddies with a platoon of GIs when we came on a solitary grass hut perched on a small dry spot. The troopers were operating in what the U.S. command called a "free-fire zone," which meant that it had been labeled as probable enemy territory and that the United States had warned all Vietnamese to get out. The men of our platoon assumed the little hut was abandoned and prepared to light it afire and burn it down. But first, just to be sure, they routinely kicked at the walls and shouted—expecting no response.

They were wrong. A figure suddenly emerged from inside. A young Vietnamese woman, eyes wide with terror and confusion. She held a baby in her arms. The infant clutched against her. And now two more children appeared, cowering behind the woman. There was a young girl and a young boy. It was then that I saw that the boy was using homemade crutches. His leg above the knee was wrapped in a bandage. Below the knee, the leg was gone. It was not hard to imagine how this might have occurred. All around us were huge craters that had been gouged in the muck by explosives. The area's designation as a free-fire zone meant American B-52s would likely have flown over often at night, dropping their huge bombs. It also meant artillery batteries from afar would have pounded the area with shells fired at random, hoping to hit any stray Viet Cong guerrillas hiding in the vicinity.

The woman before us, shivering with fright, might have been a guerrilla's mistress. Or she might have simply been a bewildered peasant who didn't understand the gravity of her location and predicament. The GIs tried to communicate. She didn't understand.

I tell this story not because it was unique—not unique to what I saw in Vietnam, and probably not unique to any war. For example, commanders have a label for what happens to victims such as the youth with the missing leg. They call it "collateral damage." That day back in 1969, the men of the platoon soon moved out, and I moved with them, continuing through the muck of the rice paddies. The woman and her three youngsters stayed in the free-fire zone. I knew the B-52s would come back, and I knew the artillery would commence again. As we left, I could only think, "God help them."

I didn't want to go to Vietnam, but in the end I was glad I did. I learned a lot about my profession. I learned a lot about that particular war. And I learned a lot about warfare in general.

Following his Vietnam experience, Robert Hager went on to a thirty-five-year career with NBC News. He covered the Cold War from bureaus in Berlin and Moscow, the 1979 ouster of the Shah and revolution in Iran, and the "troubles" in Northern Ireland. Later he covered the loss of the space shuttles *Challenger* and *Columbia*, the bombing of the Federal Building in Oklahoma City, and the terrorist attacks of 9/11. He is now retired and lives with his wife, Honore, in his hometown of Woodstock, Vermont.

Fighting the War on the Home Front

JOHN TOPPING : U.S. AIR FORCE

My two years of service during the Vietnam War were much less heroic than those of many of my Dartmouth veteran classmates. Mine were spent as a young legal officer at Bolling Field, a Washington, D.C., air base with no airplanes, some nice housing for generals, and an officers' club with a capacious swimming pool. The closest brush I had with combat was preparing wills for numerous fliers who were shipping out to Southeast Asia, where they would be exposed to hostile fire, and a few occasions when I went out as a casualty notification officer, accompanied by a chaplain, to notify families that one of their loved ones was a war casualty. Perhaps the riskiest venture was carrying out an animated discussion on the merits of the Vietnam War in the living room of a three-star general who commanded the Defense Intelligence Agency and whose daughter I was dating briefly. Despite the relatively peaceful nature of my Vietnam War–era service, my two years in the Air Force left a lasting imprint on me, forged my closest friendship, and set me on a career path that endures over four decades later.

My father was an Air Force officer, who had been a navigator. In World War II he was awarded medals, including a Silver Star, for service aboard a B-24 in New Guinea and later served in the Military Air Transport Service in support of the Berlin Airlift and many more-pedestrian assignments. He spent the last decade of his career as a special weapons officer, minding scores of hydrogen and atomic bombs. Ever the Air Force brat, it is no surprise that in high school I developed a fascination with texts on strategic theory and read several books by Herman Kahn. This military upbringing was leavened a little by my mother's background as an artist. When I arrived at Dartmouth in September 1960, despite the fact that I seemed to have two left feet on the drill field, I signed up with the Air

Barbara Topping pins Air Force
second lieutenant wings on her
son, John C. Topping Jr., as Air
Force Lieutenant Colonel John C.
Topping looks on.

Force ROTC and found my niche as the social program leader, organizing
unit bowling alley trips and other forays. For this hazardous service I received a medal from the Green Mountain Chapter of the Reserve Officers
Association.

Commissioned as an Air Force Reserve officer at Dow Air Force Base
in Maine soon after graduation, I entered Yale Law School, knowing that
if I completed law school and managed to get admitted to the bar, I would
be entering the Air Force Judge Advocate General Corps (JAG). This took
tremendous pressure off me. I suspect I was one of the few in my law
school class who never interviewed with a law firm. I spent much of my
first year in public policy work and lobbying to get Republican support for
what was to become the Voting Rights Act of 1965. Raising funds from the
family foundation of former Minnesota governor Elmer Andersen, I led a
three-member team through the eleven states of the former Confederacy
in the summer of 1965, interviewing Republican leaders, civil rights leaders, and journalists. Our objective was to assess how the southern state
Republican parties would respond to the emerging black vote in the wake

of the Voting Rights Act. Our book *Southern Republicanism and the New South* was published in October 1966 during my third year at law school and received front-page attention in the *New York Times* and many southern papers, but our advice to seek actively to compete for the rapidly growing African American vote was heeded by only a handful of state parties, most of which were happily welcoming hard-core Dixiecrats into the fold. Having spent my first three years after Dartmouth at Yale Law School, juggling my time between law school work and civil rights and political activity, I had to do an about-face after graduation, cramming for the bar. I was making up for my three years of avoiding black-letter law courses as much as possible, having opted instead for such Yale offerings as "Psychiatry and the Law" and "Social Legislation," all about as useful on a bar exam as tea leaves might be for athletic predictions. Nevertheless, I managed to squeak through both the Massachusetts and D.C. Bar and was admitted in both jurisdictions.

Reporting to duty in February 1968 at Bolling Field in D.C., just across the Anacostia River from what the real estate industry was to call Greater Capitol Hill, I found myself commuting from a small apartment on Capitol Hill in my electric transmission-powered Renault, purchased as was my TV set with an advance on my first lieutenant's salary. Only seven weeks into my service in the Air Force I suddenly had the sense that I was almost in a war zone. On April 4, 1968, Dr. Martin Luther King Jr., whose inspiring "I Have a Dream" speech at the Lincoln Memorial I had witnessed on August 28, 1963, along with about 250,000 others, had been slain in Memphis, Tennessee. Rioting erupted in many cities, with some of the worst in the nation's capital. Thousands of people were reportedly involved in the rioting that resulted in twelve deaths, over a thousand injuries, and extensive property damage, mostly from burning stores. With the police force overwhelmed, President Lyndon B. Johnson sent 13,600 federal troops, including 1,750 federalized D.C. National Guard troops, as reinforcements. Marines mounted machine guns on the Capitol steps, and the Third Infantry guarded the White House.

I lived only a block from the Capitol and was transfixed by images of U.S. troops on the Capitol steps. I was also involved in a swirl of emotions. Having spent five years in civil rights activity, I had deep affection for Dr. King and shared some of the anger of the rioters, although I was heartsick over how they were expressing it. Although Caucasian, I was in no fear of personal harm, as the anger of the black community was directed very little at individual whites and mostly at shops. Still, I was deeply troubled by these scenes from a city I dearly loved. Our nation seemed sundered by growing disagreements over a war thousands of miles away and now potential racial polarization as these images of violence belied the non-violent strategies that had made possible enactment of the Civil Rights Act of 1964 and the Voting Rights Act of 1965.

About this time I met a lanky young second lieutenant, Dan Power, from Nashville, Tennessee. He was ultimately to become my best friend and partner in both climate and clean energy activities, and become "Uncle Dan" to my yet to be born three children, John III, Elizabeth, and Alexandra. A civil engineering graduate of Vanderbilt with a master's degree in planning from the University of Tennessee, Dan had Lincolnesque storytelling skills and a rollicking sense of humor. We immediately hit it off and decided to seek with friends to rent a house on Capitol Hill. A house owned by the parents of a law school classmate became available for rent when his father retired from Congress. Soon Dan and I, both irreverent junior officers chafing at a war that seemed increasingly senseless, teamed with two housemates, an aide to a Pittsburgh-area congressman and an analyst at the Securities and Exchange Commission.

Over the next year and a half our Capitol Hill home, only a block from the Senate Office Building, became a gathering place for a diverse assemblage of largely twenty-something Air Force junior officers, Hill aides, and members of the female gender who could put up with our Inaugural spoof party, Groundhog Day party, and other festivities. On a few occasions when Washington was overwhelmed by tens of thousands of antiwar protesters, many of them our classmates, our living room floor sometimes served as accommodations for our contemporaries. Yet this generational split that was creating a chasm between a college and immediate post-college generation, on the one hand, and older blue-collar workers on the other, was also mirrored in sharply different perspectives between my fellow Air Force junior officers and officers ten to fifteen years older. Many of the junior officers who served with Dan and me were inclined to question higher-ups, both civilian and military, who seemed to be marching our peers to oblivion.

This worked much to my professional advantage as, the most junior JAG in the Bolling Air Force Base legal office, I soon settled into a position as defense counsel on courts-martial and the much more plentiful administrative discharge boards that seemed the principal means that Headquarters Command brass used to deal with what they perceived as serious infractions. The members of these courts-martial and discharge boards were largely junior officers, who shared with Dan and me an instinctive tendency to question authority. (Only an ill-advised accused airman would avail himself of his right in courts-martial of having a third of the court be noncommissioned officers, as these noncoms were much more likely, even than senior officers, to be "hard-asses.") One of my clients was a comely Air Force WAF receptionist to Defense Secretary Melvin Laird. She was charged with smoking marijuana with her boyfriend. Much to the distress of the two-star general heading Headquarters Command, the board of junior officers found that she had smoked pot, she was patriotic, she had promised not to smoke it again, and therefore it was absurd to kick her out of the Air Force. The dismay with this decision was nothing compared with the eruption from above when an administrative discharge board, composed largely of junior officers, found for my young airman client who had been spotted peddling drugs in the supersecret National Security Agency at Fort Meade, Maryland. The government's key witness was a fellow airman, who had worked closely with the Air Force's Office of Special Investigations (OSI) to nail my client. In cross-examining the accusing witness, I was able to draw him out. He came across like a junior G-man in a Dick Tracy comic strip. He proudly described how he had worked with the OSI to set up my client. Though called as a prosecution witness, he was so overemphatic in his testimony that he unwittingly became a defense witness, and I was able to resort to a "Hail Mary Pass." My client had been entrapped and was induced into drug peddling by the collusion of the OSI and their key witness. Even in a civilian setting, the chance of winning a case on an entrapment claim was just slightly greater than that of winning the Power Ball today. Yet the administrative discharge board found that my client had been entrapped, and therefore the discharge action could not be sustained.

These cases hardly endeared me to the Air Force brass, but they had one personally beneficial effect. Although I had started my Air Force legal service under a superb staff judge advocate, who exemplified all the finest traditions of military justice, he was reassigned, and his replacement was the kind of individual who made "military justice" seem like an oxymoron. Bolling's new chief legal officer, although a self-proclaimed liberal, told the young JAG captains staffing his office that all the accused we were representing as defense counsel were "rotten apples" and we shouldn't overexert ourselves on their behalf. This redoubled all our efforts in defense, helping to produce a series of results that were highly displeasing to the general. At the same time I found this an untenable situation and began casting about, using my political antennae to locate other positions in the D.C. area. Drawing on my links from five years in the civil rights movement and even longer in moderate Republican activity, I discovered that the President's Advisory Council on Minority Business Enterprise was scouting for a legal counsel, and I threw my hat in the ring. After winning the nod from the Advisory Council's executive director, Alan Steelman, who went on to be elected to Congress from Dallas in 1972, I found the White House contacting the Air Force to work out a detail assignment to the Advisory Council. Instead I received an early release (roughly two years early), with the Commerce Department picking up my salary. I suspect that my modicum of success as defense counsel was helpful in getting a green light from the Air Force (probably few individuals are more dispensable to a war effort than an aggressive JAG defense counsel). The mustering out went through in near record time, with the Bolling brass insisting only that my checkout in January 1970 be at about 6 a.m. so word would not get around too widely.

Still, my Air Force service left a lasting imprint. In late spring 1969 I served as a sword bearer at the wedding at the Bolling Air Force Base chapel of the daughter of a three-star general. Attired in my Air Force dress uniform, something that happened only a handful of times in my military career, I met at the reception an attractive George Washington University student, a friend of the bride. We soon began dating and within about fifteen months were married. The marriage lasted slightly less than four years, a casualty perhaps of the youth of my bride (barely twenty-one when we marched down the aisle), the fact that a shared passion for politics was our one overriding common interest, and the tenor of the early '70s, which seemed to be wreaking havoc with the marriages of many of my contemporaries.

Yet this grave disappointment also laid the groundwork both for my closest friendship, as my Air Force buddy Dan Power took me under his wing as I rebuilt my shattered self-confidence, and for a happy (for me

John Topping representing the Climate
Institute in Mexico City

at least) second marriage that was to produce my three wonderful children and great memories before it ended in divorce after just over a quarter century.

In 1979 my friend Dan, drawing on his knowledge from his city planning days, launched a long-shot bid to upset a strongly entrenched incumbent mayor of Nashville, Richard Fulton, who had served for many years before as congressman. After providing some political counsel from a distance, I traveled to Nashville to serve for the last eight days of the campaign as Dan's campaign manager. Outspent about four-to-one, Dan came within an eyelash of forcing Fulton into a runoff where Dan would likely have won. Although he wasn't quite able to pull off this stunning upset, his campaign cemented what had begun in our Air Force days and has gone on to become the closest friendship of my life. It was only natural that in 1986, when I launched a National Council for Clean Indoor Air (which lasted about two years) and the Climate Institute (which is still vibrant), Dan was a founding board member of both. He led the institute's effort to promote energy efficiency in city, county, and state governments and later our effort to prod the United Nations to green its facilities.

Life in the environmental nonprofit community has its psychological compensations, but financial prosperity is generally not among the likely rewards. Nevertheless, thanks to Dan's entrepreneurialism and insight as an engineer, there is a realistic chance that I won't have to worry about the solvency of Social Security, except perhaps as a policy wonk. In early 2003 Dan and I visited an energy entrepreneur in northeast Florida to provide advice on his ocean energy business. We both became excited about the potential of harnessing energy from the Gulf Stream, tidal waters, and rivers to generate electricity. In 2005, together with some close friends, we launched Oceana Energy Company, with Dan Power as president, CEO, and chief technology officer. Although a director of Oceana, I have spent only an hour or two a week on it, spending most of my waking hours on the Climate Institute. As an original investor in Oceana Energy, I should live comfortably, if we succeed. Although in business ventures, as elsewhere in life, there is a lot between the cup and the lip, we are guardedly optimistic that between a strong and well-patented technology and some promising sites (e.g., San Francisco Bay around the Golden Gate Bridge, the East River in New York City, some rivers in Alaska, and sites in Scotland and England), Oceana may pioneer in what could become a major clean energy source.

My two years in the Air Force and my lifetime before as an Air Force brat have profoundly shaped my life. A few years ago I became acutely aware of the latter on reading *Military Brats: Legacies of Childhood Inside the Fortress*, by Mary Edwards Wertsch, daughter of an Army brigadier general. The book resonated with me, bringing me to tears and even providing some insight on my two years on active duty. Based on her surveys of "military brats," dozens of children of both officers and enlisted personnel, she found some common characteristics. Although "military brats" spanned the political spectrum, most had a strong patriotism and sense of mission. An unusually high proportion became entrepreneurs, either in business or in the nonprofit sector. Except for those who followed their fathers into a military or naval service career, most seemed averse to working in large hierarchical organizations, perhaps sensing what a toll it can inflict on family life.

My time at Bolling Field, while far less harrowing than that of most of my classmate veterans, reinforced the mission consciousness and questioning of authority that had been imbued in me by growing up a child of a warrior and an artist.

From 1989 to 1990 John Topping served as editor of the portions of the Intergovernmental Panel on Climate Change (IPCC) First Assessment Report concerning impacts of climate change on human settlement, industry, transport, energy, human health, and air quality, and on impacts of climate and UV interactions. He was lead author of the portions concerning impacts on human settlement, industry, and transport. Topping received a certificate from the IPCC "for contributing to the award of the Nobel Peace Prize of 2007 to the IPCC." Topping was the former staff director of the Office of Air and Radiation of the U.S. Environmental Protection Agency under the Reagan administration. In 2002 he received Dartmouth's first Dr. Martin Luther King Jr. Social Justice Award for Lifetime Achievement. Topping is the editor of two volumes on climate change, *Preparing for Climate Change* (1988) and *Coping with Climate Change* (1989), and coeditor of *Sudden and Disruptive Climate Change: Exploring the Real Risks and How We Can Avoid Them* (2008). Now spending the bulk of his time in Hanover, two blocks from the Dartmouth campus, he is working with some 1964 classmates and students from Dartmouth, Yale, and other schools to develop a virtual Center for Environmental Leadership Training (CELT); its current mission is to empower students to gather and design environmental problem-solving games in many languages and create a multimedia Smart Solutions blog.

Nobody Knows and Nothing Changes

LYNN MCCANSE : U.S. ARMY

Several years ago a surgeon friend of mine gave a presentation at a trauma conference regarding his deployment to Iraq, which occurred in the middle part of that war. At that time, it was still the U.S. policy not to acknowledge returning fatalities, and while the war was well publicized, the injuries occurring there were not. The Iraq War was the first to have an improved mortality rate since World War II, meaning soldiers were surviving more serious wounds than ever before. After watching thirty minutes of the most horrendous injuries I had ever seen, I remember leaving the meeting thinking, *if pictures like those were publicized, the war would be over tomorrow.*

By the time I arrived in Japan in the summer of 1969, if a soldier was injured seriously enough in Vietnam to be sent elsewhere for care, his tour was over and he was eventually headed home, although not necessarily whole. My yearlong war experience was providing this intermediate care at a time when, fortunately, the number of casualties was decreasing. The Tet offensive had occurred more than a year before, but an operative schedule from that time was still taped to the door to surgery. It went from the ceiling to the floor.

I was one year out of medical school, with no specialty training. There was a need for orthopedic surgeons, and I was placed in that job category, although as a class D (no previous training). I was given on-the-job training, which consisted of spending a day with someone with experience and then being given an operating room of my own. I spent the next year closing open wounds of soldiers with associated broken bones. If there were no broken bones, then the general surgeons closed the wound. These DPCs (delayed primary closures) were necessary to prevent infection, as almost all "in-country" wounds were "dirty" and if closed at the time of

Lynn McCanse

injury would become infected, but if left open for one to two weeks could be closed safely with good results. Basically I was a glorified seamstress who coated his finished work in plaster.

Life was good in Japan, the war was a long way away, and I was too young and immature to appreciate the horrors of what had happened to the young men I was caring for, soldiers with multiple open wounds and fractures and frequently with one or two limbs missing, and occasionally three or four. They would usually stay with us for one to three weeks, depending on the bed status in the "States" and the availability of flights. Being young and healthy to start with, they usually did well with our surgery, and were surprisingly upbeat. I still have a film of a smiling young man demonstrating, with his only remaining limb, the trigger mechanism to the Claymore mine booby trap he had triggered.

They were probably happy because they knew they were going home, and unlike today, single tours of duty were more the norm. This equanimity, among other things, allowed me to be fooled and minimally affected by what was going on around me. The significance of mini-concussions from exploding ordinance was only first noted and diagnosed during the Iraq War. Harmful effects from Agent Orange were suspected then, and, as now, the whole subject was controversial. "PTSD" was not the buzz term it is now, but I cannot imagine that the incidence was not as high, if not higher than it is now. Forty years after being intimately involved with these men, I read *Matterhorn*, a novel of the Vietnam War based on true experiences, and I was overwhelmed to think of how clueless I had been about the experiences of the soldiers I had treated.

Helicopters landed in the parking lot all day, transferring casualties from the nearby Air Force base to our hospital, where they would be evaluated one day and usually operated on the next. Sometimes when inside one of the surrounding buildings, it was hard to differentiate the vibrations from the helicopters from one of the frequent earthquakes. Our

McCanse family at
Fort Sam Houston, San
Antonio, Texas, 1968

work was so routine that we were able to live fairly normal lives outside the hospital, and most of us were accompanied by our families, enjoyed exploring the country, and had very little hardship.

The movie *M*A*S*H* came out during this time, and our hospital's commanding officer walked out halfway through, declaring it subversive. It was interesting to hear comments at the child care center after the movie when picking up our son. Some thought that the movie was very realistic except for the operating room scenes, which in fact were the only highly realistic scenes. At the time, I was just finishing the editing of a super-8 movie of my own that did poke a little fun at the military, but was well received by my peers. I was encouraged to show it at the officers' club by the chaplain, who thought it would improve morale. This was apparently not the opinion of everyone, including the same commanding officer. Though he did not attend the showing, word-of-mouth reports persuaded the CO to happily sign early transfer orders, sending me back to the States before my time was up.

The war, while winding down, still had several years to go, and protests were rampant and a contributing cause to the ending of the Vietnam War. In my further medical training, I spent four months a year for three years working in VA hospitals, where I was surprised to see only three Vietnam veterans during that whole time. I suspect that had the returning, permanently injured veterans been more publicized at the time and not absorbed so easily into the general population, public opinion against the war would have been greater, earlier, and even more effective. Yet I was there and, while in favor of ending the war, was blinded by the trees and not able to see or feel the forest.

It would seem that little changes.

After returning from Japan, Lynn McCanse competed his military service as a GMO (general medical officer) at Fort Jackson, South Carolina. He then returned to Kansas City, where he trained to become a urologist and was in private practice until 2011. He served as chief of surgery and president of the medical staff while being very involved in coaching soccer and skating with his three children. He has continued to seek escapism, and is still an avid cyclist, kite sailor, and snowboarder. He has not been involved in political activism or antiwar protests, but he continues to worry about our military involvements.

Rear Guard

BILL RIGGS : U.S. ARMY

T he Army had me from 1968 until 1970. I did not go to Vietnam, although I was scheduled to be trained for a job that surely would have shown me more of that part of the world than I had any interest in seeing. I am proud of my service. I imagine that most of the chapters in this book tell stories of those who did serve in Southeast Asia, and I salute them and their sacrifice.

Drafted!

I came of age in Hamilton, Ohio. One day during my Christmas break from architecture school, in 1967, I went down to my local draft board office to straighten out what I was sure was a clerical error that had canceled my graduate student deferment and had reclassified me I-A. The draft board office was in a small two-story building on Main Street, above a butcher shop. When I entered the office it was bedlam! A long counter bisected the room, separating the draft-age (all-male) public from the (all-female) employees. The place was packed with young men, all shouting at once in angry panic. On their side of the counter, frightened clerks raised their hands to shush the unruly youths. In all the noise I could just barely make out the nature of the young men's complaints: like me, they *all* had just been reclassified I-A. Finally (I am not making this up), one of the clerks climbed on top of her desk and began shouting, "Calm down! We just sent out these notices because we needed to update our records, and we thought this would be a sure way to get you to come into our office!" "Great," I thought. This was just somebody's boneheaded idea gone bad—a stupid mistake. I managed to catch the attention of one of the clerks as the mob took in the news it had just received and began to quiet down. "See here," I said. "I'm a graduate student at Ohio State.

I'll just have my II-S student deferment back, thank you." She seemed to think this was a reasonable course of action, until she pulled out my file and noticed that I was twenty-five years old, had spent the previous year working in Austria, and had been classified II-S since I was eighteen. Under rules then in effect, once I turned twenty-six I would no longer be eligible for the draft. This did not seem fair to her, and so my I-A status stuck. I was able to finish the academic year, but my civilian life was about to be interrupted.

Private Riggs

I was inducted in Cincinnati June 19, 1968. When I got to basic training in Fort Benning, Georgia, I soon figured out that, at twenty-five, I was older than my company commander and my drill sergeants. My company commander, however, had already been awarded a Silver Star for valor in combat during his first tour in Vietnam. He and his cadre of drill instructors had already seen and done things in their short lifetimes that I could not even begin to imagine . . . things that, as my dad would have said, would "curl your hair."

During basic training, like almost everyone who goes through it, I was tested physically; I dropped about thirty-five pounds in my first three weeks; I qualified as "expert" with an M14 rifle; I managed not to kill or injure anyone on the grenade range, with my left-handedness and poor pitching ability; I was in the best shape of my life; and I was promoted to private E-2. I had also lived the summer of 1968 in a virtual vacuum. I got letters from home, friends, and my girlfriend, of course, but I had no inkling that the country was in turmoil, great cities were in flames, and the social fabric of the Republic was stretched and tearing.

After basic training, the Army decided I should go to the U.S. Army Intelligence School at Fort Holabird, in Baltimore, to be trained as a prisoner of war interrogator. I've long suspected that this path was chosen for me because I spoke German, and we used to fight the Germans. The fact that this makes no sense is irrelevant.

Setting the Scene

It will be helpful at this point to recall the temper of the nation in 1968. There were widespread riots after the assassination of Dr. Martin Luther King Jr. in April of that year. Devastation in Baltimore was particularly severe. The city was under curfew; many citizens were killed; and large sections of the city were burned to the ground. The man who would become my boss at Fort Holabird lived in a downtown high-rise apartment building with two roommates, also young Army officers. They would later tell me of living under curfew, with elements of the Eighty-Second Airborne from Fort Bragg bivouacked outside the Fifth Regiment National Guard Armory less than a block from their building in downtown Baltimore and visible from their apartment balcony.

The Tet offensive in February 1968 and further escalation of military activity in Southeast Asia generated a large increase in draft notices and the cancellation of many student deferments.

The assassination of Bobby Kennedy, and the riots surrounding the Democratic National Convention in Chicago added further to the general feeling—no, the reality—that the country was in great peril, both here at home and overseas.

Movie Night

A few days after I arrived at Fort Holabird, a group of us left the post one evening to see a movie at a theater that was a short walk away. The other fellows had already completed a tour in Vietnam. We were talking as we walked, when a passing truck backfired, and suddenly, quicker than you could shout "Incoming," I was the only one talking, and the rest of the group had vanished. They were nowhere to be seen! They had all thrown themselves to the ground and were low-crawling under parked cars and nearby bushes for cover. Those quick reflexes no doubt kept them alive in Vietnam, but it was incongruous behavior on Dundalk Avenue.

School Overcrowding

Draft deferments for students were being canceled wholesale in 1968, and many college students and graduates were sent to the Intelligence School (because college education = intelligence, of course). This resulted in over-crowded schools and longer waits to get into a class. The school itself was housed in one medium-size building (it looked a bit like Fillmore Elementary in my hometown), and there weren't that many classrooms. This meant that most of us who were waiting to take our places in class had to wait much longer for that day to arrive. We who had not yet begun classes were on what was known as "casual" status, which meant that we spent our days painting rocks, picking up cigarette butts, pulling KP, or doing a dozen other mindless chores.

Do You Know Any Communists?

Many who went into the military in the '60s, either voluntarily or by conscription, will remember the forms we had to fill out, with their Cold War–tinged questions: "Are you now, or have you ever been a member of the Communist Party?" "Do you now know, or have you ever known anyone who was a member of the Communist Party?" I answered no to the former and yes to the latter; then I crossed out my yes and wrote no. During the year I spent in Europe I traveled through East Germany, Czechoslovakia, and Yugoslavia, and my traveling companions and I had been detained in Yugoslavia for three weeks following an automobile accident in which a local farmworker was struck and killed. Tom Illick (Dartmouth '64) was one of my traveling companions; the other was the woman who would become my first wife. I figured I was bound to have met a Communist or two during my travels, so I checked the yes box initially; later I figured that the U.S. government might not have been interested in that explanation, so I changed my answer to no.

S-2

Someone in the security office (known as S-2) at the Intelligence School saw my questionnaire with its equivocating about Communists, and I was called in to explain my answers. The warrant officer who interviewed me was a nice guy, and he seemed to buy my story. He then allowed that he was pretty busy just then, and would I mind writing out a statement repeating everything I had just told him. I, who had been painting rocks only a few minutes earlier, and who was not interested in returning to that chore any sooner than necessary, said, "Sure, Sir." Toward the end of this essay, I wrote that it was during my travels in the Eastern Bloc that I might have met someone whose interests were inimical to those of the United States. The warrant officer said he had never met another soldier who had ever used the word "inimical," and he offered me a job on the spot. I was to be a clerk in his office, and I wouldn't have to pull KP anymore, or paint rocks, and I would wear my "Class A" uniform to work every day, rather than my funky fatigues.

The job in S-2 was great. It was under the direction of a ROTC captain who was a graduate of Bowdoin ('64) and Harvard Law ('67). As I later learned, one of his roommates was a graduate of the University of Vermont, and we all knew a lot of the same people. We became friends when I chanced to run into them at a civilian party off-post. My only nonmilitary contact in Baltimore at the time was Bob LeResche (also a member of the Dartmouth Class of 1964), who was "pushing back the frontiers of science" (his words) working on his doctorate (studying Adélie penguins!) at the School of Hygiene and Public Health on the Johns Hopkins medical campus.

My work in the S-2 office involved a lot of contact with my counterparts in the school's personnel office, which was right next door to ours. Most of their clerks were draftees like me, and *all* of us below the rank of E-6 staff sergeant were extremely disaffected with Army life. I didn't even know what disaffected meant until I was taken into the Army.

Anyway, I started sharing my story with the guys in personnel. I told them that I was awaiting a slot in a class to be trained as a POW interrogator. I mentioned that I thought I might be better suited for a job involving art or architecture, in which I had majored at Dartmouth. And, perhaps miraculously, they told me that they had four slots open for military illustrators in the Training Aids Division of the school. I was interviewed by the civilian in charge of the office, and I got the job! Now, instead of sleeping in a tent and being shot at, I could ride the No. 20 bus to the war every day!

Training Aids Division

The Training Aids Division was a cool place. I worked in a studio preparing illustrations for training manuals and for the various classes offered by the Intelligence School. In addition, we had a publishing plant in-house, which printed and bound the manuals and textbooks, and a cabinetry shop staffed by civilians who could make *anything*! The school taught certain students the black arts of spy craft, and the cabinetry shop made devices that were large enough to be seen and understood by everyone in a large auditorium. My favorites were the giant locks they made out of translucent Plexiglas in different colors. They were made so that one could actually look inside the lock to see how the combination mechanism worked. For "picking" keyed locks, the cabinet shop guys made oversize replicas out of Plexiglas, and they made giant picks for opening the locks without a key. The picks looked like harpoons!

COL Sanders

In my shop, instructors would come in and tell us what illustrations they wanted for their classroom presentations, and we would produce them. These illustrations were transferred to sheets of clear acetate by a process similar to that for making blueprints. Each color was printed on a separate sheet; then all the sheets were aligned and taped to a cardboard frame, which would then be put on an overhead projector so that the entire class could see the picture. These were called "Vu-Graphs." The instructors would usually give us *very* rudimentary sketches, literally with stick figures and scrawled captions. They were big on organizational charts, too, of course.

My colleagues and I always had our tongues placed deep in our cheeks when we took these assignments, but the instructors were always grateful for the results we produced. Except for one. I prepared a slide showing a chiseled colonel who resembled Kirk Douglas in his better days. Because he was a full bird (or "chicken") colonel, I named him "COL Sanders." I had to change that in the final version.

I also developed a cartoon superhero to represent the Military Intelligence (MI) branch. I called him "SuperSpook" because the intelligence

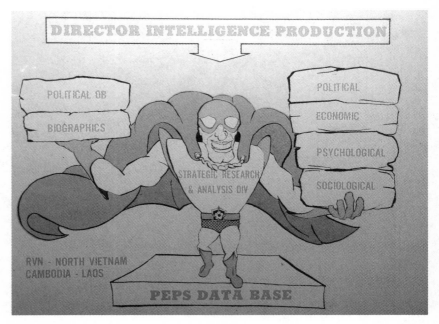

SuperSpook

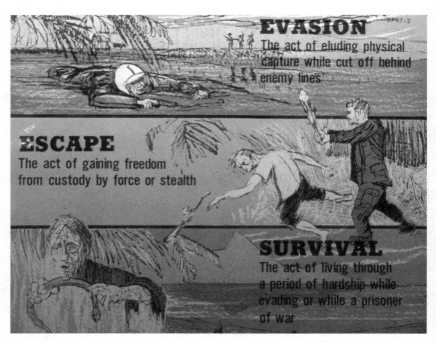

Eating snake

operatives referred to themselves as "spooks." The iconography of the MI crest includes a stylized compass, a rose, a dagger, a chessboard, and a sphinx. As you see, SuperSpook proudly wore it all, and he helped make org charts fun for everyone.

For a special forces class on Evasion, Escape, and Survival, I drew a picture of a soldier taking a big chomp out of a raw snake he had just caught for dinner. I thought this might meet the same fate as COL Sanders; however, the colonel who was teaching *this* class pronounced the slide "Outstanding, Riggs!" and told me how his troops' wives were often squeamish at barbecued snake picnics that they held each summer.

Even in those early days, the Intelligence School had a closed-circuit TV station that broadcast lectures to satellite classes at other Army installations. I prepared illustrations directing viewers to be patient when the audio conked out, or to "please stand by" when some other glitch occurred.

I learned a lot about graphic design, illustration, publishing, reprographics, model building, cabinetmaking, and problem-solving during my two years at Fort Holabird. And I was respected and appreciated in my job.

Cogs in a Machine

Training aids did not just mean Vu-Graph slides and Plexiglas locks. Although the training offered at the Intelligence School was deadly serious, its execution sometimes left me wondering about its effectiveness. The school had a fleet of Plymouth sedans, all the same year, model, and color. Students would use these cars to practice tailing each other through city traffic. Anyone seeing such a car would know instantaneously that it belonged to the Intelligence School. Students also would tail each other on foot through downtown Baltimore. Even though they were wearing civilian clothes, they all had military haircuts in the age of flower power and hippies. They weren't *too* obvious. The school also constructed a mock Vietnamese village on a remote part of the Fort Howard VA Hospital grounds, on the shores of Chesapeake Bay, at the entrance to the Baltimore harbor. Students would practice amphibious landings from a harbor patrol boat that the Army owned. Then they would sneak up to the fake village and try to free a prisoner, or learn the enemy's secrets, or who knows what. I imagine these students still had the steep part of the learning curve ahead of them when they first attempted to practice their new skills in the real world.

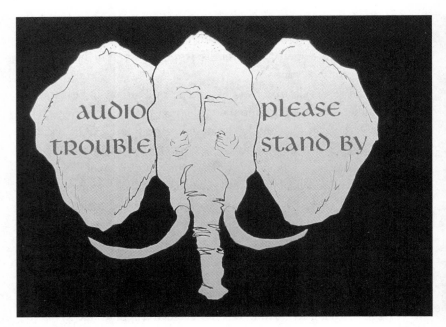

Audio elephant

Stand by your dike

War Protester

Serving in the Army in the middle of a large urban area in a time of such pervasive tension meant that my life, and the lives of many of my friends, became dichotomous. We were soldiers by day and civilians by night and on weekends. We were educated. We read the newspapers and watched the news. And we were antiwar, even as we respected and honored our brothers serving in Vietnam. We took the train to Washington to participate in protest marches. Our experience in basic training had taught us that tear gas would not kill us or even hurt us much. When we were gassed at Union Station in Washington, we just kept walking and boarded our trains back to Baltimore.

Guard Duty

One of the rituals of military service is guard duty. Because we were inside the city limits of Baltimore at Fort Holabird, none of our leaders wanted us carrying loaded weapons, so we were issued wooden dowels about three feet long and 1 ½ inches in diameter to defend ourselves or to suppress any bad guy who might want to get into the commissary after hours or urinate in the bushes outside the PX. One weekend afternoon there was a rugby game under way near my guard post, and a civilian friend of mine saw me. He had been a Navy SEAL in an earlier life and was playing on one of the rugby sides. We exchanged greetings, and he allowed that he was so glad that I was out there to protect him with my stick. Imagine the pride I felt.

Personal Observations

As I reflect on the people I knew who had served in Vietnam, I did not know *anyone* who was not emotionally scarred by the experience. A drill sergeant at Fort Benning with whom I became friendly after I completed basic training offered to kill anyone for me if I thought that person needed killing; it didn't matter who the person might be (the sergeant might have been a bit drunk at the time). An officer came into the S-2 office one day and asked my boss if it was OK for him to run over war protesters with his car. This was during one of several periods when we had protesters at the main gate. Soldiers' personal relationships with women almost always seemed to be tense and troubled. Drug use was endemic; be it Robitussin, marijuana, hashish, Freon, or anything in the panoply of psychedelic ingestibles, and of course alcohol—all were as common as cigarettes, and I was not immune. I probably drank more during my two years in the Army than in my four years at Dartmouth. Marijuana and hashish were abundant—on and off the reservation—nor was I immune to their blandishments, either. I am not proud of my behavior, but I am glad to say that I have lived clean and sober for many years.

Completing the Circle

My office at Fort Holabird was in Building 1. In the final full-time job of my civilian career, my office was again in Building 1—at Walter Reed Army Medical Center, in Washington, D.C., where I worked as the master planner until the hospital closed on September 15, 2011. Building 1 at Fort Holabird was originally a locomotive repair shop and is now but a memory. Along with everything else on the ninety-acre post, it has been torn down, and the place converted into a business park. My office at Walter Reed was in the original building on the post. It was directly below the rooms where President Eisenhower and General Pershing had spent their final days and died.

Having been away from Army life for more than forty years, I was struck by how many things had changed, and how many had not. Most markedly, there are many more civilians working for the Army now than there were then. The spirit seems different now. What I referred to earlier as disaffection doesn't seem to exist to the same extent in this all-volunteer world. That disaffection manifested, in my view, a healthy skepticism that eventually affected national policy positively, and such critical thinking could benefit military service greatly today, I believe.

I am proud to have served in the Army. I received very good training; I met wonderful people across the full spectrum of American society and saw the goodness and native intelligence in most of them; I was tested physically and mentally, and I passed(!); I learned useful skills that benefited me in my civilian career; I learned that by advocating strongly for oneself, it was and is possible to achieve a desirable outcome; I learned (and have remembered) that everything is not all black and white—that the full spectrum is beautiful; I learned that conflicting emotions, philosophies, and politics may never be resolved fully, but that conflict can build one's strength and broaden one's vision. Finally, I learned to appreciate respect when it is bestowed, to show respect when it is deserved, and to know that the journey teaches its lessons and bestows its rewards day by day, and not just when the final destination has been reached.

Bill Riggs was released from active duty in June 1970. He spent most of that summer on unemployment, whereby he received more money per week than he had earned as an E-4 in the Army. Things have improved since then. Bill remained in the Baltimore area, where he became an architect. He was privileged to participate in the rebirth of the Inner Harbor, participating in the design of the Maryland Science Center and the Baltimore World Trade Center. He also served as project architect for the Hyatt Regency Baltimore, the Inner Harbor Center office building, and the pedestrian bridge network in the Inner Harbor. He now maintains a consulting practice on Maryland's Eastern Shore, where he lives with his wife, JoAnn Kulesza, who is interim chair of the Opera Department at Peabody Conservatory in Baltimore. They enjoy sailing on Chesapeake Bay and their two amazing young grandchildren, Thomas Murphy Riggs and Abigail Wallace Riggs, who live in Baltimore with their parents, whom they also enjoy.

An Air Force JAG Desk Jockey

DAVID W. HESS : U.S. AIR FORCE

After I graduated from Dartmouth and Air Force ROTC as a second lieutenant, my active duty was deferred so that I could attend law school and get admitted to the bar. I accepted a job offer from a Wall Street law firm and was patiently waiting out my residency requirement when President Johnson announced in the fall of 1967 that he was calling up fifty thousand reservists, including intelligence specialists, to augment the substantial buildup in forces in Vietnam. Since my specialty at the time was as an intelligence officer, pending admission to the bar, I did not relish the thought of spending my four years on active duty in that role rather than in my chosen profession. But with the intervention of a senior partner at my firm, my admission to the New York State Bar was accelerated, and I reported for duty at Shaw AFB in Sumter County, South Carolina, on April 15, 1968. I entered as a first lieutenant and was promoted (automatically, I might add) to captain six months later.

Stateside Duty

Our lives in uniform stateside were not significantly affected by the war —or much different from life as a civilian. Shaw AFB was a Tactical Air Command training base for reconnaissance pilots headed for Vietnam, but outside of our having to draft wills and powers of attorney for men headed for combat, the war may as well have been occurring on another planet. However, arriving in South Carolina was a cultural shock. More than a decade after *Brown v. Board of Education,* this area of the Deep South was still completely segregated—"whites only" drinking fountains, medical waiting rooms, the whole gamut. The only desegregated school in the region was the one attended by base dependents! Before moving onto base, we lived in half of a duplex trailer in a segregated park. During that time,

Dave Hess at commissioning

my wife, Judi, had what in retrospect was a hilarious experience. Since we didn't have a clothes washer and dryer, she needed to use the local laundromat. The first time she did so, she dutifully followed the instructions on the wall, placing all our white wash in the machines marked "white," and all of our colored wash in the machines labeled "colored"—only to be corrected by a heavy, jolly black woman who pointed out that the labels referred to the *patrons* using the machines, and not to the color of the garments to be washed!

During my two years at Shaw, I performed routine JAG duties and tried as many courts-martial as I could. My most memorable case arose out of the war. I was assigned to defend a senior NCO who had just returned to Myrtle Beach AFB after serving a year as the NCO in charge of the officers' club at our major air base—Tan Son Nhut—just outside Saigon. At this time, a massive series of scandals had been uncovered at such clubs throughout Vietnam, with the officers and NCOs commanding the clubs reportedly having received vast bribes for granting favors to particular vendors, entertainers, etc. However, the military had had a poor record in prosecuting these people directly for corruption. When my client returned home, he suddenly appeared to have far greater financial resources than his pay would account for. Learning from its past failures, the Air Force decided to try him on a novel theory—income tax evasion. It was the first prosecution for that alleged criminal behavior in the twenty-year history of the Uniform Code of Military Justice. After an extended trial, he was convicted. Years later, however, one of my arguments was vindicated when the Court of Military Appeals overturned the conviction, ruling that the UCMJ did not vest the military with the jurisdiction to charge and try that crime.

But despite the escalation in the war effort and the trauma of our apparent setback during the Tet offensive, our lives stateside were pretty routine. I managed to get my private pilot's license, and almost got myself killed in my first cross-country solo over South and North Carolina. And Judi and I did our first sky dives. I landed successfully, but rather than doing a PLF—parachute landing fall—she hit the ground in a PFL ("poor f___ landing") and broke her back. Fortunately it fused successfully with no disability, and proved, in hindsight, to be a godsend. Within weeks, I received orders assigning me to Clark Air Base in the Philippines, and shortly after that, we learned Judi was pregnant.

The Philippines: Around the War, but Hardly in It

I arrived at Clark in April 1970 with two other JAGs. The three of us were transferred to try a backlog of some fifty courts-martial. At the time, Clark, like so many of our military installations, was wracked with racial tension and violence. Because of our trial experience, all of us were certified as military judges. Having met during the flight across the Pacific, we all moved in together and starting tackling the case backlog, but in a rather unorthodox way, which would be considered most politically incorrect today. In one trial, I would be the prosecutor while Steve would be defense counsel and Gary the judge. The next trial, we switched roles, with me as defense counsel, Gary serving as prosecutor, and Steve presiding as judge. The next case we would rotate again—I would be judge, Steve would prosecute, and Gary would defend. Over six months, we eliminated the backlog—all the while living, eating, and partying together! And while the appearances are highly suspect, I don't recall a single instance in which our personal lives entered one bit into our professional duties and responsibilities.

At that time, the normal wait for spouses to follow their husbands to Clark was ten months. However, because of Judi's broken back and pregnancy, she got a special medical dispensation (courtesy of our good friend, her orthopedic surgeon) and was able to join me after only three months. Thus the unexpected benefit of breaking one's back while jumping out of an airplane!

Following that, I was assigned to a special prosecution team in Thirteenth Air Force to try a number of senior Air Force enlisted men charged with massive money laundering and theft associated with NCO clubs on various air bases in Thailand. It resembled an Air Force extension of the club scandals that led to my earlier defense role at Myrtle Beach. This time, I came up against F. Lee Bailey and his law firm. At the time, Bailey was probably the most renowned criminal defense attorney in the United States. We lost, of course! But it was a memorable learning experience.

In my second year at Clark, I was assigned as head of the International Law section. In that capacity, I had a number of diverse but uniformly interesting and exciting responsibilities. First, I served as Air Force liaison to the U.S. Embassy in Manila in renegotiating our U.S. Bases and Status of Forces Treaty with the Philippines. I don't recall making a single contribution to that process, but it sounds impressive. And in that capacity, I had occasional private helicopter rides to and from the U.S. Embassy on the waterfront in Manila.

More significantly, I was also responsible for the administrative detention program on base. This requires some explanation. As you may suspect, a large military base with thousands of single men far from home creates the environment for a thriving sex trade. It also encourages reverse exploitation. Thus, Filipino women catering to the sexual drives of young USAF men quickly realized that a marriage was a ticket to the States and economic nirvana. Hence, when casual sexual encounters failed to result in meaningful relations, the young ladies quickly alleged rape and other crimes. Philippine courts necessarily honored such complaints and initiated criminal actions against the airmen. To ensure that the named defendants remained in the Philippines, we were obligated under our Status of Forces Agreement to ensure that no Air Force personnel charged with crimes in the Philippine judicial system left the country. And while we conscientiously tried to fulfill our duties under the treaty, an occasional defendant would evade our procedures and return to the United States. As a result, I was subject to the jurisdiction of the Philippine courts, and in one instance was almost held in contempt of court and thrown into a Philippine prison by an irate Philippine judge. Let me tell you, that focuses one's priorities quite quickly!

I was also involved in what I believe was the most serious espionage case of the Vietnam War. I'm not sure how much of it is still classified, but it is now more than forty years old, and the Soviet Union no longer exists, so I believe some generalities can be discussed. The case involved a ranking NCO at the U.S. Embassy in Thailand who was charged with selling our highest classified military secrets to our major enemy at the time. The information involved contingency U.S. military plans in Southeast Asia in the event of a nuclear war. The defendant was whisked out of Thailand and landed at Clark en route to U.S. soil in Guam. I was appointed his chief defense counsel. As a result, I worked closely with high-ranking counter-intelligence officers and obtained a "Specat Eyes Only" security clearance, which gave me access to some of the most highly classified contingent war plans then in existence, but which prevented me from copying or taking any written notes of anything I saw or read. I also became an occasional passenger on the CIA's in-house airline—Air America. The trial was held at Anderson Air Force Base on Guam. Most interesting was the fact that the day before the trial began (it had received no publicity in advance, for obvious reasons) a Soviet trawler armed with multiple antennae suddenly appeared just beyond Guam's three-mile territorial limits—and sat there, listening for the duration of the trial. The day the trial ended, the trawler disappeared. My client was convicted. But there is a "rest of the story." Before the trial, my co-counsel and I had a private audience with the lieutenant general commanding Thirteenth Air Force. (Believe me, approaching a three-star general as a lowly captain to propose a plea deal is a rather unnerving experience.) At our meeting we pointed out several constitutional flaws we saw in the prosecution's case and offered a negotiated plea bargain of ten years' incarceration. That offer was rejected. Two years after I had returned to civilian life, the Court of Military Appeals overturned the conviction for some of the very reasons we had pointed out. Ultimately, my client served ten years for his indiscretions. The point is: the system worked—even in wartime with heightened emotions.

Finally, I actually did get into the war zone—once, for less than twenty-four hours, spent entirely at the officers' club at Tan Son Nhut Air Base. It was a routine "perk" for some of us on the war's periphery. I got TDY (temporary duty) orders cut to fly into Saigon on the last day of one month, stay overnight, and fly back to Clark the first day of the next month. I spent the night at the O Club Bar watching the artillery flashes on the horizon, and collected two months of combat pay in the process!

Last Reflections on a War

I think it is generally accepted today that the "tip of the spear," the men and women actually in combat, or in "harm's way," as it is euphemistically described by our politicians these days, are only about 10 percent of our active duty military. In the Air Force, it is probably only about 0.5 percent. I was certainly not part of our "tip of the spear" during the

Vietnam War. Quite the opposite. I was part of the rear echelon—those who enjoyed a safe and very interesting life experience, and not without a few luxuries. While we were stationed at Clark, we enjoyed the life of nineteenth-century white colonial-imperialists. We were able to hire a house girl (some thirty-five years old with three daughters) for twenty-six dollars a month to relieve us of all our household drudgeries and parental responsibilities for six days a week. And for another ten dollars a month we could hire a "yard boy" (about the same age and also with a family) to do all our gardening and yard work.

·Clark was the hub of all Air Force activity in Southeast Asia. As a result, there were flights constantly coming and going, often with empty seats. Those seats became "space available" for us to use while traveling on leave. All you had to do was sign up, get your CO's permission, be prepared to take off on two hours' notice, and then ask where you were going. As a result, Judi and I visited seven countries during my tour, including Nepal and India, with all travel expenses paid for by the American taxpayers. That exposure imbued us with a love of traveling on our own, especially to remote regions of the Third World—a love affair that has continued to this day. One of our most memorable experiences in that regard was spending an afternoon with the king and queen of Thailand at a remote Red Meo tribal village in the Golden Triangle—where Judi was offered a brick of opium at a super-wholesale price! (It was declined, of course.)

We also developed deep friendships with people from all over the States—from the Deep South to Wyoming to California—friendships that continue to this day and would not have occurred otherwise.

Further, with the level of responsibility delegated to me, which was far beyond my experience or any opportunities then open to me in civilian life, I think I acquired the self-confidence to believe that I could do and be anything and anyone that I wanted to, and that I did not have to follow a stereotypical career path. Finally, it starkly revealed the gross economic waste and the value of "who you know" in any massive undertaking—especially war.

Postscript

I deliberately chose to caption my previous section with the title of Bernard Fall's last book—a book about "our" Vietnam War rather than the earlier war he was so famous for covering. I did so as a way to highlight the ironies and absurdities of war in general, and the two Vietnam Wars in particular. My experiences recounted here are so remote from Fall's extensive and voluntary combat exposure as to defy explanation, much less justification. Sherman was right—but perhaps only for the men and women at the "tip of the spear."

After graduating from Dartmouth, David Hess attended Yale Law School, where he was on the board of editors of the *Yale Law Journal*. After graduating from Yale, he worked for nine months as an associate at White & Case on Wall Street. Following his active duty in the Air Force, he was an assistant attorney general in New Hampshire, prosecuting homicides and other major felonies under then attorney general Warren Rudman and deputy AG David Souter. He practiced law privately as a litigator in New Hampshire until 2003, when he retired. He was a Fellow at the Kennedy School of Government at Harvard in 1996, and is now serving his twelfth term in the New Hampshire House of Representatives, where he has served as majority leader, Republican leader, and chair and vice chair of multiple committees. He and Judi were married in 1966 and have two sons—Scott, born in 1970 (in the Philippines), and Topher, born in 1978.

1969-1971

1969

President Nixon authorizes covert bombing of Cambodia.

1970

Ohio National Guard fires on protesting students at
Kent State University--four students killed.

1971

Pentagon Papers published.

Legacies of the Vietnam War

JOHN T. FISHEL : U.S. ARMY

The orders came in the spring of 1969. They said report to USASSG-ISB, Room 2A514, the Pentagon, Washington, D.C., on or about August 1,1969. They ordered me to report first to Engineer Officer Basic Course (OBC) at Fort Belvoir, Virginia, with a report date of May 26, 1969. I only recall a little from OBC: The secondary mission of the engineers is to fight as infantry. To build a good timber trestle bridge, consult your platoon sergeant and nod wisely. River recons are conducted from LFRBs (a lieutenant asked what an LFRB was and was informed it was a Little F——ing Rubber Boat!). And then there was the "infiltration course"—a low crawl under barbed wire with live machine gun rounds whizzing overhead.

During the twelve weeks of OBC, my assignment was a mystery to me and everybody else. No member of the class or cadre had ever heard of USASSG-ISB.

ISB

I reported to the Pentagon, Room 2A514, on August 1, and, behind the cipher-locked green door, was "read on" to the highly classified intelligence discipline of signals intelligence (SIGINT) by our classmate Dave Krueger. After the "read on" I crossed the hall and entered another cipher-locked room, the Intelligence Support Branch (ISB), where I would be working.

ISB was the Army's "all source" current intelligence shop. It was our job to produce the Black Book, a kind of daily classified newspaper for the Army chief of staff, the secretary of the Army, and all the senior military and civilian staff of the Army. The articles ranged from the relatively low-level classification of "secret" to "top secret," with a SIGINT code word to indicate that only those with access to that particular compartment of "top secret" were authorized to read the article. Not only did we analyze the intelligence and write the articles, but we also were the couriers of the Black Book, carrying it each morning to the one-, two-, three-, and four-star recipients, as well as the under and assistant secretaries of the Army.

On my first duty day, my immediate boss made me the primary West Europe analyst with secondary duties for the Soviet Union and Eastern Europe. The then China desk officer, Captain Len Bickwit (who would later have his fifteen minutes of fame when, as a congressional staffer, he pushed Nixon spokesman Ron Ziegler into a swimming pool), showed me "ground zero" in the heart of the "military industrial complex"—the hamburger stand in the center of the inner courtyard.

I served my first year in ISB as a first lieutenant. Then, on May 24, 1970, I was promoted to captain and became the new China desk officer. I also worked the Koreas and other countries of the Far East. During that year, I got a taste of Vietnam when I was detailed to work on a project directed by the assistant chief of staff for intelligence, Major General Joseph A. McChristian III. The project was focused on documenting McChristian's discovery in Vietnam that a majority of the supplies for the North Vietnamese Army were coming through the port of Sihanoukville, Cambodia, and not down the Ho Chi Minh Trail through Laos.

During my second year I had to make a major decision as to my own future. I was seriously tempted to stay on active duty. The Army was willing to give me time to finish my dissertation (with full pay and allowances). However, that would have been followed by a "short tour" to Vietnam just as the war was beginning to wind down. Having invested a lot of time and effort in an academic career and being unsure about a year in Vietnam, I decided not to accept the offer, but I did stay in the reserves. Little did I realize how the Vietnam War would inform my subsequent academic and military careers.

Legacies

I spent the next fourteen years in the reserves in a variety of assignments, with tours of active duty ranging from three days to two months. In 1985 I began a year and a half that would lead me back onto active duty full time and into the middle of several wars that would draw on the lessons of Vietnam. This started in January when I moved to Fort Bragg, North Carolina, to teach in the Army's Foreign Area Officer (FAO) course. I was codirector of the Latin American seminar, and during the summer of 1985 my fellow codirector (another lieutenant colonel) and I traveled extensively in the region. As a result, I got my first visits to Central America, including El Salvador and Honduras, where the Cold War was clearly in a hot phase. Another stop was Peru, where the Shining Path guerrillas were beginning to mount a real challenge to the government, along with the drug-traffickers in the cocaine trade.

In El Salvador we met with the commander of the military group, the defense attaché, the chargé d'affaires at the embassy, and the Salvadoran commander of the Atonal Immediate Reaction Battalion. In all cases we saw a war that was tactically reminiscent of Vietnam but where the United States played a very limited but critical role.

By June 1986 I was back on active duty for what would be a five-year series of tours with short intervals in between. I reported to the Policy, Plans and Strategy Directorate (J-5) of the U.S. Southern Command (SOUTHCOM) in Panama as the co-chief of the Civic Action Branch. Our focus was largely on the Central American wars, especially the ones in El Salvador and Honduras. In the latter we addressed mainly preventive activities designed to assist the Honduran government in not losing the hearts and minds of its people. To that end, SOUTHCOM was controlling a series of joint road-building exercises, known as Blazing Trails, which were building a major road in an isolated part of the country. The road building was done by an Army engineer task force from the reserves and National Guard during its annual training each summer. The Civic Action Branch coordinated ancillary activities like well drilling, and rural health and veterinary clinics designed to maximize the impact of the overall project. Both the road building and the civic actions were conducted by a combined U.S. and Honduran force including Honduran civilians from the appropriate ministries.

"Civic action" is a concept that dates back to before the earliest days of our involvement in Vietnam. The term was coined by then Colonel Edward Lansdale for the tactics used in the Philippines against the Communist Huk Rebellion. Then Lansdale brought it with him to Vietnam when he headed the Saigon Military Mission. It was central to presidential assistant Robert Komer's Civil Operations Revolutionary Development Support (CORDS) and the Marines' Combined Action Platoons. In SOUTHCOM it was a major component of our strategy for keeping the insurgents from gaining a foothold in Honduras and was an important adjunct in El Salvador. That summer I led a civic action site survey team to Honduras to plan the civic actions for the following year's Blazing Trails exercise.

Certain key insights came out of the site survey. First, we were to conduct it with Honduran counterparts who never showed up; as a result, I had to improvise by recruiting available Hondurans. A critical volunteer was a Honduran army engineer lieutenant. The next issue focused on where the Blazing Trails 87 exercise was to work. It became obvious that the engineers were not going to get as far as they expected. Worse, the people of the villages along the route had been told that the road would reach them the next year (1987). The result was that we prioritized the civic actions for BT 87 to those villages that had expected the road to reach them but where it would fall short. Discovering the problem and coming up with this solution would not have been possible without improvising Honduran participation.

SWORD

Later that summer, a longtime friend, an active duty colonel, was assigned to SOUTHCOM to head a new staff element, the Small Wars Operations Research Directorate (SWORD). He brought another mutual friend to be his deputy, while I would run his research and analysis shop. One of our first tasks was shades of a peripheral issue in Vietnam, illicit drugs. SOUTHCOM was supporting an interagency mission in Bolivia called Operation Blast Furnace. SOUTHCOM provided six helicopters and an intelligence cell to work with a Drug Enforcement Administration (DEA) task force and the Bolivian rural police to deal with cocaine traffickers. SWORD was tasked to analyze the mission in terms of its successes and failures.

We flew in a USAF C-130 to the eastern Bolivian city of Trinidad, site of the operational headquarters of the task force. In the next few days, it became obvious that mission success derived from superior intelligence analysis. This identified the tactical center of gravity as the drug lab where coca paste was refined into cocaine. The process produced measurable traces in the atmosphere that could be collected and analyzed to pinpoint a target for the Rural Police and DEA strike force. Operational success was achieved by attacking the drug labs and stopping the flow of cocaine out of Bolivia without the farmers blaming either the government or the foreigners for disrupting their livelihood. Unfortunately, DEA could not be satisfied with success and struck a town where the farmers lived, alienating the people. It produced a riot that drove the police, DEA, and the U.S. Army helicopters supporting them away, in a rout.

As in Vietnam, the strategic center of gravity was the population, and alienating the farmers and villagers doomed the mission in the long term. Over a quarter century later, Bolivia is still producing large amounts of cocaine for U.S. and European consumption.

Several other trips over the next year involved Peru. At the time, Peru was suffering through the Shining Path insurgency whose leader, Abimael Guzman, claimed inspiration from the late Chairman Mao Zedong. However, this "Maoist" insurgency had more in common with Pol Pot's Khmer Rouge than with Mao's People's Liberation Army. We did our best to provide useful support against a very real threat. Nevertheless, the best we could do was to learn as much as possible about the insurgency and share what we had learned in a series of discussions with the Peruvian National Intelligence Service, the Peruvian army, and the Center for Higher Military Studies (CAEM—Peru's prestigious military think tank). One of the highlights of my service was lecturing at the CAEM on counterinsurgency.

Bolivia and Peru were secondary to Central America. There, SOUTHCOM was directly engaged in El Salvador and Honduras.

In February 1987 I made the first of what would be many visits to El Salvador over the next year as SWORD focused on what became the Combined Assessment of the El Salvador Armed Forces. On this trip, three of us flew out to the field as military observers. We were to link up with the Bracamonte Immediate Reaction Battalion, which was operating in the Department of Cabañas. Soon after the U.S. Army helicopter dropped us on a ridge, a Salvadoran soldier appeared in front of me saying we had landed in the wrong place. Fortunately, we called the helicopter back, reboarded, and landed in the proper location. There, the deputy commander of the battalion briefed us. He explained how the battalion operated continuously with about a third of its twelve hundred troops in the field under his command, with the operations officer as his deputy, or the commander and the intelligence officer in charge. A second third was recovering under the command of the administrative officer and supply

John Fishel (left) with deputy commander of the Bracamonte
Immediate Reaction Battalion, February 1987

officer, while the last element was in training at home station under the alternate command team.

As we were about to depart, and the battalion was going to move forward, we saw a puff of smoke on the ridge where we had first landed. A radio call reported that a trooper had stepped on a guerrilla mine and had blown off his foot. A medevac helicopter arrived about the same time as ours did. The battalion continued its operation.

A month after our trip to the Bracamonte, the FMLN launched a spectacular attack on the headquarters of the Fourth Brigade at El Paraíso in Chalatenango department, killing more than one hundred troops and an American trainer. There were reports that the FMLN had used mortars for the first time in the conflict. SWORD was asked to investigate what had happened. We flew out to Fourth Brigade, saw the damage done, and talked with Salvadoran officers, the senior U.S. trainer, and the military intelligence officer detailed to the CIA to work with the Salvadorans in the Regional Intelligence Center. At the time of the attack, the trainer had been in San Salvador on business. The U.S. casualty was killed by a rocket-propelled grenade whose trajectory matched exactly the path of the supposed mortar rounds. No mortars. The other interesting fact, however, was that the U.S. intelligence officer had been sent by his CIA superior on a wild goose chase away from the site the day before, creating the suspicion that the CIA knew the attack was coming and chose not to inform the SF trainers.

The Combined ESAF Assessment

In June 1987, there was a change of command in SOUTHCOM. General Fred Woerner replaced General Jack Galvin as the commander. Woerner had led a team to El Salvador in 1981 that developed the supporting strategy for the government and the El Salvador Armed Forces (ESAF) that we had followed ever since. In SWORD, we felt it would be timely to relook the situation, and my colleague, Max Manwaring, and I met with the general to propose a new assessment. He liked the idea and followed up, naming a brigadier general to lead the team. I was the executive officer. My first task was planning the conduct of the research.

Our first steps were to coordinate the idea with Ambassador Ed Corr in San Salvador and the U.S. Military Group (MILGP) commander. The latter would work with the ESAF high command and his own team, the fifty-five trainers. Meanwhile, I proposed to base the assessment on research that Manwaring had conducted since 1984 on the correlates of success in counterinsurgency. The assessment took place over the six months between the fall of 1987 and the spring of 1988.

Our findings, not surprisingly, supported Manwaring's research on counterinsurgency success—what we would call today a population-centric approach. We did discover that the ESAF was following a four-part strategy that was not immediately apparent: (1) static defense of key sites (like bridges and dams) with regular battalions; (2) continuous military operations conducted by the six immediate-reaction battalions and the parachute battalion to keep the FMLN off balance, like the one we had witnessed; (3) intelligence-driven strike operations by ESAF special operations forces; and (4) a rural development program and civil defense force that was most successful in the form that Ambassador Corr and Salvadoran President Duarte worked out, called Municipalities in Action, where funding was given directly to the local governments to build the kind of infrastructure they decided they needed.

The most memorable moment of the assessment came the day we briefed President Duarte on our results. We all assembled in the auditorium of the headquarters with ministry officials, ESAF high command

and staff, embassy officers, the MILGP, and our team, General Woerner and U.S. ambassador Corr next to him, in the front row.

El Salvador had just had elections for mayors and the legislative assembly, and President Duarte's Christian Democrats had been thoroughly trounced by the right-wing ARENA party. The newly elected *Arenista* legislators were feeling their oats and trying to influence sympathetic high military officers even before they were sworn in. During the wait for President Duarte to arrive, Ambassador Corr took the opportunity to politely but firmly remind the high command that they still worked for the president and minister of defense and not the yet-to-be-sworn-in legislature. It was hardly lost on the Salvadoran generals and colonels that next to the ambassador was seated a U.S. four-star general in uniform giving his full support.

Panama: Just Cause and Promote Liberty

For the next six months, back in Panama, I was editing the final report of the Combined ESAF Assessment and supervising its translation into Spanish. By the time it was completed in the fall of 1988, SWORD was being dismantled and I was transferred to the J-5, where I headed the Policy and Strategy Division. On May 18, 1989, I was handed a new additional duty: to upgrade SOUTHCOM's plan for post-conflict reconstruction in Panama, if that should become necessary. When Operation Just Cause was executed on the night of December 19–20, 1989, I was on leave in the States. When I finally reached my roommate on the day after Christmas, I was told to "get your butt back here; they are executing your plan!" When I returned on December 28 I found I had no job but was able to get assigned to the U.S. Forces Liaison Group (USFLG) to assist the new Panama security forces in becoming organized, trained, and equipped.

As the deputy chief of the USFLG, I found myself very much engaged in working with Panamanian police officers (former military) as a military adviser and with our own people. I had several close working relationships with key Panamanian officers and watched other U.S. officers perform advising duties in ways that ranged from highly successful to disastrous. Initially, the principal adviser to the police commander was a textbook case in how advising should be done. He spent most of his time with the commander, becoming his confidant. When he rotated, his role was to be passed to the head of the interagency State-Justice International

Criminal Investigation Training Assistance Program. Unfortunately that gentleman never took ownership of the role, and it went largely unfilled. As the officer in the USFLG with the best relationship with the police commander, I inherited a piece of the advisory role by default but without the authority to really carry it out. As it turned out, we left that colonel to twist slowly in the wind, resulting in his relief for cause. It was a result that was reminiscent of our dealings with President Diem in the early days in Vietnam but without the totally tragic ending. It also foreshadowed how we have dealt with President Karzai in Afghanistan with less than total success.

John Fishel stayed in the Army Reserve for a full twenty-eight years, serving two years active at the front end and five at the back end. He retired as a lieutenant colonel in 1992. He also had a full academic career teaching political science and international relations at the University of Wisconsin–La Crosse, the Army Command and General Staff College, National Defense University (NDU), and currently at the University of Oklahoma. He retired from NDU in 2006 and moved to Oklahoma, where he found his true calling as a cowboy. John is the author and editor of several books and numerous articles. He rides his horses with his wife, Kim, and takes pride in her piano artistry as well as that of their thirteen-year-old daughter, Karina.

Drafted

ROBERT J. ROSE : U.S. ARMY

I graduated from the University of Wisconsin Medical School in 1968 and subsequently started my internship at Mary Hitchcock Memorial Hospital knowing that I was subject to the "doctor draft" of the Vietnam era. At that time Betsy and I already had three children. Because I had been accepted into a residency in orthopedic surgery at the Hitchcock Clinic, I wanted to enter the military on terms other than those of that draft. I therefore applied for a Navy commission and entered the lottery known as the Berry Plan. This program determined into which branch of the service one would be commissioned and in what specialty one would be trained. I "bought the ticket" for Navy / orthopedic surgery. I have never won a lottery and didn't win this one. I did get the default, which entailed one year of general surgery training and then active duty as an Army battalion surgeon. That meant a year in Vietnam rather than my desired "accompanied assignment" as an orthopedic specialist in a stateside naval hospital. A good friend was on the faculty in anesthesiology at Dartmouth Medical School. He made the suggestion that as the Army needed anesthesiologists, and as I wanted to defer active duty until I had additional training, I should reapply to the Berry Plan. I did. Within a month I had a reserve commission in the Army and a residency in anesthesiology at Dartmouth.

When I went on active duty with the First Infantry Division in the early summer of 1971, the drawdown of troops from Southeast Asia had started and the division had returned to Fort Riley. As a result, Betsy, our daughters, and I spent the majority of the next three years there. Unlike so many others who truly suffered during their military service, for me these were enjoyable years. I was assigned significant leadership responsibility in addition to clinical work and found it exciting and stimulating.

Bob Rose with daughter
Marta at Fort Riley,
Kansas

Most of the medical officers were "doctor draft" physicians and, like me, fresh out of training and eager and competent to apply new skills. There were many other Army families of our age, consequently social life on the post was good. There was adequate free time to spend with my young family and to enjoy bird hunting on the prairies. We also undertook family camping trips in the Rockies.

Fort Riley Army life wasn't all country club existence. A great deal of unpleasantness was a direct result of the wartime draft. Most of the enlisted medical personnel were high school graduates or those who had some college and were motivated to provide good care to their charges. Unfortunately, a large proportion of the enlisted infantry force were less qualified draftees who were just marking time until discharge. They did only what was necessary to avoid a dishonorable separation. This lack of motivation resulted in a great waste of time and resources. The draft resulted in a disproportionate number of African Americans at my facility, and while the Army was nominally racially integrated, social segregation was obvious. Racially motivated incidents with injuries were common. Drug abuse was rampant, especially among those who had spent their year in Vietnam. I received a medical needle-stick injury while caring for a hepatitis-infected drug abuser and spent three months on sick leave.

"McNamara's 100,000" was a program designed to avoid the political horror of eliminating a similar number of student deferments. It was a disaster. A large number of those substandard draftees ended up in the stockade of the U.S. Army Retraining Battalion in Camp Funston at Fort Riley. I worked with these recruits in my assignment as stockade medical officer and experienced how misguided it was to have dropped the entrance mental capacity testing standards to scores that would result in an additional one hundred thousand draftees. These were unfortunate draftees who would end up serving as cannon fodder in Vietnam. They would be among those who over the long term would adapt most poorly to the subsequent return to civilian life.

There is no question that my military service was a positive experience. The most notable benefit to me was the serendipitous choice of anesthesiology as my medical specialty. That choice led to a very satisfying professional career on the faculty of Dartmouth Medical School and the staff of DHMC.

I feel privileged to have served.

On June 30, 2011, Robert Rose retired following forty years of service at the Dartmouth Hitchcock Medical Center. He is grateful for having realized all he could possibly hope for in his professional life, having been able to look forward every day to rewarding interactions with colleagues and staff, wonderful patients, Dartmouth Medical students and residents, and fellows in anesthesiology.

He and Betsy recently celebrated fifty-one years of marriage. They live in the rural New Hampshire village of Haverhill Corner, thirty miles up Dartmouth College Highway (NH Route 10) from Hanover, enjoying close relationships with other members of their community, a calendar full of church and community volunteer activities, and a great variety of northern New England outdoor recreation.

Missing from Action

C. DEAN RAZZANO : U.S. NAVY

A fter receiving an MD from the University of Kansas in Kansas City in 1968, I went to the Cleveland Clinic to embark on a career of either cardiology or heart surgery. The clinic had recently pioneered cardiac catheterization and revascularization heart surgery. After one year of internship and one year of general surgery, both prerequisites, I chose to rotate through orthopedic surgery for one month. The chief of orthopedic surgery, Dr. Mack Evarts, had just returned from three months in England, where he worked with John Charnley, who had originated the modern "cement-fixated total hip" procedure. Through Dr. Evarts's efforts, the clinic was designated to be one of three institutions chosen by Uncle Sam and the Food and Drug Administration to start a trial program to begin the surgery of total joint replacements in America for an exclusive period of two years. Europe had been replacing total hips for ten years with cement fixation. Our FDA was hesitant but permitted three programs to begin this new surgery in the United States. This was late in 1970. I saw the light and my future. I applied for the Berry Plan, which enabled me to complete three additional years in orthopedic surgery without being drafted into our military and shipping off to Vietnam. The Berry Plan guaranteed Uncle Sam a needed number and quota of fully trained orthopedic surgeons yearly. Two years later, at the close of 1972, total joint replacements—with cement fixation—were permitted throughout the United States. It was the surgery of our future. I completed my residency training six months later, in June 1973, at the clinic.

Because of my gratitude for being selected into the Berry Plan and being temporarily deferred from Vietnam, I volunteered to work once a month for the U.S. Navy for the last three years of my residency. I was stationed—inactive duty—for two and a half weeks in 1971 at the Philadelphia Naval Hospital, a three-thousand-bed facility at the time, on loan from my residency program in Cleveland.

At this time in the Vietnam conflict, the Philadelphia Naval Hospital was designated to be the evacuation center for the Eastern Seaboard for amputees from 'Nam. Primary amputations were frequently performed—guillotine fashion—in the field of conflict in Vietnam or later in Germany or Japan, which were the immediate secondary evacuation medical locations for such injuries. Initial lifesaving measures were performed immediately on the field of battle or close by. Traumatic wartime amputations were, by nature, dirty and contaminated when sustained in battle, hence the need for guillotine amputation as a first stage. A guillotine amputation is not closed primarily, and the terminal portion of the limb is left "open." Major vessels are ligated, and the open wound is packed with gauze and wrapped in compression dressings or plaster. Primary or revision closure was delayed until infection was not only controlled, but completely eradicated. Germany and Japan handled the majority of such injuries with delayed revision closure after infection was controlled. Only those amputation cases that could not be sterilized or were otherwise so horrendous because of other circumstances were sent to the Philadelphia Naval facility for final tertiary treatment.

The original Philadelphia Naval Hospital was fifteen stories high, and was later expanded to house three thousand patients in fingerlike, rapidly constructed wards extending out from the primary facility to accommodate all the severely disabled amputee casualties from all the services. One, two, three, and four-limb amputees were all present there. Four-quadrant amputees were sometimes transported in nothing more than modified baskets. The coordination between naval doctors, nurses, corpsmen, professionals in prosthetics and orthotics, rehabilitation, physical therapists, psychiatrists, and many other areas of expertise was an experience that is impossible to relate or write about. I revised and performed countless more amputations in two weeks in 1971 than I was exposed to in my entire career as an orthopedic surgeon after the war. This form of surgery is very sobering and unhappy work. It is work that a surgeon never looks forward to and doesn't enjoy thinking about in present or past tense. Amputation work is almost impossible for the average lay person to comprehend.

What is far more incomprehensible and unexplainable is the utter absurdity and inanity of WAR and its consequences that all too often lead to amputations. War has no mercy on soldiers, their families, or their loved ones. Yet civilization continues to breed wars. Words cannot paint the pictures that wars create. Young men and women with no arms and legs are our living testimonials. What do these atrocities accomplish, and what lessons do we and have we learned from them?

When I finished my orthopedic residency training in June 1973 at the Cleveland Clinic, the Navy commissioned me a lieutenant commander and asked me to start a "total hip and knee" program for them in July 1973 at Bethesda Naval Hospital. I politely declined, but offered to do the same at the Philadelphia Naval Hospital. I did so, and the Navy supplied me with every operating room facility and surgical instrument that I needed upon my arrival for my two-year period of service. The Navy did not require my services in Vietnam with my background at that time. President Nixon ended the war about six months after I went on duty with the Navy. While completing my two years of service with the Navy, I became board certified in the field of orthopedic surgery.

I had the occasion to perform a total hip replacement on a general from the Walter Reed Army Hospital, who wrote me a kind letter, on her discharge: "I spent my career in the Army only to come to the Navy for 'spare parts.'"

I never saw a battle, never heard a shot, but I was horrified to experience and see just what the realities of war can do to mankind. Our leaders don't seem to comprehend these truths or learn from them. They would benefit from seeing such realities under one three-thousand-bed roof. In 1976, one year after I had left the Navy, when I had returned to teach and practice orthopedics at the Cleveland Clinic, Uncle Sam closed the doors on the Philadelphia Naval Hospital for good. Vietnam was in the history books and her atrocities apparently forgotten. Our next wars were yet to come.

- -

Honorable discharge, U.S Navy lieutenant commander, 1975; board certified orthopedic surgery, 1975; Fellow of American College of Surgeons, 1977; Fellow of American College of Orthopaedic Surgeons, 1977; Cleveland Clinic staff surgeon, 1975–78, specializing in total hip and total knee replacements; Orthopaedic Research Society, 1977. Authored medical papers. Private practice Marion, Ohio, 1978–98; Fellow of the International College of Surgeons, 1980.

Dean Razzano retired January 1, 1998, at age fifty-five, to Naples, Florida, on Naples Bay, and Port Clinton (Catawba Island), Ohio, on Lake Erie, and recently moved to the Villages in Central Florida, a golf course and golf-cart community north of Orlando.

He married his wife, "Sandy," in 1972 ("My best career move"). They have three daughters: Molly (Ohio), Carrie (Kansas City), and Suzanne (Virginia), and six healthy grandchildren (four boys, two girls).

Epilogue
The Plan

WILLIAM PETERS : U.S. ARMY

Editor's note: By way of concluding this collection and to remind everyone that Dartmouth's participation in and support for the military continues to this day, we are proud to present an essay by a veteran of the Iraq War and a current Dartmouth student (Class of 2015) who is a beneficiary of the efforts of President Emeritus James Wright to bring recent veterans to Dartmouth.

Always have a plan, they told us. A good plan keeps the mission together. But then they would tell us that the plan could always go out the window. Later, they would tell us, the lower enlisted, not to concern ourselves with the plan, that we'd be given orders and we only had to follow them. To this day, I'm convinced that much of military consists of clueless men passing down orders to even more clueless men.

Two months into the deployment to Iraq, C Company 4–31 of Second Brigade, Tenth Mountain Division, was settling into a new area of operations. We'd already survived some volatile and filthy situations, so the higher-ups were confident that we would be able to handle this next mission. The plan was to leave Yusufiyah, a dusty shithole south of Baghdad that is surrounded by farmland along the Euphrates, clear some routes, and provide a military presence in the area. The operation was supposed to last two days, so we only took our assault packs and a few boxes of MREs (meals ready to eat) for the truck, leaving our rucks at a nearby base where battalion was set up. We didn't return to Yusufiyah for three months.

I remember when everything changed, when the plan went down the toilet. It was the morning after the raid on the village, the one where guys were so exhausted they were kicking in doors and vomiting on terrified

William Peters (left), Patrick Batsford, and Duval Patel on M1151 Humvee

children. That morning, we set up overwatch with four Humvees along a high road that ran along the canal so that we could provide security for the men who left the vehicles to patrol the fields. I was one of the guys who left the vehicles. The vehicles were separated by about a hundred meters. We fanned out along the fields in wedge formation, and it didn't take long before we began to find the weapons caches. That day we discovered the mother lode of weapons and bomb-making materials, the likes of which hadn't been seen since the invasion. Those fields were like Candy Land. At one point I kicked over some dried brush and found a ditch with five five-hundred-pound bombs, the kind dropped from planes, packed with homemade explosives. I will not deny wanting to run for my life at the sight. Later that night, I accompanied my buddy while he had to answer nature's second call. I stood with my back to him pulling security. He gave a sudden yelp that startled me. When I turned around I saw that he was shining a light on a ditch filled with some two hundred mortar rounds.

We continued to find more caches, and the plethora of weapons grew larger and larger. The two-day operation grew into something indefinite, especially after the insurgents began shooting at us. It began with some sporadic sniper fire and light mortaring; then we encountered direct contact with enemy combatants. For ten days, our platoon stayed on that road and patrolled the nearby villages, occasionally taking contact or apprehending someone trying to set up an IED at night. It seemed battalion command didn't see fit to send more people to secure the area, or could not, so we were stretched thin, logistically, physically, and mentally. We averaged about three hours of sleep a day, and we were running low on MREs and water. Our minds were working against us much of the time. I think the lack of direct contact with the enemy did more harm to us than the lack of sleep. We began to grow paranoid, and I think we began to say completely unintelligible things to each other that seemed to make complete sense at the time. The memory of those days comes to me in a maddening yellow haze that makes me think how I would grit my teeth hard or laugh aloud at nothing at all. One day, my squad was moving through a tiny farm and we stopped for a rest in a cow pasture. Oh, how the cows in Iraq were so sad! Their shoulders protruded from their backs like two misshapen elbows. This particular cow pasture had only one cow. I remember my squad leader saying, "Look at this cow. I wanna punch it in the face." I don't know if he was joking, but it didn't seem to matter much when I stood in front of the cow and thrust my fist into its face. My friends laughed, and it makes one hell of story over drinks, but I truly feel remorse for striking that poor creature. It seemed so logical at the time.

When we were relieved on the road by one of the other platoons, I remember everyone thinking how the men replacing us would screw up all the progress we had made, but we left them to it all the same, not that we had a choice. Our company had set up at an imam's house. Seventy people crammed into a house manning radios, cleaning weapons, making coffee, giving reports, receiving reports, sleeping on muddy floors, eating, shaving, pulling guard, packing, unpacking . . . all in shifts. There was a mosque attached to the house, very spacious, but only Muslims could go inside. It was almost dark by the time we got there, and the good people from the other platoons decided to leave us some of the food brought by battalion. "Hot chow," which consisted of stale bread, cold mashed potatoes, and something that resembled a beef patty. We ate without complaint, and then guys began guard shifts. Mine was in the turret of a truck posted in the southern yard. The chaotic orchestra of dogs, chickens, cows, goats, and Arabs crying through the night air kept me company on my watch. Two hours into in my shift, I began to doze, but my squad leader came just in time and banged on the trunk of the Humvee. "Don't fall asleep, Pete," he said, "or they'll cut your head off and sew a dog's head in its place like those 101st guys. You hear?" I heard. We all knew about that. The battalion we'd relieved had some guys who stayed up late getting high and decided to rape a fourteen-year-old girl, murder her family, and burn the bodies. The locals retaliated by kidnapping a few of them when they took some Valium and fell asleep in a truck that was left far away from the rest of the unit. It was a fair assumption that Americans were not the most popular people in this area.

After my watch, I made my way to the flat rooftop, where I would finally get more than two hours of sleep for the first time in almost two weeks. When I arrived, I found the hard, flat floor of the rooftop covered in sleeping bags. They looked like large black cocoons in the moonlight. I was far too tired to be unpacking, so I simply laid out my sleeping pad and my poncho liner, then balled my sweat-salt-stiffened uniform into a pillow. I looked up at the Iraqi sky, speckled with stars shining ever so brightly. It was my first peaceful moment in quite some time, and it pulled me down to sleep like an anchor.

At 0500, I was awoken by a loud clack followed by a faint hum. It was as if God had struck a giant match far up in the heavens and I could hear it burning. Then the prayer started blaring and I knew it wasn't God, not mine at least. I opened my eyes to see the pink and yellow sky and the dull gray loudspeaker towering right above me. You've got to be kidding me, I thought in a disgruntled fashion. I'd say the imam was laughing at us as he paused his praying every now and then to hack up half a lung. I'm sure the Iraqi soldiers had a chuckle over our wonderful wake-up call. I got up and took my boots off, realizing I hadn't removed them for at least four days. The once dark green socks were bleached into a sickly orange, and the stench was horrific. My uniform felt as if it had been doused with way too much starch because of the amount of sweat that had soaked into it. Our medic, dearest Doc, had the pleasure of raking my ID card down my back to scrape away the salt crystals that had formed in my pores. It was a splendid morning indeed.

We spent that morning and afternoon patrolling the area and finding more weapons caches. We cleared some houses and even took some detainees, mostly for running away from us. I had the luxury of carrying the M240B (a heavy machine gun that included eleven hundred rounds of ammunition), so luckily I didn't have to do any of the chasing, just hauling a twenty-seven-pound necklace all day. When we got back to the house, we found that the Fourth Infantry Division Bradleys (heavily armored vehicles with a 25 mm canon) had finally shown up to provide overwatch and ease up some of the security burden on us. It only took the Fourth Infantry guys a few hours to open fire on our scouts. Fortunately, none of the 25 mm rounds caught any of the scouts before someone got on the radio to let them know they were firing at friendlies. At least we knew they were partially awake.

At dusk, a dozen or so armed Iraqi men rolled up in pickups and came on the house and attempted to catch us unawares. They stopped about a hundred meters from the house and began to open fire. Their surprise was met with every SAW (a light machine gun) and M240B at the house raining hell upon them from the rooftop. My buddy lobbed a few 60 mm mortars from the hip just for the hell of it. That was the last time anyone decided to attempt direct assault on the imam's house while we were there.

I think that the amount of enemy contact we were taking, mixed with the overwhelming amount of cache finds, attracted the attention of some high-ranking individuals, because a few days later they sent us a platoon from A Company and our own EOD (explosive ordinance disposal) detachment. Afterward we consolidated more than six hundred pounds of explosives in a barren field. The explosion was gigantic, and the shock shattered all the windows in the house. Not everyone was happy about the mess, but they had let me pull the detonator, so those guys were OK in my book. The A Company guys, on the other hand, well, they ate all our food and weren't exactly good at following the orders from another company's officer. We all moved out to the high road again, this time farther down. The A Company guys did as they pleased, driving too far ahead without paying much attention, until they got a Humvee stuck in the canal. Then they got another one stuck in an attempt to tow the first one. After that, they listened to us a little more.

I remember a few days later, just after dawn, I was walking with the M240B slung around my shoulders with three other soldiers. We were going to set up an observation point, but an explosion stopped us, sending us to cover. We weren't under attack—one of the A Company vehicles had hit an IED that destroyed its front end and blew both front doors and tires off. They called us back, and we sprinted to them as fast as we could. I felt as if I were breathing fire as I hauled that machine gun hard and fast. By the time we rallied, my legs felt like jelly. They eventually went numb when I saw that doors and tires weren't the only thing the blast blew off. I looked at the young man being cradled in one of the sergeant's arms. He was bleeding from his face and crying for his mother as the medics tried to stop the bleeding from the place where the rest of his leg used to be. I remember watching them try to calm him down as he went into shock. I stood there holding the machine gun; my eyes locked on the terrified soldier who was barely nineteen. A firm hand took my shoulder and yanked me away. It was my squad leader. He ordered me to pull security while we waited for the air medevac to arrive. Lying prone with my eyes fixated down the barrel, I listened to him continue to scream helplessly, unintelligibly. When the Black Hawk arrived, the sound of engines and propellers drowned out his cries. But when the bird left with the injured soldier, I started hearing them again. I heard those screams for a while. I remember thinking to myself, I want to go home. It was the first time during the deployment that I thought that, but not the last.

Bill Peters joined the Army in 2005 at age nineteen. He served in the Fourth Battalion, Thirty-First Infantry Regiment, Tenth Mountain Division, in Yusifiya, Iraq, from August 2006 until November 2007. He was discharged from active duty in 2008, whereupon he joined the National Guard, in which he served until 2011. From 2009 to 2011 he was a student at Bunker Hill Community College (Boston). President Emeritus James Wright visited his school, and subsequently one of Bill's professors encouraged him to apply to Dartmouth. He has been a student at Dartmouth since September 2012. He is majoring in government and creative writing. After graduation he plans to be a writer and possibly seek a career in international relations.

Veterans from the Class of 1964

Lockwood C. Barr, Army
Robert I. Bayer, Army
Ivars Bemberis , Army*
Peter H. Benzian, Army*
Thomas D. Bird, Navy
Robert B. Blagden, Army*
Steven D. Blecher, Army*
John T. Booker, Army*
John Boynton, Marines
Douglas P. Brandt, Army*
Timothy H. Brooks, Army
Donald C. Bross, Navy*
Gardner L. Brown Jr., Navy
Stewart T. Brown, Army
Lawrence C. Cabell, Army*
Robert M. Cahners, Coast Guard
E. Bruce Campbell, Army Reserve
Gregor A. Campbell, Army*
Richard S. Carey, Navy*
Nelson O. Carman Jr., Navy*
Peter D. Carney, Army*
John H. Carpenter, Army
Charles E. Carroll III, Army*
Lee A. Chilcote, Marines*
Laurence A. Clark, Army*
Henry E. Clay Jr., Army*
Philip B. Cleaves (deceased), Army
Stephen T. Cochrane, Army*
David K. Combs, Army*
Willard E. Cook Jr., Navy
Fredric W. Corrigan, Army*
Alan F. Davis, Navy
David S. deCalesta, Army
Derick V. Denby, Army*
James A. Dull, Army
Carl S. DuRei, Army*

John E. English, Navy
G. Jay Evans, Navy
R. Bradford Evans, Navy
Alan E. Ferris, Army*
George J. Fesus, Army*
John T. Fishel, Army*
William W. Fitzhugh IV, Navy*
William E. Flowers, Army*
Edmund B. Frost, Army*
Don Michael Gamel (deceased), Navy
Frederick W. Gerbracht Jr., Army
Newell M. Grant, Army*
Kenneth E. Graves, Navy*
John N. Gridley III, Air Force*
John W. Griffin III (deceased, Agent
    Orange), Army
Russell L. Grohe, Air Force*
Peter G. Guerrini, Navy
Paul E. Hale, Navy
James H. Harris III, Navy
David B. Heroy, Army*
Stanley C. Herr, Air Force*
David W. Hess, Air Force*
David C. Hewitt, Army
David S. Hope, Army*
Alfred L. Horowitz, Army
William D. Howey Jr., Navy*
Roger H. Hull, Army*
Glen R. Kendall, Army*
Gerard E. Ketz, Army
John F. Kindergan (deceased), Army*
Ronald C. Kinsey Jr., Army*
George R. Kinzie Jr., Air Force*
George G. Kitchen, Army
Peter J. Koenig, Navy
M. William Krueger II, Army*

*Including ROTC.

David W. Kruger, Army*
Bruce R. Kuniholm, Marines
John T. Lane, Army*
John W. Larsen Jr., Army
James Laughlin III, Army*
William R. Lewis, Coast Guard
Nicholas J. Listorti (deceased), Marines
Curtis W. Little Jr., Army*
James A. Long, Navy
Mark L. Lowmiller (deceased), Army
Richard Luca, Army*
Peter E. Luitwieler, Army*
Richard S. Mack, Air Force*
Michael M. MacMurray, Navy
Charles L. Marsh Jr., Navy*
Lynn Raymond A. McCanse, Army
Philip N. McFerrin, Army*
Arthur McGinnis, Army
Francis C. McGrath, Army*
Alan R. McKee, Army*
John W. McLaughlin, Army*
John Merrill, Air Force*
Robert L. Merrill, Navy
Edward A. Miller Jr., Marines
Larry D. Mitchell (deceased), Army*
George M. Morrow, Navy
Alan M. Nadel, Navy
Ronald J. Naso, Army
Roger G. Nastou, Army
Richard F. Neely, Army*
William B. Nickerson (deceased, casualty), Navy*
Ernest J. Notar, Navy
Peter W. Morrison (deceased, casualty), Air Force*
Gerard J. O'Brien, Navy*
David H. Osborn, Army*
Eric H. Oxboel, Navy*
Michael W. Parker, Navy*
Robert Parkinson, Navy
John E. Peltonen, Air Force*
Park L. Price, Navy*
Brian F. Randall, Air Force*
Frank H. Rath Jr., Army*
C. Dean Razzano, Navy
Gerald L. Reichwald (deceased), Navy

William C. Riggs, Army
William O. Ringham (deceased), Navy
James M. Rini, Air Force
Kenneth A. Ritchie, Army*
Robert J. Rose Jr., Army
Frederick M. Rothenberg, Army*
Dexter R. Rowell, Navy*
Edward A. Rubel, Navy
Hugh P. Savage, Army*
Charles J. Savoca, Army
Howard J. Seaver, Army*
Gabriel M. Serenyi, Navy*
Thomas F. Seymour, Marines
David K. Shipler, Navy*
Kevin J. Shore (deceased), Army
Barry S. Shultz (deceased), Navy*
John D. Shuster Jr., Navy*
Thomas E. Sliney Jr., Navy
Walton N. Smith, Army*
Furman K. Stanley Jr., Army*
Edward W. Stern (deceased), Army*
James P. Stewart, Army*
Jeffrey P. Swain, Navy*
Robert J. Szakonyi (deceased), Navy
William W. Teahan Jr., Army*
Anthony B. Thompson, Army
Stephen M. Thompson, Navy
John C. Topping Jr., Air Force*
George R. Turmail (deceased), Navy*
Chris Vancura, Marines
Frederick F. Wangaard Jr. (deceased), Navy
Arthur W. Ward Jr., Navy
Harold H. Weiler, Navy
William K. Westling, Marines*
John H. Whitmoyer, Marines
Charles G. Williams Jr., Marines*
Edward G. Williams, Army*
Karl F. Winkler, Army*
Alan S. Woodberry, Navy*
Robert J. Woodruff III, Army
William F. Woods, Navy*
William P. Woods Jr., Navy*
Peter F. Wulfing Jr., Navy
James A. Zurn, Army

*Including ROTC.

Index
